HITLER'S SOCIAL REVOLUTION

DAVID SCHOENBAUM attended the universities of Wisconsin, Bonn, and Oxford and worked on the staffs of the Waterloo (Iowa) *Daily Courier* and Minneapolis *Tribune* before leaving for Europe on a Fulbright grant. From 1962 to 1966 he was a free-lance reporter in West Germany; in 1966–67 he taught history at Kent State University, and he now teaches at the University of Iowa.

Hitler's Social Revolution

CLASS AND STATUS IN NAZI GERMANY 1933–1939

by David Schoenbaum

W · W · NORTON & COMPANY

New York · London

HITLER'S SOCIAL REVOLUTION
was originally published by Doubleday & Company, Inc.
in 1966.

W. W. Norton & Company, Inc., 500 Fifth Avenue,
New York, N.Y. 10110

W. W. Norton & Company Ltd., 37 Great Russell Street,
London WC1B 3NU

Published simultaneously in Canada by
Penguin Books Canada Ltd,
2801 John Street, Markham, Ontario L3R 1B4.

Printed in the United States of America.

First published as a Norton paperback 1980
by arrangement with Doubleday & Company, Inc.

Library of Congress Cataloging in Publication Data
Schoenbaum, David.
Hitler's social revolution

(A Norton paperback)
Reprint of the 1st ed., 1966, published by
Doubleday, Garden City, N.Y.
Based on the author's thesis, Oxford.
Bibliography: p.
Includes index.
1. Germany—History—1933-1945. 2. Germany—
Social conditions. I. Title.
[DD256.5.S336 1980] 943.086 80-11579

ISBN 0-393-00993-9

6 7 8 9 0

FOREWORD

In the fourteen years since *Hitler's Social Revolution* first appeared, it has become something of a classic. Rare indeed is the syllabus of a course on modern German history, on fascism, or on the social history of twentieth-century Europe that does not include it as required reading. Rare, too, is the recent book on these subjects that does not reflect Schoenbaum's findings.

What accounts for the book's success? Largely, I think, the questions Schoenbaum posed. When he began writing, a small army of researchers had for more than a decade been exploring the history of the Third Reich. The availability of unprecedentedly rich and voluminous documentation on the recent past made possible an impressive array of informative monographs on many aspects of Nazi tyranny, aggression, exploitation, and mass murder. But as Schoenbaum noted, something of great importance was in danger of being overlooked: the lasting impact of the Nazi regime on the social order of one of the world's most advanced and dynamic countries, Germany itself. While others burrowed industriously, and often with illuminating results, into particular topics, Schoenbaum set himself the task of establishing the overall direction and extent of social change in the peacetime Third Reich. While others pursued the secrets entombed in truckloads of Nazi documents, he concentrated on evidence in danger of going unnoticed precisely because it had been in the public domain all along. The result was a startlingly fresh look at the effects—the unintentional and inadvertent as well as the deliberate and calculated—of Nazi rule on German social life and the social attitudes of a generation of Germans.

The book's success cannot be adequately explained solely in terms of Schoenbaum's choice of subject matter or his skill in marshaling relevant evidence. Also important was his skill in devising unobtrusive strategies for arriving at answers to the questions he posed and his ability to express his findings in a prose that is at once concise and precise, sprightly and stimulating. A model of careful organization, insightful analysis, and fine writing, *Hitler's Social Revolution* retains a thought-provoking freshness that makes it just as accessible and rewarding to a wide variety of readers in the 1980s as in the 1960s. Its republication is to be welcomed.

Henry Ashby Turner, Jr.

Yale University
New Haven, Connecticut
January, 1980

PREFACE

This book originated as a dissertation at St. Antony's College, Oxford. The Warden and Fellows of St. Antony's, and their librarian, Miss Anne Abley, are entitled to sincerest thanks for supporting me in it. This applies particularly to James Joll, without whose patience this book might well not exist at all.

Thanks are also due to the Alexander von Humboldt Foundation, Bad Godesberg; to Mrs. Ilse Wolff of the Wiener Library, London; to Drs. Thilo Vogelsang and Anton Hoch of the Institut für Zeitgeschichte, and the Inter-Library Loan Department of the Bayerische Staatsbibliothek, Munich; to Dr. Heinz Boberach of the Bundesarchiv, Koblenz; and to Miss Lucille M. Petterson of the U. S. Document Center, Berlin.

I owe a special word of thanks to my colleagues T. W. Mason and P. G. J. Pulzer for their criticism and stimulation; to Professor K. D. Bracher for setting me on my way, and to Professor Kurt Schmidt for whatever statistical inspiration I might have to show.

I also want to thank Lieutenant General Hermann Boehme and Dr. Otto Strasser, Munich; Herr Hans Schwarz van Berk, Stuttgart; and Herr Hans Schaumann of the Deutsche Angestellten-Gewerkschaft, Munich, for submitting to interviews.

A final word of thanks is due my wife, who in 1945 knew more about the Third Reich than she ever wanted to know, but who now knows still more.

CONTENTS

INTRODUCTION

Three decades since its fall and over four since its rise, we know much about the Third Reich. The careers and personalities of its leaders have been reviewed at length. Its foreign policy, military operations, ideology, institutions, press, economy, and art, schools and universities, its conduct of justice and mass extermination—all have captured the historical imagination, all have been analyzed and reported in detail. In turn, they have been subsumed in the common denominators of totalitarianism and fascism. What remains is more detail. The odds are against a documentary Rosetta stone, capable by itself of casting new and pervasive light on what till now has been unrelieved darkness.

Despite all we know, a lot remains to be understood. The Third Reich was the closest approximation to date of those "last days of mankind" that Karl Kraus had already anticipated a decade before Adolf Hitler's appointment as Reichskanzler. This is presumably self-evident to all but the ignorant or the willful, and acceptable to Germans and non-Germans, East and West alike. But how it happened, why it happened, what it specifically meant to those to whom it happened—these are matters of understanding. They are no less matters of controversy.

Characteristically, East and West tend to different answers, but both predate the Cold War. They have dominated discussion since 1933. Both, in their historical derivation, point to the obvious limits and even dangers of historical interpretation. One answer identifies the Third Reich as a class phenomenon: the victory of capital over labor with its inevitable capitalist consequences. The other identifies it as a national phenomenon: Hitler's victory as the victory not of German capitalism but of the German character, with Hitler as the proto-German. With amusing consistency, the latter thesis unites those, like William L. Shirer, who would indict Hitler as the gaudy consummation of German history and those, like A. J. P. Taylor, who would in effect exonerate him as a vigorous but basically typical manifestation of it.

Neither theory is easy to dismiss. After a slow start, Hitler fought communism.[1] He opposed the Socialists from the beginning. De jure and de facto, his victory meant the end of the working-class parties, of unions, worker representation in industry, and collective bargaining. On the other hand, capital and industry financed Hitler's party and went on to finance, and profit from, Hitler's war.

That Hitler, whether in his weakness for pastry, for shepherd dogs, for national self-glorification, or for continental expansion, was in the main stream of modern German history is no less obvious. However eccentric his interpretations, his sympathies and antipathies were of the stuff of German life, whether they affected art or politics. Of his millions of voters before 1933 and his delirious mass audiences afterward, very few were consciously endorsing his originality.

The questions remain. As they had been in 1914, Germany's working classes in 1933 were the best organized in Europe, the best educated, and among the larger European nations, the strongest. They nonetheless folded overnight without even the shot of protest that salvaged the self-respect of their Austrian comrades a year later. Why? In the twelve years that followed, they produced heroes. But they failed, in any effective sense, to produce resistance. Their marginal protest in the years 1933–39 was economic, not political, a matter of wages and hours and not, it seems, of fundamental opposition. Why? In September 1939 they marched like everybody else. Between 1916 and 1918, in the midst of the first total war, they had struck. There were no strikes between 1943 and 1945. Why?

The role of capital poses similar problems. However it allowed itself to be bullied, German business helped itself to a large piece of cake. Fritz Thyssen nonetheless fled. The Krupps, whatever their policy afterward, did not finance Hitler before 1933. Does class interest account for both Siemens' co-operation with the Third Reich and Bosch's opposition to it? Apparently underrepresented in the ranks of the organ-

[1] Cf. Walter Laqueur, "Hitler and Russia, 1919–23," *Survey*, October 1962, pp. 93–95.

ized opposition, leaders of German business covered Carl Goerdeler and Ulrich von Hassell for years on end in their efforts to organize the most effective opposition the Third Reich had to show. Why?

If the projection of presumable class interests fails to answer these questions, the alternate solution, "the Germans," is no better. Between 1933 and 1941, an estimated thirty-five thousand non-Jewish Germans, not all of them Socialists, went into exile. In April 1939, over three hundred thousand Germans were in concentration camps, among them Kurt Schumacher who ten years later was to accuse Konrad Adenauer of being "The Chancellor of the Allies." Can we assume that the Germans inside the concentration camps were somehow less German than those outside? Did the formula "German equals Nazi" occur to the foreign inmates of Buchenwald who spontaneously honored their German comrades on their common liberation in 1945?

The subsumption of the Third Reich in the larger categories of totalitarianism and fascism again introduces as many questions as it answers. The concept of totalitarianism undeniably does justice to the last stages of Hitler's Reich, as it does to Stalin's. Even here there are important differences, among them the role of the parties in the respective one-party states, in Stalin's relative weakness for purges and Hitler's relative indifference to them, in Hitler's uniquely dynamic foreign policy and Stalin's characteristic diplomatic conservatism.

But does "totalitarianism" really tell us what we need to know about how this final stage was reached? Can we assume a meaningful identity between a conspiratorial group of highly intellectual professional revolutionaries and a heterogeneous collection of provincial cranks; between an underdeveloped country with a vast rural population in the throes of industrialization and a well-developed industrial society in the midst of a worldwide economic crisis?[2]

"Fascism" causes similar problems. For all the difficulties

[2] Cf. Alec Nove, "Was Stalin Really Necessary?" *Encounter*, April 1962, pp. 86 ff. Nove suggests that some aspects of Stalinism, in any case, were directly related to industrialization. Does this apply in any comparable sense to Nazi terror?

in its definition, there can be no doubt that it existed—and perhaps still does.[3] It is distinct from Communism, it is no less distinct from the older systems it superseded. It is not inevitably totalitarian despite certain basic tendencies in that direction. But the similarities of its various manifestations extend beyond the negative. It is not only anti-Marxist, anti-liberal, anti-Semitic. Its positive affinities affect both style and content, shirts, march steps, economic organization, and political objectives.

Hitler's National Socialism was well within the fascist model. Hitler himself acknowledged Italian inspiration and indicated sincere admiration of Mussolini long before Mussolini reciprocated. To the viewer of the 1920s and early '30s, Nazi affinities to Bolshevism would have been next to invisible, despite marginal evidence of a vacillating Nazi-Communist vote in Berlin before 1933. The left, having repressed the memory of the common Ruhr effort against the French in 1923, would have overlooked the affinities or denied them. But by and large the right would have done the same. If occasional German industrialists opposed the Nazis as socialists, their French and British colleagues were more likely to oppose them—if at all—as Germans. Nazi affinities to Italian and French fascist predecessors, on the other hand, would have struck all contemporary viewers between the eyes.

But is this enough? Fascism appears to have been a product of industrially underdeveloped, but not undeveloped, countries where parliamentary-democratic pegs failed to fit in vacant feudal or absolutist holes. Can this be said of Germany in the same sense that it can of Italy, or in a more limited sense of France, Hungary, Romania, or Spain where fascism never came independently to power at all?

In Italy, where it did come independently to power, fascism appears to have been more or less congruent with the Fascist party. Was German fascism congruent with Hitler's party? Germany was full of ideological fascists, "conservative revolutionaries," "national Bolsheviks," bündische Jugend. All of them could have communicated with Charles Maurras or

[3] See Ernst Nolte, *Der Faschismus in seiner Epoche,* Munich, 1963, for the best discussion to date of its theoretical, if not its practical, premises.

Mussolini. Communicating with Hitler was not so easy, either before 1933 or after. Richard Scheringer, a Nazi supporter in 1930 while he was still a regular officer, switched to the Communists in 1931. Otto Strasser broke with Hitler in 1930 and went on to denounce the Nazis, first in Berlin, then in Prague, and finally in Canada. Ernst von Salomon had nothing to do with the Nazis at all. Instead, he wrote harmless film scenarios and indulged a historical nostalgia for the defunct Freikorps, bands of volunteers armed by the Reichswehr in 1918 to guard Germany's eastern borders. Ernst Jünger collected insects.[4] In its fantastic ramification, the Youth Movement maintained its spiritual independence with a tenacity that can otherwise be matched only by various species of splinter communists a decade later. It was finally absorbed in the Third Reich only by direct executive action. Similarly German Catholics, a large minority of the population with a susceptibility to fascist ideas at least equal to that of their neighbors, resisted Hitler with impressive unanimity until at least 1933.[5]

[4] None of them, it can be assumed, might be very happy to be characterized as fascist, and their reservations would be legitimate. Their own careers, like the definition of fascism itself, are necessarily colored by what subsequently happened. It is hard to conceive of them today without reference to the years 1933–45, to the consummation, so to speak, of what we generally assume to be fascist history. But the association is not altogether fair. However we might feel about them, we can scarcely make them responsible for, say, Auschwitz. Whether they would have thought of themselves as fascists at the time is another question. But in any case, their criteria would have been different. It is also safe to say that these would not have included Auschwitz. After the event, in an interview with the author in Munich in early 1963, Otto Strasser defined fascism as arbitrary use of executive power. He was of course against it. But the "fascist" he appeared to have in mind was John F. Kennedy who had recently imposed a price ceiling on the U.S. steel industry and integration on the University of Mississippi. On the other hand, their respective social origins, their military and Freikorps experience, their political sympathies and antipathies, and, in the case of Salomon, his participation in the murder of Rathenau, make it hard not to think of them as fascists at least within the categorical limits suggested, for instance, by Nolte, op. cit.

[5] Cf. Walter Dirks, "Katholizismus und Nationalsozialismus" *Die Arbeit*, March 1932, reprinted in the *Frankfurter Hefte*, August 1963.

Can anything comparable be said of Spanish, French, or Italian Catholics?

Nor is this all. Mussolini's victory, like Franco's, can be traced to a direct clash with the left. Maurras' *Action Française* was a by-product of the Dreyfus affair and the victory of anti-clerical, republican forces. With some precision, all three can be called reaction: reaction to impending—or in any case anticipated—socialist revolution. Mussolini's and Franco's forces won; in two years in Mussolini's case, in three years in Franco's. The corresponding phase in the history of National Socialism was the period 1919–23. It was Freikorps and Reichswehr, however, who put down the Spartacists in Berlin and the revolutionaries in Munich. Hitler was not yet in sight. In the skirmishes in the Ruhr, in Saxony and Thuringia in the years 1920–23, the Nazis were not *primi* but *pares inter pares*, in fact a provincial minority. The putsch of November 1923, it was assumed, was a chorus, not a solo. Because it wasn't even this, Hitler's "March on Berlin" ended before it had ever reached the Munich city limits.

It was only a decade later that Hitler came to power, fourteen years, more than half a generation, after his entrance on the political stage. He then came to power legally. There was no serious threat of force, no civil war. In the meanwhile his following had changed, in geographical distribution, in social constitution, above all in size. The *arditi*, the Freikorps representation was still there. But quantitative changes had qualitative effects. Hitler had not marched to power. He had, if indirectly, been voted there. And it was the depression that motivated his new followers. The consequences of the ten-year wait were visible in the party leadership. The ideologists, Alfred Rosenberg and Gottfried Feder, were being crowded to the edge. Gregor and Otto Strasser were gone, their followers isolated. Such curious and, by any standard, proto-fascist types as Dietrich Eckart and Max Erwin von Scheubner-Richter, both of them close to Hitler in Munich before 1923, were dead.[6] Of the Munich faithful, only Her-

[6] Scheubner-Richter, according to Laqueur, was actually a monarchist at heart, and it is hard to say what might have become of him after 1933. Cf. Laqueur, "Hitler and Russia," op. cit., p. 103. But Röhm too was a monarchist and so was Maurras. Monarchism

mann Goering went on to Nazi greatness and Rudolf Hess to a kind of conspicuous oblivion. Others, like the party publisher Max Amann, made money. But they never made policy. Ernst Röhm, who again might have been conceivable in Italy, made a bad end scarcely a year after nominal victory.

Even supposing that fascism was an adequate characterization of Hitler's movement in 1923, was it still adequate to the radically different circumstances of 1933? Does it define a meaningful identity between Italy, which, it is generally agreed, was not a totalitarian state, and Germany, which was one? Does it account for the notable unwillingness of the Italians, the crucial willingness, if not enthusiasm, of the Germans, to fight once war had begun?

The willingness of Germans to support Hitler in 1933 and to fight for him in 1939 are the basic questions now, as they have been since 1933 and 1939 respectively. But they are questions that the tremendous historical literature of the past quarter century, whether in its preoccupation with German-Nazi continuity, with an unqualified German capitalism, with the ideology of fascism or the phenomenon of the total state, has failed to answer. That the Third Reich was "dynamic" has been part of the conventional wisdom of its historians since the beginning. But until the implications of this dynamism have been further examined with respect to social groups and individuals in their social roles, new answers are unlikely.

This work is conceived as a new answer; still more as an indication of where more answers might be found. The problem it poses is the impact of National Socialism not on German thought or statecraft, but on German society. Its method is analytic. It subdivides German society into constituent groups and examines their development—principally between 1933 and 1939. But its purpose is synthetic, to explain those social processes in a way that might help answer the basic questions.

Neither a comprehensive economic history nor a sociology of the Third Reich, this book is, at the very least, an appeal for both of them. With all respect for Franz Neumann's

---

might well have disqualified a man for a career in the Third Reich—unless he happened to be a general. But it disqualified him neither as a Nazi nor as a fascist.

Behemoth (1942), neither really exists. But while no substitute for either, this work, it is hoped, is an approach to both. Formally a social history, it is intended as the social history of a revolution. But even here it has definite limits, both in dimensions and contents. A complete social history of revolutionary Germany would necessarily be a history of twentieth-century Germany. The revolution did not begin in 1933, nor in 1918. This work makes no claim to such completeness. While it begins with a review of the Weimar Republic, it is primarily a description of six years.

There are a number of reasons for its limitations. One of them is documentation. The years 1933–39 have been well studied and are enormously well documented. But fundamental material is still only relatively accessible, or, in fact, nonexistent. Tons of basic material are available—or not available—in Potsdam. Among them are the files of key ministries and institutions. More tons, in the form of local party files, went up in smoke at the end of the war. Others were never produced. The only *Führerlexikon*, the Nazi Who's Who, appeared in 1934, the only Party census in 1935. In part, the limits of the present work are absolute. Basic sources are either non-existent or not to be found. In part, the limits are practical. They coincide with the limits of Western archives, specifically the files of the Bundesarchiv, the Berlin Document Center, the Institut für Zeitgeschichte, the Wiener Library, and the microfilms of the U. S. National Archives.

The result is blind spots. It was the ministries whose files are now in the East German archives in Potsdam that, in their prosaic way, governed daily life, and local party officials who both colored and reviewed it. There is a lot more to be learned about them and also—to name other examples—about the police, the Protestant churches, the administration of state industry, managerial selection in private business, the selection of military officer candidates, and of candidates for the Nazi academies.

For the period after 1939, the documentation problem is exacerbated. With the beginning of the war, material is neither more nor less accessible in principle, but different. From 1939 on, statistics, to name one fundamental documentary source, are harder to find. With the fundamental revision of borders and priorities, they are also harder to interpret. Most important, they reflect a different situation. War by its nature accelerates social change. Wartime society is both more egalitarian and more mobile than society in peacetime. Its goals and priorities are set by the war itself; this was also true in Nazi Germany. Goals and decisions are no longer free in even the relative sense they are when the nation is at peace. From September 1939 on, the initiative in German decision-making gradually left German hands.

Between 1933 and 1939, decisions were made largely in Berlin. The decisions made in these years were not only relatively free, but crucial. They determined the quality and structure of German society in ways whose consequences can still be felt. What followed, through 1945, was only a logical development of decisions already taken, whether on labor, business, agriculture, civil or military administration. Methods changed rather than policy. Apparent exceptions, like the recovery of Party strength late in the war or the colossal growth of the SS (Schutzstaffel—"black-shirts"), were optical illusions. The growth of the SS was latent from its creation. The war only accelerated it. The recovery of the party was an aspect of the institutional anarchy characteristic of the Third Reich from 30 January 1933 on. It was, in the hands of Martin Bormann, a matter of skillful management, not of fundamental social changes. Where this work transgresses the limit of 1939, it does so for the sake of detail and consistency. A social history of the Third Reich can no more leave the SS, say, at 1939 than a biography of its Führer can leave the young Hitler in Vienna. But the few cases so pursued describe consistent developments, not new departures.

The basic problem of a social history of the Third Reich, however, is neither a matter of documentation nor context. Among the reasons we know relatively little about German society after 1933 is that German social science disappeared. But this only makes historical reconstruction difficult, not impossible. Even without serious contemporary studies by Germans in Germany, the available material is enormous, for all its limitations. Statistics continued to be published; there is no reason to doubt their legitimacy. Newspapers and periodicals were informative, despite their official regimentation and endless doses of propaganda. Since on many of the most fundamental social issues there was no official line, there were consequently few secrets. The problems of agriculture, small business, and industrial labor, for example, were thrashed out in a fog of ideological phraseology. But they were nonetheless thrashed out in public. It is scarcely exaggerated to say that a file of the *Völkische Beobachter* and the statistical yearbook suffice to know all that was essential about them.

The real difficulty is understanding what we know, a difficulty most contemporaries also failed to solve. Their failure has dogged us ever since. Neumann concluded that the Third Reich was a class society, Emil Lederer that it was classless. Their analyses are among the best we have, but also among the most unreliable. Neither of them was short of information. What was lacking were concepts adequate to interpret it. With far less specific information, Sebastian Haffner produced a better book.[7] So did Richard Löwenthal, writing in 1935 as "Paul Sering" in Hilferding's *Zeitschrift für Sozialismus.* What distinguished both Haffner and Lowenthal from most of their contemporaries is that they asked better questions.

The best formula of all was Hermann Rauschning's *Revolution of Destruction.* It is surely no coincidence that it was also the furthest from the socialist-capitalist, revolutionary-reactionary, elitist-egalitarian categories that make so much contemporary analysis misleading. With all its limits, Rauschning's book described the Nazi revolution as the novelty it was.[8]

[7] This applies to the analytical part of Haffner's book, *Germany: Jekyll and Hyde,* London, 1940, not necessarily to its conclusions which might well have haunted him now for over two decades. Beginning with an admirably differentiated description of German society under Hitler, Haffner concludes with a recommendation that postwar Germany be reduced, practically, to the status quo of 1870.

[8] It is worth mentioning how Professor Stuart Hampshire, in conversation, recalled what an enormous impression Rauschning's book had made on him and his acquaintances on its appearance in 1938. This is a revealing testimonial to Rauschning's originality, but also to the intellectual habits of his readers who had evidently failed until then to recognize the novelty that Rauschning described.

But without empirical demonstration, it remained an hypothesis, at best an inspired guess, and potentially a logical paradox. Among historical generalizations, "revolution" has been relatively precise. The events of 1776, 1789, and 1917, for example, were revolutions; whether for them or against them, neither historians nor contemporary observers would have argued about this. In each case, a conjunction of ideas and events had taken a more or less consistent course. Their objective reality was confirmed by their permanence. The revolutions of 1776 and 1789, to say nothing of 1917, are still around us.

None of this applied in the same sense to the "revolution of destruction." It began legally. There was neither a declaration of independence nor an attack on a Bastille or a Winter Palace. The revolution led to neither the expulsion of a colonial regime, a declaration of rights, nor the introduction of new relations of production. Its Thermidor, its constitutional convention, its New Economic Policy was not self-imposed, but imposed from without and after the event—at Nuremberg in 1945–46, at Frankfurt and Bonn in 1948–49.

Between its ambiguous beginning and its spectacular end, the courses of events and ideas ran not parallel but apart. At crucial points they ran in opposite directions. Hitler no more questioned the revolutionary purpose and significance of the events he set in motion than had Jefferson, Robespierre, or Lenin before him. But his revolution was different from theirs, in ways he himself scarcely realized. In the cases of Jefferson, Robespierre, and Lenin, contemporaries were in basic agreement about what they represented. In Hitler's case, neither contemporaries nor posterity altogether agree that there was a revolution at all.

Without the *post facto* evidence of an unambiguously capitalist, unambiguously industrial, and basically democratic Federal Republic of Germany, it might be hard to prove even today that there had been a revolution. The Federal Republic gives Rauschning's formula concrete meaning. It confirms and demonstrates what Hitler's revolution destroyed. There were nonetheless those, like Haffner and Lowenthal, who were right at the time.

The major thesis of this work is that the Third Reich was a

double revolution. This was, in fact, the source of its anomalies and helps explain why so few of its contemporaries understood it. It was at the same time a revolution of means and ends. The revolution of ends was ideological—war against bourgeois and industrial society. The revolution of means was its reciprocal. It was bourgeois and industrial since, in an industrial age, even a war against industrial society must be fought with industrial means and bourgeois are necessary to fight the bourgeoisie.

Neither revolution began in 1933 or ended in 1939. But it was the combination of the two revolutions that made Germany not only a different place than it had been in 1914 or even 1932, but a kind of mad dog among nations. Because both revolutions, in their fullest implications, dominated German life in these years, the period 1933–39 is of absolute importance.

But it is also of relative importance. If National Socialism in its Central European form is a thing of the past, the model remains—and we need only look beyond Central Europe to cure any excessive optimism. In 1946, Friedrich Meinecke traced "the German catastrophe" to a synthesis of nationalism and socialism. Since then, these, "the main currents of Western history"[9] have reached new states and continents with no less impact than Western technology and medicine. The Swiss psychologist Max Picard declared that there is a Hitler in us all. If we reconsider the history of German society between 1918 and 1939, there are reasons to suspect that there might be a Third Reich in every industrializing society. We need not assume that history repeats itself. But we need only look again at the world around us, a world of disintegrating patriarchal societies, of revolutionary ideas, of non-ethnic borders, of commercially active minority groups surrounded by partly agrarian, partly proletarian majorities, to question the prudence of forgetting history altogether.

[9] Friedrich Meinecke, *Die deutsche Katastrophe,* Wiesbaden, 1949, pp. 9 ff.

WEIMAR PARTIES REFERRED TO IN TEXT

Nationalsozialistische deutsche Arbeiterpartei (National Socialist German Workers' Party) NSDAP	Hitler's party
Deutschnationale Volkspartei (German Nationalist People's Party) DNVP	Hugenberg's conservative nationalist party
Deutsche Volkspartei (German People's Party) DVP	Stresemann's rightist liberal party
Deutsche demokratische Partei (German Democratic Party) DDP	Bourgeois left-liberal party
Wirtschaftspartei (Business party)	Party of small business interests
Zentrum (Center)	Party of German Catholics
Sozialdemokratische Partei Deutschlands (German Social Democratic Party) SPD	Majority socialist party
Kommunistische Partei Deutschlands (German Communist Party) KPD	Communist party

HITLER'S SOCIAL REVOLUTION

I

The Third Reich and Its Social Promises

The concept of a sick society causes problems if only because no one knows exactly what constitutes social health.[1] But to the extent that the concept has meaning, Germany after 1918 was an appropriate place for its application. The most spectacular symptoms—the propensity to physical violence, the hyperbolic inflation of 1923, and the near-overnight disintegration of the economy in 1929–30—had their equivalents elsewhere. But elsewhere they led to crises and convalescence recognizably within the limits of previous historical experience and the status quo. In Germany, however, the permanent disaffection of major social groups, the alienation of those groups who presumably support a liberal republic, was reflected in the progressive and total collapse of all liberal parties, and in the discrepancy between social reality and its political interpretation. They testify to a latent malaise whose consequences, even without Adolf Hitler, would have led to major social and political transformation. This need not have led to war and Auschwitz. But with high probability, it would have been fatal to the Weimar Republic in the form envisaged by the authors of its constitution.

National Socialism was not the cause of the malaise, nor was its ultimate totalitarian, imperialist form the inevitable consequence. Its programmatic demands were neither original nor peculiar to Hitler's Party. The Nazis came to power by miscalculation rather than by some exclusive popular demand focusing on the person of Hitler or his Party. The mandate

[1] Cf. Harry Pross, *Vor und nach Hitler*, Freiburg im Breisgau, 1962, pp. 9 f.

with which Hitler took office was a conglomerate of disparities and contradictions long apparent to anyone interested in politics, both outside the party and in it. The common denominator of Nazi appeal was as remote as the smile of the Cheshire cat. In its negative form, it was a promise to make things different, in its positive form, a promise to make things better. But as far removed as it was from the unitary political will Hitler claimed to see in the uniform columns of the SA (Sturmabteilung—Storm Troopers, "brown shirts") or the ecstatic acclamation of a mass audience, there was in it nonetheless a homogeneity great enough to cover the yawning cracks in the Party program with ballot papers. This was the homogeneity of common disaffection.

The disaffection was structural, endemic in all Western industrial societies, but intensified in Germany by special historical factors: a non-competitive, highly concentrated, high-priced industrial economy, the disproportionate influence of a small class of large landowners, a high birthrate until World War I, too many rural smallholders, an inflated urban petite bourgeoisie. All of these had been built into Bismarck's Reich. Carried along on the winds of economic expansion, they formed a fair-weather constellation whose stability was virtually identical with the success of its political leadership in balancing the conflicting demands and requirements of industry and agriculture, labor and capital, West and East, centralism and particularism, Catholic and Protestant, rich and poor. Success created a clientele that included even the nominal enemies of the established order. Their own vested interest in this order was certainly an important factor in the SPD (Social Democrat) decision to vote war credits in 1914.[2] But the compromises of the old order failed to solve, even precluded solving, the problems of an industrial society. The collapse of the monarchy in 1918 with its chaotic "return to normalcy" only reintroduced the problems of the prewar era after four uneasy years of civil truce. But they were now complicated by the by-products of defeat: a "lost generation" of demobilized soldiers; a floating population of eastern

[2] Cf. Julius Leber, *Ein Mann geht seinen Weg*, Berlin-Schöneberg, 1952, pp. 196–201.

refugees, many of them aristocrats; the liquidation of millions of war loans floated with middle-class savings; and a large disproportion in the demographic relationship of women to men. Finally, there were the economic consequences of the war: reparations, loss of export markets, exhaustion of both plant and raw materials, and inflation. The latent social problems of the prewar era were further complicated by a crisis of legitimacy in the political order coinciding with economic disintegration. The results were paradoxical; on the one hand, consistent and uninterrupted extension of the social tendencies of the prewar era, on the other, an ideologized misinterpretation of these tendencies that effectively prevented the solution of the maladjustments they caused.

A statistical résumé leaves no doubt about the unambiguous course of social development (see Table 1).

TABLE 1

GERMAN OCCUPATIONAL DISTRIBUTION IN % OF POPULATION[3]

Year	*Agriculture*	*Industry & Handicrafts*	*Services*
1882	42	36	22
1895	36	39	25
1907	34	40	26
1925	30	42	28
1933	29	41	30

This was the classical pattern of industrialization, urban growth, industrial rationalization, and the development of distribution and service industries. While only 5 per cent of the German population had lived in cities of over 100,000 in 1871, the proportion had grown by 1925 to 27 per cent.[4] Equally striking was the relative redistribution of ownership and economic status (see Table 2).[5]

While the figures were neutral as economic indicators—pointing only to advancing industrialization and relative only to success in feeding, housing, and clothing an industrial pop-

[3] Quoted in Fritz Croner, *Soziologie der Angestellten*, Cologne and Berlin, 1962, p. 196.

[4] Joseph A. Schumpeter, "Das soziale Antlitz des deutschen Reiches" (1929), *Aufsätze zur Soziologie*, Tübingen, 1953, p. 217.

[5] Quoted in Croner, op. cit., p. 196.

TABLE 2
GERMAN OCCUPATIONAL STATUS IN % OF POPULATION

In %	*1882*	*1895*	*1907*	*1925*	*1933*
Independent	38	35	27	21	20
Their employed dependents	4	4	8	10	11
White collar including civil service	8	11	14	19	18
Workers	50	50	51	50	52

ulation—they were full of implications as a reflection of social and political tendencies. The loss of economic independence, the employment of family members, the ballooning white-collar population characteristic both of the big city and the bureaucratic state and economy all affected the self-respect of the people they touched—or at least were capable of doing so as soon as they seemed to coincide with a decline in the standard of living. If the processes themselves were characteristic of capitalism, it stood to reason that those affected by them would come to consider themselves anti-capitalistic, without, however, accepting the theoretical Marxian implications of their misery and disappearing in the traditional proletariat. Theodor Geiger estimated, on the basis of the 1925 census, that 25,000,000 Germans could be classed, socially, as proletarians. But 45,000,000, roughly three quarters of the population, were living—during a period of increasing prosperity nearly five years before the depression—on proletarian incomes.[6]

Particularly characteristic of this tendency were the retail traders, a bumper crop sown by the imperial order and in constant fear of being mowed down by the economics of the Republic. Between 1882 and 1907, the number of small retail traders had grown faster than both population and the national product as people sought to exploit urban growth and a rising living standard in tobacco shops, groceries, drugstores (Drogerien), and delicatessens (Feinkostgeschäfte). Even before the war, existing statistics pointed to a decline in professional quality. A survey of Brunswick grocers (Ko-

[6] Theodor Geiger, *Die soziale Schichtung des deutschen Volkes*, Stuttgart, 1932, pp. 72 f.

lonialwarenhändler) in 1901 established that only 34 per cent had had any vocational training compared with 67 per cent in 1887. Even before the depression, the economic consequences of the peace had revealed the weaknesses of the small shopkeeper, exposed to the business cycle, unresponsive to shifting population, and inadequately trained for either successful competition or other employment.[7] Added to his problem on the one hand were the price-sinking creations of advancing technology and concentrated capital, the chain and department stores, and on the other, the vast overaccumulation of non-competitive manpower in retail trade. Between 1907 and 1925, the number of retail outlets rose from 695,-800 to 847,900, an increase of about 21 per cent. Between 1924 and 1929 it increased another 3 per cent. Geiger estimated that in 1925 nearly 45 per cent of those engaged in retail trade were already living on proletarian incomes.[8]

Meanwhile the number of department store subsidiaries rose from 101 in 1925 to 176 in 1929. While their absolute share of retail turnover was still small enough, their relative share by 1928 was growing 22 per cent faster than the total volume of retail trade.[9] Between 1925 and 1931 so-called "specialty" shops lost 5 per cent of their share of retail volume, a relatively small figure but one magnified by higher operating costs, lively imaginations, and then by the depression. A 1929 tax study showed that the department stores had, in fact, taken over only 4 per cent, the chain stores at most 1.1 per cent of retail trade.[10] This included, however up to 6 per cent of the turnover in clothing and 20 per cent in household goods and furniture. By 1928 retail pressure groups were pressing for increased taxes on department stores, a goal achieved by 1929 in Munich and Frankfurt, Main.[11] In 1932, the Brüning government declared a limit

[7] L. D. Pesl, "Mittelstandsfragen," *Grundriss der Sozialökonomik*, Vol. IX, Tübingen, 1926, pp. 104 ff.

[8] Geiger, op. cit., p. 73.

[9] Heinrich Uhlig, *Die Warenhäuser im Dritten Reich*, Cologne-Opladen, 1956, p. 25.

[10] Ibid., pp. 47 f.

[11] Ibid., p. 39. Uhlig thought, however, that this had more to do with considerations of local finance than with effective pressure by the shop owners.

on further department store expansion, followed before the year was out by a similar ban on chain stores. Whether his misery was caused by his own inefficiency, his aversion to co-operatives, to the methods, economics, or good advertising of larger units within his own line, or by the department stores was a matter of indifference to the retail merchant whose effective desire was a self-contradiction: free enterprise minus its attendant risks.

But while the economic implications of retail trade seemed to point in the direction of the Marxist prognosis, toward concentration, intensified competition, and the strangulation of the small, independent proprietor, another development pointed in the opposite direction. This was the rapid growth of the white-collar population, "sociologically perhaps the most significant development of the last decades," as Ferdinand Fried called it in 1931.[12] It was indeed characteristic of the period that the white-collar workers formed one of the best-observed of all social groups, their origins, attitudes, and habits becoming a subject of considerable public interest. Siegfried Kracauer's Marxist phenomenology of the white-collar worker ran for weeks in a daily newspaper[13] in 1929 while the white-collar "little man" became in 1932 the hero of a fictional best seller, Hans Fallada's *Little Man, What Now?*

Coming as they did both from the ranks of the traditional bourgeoisie and from the proletariat, it was nonetheless clear that the white-collar workers were neither workers nor middle class in the traditional sense. Contemporary social science begged the problem of categorization rather than solved it by calling the entire group, from shop clerks to graduate engineers, "the new middle class."[14] But this was hardly a guide to their behavior, which was, from the Marxist point of view from which they were most often observed, a collection of anomalies.

[12] Ferdinand Fried, *Das Ende des Kapitalismus,* Jena, 1931, p. 97.

[13] Reprinted as *Die Angestellten, Eine Schrift vom Ende der Weimarer Republik,* Allensbach and Bonn, 1959.

[14] Cf. Emil Lederer and Jakob Marschak, "Der neue Mittelstand," *Grundriss der Sozialökonomik,* Vol. IX, Tübingen, 1926, pp. 122 ff.

The white-collar worker was usually employed in a big city and by a big employer. He—or still more likely, she—was often of working-class origins, even before the war. Hans Speier quoted a number of surveys (see Table 3).[15]

TABLE 3

Year	*Job classification*	*Working class origins*
1906	Berlin saleswomen	33.6%
1909–11	Young Munich saleswomen	66.9
1932	Cologne saleswomen	51.5
1929	Apprentices of Gewerkschaft der Angestellten (clerical union):	
	Male	33.6
	Female	42.9

White-collar workers showed a progressive tendency to organize, and in a relatively militant organization from which employers were excluded. But both the form and the objectives differed from the traditional union pattern, corresponding in part to the different social origins of the membership, in part to the nature of their employment. While Geiger estimated that less than 4 per cent of the working-class population was skilled (qualifiziert), he estimated that 70 per cent of the white-collar population had some professional qualifications.[16] This alone might have led them away from the traditional union demands. While 80 per cent of the workers were organized in the so-called "free" socialist unions in 1931, only 25 per cent of the white-collar workers were organized in the socialist Gewerkschaft der Angestellten (clerical union), while 22.6 per cent were in the national-liberal Hirsch-Duncker unions and 34.1 per cent in the so-called "Christian-National" organizations like the Deutschnationaler-Handlungsgehilfenverband (German National Sales Clerks Association) (DHGV), perhaps the only economic-interest organization in Weimar Germany that combined a racist-nationalist

[15] Hans Speier, "The Salaried Employees in German Society," mimeographed, Columbia University Department of Social Sciences and WPA, New York, 1939, pp. 97–99.

[16] Geiger, op. cit., pp. 74 f.

(völkisch) program with mass membership.[17] It is also of interest that 39 per cent of the DHGV membership came from working-class origins.[18]

While the white-collar union was a tough negotiator and the pressure of economic circumstances could bring about a professional solidarity great enough to overcome the ideological divisions separating the white-collar groups, white-collar consciousness made itself felt in a preoccupation with salaries instead of wages, long-term contracts, and pensions;[19] reflections of a concern with security—including the security of social status—that distinguished it from the blue-collar unions. Weimar legislation continued to distinguish white collar (Angestellten) from blue collar (Arbeiter), granting the former special job security, separate status in wage contracts, and a separate insurance fund.[20]

Both Schumpeter and Lederer-Marschak claimed to see the line between blue collar and white collar fading, Schumpeter because the workers were coming to live like petits bourgeois,[21] Lederer and Marschak because the white-collar workers were coming to behave like other workers.[22] The depression proved the contrary. Unemployment hit blue collar and white collar alike, but psychologically it hit the white-collar worker harder. Speier quotes an unemployed white-collar worker: ". . . one is immediately ostracized, one is déclassé, without means of support, unemployed—that's equal to being a Communist."[23] Déclassé is clearly the important word, reflecting a sensitivity of self-esteem different from that of the traditional working class. The increased employment of women—between 1913 and 1921 the proportion of women in the white-collar organizations had grown from 7.7 to 23.8 per cent[24]—tended to increase the tension by making

[17] Speier, op. cit., p. 76.
[18] Ibid., p. 87.
[19] Lederer and Marschak, op. cit., p. 131.
[20] Cf. Kunibert Piper, "Das Wesen des Angestellten," Greifswald dissertation, 1939, pp. 31 ff.
[21] Schumpeter, op. cit., p. 225.
[22] Lederer and Marschak, op. cit., p. 141.
[23] Speier, op. cit., p. 20.
[24] Lederer and Marschak, op. cit., p. 131.

higher paid male jobs more vulnerable and compounding class war with sex war.

A key group in the white-collar population was an academically trained class, multiplied by postwar circumstances beyond its prewar numbers and increasingly absorbed in salaried employment in an economy that placed growing demands on technically trained manpower. The economic crises of the first Weimar years fell with particular weight on them, a group already sensitive to its exclusion, in part real, in part apparent, from traditional careers in the Army and civil service. While the social structure of Germany's political leadership changed significantly, the structure of the university population changed little except to the extent to which it grew and suffered. The 1922 Who's Who revealed that 20.3 per cent of the political entries came from the working class and 30.8 per cent from lower-income groups while only 40.8 per cent came from the old upper classes (Oberschicht).[25] But the universities were peopled by the sons of the groups most conscious of the loss this revolution had caused them. The relative frequency of sons from the families of professional men went up in proportion to the restrictions imposed on business and the military.[26] But while the sons of lawyers cautiously chose to make their ways in other areas, considerable numbers in medicine, pharmacy, and the natural sciences, the law faculties were filled with the sons of the petite bourgeoisie seeking the traditional prewar way to the top.[27] In 1929, 23.4 per cent of all students were from the families of university graduates, 11.5 per cent from the homes of the rich—big landowners, company directors, etc. But 64.2 per cent came from the middle class[28] intent on making their way in a world whose political direction was increasingly dominated, as they would tend to see it, either by the discredited representatives of the old order or by their social and cultural inferiors.

"The age of the self-made man is past," Robert Michels

[25] Quoted in Robert Michels, *Umschichtungen in den herrschenden Klassen nach dem Krieg*, Stuttgart, 1934, p. 79.

[26] Ibid., p. 60.

[27] Ibid., p. 59.

[28] Ibid., p. 62.

claimed.[29] The only career open to the talented working-class boy was political. At the same time there was every evidence of dissatisfaction in a university graduate population of 840,000 while the student population tended to grow by 10 per cent a year. Since the routes to the top narrowed, and the traffic increased, the result appeared to be fewer and fewer rewards for higher and higher qualifications. Fried, who clearly felt himself a victim of the process, was eloquent in his description of its consequences: four to six years of university study, costing from five to nine thousand marks, rewarded with starting salaries ranging from two to four hundred marks monthly and advancing to a level commensurate with family obligations and social status only when its recipient reached the age of forty or fifty.[30] The university graduate, Fried declared, felt as he had once felt during his first weeks of military service: spiritually and physically exploited. But while he might once have become a reserve officer for his pains, his civilian occupation under present circumstances offered him the chance of one day becoming—with the best of luck—a prokurist, a kind of economic sergeant. "The way to the top is blocked off,"[31] he concluded, including among the obstacles the oligarchy of age. Reichstag deputies were, on the average, fifty-six years old, the two hundred leading economic figures, sixty-one years old—"rigid, dead, outdated and reactionary like the SPD."[32]

One other major social group, the farmers, shared the general disaffection. Geiger estimated that nearly 60 per cent of them were living on proletarian incomes.[33] The intensity and quality of their disaffection varied according to region and market conditions but was ultimately reducible to the classic problem of agriculture in an industrial society: the farmer's inability to control prices and production in an otherwise manipulable economy. The result was a curious dilemma. Massive economic disintegration might bring him short-term advantages, as it did during the 1923 inflation which liqui-

29 Ibid., p. 64.
30 Fried, op. cit., pp. 105–8.
31 Ibid., p. 100.
32 Ibid., p. 127.
33 Geiger, op. cit., pp. 72 f.

dated his debts and brought him the short-term benefits of a barter economy and a sellers' market. But in the long run, the farmer suffered as the general economy suffered. On the other hand, prosperity, even as it brought him higher prices, tended to increase the lag between farm and industrial income on one side and farm and industrial prices on the other. His efforts to overcome this gap resulted in overproduction with a consequent decline in prices.

The basic problem of German agriculture was not really a problem of water, climate, or soil chemistry. Nor was it necessarily a problem of education or administration. German farm administration was respected, its research stations admired, its statistics exemplary. A growing number of farmers were aware of scientific breeding, crop rotation, soil chemistry, and mechanical rationalization. The chronic problem was relative—too much rural population to guarantee all of it an acceptable income. While grain constituted up to 40 per cent of German agricultural production, German conditions all but precluded competitive operation against overseas imports, and milk, butter, meat, eggs, which could be produced more economically, were vulnerable to the wide fluctuations in purchasing power in the Weimar economy. The solution, as in any other industrial country, was inevitably the creation of alternative forms of employment. But it was this that the Republic, for various reasons, avoided. On the contrary, among its earliest economic measures was a homestead act intended in the short run to drain off demobilized military manpower by redistribution of defaulted eastern estates, but, in the long run, intended to reverse the prewar trend toward urban concentration. It was characteristic of Weimar economic policy that subsidized industrial development of East Germany through exploitation of its plentiful waterpower sources was never seriously considered.[34] But while Prussia's eastern provinces stagnated in industrial underdevelopment, the farm problem west of the Elbe was one of rural overpopulation. In 1925 30 per cent of the German population was engaged in agriculture. To be sure, as Schumpeter observed, one and a half million had left the land between 1882 and 1925 while

[34] Henning von Borcke-Stargordt, *Der ostdeutsche Landbau zwischen Fortschritt, Krise und Politik*, Würzburg, 1957, p. 46.

the number of farm owners had remained constant.[35] During the same period there had also been a relative decline in the number of large holdings and consequent increase in "healthy" middle-sized units. But a survey of land ownership in a relatively average, prosperous West Elbian landkreis (county) indicates the narrowness of the productive base. Nearly 40 per cent of the farms around Kassel were under 12½ acres,[36] only 4.7 per cent of all holdings had any sort of power-driven machine, only 25 per cent machines of any sort.[37] A labor shortage that required the importation of Polish help, alternating with spasmodic phases of severe rural unemployment, reflected the general instability.[38]

The farmer reacted to all this as he always had, in two ways, by intensification that often transgressed the law of diminishing returns, and by expanded production. During the years 1919–30 German and Prussian wheat yields per hectare (abbr. ha., equal to 2.471 acres) exceeded comparable American yields by 100 to 150 per cent.[39] Given 1880=100 as a base, general productivity per hectare, 186 in 1913, had reached 188 by 1927 and 212 by 1933.[40] The milk output of a farm in Lower Saxony nearly doubled between 1925/26 and 1932/33 while the price fell by nearly half.[41] By 1933 when the price of wheat had fallen by nearly 50 per cent, of swine by nearly 65 per cent, of cattle by 55 per cent of their 1929 level[42] and the farm debts that had financed both the intensification and the surpluses had reached unprecedented

[35] Schumpeter, op. cit., p. 218.

[36] Walter Schreiner, "Agrarpolitische Untersuchungen im Landkreis Kassel," Giessen dissertation, 1929, p. 35.

[37] Ibid., p. 80.

[38] Ibid., pp. 50–52. In April 1926 unemployment was estimated at 3320, in October 1927 at 209, during the winter of 1927/28 at 1400.

[39] H. W. Graf Finck von Finckenstein, *Die Entwicklung der Landwirtschaft in Preussen und Deutschland, 1800–1930*, Würzburg, 1960, p. 68.

[40] Elisabeth Steiner, "Agrarwirtschaft und Agrarpolitik," Munich dissertation, 1939, p. 18.

[41] Ludwig Preiss, "*Die Wirkung von Preisen und Preisveränderungen auf die Produktion in der Landwirtschaft*," Berichte über Landwirtschaft, Vol. XXIII, No. 4, Berlin, 1938, p. 639.

[42] Ibid., pp. 637 f.

heights, the Weimar Republic had fully lost the confidence of its farmers. The state of emergency declared in East Prussia in May 1929 had, by July 1932, extended to all of East and Central Germany, Lower Bavaria and the Upper Palatinate, and by 1933 to all of Germany.[43]

None of these problems was new or unique to Germany. In one form or another they had been, since the middle of the nineteenth century, not only the raw material of German politics but in varying degrees of the politics of all industrial and industrializing countries. In America similar phenomena had fueled political controversy since at least the election of Jackson in 1828 and formed the bases of the mass Populist and Progressive movements before World War I and later the basis of the New Deal.[44]

What complicated solution in Germany was not a failure to recognize the structural inadequacies of industrial society, but rather a failure to find an alternative social model adequate to correct them. Advancing literacy, urbanization, industrialization, and the development of overseas agriculture all pointed to the liberal society envisaged by the Weimar Convention. But the main currents of social thought since at least the constitution of the Reich pointed away from it. They aimed instead at what René König calls "the two revolutions that didn't occur."[45] One of these was Marxist. The other was what Fritz Stern has called "the politics of cultural despair,"[46] a kind of Peter Pan ideology for a society that didn't want to grow up. As aware as the Marxists of the evils of industrialization, the cultural pessimists saw their correction not so much in a redistribution of ownership as in the elimination of industrial society itself. They waged war against the city, turned rural emigration into the pejorative "Landflucht" as though it were a form of desertion, created a

[43] Cf. Leo Drescher, *Entschuldung der ostdeutschen Landwirtschaft*, Berlin, 1938, pp. 7 f.

[44] Cf. Arthur Schlesinger, Jr., *The Age of Jackson*, Boston, 1945; Richard Hofstadter, *The Age of Reform*, New York, 1955.

[45] René König, "Die Soziologie der zwanziger Jahre," *Die Zeit ohne Eigenschaften*, ed. Leonhard Reinisch, Stuttgart, 1961, pp. 82–118.

[46] Fritz Stern, *The Politics of Cultural Despair*, Berkeley, 1961; Anchor Books, 1965.

distinction between Gemeinschaft, the Arcadian community of the rural village, and Gesellschaft, the soulless rat race of urban society, and turned the sociological discussion of the period into an exhaustive analysis of "class" and "estate."[47] The homestead act of 1919 and the economic parliament foreseen by the Weimar Constitution were testimony to their influence even during the brief honeymoon of popular support for the liberal Republic. In the form of land reform and conventions of estates (Ständekammern) and supplemented with demands for industrial profit sharing, nationalization of trusts, and redistribution of department store properties to small business, both measures found their echo only a few months later in the "inalterable" Nazi program of 24 February 1920.

This was less evidence of Nazi originality than of the Zeitgeist. The infant Party was obliged to climb on the bandwagon to remain in the race. What subsequently turned the NSDAP into a mass organization with a voter potential of fourteen million, and finally into Germany's governing Party, was at no point its programmatic command of the issues or pseudo-issues, but its manipulation of them. It was the mobilization of disaffection.

A form of this general disaffection had created National Socialism even before Hitler discovered it. In its original form, National Socialism was a phenomenon of the South German border areas,[48] an organization of "little men," frequently handicraftsmen, frequently of small-town origin, all of them hungry for the respect of their German-National social betters. An outline of its general premises can be found in the unassuming autobiographical essay of Anton Drexler, the chairman of the little German Workers Party Hitler discovered in Munich in 1919. Drexler described with horror his youthful experiences in Berlin, his ostracism for unstated reasons by Socialist unionists, and the humiliation of having to play the zither in a restaurant.[49] With the querulousness of the born crank, he was quick to find a Jewish-capitalist-

[47] Cf. Käthe Bauer-Mengelberg, "Stand und Klasse," *Kölner Vierteljahreshefte für Soziologie*, 1924, p. 287.

[48] Cf. A. G. Whiteside, "Nationaler Sozialismus in Oesterreich," *Vierteljahreshefte für Zeitgeschichte*, Vol. IX, No. 4, 1961.

[49] Anton Drexler, *Mein politisches Erwachen*, Munich, 1937, p. 10.

Masonic conspiracy at the root of all problems, to appreciate its diabolical exploitation of existing class differences to plunge Germany unprepared into World War I and then to secure its defeat. While addressing himself to the working class,[50] he was careful to avoid offense, to declare the worker a Bürger, and the officer and civil servant non-bourgeois.[51] He declared himself in favor of capitalism but "healthy" capitalism,[52] and drew a line between the Bürger, the farmer, the worker, and the soldier, on one side, and their common enemy, the capitalist Jew, on the other.[53]

In industrially underdeveloped Munich at the end of the war and after the left-wing putsch that followed it, this was an ideology with a certain appeal. The following it attracted was not as limited as Hitler later tried to suggest. Hitler, who joined with membership card No. 555,[54] found both a rudimentary party program and a potentially expansive membership. The ideology was the work of a kind of Central European William Jennings Bryan, the engineer Gottfried Feder, whose specialty was inflationary fiscal policy and who had previously tried without success to sell his schemes to Kurt Eisner, the Socialist leader of the 1918 Bavarian revolution.[55] The membership was mixed, in part a combination of desperate small shopkeepers, professional men, and workers like the machinist Drexler and his friends from the railroad, in part of demobilized soldiers like Hitler himself, at loose ends and unable to find their way back into civilian life.[56] There being potentially large reserves in both the "civilian" and the "military" groups, this was a combination with a political future, provided that it found leadership capable of holding it together, and that economic and political stabilization did not undermine its attractiveness.

Relying on Feder and the völkisch bohemian Dietrich Eckhart for intellectual sophistication and social introductions,

[50] Ibid., p. 9.
[51] Ibid., p. 38.
[52] Ibid., p. 63.
[53] Ibid., p. 48.
[54] Georg Franz-Willing, *Die Hitler-Bewegung, Der Ursprung 1919–22*, Hamburg-Berlin, 1962, p. 63.
[55] Ibid., p. 128.
[56] Ibid., p. 126.

Hitler made leadership his own task. Bavaria's particularist struggle with Prussia, its economic underdevelopment, the influx of the refugees and social déracinés attracted to Munich by its seemingly infinite tolerance and its relatively low cost of living, postwar inflation and the trauma of the Bavarian soviet republic of 1919, maintained the necessary instability. Appreciating from the beginning that his objective of turning his organization into a mass party could be achieved only by exclusiveness, by making it distinct from the many comparable groups already fishing in the same troubled waters, Hitler avoided coalition and set out to manipulate techniques instead of ideas. The program of February 1920 was broad enough to appeal to everyone but Jews, capitalists, and war profiteers. It was then declared final and unalterable. The immediate task, as Hitler saw it, was not the creation of a program but of an "image."

The image he created was double, a combination of conciliation indoors and violent aggressiveness on the street, of tactical flexibility and direct intimidation. To separate his own group from its völkisch competitors, Hitler, by his own statement, was assiduous in calling his organization a "party," retaining "Worker" in its name, flying a red flag, adopting "comrade" as the official form of address,[57] and appearing in public without a tie.[58] But from the beginning he was careful to avoid the one-sidedness that might bring his party into direct competition with the established workers parties or alienate any other potential sources of mass support. While Feder campaigned against "predatory capital," Hitler cultivated contacts with it, reaching variously to the local haute bourgeoisie, the University of Munich, and officers of the Reichswehr garrison. He let himself be seen, as a skeptical scout from Julius Streicher's Franconian group described him, "riding around in automobiles with women who smoke cigarettes";[59] the Franconian group nonetheless merged with Hitler's on Hitler's terms.

[57] Adolf Hitler, *Mein Kampf* (1925, 1928), Munich, 1939, p. 478.

[58] Henry Picker, *Hitlers Tischgespräche,* Bonn, 1951, p. 422.

[59] Quoted in Franz-Willing, op. cit., p. 92; cf. Oron James Hale,

As early as 1920 Drexler answered a suspicious query from Berlin with the assurance that "whether one works physically or intellectually (geistig) for the well-being of the fatherland, he is a worker. . . . There is therefore no reason to take exception to our name. A glance at one of our meetings would convince you that the most highly qualified intellectual workers (Geistesarbeiter) are joined in the greatest mutual agreement and co-operate loyally with men from the workbench. We have no intention of being a "Workers' Party" in the narrow sense, but rather a party of all who work (Schaffende)."[60] According to the earliest available membership list, the Party in January 1920 consisted of 33⅓ per cent handicraftsmen and skilled workers, 14½ per cent from the liberal professions, 7 per cent students, 14 per cent civil servants and white-collar workers, 13 per cent soldiers and officers, 12 per cent shop clerks, 4 per cent shop owners, 2½ per cent unskilled workers. The average age was thirty to thirty-two,[61] corresponding to the age of Hitler himself who was thirty when he arrived in Munich. A war of the young against the old was as great a possibility as the mobilization of the déclassé against the established. This opportunity Hitler was quick to exploit with his organization of an "active" Party auxiliary, a "sport" group organized from the remnants of the anti-Communist militia of the first postwar months and the Upper Silesian Freikorps Oberland, to ride around in trucks, pick fights with the Communists, and be seen.[62] Of the twenty-five members of the first SA group, formed in 1921, only one was over thirty, and fifteen were under twenty, too young even to have been in the war.[63] According to a Munich police report of July 1921 these "actives" were in a relative majority at the meeting where Hitler seized sovereign control of the Party, numbering 200 out of 350—"Upper Silesian adventurers flashing medals, badges, and swastikas." The

---

"Gottfried Feder Calls Hitler to Order," *Journal of Modern History*, December 1958, pp. 360–62.

[60] Quoted in Franz-Willing, op. cit., p. 104.

[61] Ibid., p. 129.

[62] Ibid., p. 138.

[63] Archive of the Institut für Zeitgeschichte, Munich, F107, 391.

other 150, fifty of them women, were identified as commercial middle class (Mittelstand).[64]

These two elements, youthful "actives" and "passive" Mittelstand, distinguishable to an extent as an "SA" group and a "Party" group, reinforced respectively by unemployment and inflation, were the basis of Hitler's support. But while both groups shared a common antipathy for Jews and the republican status quo, there was no particular ideological common denominator. Indeed ideologically they were diametrically opposed, though this seems to have remained latent at least until the putsch attempt of 1923, as both sides were united by a common republican or Prussian or Social Democratic or foreign enemy. But while the "passives" were basically concerned with finding their way back into bourgeois society, the "actives" were interested in destroying it, with no particular scruples about ideological affiliation. "Colonel," Hitler is reported to have told the chief of the Bavarian police in November 1923, "either we act now or our SA people will go over to the Communists."[65] Despite the implied bluff, the threat was plausible enough to be taken seriously.

The clamp holding the groups together was Hitler himself who belonged to both of them. *Mein Kampf* left no doubt that Hitler's heart was with the "actives." But his practice, particularly after the grandiose failure of "activism" in November 1923, was, for the moment, with the "passives." The jail-born reflections of a frustrated revolutionary, *Mein Kampf* was a social-revolutionary book in the most profound sense. It was not the audacity of its insight which distinguished it. Of this there was little; nor was it the originality of its political demands, of which there was also little. Scarcely to be matched, however, were the breadth and depth of its author's contempt for bourgeois society and indeed for the human species. The book included, to be sure, the obligatory testimonials to the farmers,[66] to the loyal and patriotic German worker,[67] to the Army, school of the nation,[68] and even to

64 Franz-Willing, op. cit., p. 115.
65 Quoted in Franz-Willing, op. cit., p. 136.
66 Hitler, op. cit., p. 137.
67 Ibid., p. 171.
68 Ibid., p. 276.

monarchy as an institution.[69] It envisaged a promised land of Volksgemeinschaft and social justice where careers were open to talent[70] and the proud equality of common "racial" citizenship had replaced class hate.[71] But what was most interesting was an anthology of social resentments that included every level of society, Habsburgs, Hohenzollerns, and the princely houses in toto,[72] civil servants,[73] the bourgeoisie in every conceivable form,[74] and the working class that had humiliated him as an adolescent in Vienna.[75] But the worst of these was the bourgeoisie which Hitler characterized in terms reminiscent in part of Marx, in part of the prewar *Simplicissimus.* "Let us not deceive ourselves," he wrote, "our bourgeoisie is already worthless for any noble (erhaben) human endeavor,"[76] capable of any error of judgment, failure of nerve, and moral corruption. Bourgeois behavior, as Hitler saw it, included nationalist hypocrisy while fellow citizens were in misery,[77] exploitation of labor,[78] class snobbery,[79] the climactic subversion of the war effort in 1918 by support for democratic reforms,[80] an unholy respect for formal academic qualifications,[81] a tendency toward syphilis, defined further as willingness to marry the daughters of rich Jews,[82] cowardice,[83] indifference to the realities of race,[84] exclusive preoccupation with money and personal affairs,[85] and identification of the nation with the interests of the bourgeoisie.[86]

[69] Ibid., pp. 235–37.
[70] Ibid., p. 422.
[71] Ibid., p. 428.
[72] Ibid., pp. 235–37, 305.
[73] Ibid., p. 314.
[74] Ibid., pp. 39, 57, 216, 222, 245, 398, 399, 420, 474.
[75] Ibid., p. 55.
[76] Ibid., p. 398.
[77] Ibid., p. 39.
[78] Ibid., p. 46.
[79] Ibid., p. 177.
[80] Ibid., p. 216.
[81] Ibid., p. 222.
[82] Ibid., p. 245.
[83] Ibid., p. 327.
[84] Ibid., pp. 382, 423.
[85] Ibid., p. 315.
[86] Ibid., p. 325.

This was the world Hitler meant to fling out of its orbit, a world of daily affairs and calculated economic interests, of scruples and academic degrees, of monocles and cutaways, as he wrote in a passage of some eloquence.[87] The success of the endeavor depended, however, on finding an adequate lever. Among the possibilities, Hitler included "the vast army of those too poor . . . to view money as the regent of their existence . . . [and] the mighty army of German youth . . . destined to be either the architect of a völkisch state or to be final witness to the total collapse of the bourgeois order."[88] And he referred to a historical model, the Austrian Christian-Socialist movement of the '90s which "possessed the necessary understanding of the significance of the masses and assured itself at least a share of it by its emphasis on its social character. By its basic objective of winning for itself the petite bourgeoisie and the handicraftsman, it gained a following as loyal as it was tenacious and self-sacrificing."[89]

This was the kind of material that was already available, not only in Bavaria but all over Germany. The core in Lower Saxony included a onetime medical student, a middle-aged salesman who had spent some years in Spain and came from a völkisch splinter party, a carpenter and former policeman who had left the SPD when it failed to heed his warnings about Poles and Jews,[90] the son of a Baltic-German professor

[87] "The speaker was a dignified old gentleman, professor at some university or other. The executive committee sat on the platform. A monocle to the right, a monocle to the left, and in the middle one without a monocle. All three in cutaway, making the impression either of a court about to announce a death sentence or a particularly fancy baptism. . . . Three workers, who were there either out of curiosity or because they had been sent, were in the audience. I posted myself behind them. They looked at each other from time to time with scarcely concealed grins, finally nudged each other with their elbows, and then stole out of the hall." Ibid., p. 475.

[88] Ibid., p. 398.

[89] Ibid., p. 125. The Bavarian police reported that Oskar Körner, a toyshop proprietor who was killed in the Hitler putsch of November 1923, was nearly ruined at the time of his death because for years he had been contributing half his income to Hitler's party. Quoted in Franz-Willing, op. cit., p. 186.

[90] Ludolf Haase, "Aufstand in Niedersachsen," mimeographed, 1942, pp. 5–8.

who found Ludendorff "reactionary,"[91] and the unemployed son of an emigré German officer who had attended secondary school (Gymnasium) in Tiflis before arriving in Göttingen after the war as a farm laborer. The charter members of the Party included a printer, a janitor, a gamekeeper, three handicraftsmen and a small tradesman, two elementary school (Volksschule) teachers, and a dentist (whose Jewish wife was the cause of some embarrassment).[92] Uniting them were a common völkisch past[93] and a high level of unemployment[94] that in 1923 included up to 30 per cent of the membership.

Real workers, as Albert Krebs recalled from his experience in Hamburg, were as rare as civil servants and those with higher education. Krebs, himself under thirty, a war veteran and the holder of a doctor's degree, was named district leader (Gauleiter) in Hamburg in the mid '20s. The membership he found on his arrival came from the lowest subgroups of the middle class, people whose political outlook was rooted in the prewar world, many of them small tradesmen and handicraftsmen but many shop clerks as well.[95] Krebs was a functionary of the Deutschnationaler-Handlungsgehilfenverband. His predecessor as Gauleiter was a Silesian whose memory reached back to Adolf Stöcker's Christian-Socialist movement of the '90s, and his second in command a West Prussian blacksmith who, though employed in a Hamburg factory, continued to think of himself as a farm boy. The treasurer, a former seaman, cook, and mounted policeman, had been antagonized by the anti-German propaganda current in America where he had been during the war—and where, Krebs surmised, he might also have acquired his anti-Semitism—and felt acutely his lost opportunity to perform military service.

Of ten relatively prominent Alte Kämpfer (old fighters) whose obituaries appeared in a Party journal in 1939, seven

[91] Ibid., p. 468.
[92] Ibid., p. 94.
[93] Ibid., p. 91.
[94] Ibid., p. 81.
[95] Albert Krebs, *Tendenzen und Gestalten der NSDAP*, Stuttgart, 1959, p. 41.

listed no profession other than Party activity, one was a tailor, one a small farmer, one a physician with a völkisch past and a record in General Epp's Freikorps that had smashed the Munich Soviet.[96] All had joined the Party between 1922 and 1927. Four had been born between 1899 and 1908. The eldest, born in 1879, had lost his savings in the 1923 inflation.

These types were Hitler's lever arm. His task was to increase its weight and radius. The task was all the more urgent in the changed situation which threatened to split the Party into its latently antagonistic halves. The party to which Hitler returned on release from his Landsberg detention was drawn toward ideological poles. One was the rural, racist, anti-industrial, populist pole around Feder. The other was the urban, "socialistic," revolutionary pole around the brothers Gregor and Otto Strasser, whose followers, like twenty-one-year-old Reinhold Muchow, a Berlin sales clerk, and the young Paul Josef Goebbels, expressed open sympathy with the Communists and, in Goebbels' case, were capable of going still further. "I believe in proletarian socialism," Goebbels wrote in 1925.[97] Gregor Strasser, since 1924 a deputy in the Bavarian Landtag and sensitive to the uneasiness of his south German listeners, was no less aggressive, even when his aggressiveness took forms adjusted to South Germany's archaic economic structure. Conventionally, his demands included support for farmers and retail trade, compensation for pensioners ruined through the inflation, and prison terms, even the death sentence, for speculators.[98] But they also included declarations of "undiluted socialist principles"[99] and contempt for the quietism and cowardice of the SPD.[100] They relegated the Wittelsbachs and all other German dynas-

[96] *Der Hoheitsträger*, April 1939, pp. 36 f.

[97] Nationalsozialistischer-Brief No. 9, reprinted in Paul Josef Goebbels, *Die zweite Revolution*, Zwickau, 1926, p. 53. Cf. Goebbels, *Tagebuch*, 1925/6, Stuttgart, 1961, p. 56; Muchow, "Situationsberichte" 1926/7, ed. Martin Broszat, *Vierteljahrshefte für Zeitgeschichte*, 1960, p. 113.

[98] Quoted in Gregor Strasser, *Kampf um Deutschland*, Munich, 1932, p. 26.

[99] Ibid., p. 72.

[100] Ibid., p. 119.

ties to history's rubbish heap,[101] and endorsed the effective nationalization of both banks and land.[102] With the consequences of revolutionary radicalism still before his eyes on his release from Landsberg in 1924, and with economic recovery undermining the basis of his support, this kind of radicalism can only have struck Hitler as dangerous.

The accumulated tension was discharged in 1925 on the issue of expropriation of the princely houses, a question that forced the Nazis to make an explicit ideological stand. Strasser favored expropriation and, at a meeting in Hanover, won the support of his North German colleagues Goebbels, Karl Kaufmann (later Gauleiter in Hamburg), Friedrich Hildebrandt (later Gauleiter in Mecklenburg), Erich Koch (later Gauleiter in East Prussia), Hans Kerrl (later Minister for Religious Affairs), and Bernard Rust (later Minister of Education), despite the efforts of Feder who was sent as Hitler's emissary to oppose the decision. The only minority vote was cast by Robert Ley, later leader of the Labor Front.[103]

Hitler, however, realized that the princely properties could be identified with the principle of private property as such, and that while support for expropriation could not fail to lead the Party into competition with the SPD and the Communists and therefore to a dead end, opposition to it was a bridge to the reserves of frightened small property owners who were the Party's only potential mass following. At a hastily called Party congress in Bamberg early in 1926, he mobilized a majority of his South German followers to outvote Strasser.[104] Goebbels, who had been delegated to represent the Strasser position and who despised Feder, later claimed to have been overcome by Hitler's logic and eloquence. A few months later when tension between "actives" and "passives" threatened to lead to a real crisis in the Berlin Party organization, Hitler, recalling Goebbels' loyalty, sent him to Berlin as

[101] Ibid., p. 23.
[102] Ibid., p. 70.
[103] Cf. Otto Strasser, *Hitler und ich,* Konstanz, 1948, pp. 108 ff.; Goebbels, *Tagebuch,* pp. 55 ff.
[104] Goebbels, *Tagebuch,* pp. 60 ff.

Gauleiter.[105] Strasser demonstrated his sense of Party discipline in a speech of May 1926 declaring support for the expropriation referendum equivalent to support for plutocracy. "Finance capital sniffs profits," he said, "perhaps something like those which it won by plundering the property of the German army, may it rest in peace, or by the expropriation of the German Mittelstand."[106]

In the years between the normalization and the depression, as Germany again turned toward the center, Hitler did the same. In a speech in February 1926 to the merchant elite of Hamburg, he addressed his hearers as "Gentlemen" ["Meine Herren"] instead of "Comrades" and found warm words for the splendor of the prewar empire and for German overseas colonies.[107] He drew shouts of "bravo" with the declaration, "Those who revolted on the home front were not Bürger, but scum, traitorous scum."[108] He chastised his audience gently for its failure to appreciate either the misery of the masses or their potential political importance, for their tendency to fight with "intellectual" (geistig) weapons and their gentlemanly reluctance to answer the terror of the 1918 revolution in kind. But he promised a reward for their insight, "The promotion of individual well-being within a framework that assures an independent economy . . . and the conviction that, in that line of activity in which we find our work, all of us are workers. . . ."[109] On Hitler's reappearance in Hamburg a year later, Krebs had the impression that Hitler was genuinely displeased with the working-class location of the Party office.[110] "In the audience that heard him campaign for Nazi candidates in the local election middle-class listeners were predominant and the haute bourgeoisie was well represented."[111] At the same time, Goebbels, on orders from Party headquarters in Munich, dissolved Muchow's creation, a

[105] Muchow, "Situationsberichte," op. cit., p. 89.

[106] Gregor Strasser, op. cit., p. 127.

[107] Werner Jochmann, *Im Kampf um die Macht*, Hamburg, 1960, p. 70.

[108] Ibid., p. 82.

[109] Ibid., p. 109.

[110] Krebs, op. cit., p. 219.

[111] Ibid., p. 56.

"Central Union of the Unemployed," whose objective had been Nazi propaganda in proletarian North Berlin.[112]

These, the relatively fat years of the Weimar Republic, were correspondingly lean years for the Nazis. A Berlin police report estimated Party membership at three thousand at the end of March 1927. Feder drew an audience of three hundred. The group had a club-like quality, issued membership cards which had to be shown at the entrance to meetings, and went on excursions. Only the SA maintained the old aggressiveness, carried revolvers, and armed itself with sharpened flagpoles.[113] In Berlin Goebbels himself led them into working-class Wedding and made capital in the Party paper *Der Angriff* of every clash with the Communists. This was fun and self-advertising like the double-bottomed radicalism of his editorials. "The political bourgeoisie is about to leave the stage of history," he wrote in 1928. "In its place advance the oppressed producers of the head and hand, the forces of Labor (Arbeitertum), to begin their historical mission. This is not a matter of wages and hours—though we must not fail to realize that these demands are essential, perhaps the most important single manifestation of the socialist will. More important is the incorporation of a potent, responsible estate (Stand) in the affairs of state, perhaps indeed in the dominant role in the future politics of our fatherland."[114]

"We are not a charitable institution but a Party of revolutionary socialists," he wrote in May 1929.[115] This was qualified, however, within a few months. The Party, Goebbels wrote, "was not against capital but against its misuse . . . , against capitalism in every form, that is, misuse of the people's property (Volksgut). Whoever is responsible for such misuse is a capitalist. . . . For us, too, property is holy. But that does not mean that we sing in the chorus of those who have turned the concept of property into a distorted monstrosity. . . . A people of free and responsible owners: that

[112] Muchow, op. cit., p. 88.
[113] Archive of the Institut für Zeitgeschichte, E 114, 49–57.
[114] Editorial of 16 July 1928, "Warum sind wir Sozialisten," reprinted in *Der Angriff*, Munich, 1935, p. 223.
[115] "Einheitsfront," editorial of 27 May 1929, ibid., p. 289.

is the goal of German socialism."[116] This was a form of agitation that brought rewards of relatively little immediate political importance, but of considerable sociological interest, the first evidence of organized worker support.

Worker support had been a cause of Party friction since at least 1925. In February 1926, the *Völkische Beobachter*, the Party paper, had advanced the idea of Nazi unions only to reverse its position within six weeks with the suggestion that Party members turn instead to the existing non-socialist unions as a more effective form of resistance to the class struggle. In the spring of 1927 the choice of union was made a matter of individual choice since the level of economic stability seemed to preclude any potential support for Nazi labor organizations. At the Weimar Party congress of 1926 a special session had been devoted without results to questions of labor organization. At the Nuremberg convention of 1927 a resolution in support of Party-sponsored unions was overridden by the appearance of the second volume of *Mein Kampf*, which left the question open.[117] Adolf Wagner's appointment as advisor on union questions (Referent für Gewerkschaftsfragen) in 1928 was the first concession of any kind to the northern wing of the Party.[118]

Pressure from below in the form of spontaneous organizations of white-collar workers and technicians in a number of large Berlin plants forced the first major decision in 1928 when Goebbels granted official recognition to the worker groups at the congress of the Berlin Party in July. Muchow was then entrusted with a secretariat for worker affairs (Sekretariat für Arbeiterangelegenheiten) which, at a special session of the Nuremberg congress of 1929, was expanded into the "Organization of National Socialist Factory Cells," the first Nazi group explicitly organized for the purpose of industrial agitation. But the campaign that followed, "Into the Plants" ["Hinein in die Betriebe!"], was identified almost totally with the Berlin area, financed almost entirely by the

[116] Ibid., pp. 227 f.

[117] Cf. *Mein Kampf*, pp. 588–600.

[118] Hans-Gerd Schumann, *Nationalsozialismus und Gewerkschaftsbewegung*, Hanover and Frankfurt, 1958, pp. 30–38.

Berlin Party. Party headquarters in Munich provided fifty marks monthly for its support.[119]

More fruitful during these years was the cultivation of auxiliaries and fellow traveler organizations in sympathetic bourgeois circles. The National Socialist Student Organization (Nationalsozialistischer Deutscher Studentenbund) was organized in 1926/27—that is, given clear priority over worker organizations.[120] It was followed in early 1929 by the League for German Culture (Kampfbund für deutsche Kultur) a creation of Alfred Rosenberg's, whose opening session was held in the main lecture hall of the University of Munich with Othmar Spann, the high priest of Gemeinschaft sociology and corporatist (ständisch) reorganization of society, as the main speaker.[121]

While the Nazi vote for the Reichstag fell in 1928 to 810,000, or ninth in order of representation, the creation and combination of ideological clienteles—Feder's petite bourgeoisie, Rosenberg's cultural pessimists, Goebbels' and the Strassers' young activists—and, above all, the charisma of Hitler, sustained both a base and an image. Radical, youthful, anti-Communist, sympathetic to small business, not necessarily hostile to big business, and ferociously nationalistic, the Party, like its program, was potentially acceptable in one way or another to nearly every large social group. Even while the vote fell, membership rose steadily—from 27,000 in 1925 to 178,000 in 1929. National Socialism had its hard core, a sociological base more diversified than that of any other party except the Catholic Center (Zentrum), variously maintained by fear of the department store, fear of communism, fear of the Poles, fear of further decline in the price of farm commodities, and "the politics of cultural despair." The numbers were small but tenacious; the cadres were there.

[119] Ibid., p. 35.

[120] One of the SS defendants at the American Zone trial in 1947 told a French psychiatrist, "During four years of studies at Heidelberg I lived on twenty marks a month and asked myself if the society which permitted such a thing was still healthy. I answered the question by joining the party." François Bayle, *Psychologie et Ethique du National-Socialisme,* Paris, 1953, p. 102.

[121] Hildegard Brenner, *Die Kunstpolitik des Nationalsozialismus,* Reibek bei Hamburg, 1963, pp. 7 f.

On the eve of its first great election victory on 14 September 1930, the Party consisted of:[122]

workers	26.3%
white collar	24.0
independent	18.9
civil servants	7.7
farmers	13.2
miscellaneous	9.9

Still more revealing of its sources of support was its age distribution:[123]

18–20	0.4%
21–30	36.4
31–40	31.4
41–50	17.6
51–60	9.7
61–	4.5

In the Party groups in Berlin, Halle-Merseburg, Mecklenburg-Lübeck, the Palatinate, and Württemberg-Hohenzollern, the 21 to 30 year-olds were more than 40 per cent of the total membership.[124] In comparison to the average for the Reich, the underdeveloped areas of South Germany, Lower Bavaria, Franconia, the Palatinate, and Schleswig-Holstein with its chronic agricultural crisis were overrepresented.[125]

The Nazi deputies elected to the Reichstag in September 1930—who, under Weimar's proportional electoral system, were men who had distinguished themselves in the Party apparatus rather than men with direct public appeal—included, by their own identification, 16 in crafts, trade, or industry; 25 employees, both blue- and white-collar workers; 13 teachers; 12 career civil servants; 9 editors and 6 Party employees, together 15 full-time Party functionaries; 8 military officers; a Protestant clergyman; and a druggist, Gregor Strasser; as well as 12 engaged in agriculture. Of the 107, 12 were under 30

[122] Reichsorganisationsleiter, *partei-Statistik,* Vol. I, 1935, pp. 85 ff.

[123] Ibid., pp. 202 f.

[124] Ibid., pp. 202–6.

[125] Ibid., pp. 28–30.

(compared with 8 of the 77 KPD deputies), 59 between 30 and 40 (compared with 45 of the 77 KPD deputies, 17 of the 143 SPD deputies).[126] Roughly 60 per cent of the Nazi (and KPD) deputies were under 40, compared with scarcely more than 10 per cent from the SPD.

Hitler's course from here to the Machtergreifung (seizure of power) was, even more than before, tactically rather than ideologically defined. As Weimar's social and political supports collapsed under the impact of the depression, his object, as before, was effectively negative: to do nothing that might antagonize potential support. This went so far, as Theodor Heuss noted, as to exclude Jews as the favored target. Hitler had nothing against "decent" Jews, he is supposed to have told a foreign visitor after the September election,[127] and Heuss had the impression that Goebbels' characterization of bourgeois opponents as a "stinking dung heap" caused him genuine embarrassment. Even before the election, Otto Strasser—a "utopian socialist," as he considered himself[128]—left the Party, antagonized by a series of what he felt to be officially sanctioned harassments and outraged, he reported, by Hitler's evident opportunism. There was no such thing as social or economic revolution, Hitler is supposed to have told him; redistribution of ownership was a Marxist chimera, the economy in its existing form was inviolable, and socialism meant nothing more than State intervention to assure the prevention of conflict. He even rejected autarky. "Do you think we can isolate ourselves from the world economy?" he asked.[129] Nazis were forbidden to join a strike in Saxony in April 1930, another of Strasser's sore points. In October 1930 when the dimensions of a metalworkers' strike in Berlin made this impossible, the Party dispatched its economic advisor, the retired major Otto Wagener, to persuade Saxon industrialists that the alternative was a mass migration to the SPD. Officially Hitler announced in the *Völkische Beobachter* that

[126] *Reichstags-Handbuch,* Berlin, 1930, pp. 522 f.
[127] Theodor Heuss, *Hitlers Weg,* Stuttgart, 1932, p. 148.
[128] Interview with author, 18 January 1963.
[129] Otto Strasser, "Meine Aussprache mit Hitler," *Aufbau des deutschen Sozialismus,* Prague, 1936, pp. 118 ff.

participation in the strike was intended to teach German industry a lesson in the consequences of observing the conditions of the Versailles Treaty.[130]

At the same time, the Party permitted itself occasional displays of its old radicalism. On 14 October 1930, the newly elected Reichstag deputation presented a bill demanding confiscation of all bank and brokerage fortunes, of the property of all East European Jews who had arrived in Germany since 1914 and of all profits accruing from the war or speculation, as well as nationalization of the larger banks and a maximum interest rate of 4 per cent. But they withdrew it in the face of the SPD and KPD who threatened to support it, knowing this would frighten Hitler's financial supporters, and equally in the face of Germany's economists who bought newspaper space to testify to the bill's impracticability.[131] In early 1931 a bill in the budget committee of the Reichstag forbidding the acquisition of any further public debts and demanding the financing of all public works with interest-free Reich credit bills testified to the survival of Feder's influence and the old populist spirit.[132] So, in May 1932, did Strasser's famous proclamation of the antikapitalistische Sehnsucht (anticapitalist yearning), with its demands that Germany go off the gold standard, increase its farm productivity, break up its urban concentrations, create a rural labor service, control farm prices and wages, finance cheap credits, and lower interest rates.[133]

But Hitler's course led away from specific demands rather than toward them, even at the risk of offending potential radical support like the SA, which was already susceptible to mutiny,[134] or like the young Reichswehr lieutenant Richard Scheringer whose indignation about the Party's apparently anti-revolutionary course led him in 1931 to make a public

[130] Konrad Heiden, *Geburt des dritten Reiches,* Zurich, 1934, p. 21.

[131] Ibid., p. 20. Cf. K. D. Bracher, *Die Auflösung der Weimarer Republik,* Stuttgart and Düsseldorf, 1955, p. 375.

[132] Heuss, op. cit., p. 94.

[133] Gregor Strasser, op. cit., pp. 347 ff.

[134] Cf. Krebs, op. cit., p. 163; Alan Bullock, *Hitler,* Penguin, 1962, p. 168.

switch to the KPD.[135] The Party was becoming respectable, and Hitler, concerned very much with votes and financial support and very little with ideological consistency, did his best to ease and hasten the process. Fritz Thyssen reported later that Hitler had given him the impression that he intended to clear the way for a restoration of the monarchy,[136] while the young and foolish Prince of Schaumburg-Lippe told of Hitler's assurance that his movement had room for monarchists and republicans alike.[137] Thyssen agreed to underwrite the Party. Schaumburg-Lippe volunteered to campaign actively in its support and noted by 1931–32 that his relatives —one of the Kaiser's sons among them—already had not only accepted "high and highest" positions in the party and SA but had been sent ahead as Landtag and Reichstag deputies.[138] Krebs, at the same time, noted that the later Hamburg Gauleiter Karl Kaufmann, then close to the Strasserite wing of the Hamburg Party, had been censured from Munich for his critique of Hitler's "Harzburg Front" with Alfred Hugenberg and the Stahlhelm, and that he himself was being edged out of his position as press secretary of the Party by a man with the "best connections" to the Hamburg merchant bourgeoisie.[139]

Still presented in their "inviolability," the twenty-five points of the party program were meanwhile subjected to a creeping violation intended to reduce any remaining resistance in yet untapped electoral reservoirs. As early as 1928 Hitler had replied to a challenge from the farmers' organizations by declaring that the land reform envisaged in the Party program would not lead to expropriations. The phrase "uncompen-

[135] Heiden, op. cit., p. 38.

[136] Fritz Thyssen, *I Paid Hitler*, New York, 1941, p. 110.

[137] Friedrich Christian Prinz zu Schaumburg-Lippe, *Zwischen Krone und Kerker*, Wiesbaden, 1952, p. 87. In a speech of August 1929, Gregor Strasser declared, "that Hitler himself has declared himself a republican, that I and the majority of my friends give the republic unequivocal precedence over the monarchy, and particularly the hereditary monarchy, and that we have never made any bones about our republican sentiments." Gregor Strasser, op. cit., p. 236.

[138] Schaumburg-Lippe, op. cit., p. 132.

[139] Krebs, op. cit., p. 115.

sated expropriation," he stated, referred only to Jewish speculators. The Party stood firmly in support of private property.[140] In its practical activity, the Party went still further. When the SPD in Brunswick presented a bill granting the state automatic priority of purchase right in sales of land, a bill whose language was copied directly from Rosenberg's official exposition of the land-reform paragraph in the Party program, eight of the nine Nazi deputies voted against it.[141] As early as 1928, this combination of tactical accommodation with falling prices resulted in a steep climb in rural support, particularly in hitherto untapped North and East German Protestant areas.

Appealing to the middle class, Feder confined the problem of profit-sharing to the very largest industrial concentrations like the I. G. Farben, then redefined it as simple price-reduction, which would bring its benefits to everyone, rather than confining it to employees of the firm concerned.[142] He also distinguished between "moral" industrialists and "anonymous, depersonalized" corporations.[143] Rosenberg left the problem to the future.[144] Still more important than ideological concessions was political organization in the form of the Kampfbund für den gewerblichen Mittelstand (Small Business Action League), another fellow-traveler group, under the leadership of Theodor Adrian von Renteln, earlier the Party's first youth leader.[145] The organizing of fellow travelers was meanwhile extended to every other possible interest group—to lawyers, doctors, teachers, schoolboys, and to women whose organizers were instructed to avoid titles, uniforms, and class appeals, and to concentrate instead on Christianity, motherhood, and the family as the basis of the future Reich.[146] Hung above each subappeal—fixed prices for the

[140] Quoted in Gottfried Feder, *Das Programm der NSDAP*, Munich, 1931, pp. 4–5.

[141] Geiger, op. cit., p. 119.

[142] Feder, op. cit., p. 58. In the 1935 edition, the reference to the I. G. Farben had been removed.

[143] Ibid., p. 46.

[144] Alfred Rosenberg, *Wesen, Grundsätze und Ziele der NSDAP*, Munich, 1937, p. 40.

[145] Heiden, op. cit., p. 172.

[146] Clifford Kirkpatrick, *Nazi Germany: Its Women and Family*

farmers, jobs for the unemployed, liberation from competition with big competitors for small business, and careers open to talent for the young—was the general appeal of "Rescue Germany," an idealized form of "sauve qui peut," as Geiger said, directed at a population that had lost the self-confidence of 1848 and 1870 and was now prepared to throw itself into the arms of its own desperation.[147] Underpinning it was a style composed equally of radical activism, military hierarchy, and the grandiose hocus-pocus of a fraternal lodge, embellished with stars, stripes, oak leaves, medals, and badges.[148] Hitler's Party had become a revolutionary mass organization whose members addressed one another with the formal, plural "Sie" rather than the familiar "Du."[149]

Ideologically, in the multiplicity of its appeals, organizationally, in the multiplicity of its forms, Hitler's following simultaneously embodied a revolutionary and a conservative principle. While potentially a source of weakness, this was also one of strength. In 1932, when the appointment of Weimar's least popular government, von Papen's, coincided with the greatest popular dissatisfaction, Hitler was trapped in a dilemma, forced to choose between financial supporters indispensable to further electoral success and electors inimical to his financial supporters. He chose the latter, even risking the opprobrium of a public testimonial to "my comrades," the SA murderers of Potempa, in order to hold the loyalty of the SA. And before the year was out, speculating on the "reactionary" godsend of the Papen government, he threw the SA into a grotesque liaison with the Communists in a wildcat

---

Life, Indianapolis and New York, 1938, p. 49. Cf. Geiger, op. cit., p. 122.

147 Geiger, op. cit., p. 120.

148 Cf. Heuss, op. cit., pp. 128–32; Karl-Gustav Specht, "Die NSDAP als organisiertes soziales Gebilde," Cologne dissertation, 1948, p. 34.

149 Cf. Robert Michels, "Psychologie der antikapitalistischen Massenbewegungen," *Grundriss der Sozialökonomik*, Vol. IX, pp. 343 ff. Otto Strasser speculates that the "Sie" form might have had something to do with the Party's weakness for military forms. But it might also have been a reflection of its fundamental disunity that precluded the "band of brothers" solidarity implied by the intimate pronoun. Strasser thought it might also indicate that party members found one another basically unpleasant. Interview with author.

strike of Berlin transport workers. "The reorientation of National-Socialist agitation is being observed here with the greatest concern," an Essen correspondent wrote Gregor Strasser. ". . . one need only think of the renewed demands for socialization, the reawakening of long refuted socialistic wage theories and the proposition that 'entrepreneur' is identical with 'exploiter' . . ."[150] This was a risk Hitler was both prepared and obliged to take, as he had accepted the risk of a "socialist" defection in 1930, was to risk one again in late 1932 when Gregor Strasser considered a coalition with Schleicher, and was to risk yet another in January 1933 when he accepted the chancellorship of a bourgeois government. Despite significant electoral losses at the turn of 1932/33, it appeared to pay off at the polls.

Hitler's first major electoral breakthrough came in underdeveloped Thuringia, a land of high unemployment, home labor, and latent Protestant radicalism, where Frick was carried into a coalition in 1929. Carrying out his mandate against the twentieth century, Frick purged what remained in Weimar of the Bauhaus, the symbol of a hopeful symbiosis of craftsmanship and industrial technology.[151] In September 1930 another major electoral victory, combined with traditional bourgeois animosity toward the SPD and Hugenberg's determination to bring Hitler into the "Harzburg Front" with his own conservative German Nationalists, brought the Nazis into the government in equally underdeveloped Brunswick. While the SPD lost votes to the KPD, all other parties showed major defections to the Nazis, despite a Volkspartei campaign against the socialist wolf in nationalist sheep's clothing.[152] The base broadened as the rest of Germany turned, in effect, into a larger Thuringia, though the tendency was complicated by other, regional conditions. The conservative parties sustained their highest losses in the districts adjacent to the Polish border, where nationalism was an important issue.

[150] National Archives Microcopy, T 81, Roll 1, frames 11441–3; letter of 20 September 1932.

[151] Brenner, op. cit., pp. 24 f., 30 f.

[152] Ernst-August Roloff, *Bürgertum und Nationalsozialismus*, Hanover, 1961, pp. 115, 27, 65–76. The Nazis elected in Brunswick included a tax official, a farmer, a worker, a mechanic, two merchants, a baker, a bank employee, a teacher, and a lawyer.

Where it was less important, in districts like Schleswig-Holstein, conservative voters continued to vote conservative while small holders, who in other western and northern districts voted liberal, switched to the Nazis. But from 1930 on, the Nazi gain was effectively proportional to the liberal loss, particularly to the loss of regional and special-interest parties. Marburg on the Lahn, where support for anti-Semitism in the '90s, for the radical liberalism of Friedrich Naumann in the years before the war, and for the bourgeois triad of DDP, DVP, and DNVP in the early '20s turned into Nazi support well above the Reich average from 1930 on, is an ideal case of the social-political continuity the Nazis drew on. Between 1928 and 1932 the Wirtschaftspartei lost 93 per cent of its voters. In 1932, as Lipset writes, the ideal type of the Nazi voter was an economically independent Protestant of the middle class who lived either in the country or in a small town, and had previously voted for a party of the center or a regional party that had campaigned against both big industry and trade unions.[153] This was reinforced, particularly in 1930, by the advent of new voters in a number of districts and of previous non-voters, particularly women, who in 1932 comprised up to half of the Nazis' electoral support though only 3 per cent of the Party membership.[154] Electoral support also included demonstrable defections from the KPD.[155]

The basic elements of Nazi support were again reflected in the 230-man Reichstag delegation of October 1932, which included 55 blue- and white-collar employees, 50 farmers, 43 independent representatives of trade, handicrafts, and industry, 29 full-time Party functionaries including editors, 20 career civil servants, 12 teachers, and 9 former officers. Compared with 1930, this showed a significant increase in the

[153] S. M. Lipset, "Faschismus," *Kölner Zeitschrift für Soziologie und Sozialpsychologie,* 1959, pp. 417 ff.; Rudolf Heberle, *From Democracy to Nazism,* Baton Rouge, 1945, pp. 111 ff.; Irmgard Neusüss-Hunkel, "Parteien und Wahlen in Marburg nach 1945," Marburg dissertation, pp. 33–36.

[154] Kirkpatrick, op. cit., p. 57; Reinhard Bendix, "Social Stratification and Political Power," *American Political Science Review,* June 1952, pp. 369 ff.

[155] Geiger, op. cit., p. 110.

representation of farmers, a slight increase in the representation of the commercially independent, and a very slight increase in the representation of employees.[156] All other major groups declined. As before, the majority were under 40, 21 between 20 and 30, 121 between 30 and 40, 64 between 40 and 50. This was a 5 per cent decline in the proportion of deputies under 40, but still impressive and again comparable only to the KPD where the relationship was 62 of 75. The SPD ratio, by further comparison, was 19 of 133.[157]

Between the September election of 1930 and the Machtergreifung, Party membership rose to 850,000, an increase of over 550 per cent. Broken down into occupational groups, the Party was made up as shown in Table 4.[158]

TABLE 4

Workers	31.5%
White collar	21.1
Independent	17.6
Civil servants including teachers	6.7
Farmers	12.6
Miscellaneous	10.5

This, compared with 1930, meant a relative increase in the number of workers, clearly an effect of unemployment. From the end of 1928 to the beginning of 1931, growth in Party

[156] A letter from the general director of the Edeka grocery chain of 22 July 1932, complaining about apparent Nazi reluctance to present Mittelstand candidates, throws an interesting light on the constitution of the Party list. Edeka had made an effort to get party members in its employ accepted on the list but with no success. The director had then gone to see Otto Wagener, the Party's economic spokesman, who again turned him down, assuring him that economic representation would be dealt with in the future outside the Reichstag, in an economic parliament to be created for that purpose. Quoted in Uhlig, op. cit., p. 195. The continued heavy representation of Mittelstand deputies reveals no change of heart, of course, but testifies to the Party's effective independence of the interests it sought to exploit.

[157] Reichstags-Handbuch, *VI. Wahlperiode,* Berlin, 1932, pp. 270 f.

[158] *Partei-Statistik,* Vol. I, 1935, p. 85.

membership was parallel to growing unemployment, although from 1931 on unemployment tended to level off while Party growth continued to rise.[159] All other groups, excepting the miscellaneous, showed a relative decline. Compared, however, with the total population, there was still a striking underrepresentation of workers and farmers. The latter was a testimonial to the loyalty of rural Catholics to the Center, particularly in west and south Germany. White-collar workers, on the other hand, were represented up to 90 per cent, the economically independent up to 100 per cent, the civil servants and teachers about 25 per cent,[160] beyond their representation in the general population.

The age structure of the new membership was as shown in Table 5.[161]

TABLE 5

18–20	1.8%
21–30	40.4
31–40	27.8
41–50	17.1
51–60	9.3
61–	3.6

In Halle-Merseburg, Koblenz-Trier, Kurhessen, the Palatinate, Weser-Ems, and Württemberg-Hohenzollern, over 45 per cent of the membership was under 30. In Catholic Koblenz-Trier and Württemberg-Hohenzollern, the high proportion of youthful members coincided with absolute membership well below the Reich average, perhaps a reflection of the relative effectiveness of clerical opposition to National Socialism on different generations. An indigenous liberal tradition in Württemberg-Hohenzollern might also have been a factor. In Halle-Merseburg, the high proportion of youthful members coincided with absolute membership above the Reich average, pointing probably to the effects of industrial unemployment in a Protestant area. Common to all except Halle-Merseburg was the crisis of the small farmer.

[159] Ibid., p. 18.
[160] Ibid., p. 53.
[161] Ibid., pp. 202–6.

At the same time, a survey of Oschatz-Grimma, a light-industrial county in Saxony, showed:[162]

TABLE 6

	Population (1933)	*SPD* (1931)	*NSDAP* (1931)
18–30	31.1%	19.3%	61.3%
31–40	22.0	27.4	22.4
41–50	17.1	26.5	8.0
51–	29.8	26.8	8.3

Regionally, the relative influx of new members increased most spectacularly in the Palatinate, Danzig, and Schleswig-Holstein; fell behind in Franconia and Lower Bavaria, which had set the pace before September 1930; and was at its lowest level, as before, in the predominantly Catholic districts of Main-Franconia and Cologne-Aachen.[163] While difficult to derive from statistics, this trend would seem to point to both ideological and geographical diffusion, a transition in the direction Hitler desired, from völkisch provincialism to Volkspartei (a popular mass party). If this is so, the relative decline in Franconia and Lower Bavaria reflects the relative saturation of Nazi support in those areas by 1930; those attracted to Hitler were already in the Party. The gain in Danzig, the Palatinate, and Schleswig-Holstein, on the other hand, was obviously a consequence of economic misery and the apparent failure of all other alternatives.

Possible confirmation of this hypothesis is the influx of women members who, by their limited number—barely 6 per cent of total membership in January 1933—might be assumed to have been proportionally more "idealistic" than men and thereby a more sensitive index to the effectiveness of the Nazi appeal. Before 1930, while male enrollment in the fastest growing Gaue (party districts) Franconia and Lower Bavaria ran only 3 to 3½ per cent ahead of the Reich average,[164] the enrollment of women in Franconia exceeded the Reich average by 23½ per cent, in Lower Bavaria by nearly 10 per cent, and in Munich and Upper Bavaria by roughly the

[162] Ibid., p. 157.
[163] Ibid., pp. 28–30.
[164] Ibid., pp. 28–30.

same rate. But between September 1930 and January 1933, while the Reich average increase was over 550 per cent, women's enrollment in Franconia rose only about 30 per cent and scarcely doubled in Upper and Lower Bavaria. At the same time, women's enrollment in Danzig rose by 2100 per cent, in East Prussia by 1900 per cent, and in Westphalia-North by 1700 per cent. Unlike male enrollment, which showed considerable regional variation, there was relatively little deviation from the general Reich average in the growth of women's enrollment, save in Catholic areas like Cologne-Aachen, where membership grew by nearly 1000 per cent but, relative to the total female population, was still only about 50 per cent of the Reich average.[165]

One last aspect of interest was the constitution of political leadership in the Party relative to the general membership. Including honorary as well as salaried Party leaders, it comprised:[166]

TABLE 7

	To 14 September 1930	*To 30 January 1933*
Workers	18.5%	22.0%
White collar	25.2	23.4
Independent	20.3	19.7
handicraftsmen	9.9	9.9
trade	8.1	7.6
professions	2.3	2.2
Civil servants	11.4	10.4
public officials	8.7	7.6
teachers	2.7	2.8
Farmers	18.4	18.4
Miscellaneous	3.8	3.1
Unemployed family members	1.2	1.6
housewives	0.9	1.3
school, college students	0.3	0.3
Pensioners	1.2	1.4

165 Ibid., pp. 28–30.
166 *Partei-Statistik,* Vol. II, 1935, p. 164.

Compared with Party membership, worker representation in Party leadership lagged visibly, the gap growing between 1930 and 1933, while farmers, civil servants, white-collar workers, and the economically independent were strikingly overrepresented. Considering that particularly in the white-collar and worker groups large, if statistically non-demonstrable, numbers had been exclusively employed by the Party for long periods, the discrepancy, particularly in worker leadership, was probably still greater than it appeared.

Age distribution ran roughly parallel to that of the general membership though, as might be expected, there was a tendency toward reinforcement of the middle-aged groups.[167]

TABLE 8

	To 14 September 1930	*To 30 January 1933*
18–20	0.2%	0.7%
21–30	26.0	28.2
31–40	39.1	36.3
41–50	21.9	23.1
51–60	9.8	9.6
over 60	3.0	2.1

In both cases, 65 per cent of the Party leadership was under forty years old.

Seen against its social background, National Socialism is far too complicated a phenomenon to be derived from any single source or reduced to any single common denominator, whether it be the depression or the course of German history. Its very dynamism precluded easy generalizations. If, before 1930, the NSDAP tended to be a Party of völkisch true believers, like the Göttingen Nazis who saw their mission in the compilation of a directory of Jews in German academic life,[168] it tended after 1930 to be an organization of the economically desperate with a considerable admixture of opportunism. "When I joined the NSDAP," Fritzsche testified at Nuremberg, "I did not have the impression of joining a Party in the conventional sense since this was a Party with-

[167] Ibid., pp. 213, 220.
[168] Haase, op. cit., pp. 692 ff.

out a theory. . . . All the Party theoreticians were under fire. . . . There were already whole groups of former DNVP members in the NSDAP or of former Communists. . . ."[169]

"The formula, 'National Socialism is exclusively that which So-and-so says or does,' whereby the particular proponent was referring to himself, replaced the Party program . . . ," Hans Frank declared in his memoirs. "Any number of names filled the formula at the start: Hitler, Goering, Strasser, Röhm, Goebbels, Hess, Rosenberg, and more. There were as many National Socialisms as there were leaders."[170]

The most general theory—that National Socialism was a revolution of the lower middle class—is defensible but inadequate.[171] National Socialism had a striking appeal for the Auslandsdeutsche, Germans who had spent the impressionable years of their lives in a German community abroad.[172] Whether at the microcosmic level of the Göttingen Party or in important positions in Munich, like Rosenberg or Darré, there was an impressive number of them. National Socialism was no less a revolt of the young against the old. While a theory of National Socialism as a lower middle-class phenomenon applies very well to voter behavior, it fails to account for important sectors of Party leadership with their violent animosity toward the social forms for which their voters yearned. Himmler's contempt for the bourgeois self indulgence of railway dining cars[173] was no more a lower middle-class attitude than the longing for action, power, nights of the long knives, or a radical reorganization of society, shared by the Party's leaders. National Socialism drew unmistakably on the historical reserves of liberal support, but its leaders were unequivocally sworn to the destruction of liberal values and liberal society.

169 International Military Tribunal, Vol. XVII (German edition), p. 154.

170 Hans Frank, *Im Angesicht des Galgens,* Munich, 1953, p. 184.

171 Cf. Harold Lasswell, "The Psychology of Hitlerism," in his *Analysis of Political Behaviour,* London, 1949, p. 236; Helmuth Plessner, *Die verspätete Nation,* Stuttgart, 1959, pp. 157 f.

172 Cf. Karl Mannheim, *Mensch und Gesellschaft im Zeitalter des Umbaues,* Darmstadt, 1958, p. 111, footnote.

173 Krebs, op. cit., p. 210.

This hard core of revolutionary destructiveness existed before the depression in quantities too great to be dismissed as simple personal idiosyncrasy. The longing for security that it exploited existed before the depression as well, but sought its objectives elsewhere in unrevolutionary places. What brought them together, leaders and followers, was a common hostility to the status quo at a moment of unique desperation, a desperation only two parties, the KPD and the NSDAP were fully prepared to exploit. In promising everything to everybody, the Nazis promised nothing to anybody. The tactical pursuit of power obviated any immediate urgency in the discussion of what was to be done once it was attained. As it was to Frank and Fritzsche this was clear to the farmer who told Heberle ". . . we believe that in the Third Reich, we, the farmers, will be so strong a power that we can shape it as we desire."[174] From a contemporary standpoint, National Socialism was wide open, its disparity not a handicap but a positive advantage. What united it ultimately was not a mandate for war and Auschwitz, but a universal desire for change.

[174] Heberle, op. cit., p. 120.

II

The Third Reich and Its Social Ideology

Hitler's appointment as Chancellor was bound to have considerable effect on both the social constitution of National Socialism and the social program it represented. Hitler was obliged to carry out the mandate of change that had brought his following together, an obligation made all the more pressing by the thoroughly unrevolutionary circumstances of his appointment and the visible moral compromise of a minority coalition with the "reactionaries" he had spent the preceding summer and autumn castigating. Hitler's appointment was the fulfillment of the bourgeois revolution in Germany, if not of bourgeois restoration, a völkisch critic wrote in March. In any case, "the mortally dangerous situation of National Socialism today is a result of the fact that it has joined its destiny with that of the bourgeoisie."[1] This situation, in turn, led directly back to the Party's basic conflict, the tension between the "actives" and the "passives," with respect to both immediate distribution of the spoils and ultimate goals. With the achievement of power, the logic of Hitler's situation and his own long-term objectives led unavoidably to "revolution," where eggs would have to be broken and not, as hitherto, walked upon.

On the other hand, the movement now faced the complex of problems involved in the metamorphosis from opposition to establishment. Despite the organizational efforts of the preceding years, the NSDAP was not a miniature reproduction of the State it took over, and still less of German society. It

[1] Hans Brandenburg, "Nationalsozialismus und Bürgertum" *Blut und Boden*, No. 3, 1933, pp. 106 ff.

found itself in the position of stowaways suddenly in control of an ocean liner. The resources at hand were suitable, in fact desirable, for seizing the bridge. But despite the presence of occasional engineers like Frick, the available personnel was of rather less use in maintaining the engines or the course. This meant, in its broadest implications, that Hitler must become Chancellor of all the people, and his following, hitherto half a civil war, a "Party above the parties." But it also meant specifically a rapprochement with the representatives of the old order—army, civil service, and big business—to keep the ship afloat.

The result of these two tendencies, the one toward revolution, the other toward social rapprochement, was reflected in the Party's membership and in the course of official pronouncements on social subjects. In advancing stages National Socialism was identified with Germany, while the new Reich developed a vocabulary and a style intended to distinguish it from all other societies, whether "reactionary" and capitalist, fascist or communist, in the consciousness of its citizens.

The first task was the creation of national solidarity behind the new government. His government, Hitler told the nation in his first broadcast speech, meant to transcend all differences of class and status. It would bring the entire nation to common awareness of its ethnic and political unity and the duties this entailed. In effect, he promised a New Deal.[2] Hitler appealed specifically to the two groups, "the pillars of our Volkstum [nation]," the farmers and the workers, who had until now been underrepresented in the Party's ranks.[3] Farm recovery and employment were declared the foremost goals of the new government and the homestead program and a labor service, the foundation of their achievement.

In the course of the year, the bourgeois joined the worker

[2] By comparison, Roosevelt announced in his first inaugural speech of 4 March 1933, "We face the arduous days that lie before us in the warm courage of national unity; with the clear consciousness of seeking old and precious moral values; with the clean satisfaction that comes from the stern performance of duty by old and young alike. We aim at the assurance of a rounded and permanent national life."

[3] Max Domarus, *Hitler: Reden und Proklamationen, 1932–38,* Würzburg, 1962, p. 192.

and the farmer as an element of national existence. At the same time, in a triumph of propagandistic showmanship, the new regime declared itself heir to the Prussian tradition at the tomb of Frederick the Great in Potsdam in the presence of Hindenburg and the Reichswehr. Before the year was out, on November 9, the tenth anniversary of the Munich putsch, Hitler appropriated the nationalist estate of the old Freikorps as he collected their flags at the Brown House. The Stahlhelm was absorbed in the SA and dissolved altogether in 1935. But the social image of the Third Reich was concentrated in the forms of the worker and the farmer. Hitler declared the farmer "the most important participant at this historic turning point in our fortunes.[4] The farmer's interests were identified with those of the nation. The harvest festival became a national holiday. Similarly, National Socialism appropriated the history of the labor movement as May 1 was henceforth celebrated in the presence of the new Chancellor.

The preoccupation with the worker was one of the most striking phases of the new course, indeed the basis of a new myth. In Richard Euringer's pageant *Deutsche Passion* German society appeared on the stage in the form of two exclusive worlds struggling for the soul of a third. On the one side stood, allegorically, the union or Party boss, the pharisaical scribe, the speculator, the shareholder and the intellectual. On the other stood the student, the businessman, the farmer, the pastor, and the artist. Between them stood the undecided, the mother, the unemployed, the wife of the unemployed, the proletarian.[5] In a variant, Alfred Karrasch's novel *Parteigenosse* [Comrade] *Schmiedecke*,[6] the worker was the main protagonist. Karrasch, a functionary of Goebbels' Ministry of Propaganda, placed the burden of responsibility on the worker and Party member Schmiedecke and his colleagues who struggled to achieve National Socialism in the face of opposition from brutal foremen, spineless engineers and white-collar employees, and villainous company directors.[7]

[4] Ibid., p. 253.
[5] Brenner, op. cit., pp. 100 f.
[6] Berlin, 1934.
[7] The secret of success, one of them explains characteristically to a managerial aspirant, is "to lie without blushing." Ibid., p. 188.

In the novel the workers display their solidarity, extending their camaraderie even to those who had fallen victim to the siren songs of Marxism, and their sense of responsibility to the acceptance of a new machine that they know will cost them a number of jobs. The engineers, on the other hand, intrigue for one another's position, and the directors ostracize a colleague who volunteers to sacrifice his dividends. The National Socialist version of a happy end includes intervention by a paternalistic owner and his son, an officer in the SA; dismissal of the intriguers; and appointment of workers to fill their places in the managerial hierarchy.

Connecting the worker motif with the farmer motif was the motif of common Blut und Boden (Blood and Soil), an anti-urban animus reflected in the first days of the Third Reich in the appointment of Darré and Feder to prominent positions. Karrasch's Schmiedecke characteristically leaves his urban slum for a suburban allotment where he invites his soul in the cultivation of his modest garden. But the theme was by no means a monopoly of the official propagandists. An instructor in the newly created Department of German Socialism at the University of Cologne conceived the purpose of industrial rationalization as liberation of potential small holders.[8] A sympathetic observer of the new regime, a professor of sociology at the University of Frankfurt, expected to witness the gradual dissolution of industrial society in Germany,[9] carrying his argument to the point of redefining the farmer and the rural handicraftsman as the real workers of the future and thus as the vanguard of the new socialism.

With the advance of industrial recovery and the preoccupation with rearmament, the anti-urban tendency understandably lost its position as a practical goal but survived as the basis of a characteristic folklore. The new folklore was a kind of ideology of the "Wild East," with the small homesteader as the cowboy and the Pole as the Indian. New land was to be conquered, Kultur to advance and a new, egalitarian "socialist" society to be created. The homestead program, wrote

[8] Achim Holtz, *Nationalsozialist–Warum?*, Munich, 1936, p. 35.
[9] Heinz Marr, *Die Massenwelt im Kampf um ihre Form*, Hamburg, 1934, p. 550.

a doctoral candidate, marked "a shift of standpoint . . . from the liberal-capitalist West toward the socialist East."[10]

In these terms even the rural gentry, junkers, like the pre-industrial order they represented, could be aligned with the builders of socialism. Their typical fields of activity, the Army and the civil service, were public service, not means of private aggrandizement.[11] A dissertation on the relative efficiency of rural and urban soldiers closed a circle that began with the worker and farmer and ended with the soldier and the historical example of the Prussian reformers. The author's model, both of élan and military effectiveness, was the Prussian yeoman army of 1813–15. Granting his bias in favor of the farmer soldier, he was nonetheless forced to conclude on the basis of casualties and decorations in a Baden regiment during World War I that the worker soldier could hold his own. But he interpreted this as a triumph of surviving rural values. Appreciating the impossibility of deindustrializing Saxony or Westphalia, he recommended the widest possible distribution of allotments to keep traditional rural values alive.[12] Consistent with his argument was his conviction that the naval mutiny of 1918 was a result of the urban influence of Kiel. He praised the wisdom of the Admiralty for keeping the British North Sea fleet from temptation at Scapa Flow.[13]

Since the Third Reich was a Reich of divergent interests no less than its Weimar predecessor, the actual significance of these, or any, statements depended, as before, on who made them and when. For example, the Frankfurt sociologist very probably believed what he said. The ideological conviction of Karrasch, who had helped himself to official patronage and even found public employment for an uncle,[14] might have

[10] Walter Haas, "Bedeutung, Aufgaben und Durchführung der Neubildung deutschen Bauerntums östlich der Elbe im nationalsozialistischen Staat," Heidelberg dissertation, 1936, p. 16. For historical continuity, cf. Hans von Schlange-Schöningen, *Bauer und Boden,* Hamburg, 1933.

[11] Karl Berger, "Beamtentum und Besitz," *Der völkische Beobachter,* (VB, hereafter), 9 June 1936.

[12] Hermann Gauer, "Vom Bauerntum, Bürgertum und Arbeitertum in der Armee," Heidelberg dissertation, 1935, p. 73.

[13] Ibid., p. 65.

[14] Bundesarchiv, Koblenz, R 55/24.

been a bit less sincere. It is conceivable that the two doctoral candidates were writing, at least in part, what they thought their examiners wanted to read. It is doubtful that one of them, whose father was a locomotive engineer, felt any particular sympathy for the junkers as a class, or that the other, born in Konstanz and trained in Freiburg and Munich, felt any unqualified reverence for the Prussian tradition. The civil servant, in turn, who found socialism among the roots of the Prussian aristocracy, might well have been seeking protective coloration in a new environment.

What was revealing was that all were speaking the same language—indirect evidence of the extent to which all had accepted or acquiesced in the new order that had created it. Its elements were a set of normative concepts, "worker," "farmer," "soldier," "socialism." Each of them was undefined in varying degrees but all of them were positive in their associations and, as such, beyond criticism. By its use of these elements, National Socialism achieved a double purpose. It conducted a verbal social revolution while accommodating both the anti-capitalist following that had supported it before 1933 and those social groups that were yet to be won. Since the new regime was, by its own definition, revolutionary, socialist, egalitarian, and elitist at once, the active social issues were fought out behind the words but never against them.

The result, superficially, was a verbal radicalism in the old socialist tradition. National Socialism was henceforth the spokesman of the German worker, Hitler declared in the debate on the enabling law in response to Wels,[15] the leader of the SPD, and Hermann Goering reproached those who neglected the "socialist" in the Party name at the expense of "national."[16] As the worker was declared a pillar of the community, the bourgeois and the capitalist were excoriated as the enemies of the people. But while the relations of state and economy, labor and capital, were indeed changing in fundamental ways, the vocabulary obscured rather than clarified the changes.[17] Beneath the surface, the vocabulary was buffeted in the currents of domestic political interests until it

[15] Domarus, op. cit., pp. 244 f.
[16] Hermann Goering, *Reden und Aufsätze*, Munich, 1940, p. 37.
[17] See Chs. III and IV.

became purely affective. Each concept became the dialectical synthesis of the stresses imposed on it by respective protagonists: "revolutionary" SA and "anti-revolutionary" regime, the "socialist" Labor Front and Party and the "capitalist" economy, the protagonists of Blut und Boden and the custodians of an efficient agriculture, and finally the mutually competitive "elites" of Party, SS, civil service, Hitler Youth, and Army.

An example of the semantic consequences of this process was the development of the word "revolution." In June 1933 Hitler told major Party leaders that the dynamism of the "national revolution" was still dominant in Germany, bringing with it a total rearrangement (Neuordnung) of German life.[18] Weeks later, he warned the Statthalter, the regional proconsuls, many of them among the audience who had just heard him, that revolution was not a permanent state of affairs but that it must be directed into an evolutionary course. "It is not permissible," Hitler continued, "to dismiss a business leader when he is a good business leader but not a National Socialist, and particularly not when the National Socialist appointed to his place has no idea of business."[19] In July, his Minister of the Interior, Frick, threatened for the first time to turn his special police powers against Party members, clear evidence of latent disunity in the "revolutionary" ranks. At least as late as March 1934,[20] Hitler declared that the revolution must continue, presumably the same revolution he had spoken of before the Labor Front[21] and the Reichstag[22] nearly a year before. But on June 30, with the aid of the SS and the Army, he crushed both the "revolutionaries" of the SA and the "counter-revolutionaries" like Schleicher and Papen's secretary Edgar Jung. "We are not a fraternal lodge (bürgerlicher Klub)," Röhm had declared in a typical statement in January. "We are a union of resolute political fighters. In the SA the revolutionary line will be maintained in

[18] Domarus, op. cit., p. 280.

[19] Ibid., p. 286; cf. K. D. Bracher, G. Schulz, and W. Sauer, *Die nationalsozialistische Machtergreifung*, Cologne and Opladen, 1960, p. 474.

[20] Ibid., p. 371.

[21] Ibid., p. 267.

[22] Ibid., p. 276.

the spirit of the recent past. I have no intention of leading men popular with the Spiesser (Babbitts) but revolutionaries, prepared to carry their fatherland forward."[23] Rauschning, who met him at the Hotel Kempinski in Berlin that spring, found him comparing the SA with Danton's levée en masse of 1792.[24] The purge of June 30 was the end of all that. In his self-justification before the Reichstag, Hitler brought two charges against the SA dead. They had become revolutionaries who practiced revolution for its own sake, and they had forsaken the paths of revolutionary virtue for homosexuality, high living, and financial corruption.[25]

In September 1934, at Nuremberg, Hitler declared the revolution over. "The revolution has achieved without exception all that was expected of it. . . . in the next thousand years there will be no new revolution in Germany."[26] Yet in Hitler's terms the revolution went on, only from above and not from below.[27] As he had told a meeting of old Party members in March 1934, the victory of a Party was nothing more than a change of government. Only the victory of a Weltanschauung was a revolution. The National Socialist revolution would have achieved its final victory only when it was accepted by all Germans, something Hitler estimated might take years or even generations.[28] That National Socialism was revolutionary remained an ideological first premise. Addressing an SA audience on the third anniversary of his appointment as Chancellor, Hitler referred to the revolution of 1918, always "revolution" in his pre-1933 speeches and always strongly pejorative, as a "miserable revolt" (traurige Revolte),[29] thereby distinguishing it from the real revolution carried on under his own leadership. That the revolution was carried on against the revolutionaries, that it had effectively turned to the benefit of the military and industrial old order, in no way vitiated the new regime's revolutionary self-image

[23] VB, 22 January 1934.

[24] Hermann Rauschning, *Gespräche mit Hitler*, Zurich, 1940, pp. 142 f.

[25] Domarus, op. cit., pp. 410 ff.

[26] Ibid., p. 447.

[27] Bracher, Schulz, and Sauer, op. cit., p. 900.

[28] Domarus, op. cit., p. 317.

[29] Ibid., p. 570.

but only rendered it abstract. "Revolutionary" was ultimately a state of mind, identical by definition with support of Hitler.

Under the pressure of Hitler's supporters, the men on the street (kleine Volksgenossen) who had made the "revolution" possible, as he declared in May 1933,[30] and the pressure of economic expedience, the "socialism" represented by the new government underwent a similar semantic development. In no case did socialism mean nationalization in the conventional sense. On the contrary, it included "the right to acquire property through honest work."[31] A functionary of the Labor Front distinguished carefully between socialism and socialization. The former referred to "work and achievement, to fulfillment of duty and responsibility to the state and the nation," the latter to "collectivism, based on a materialistic view of history."[32] What characterized this socialism was not the ownership of capital but its relationship to the State. Capital remained in private hands because this seemed expedient. But the threat of intervention was always present and generally adequate to produce the desired cooperation. The East Elbian proprietors could maintain their estates, Walter Darré told a Pomeranian audience in 1934, if they were prepared to recognize the winds of change (den Geist der Zeit erkennen).[33] In a discussion of civil rights, E. R. Huber defined the right of property as a function of duty. If he did not fulfill his duty, the farmer could be forced from his land, the businessman expropriated, the worker fired.[34]

Opening the Berlin auto show in 1937 with an affirmation of German's will to autarky, Hitler made the survival of the "so-called free economy" contingent on its capacity for solving the problems this brought with it. No economic interest was justified in settling itself against the common interests of the nation, he emphasized.[35] But the stick was al-

[30] Ibid., p. 267.
[31] Holtz, op. cit., pp. 30 f.
[32] *Der Angriff*, 14 October 1937.
[33] Gerd Rühle (ed.), *Das Dritte Reich*, Berlin, 1935, p. 111.
[34] E. R. Huber, "Die Rechtsstellung des Volksgenossen," *Zeitschrift für die gesamte Staatswissenschaft*, 1936, pp. 446 f.
[35] Domarus, op. cit., p. 681.

ternated with the carrot in the form of testimonials to the initiative of the individual businessman. Vigorous encouragement of private enterprise was one of the programmatic points Hitler presented to the Reichstag in March 1933.[36] A Party editorial in 1939 declared free enterprise to be the very basis of Germany's socialism, and the social responsibility deriving from free enterprise the key to its realization.[37] Assuring the businessman of his fair profit, an official of the Factory Cell Organization refused even to think of him as a "capitalist."[38] The spectacle of Dr. Schacht defending capitalism in the name of socialism prompted a correspondent of *The Economist* to conclude, "In reality it is impossible to formulate the opposition between Capitalism and Socialism as long as Socialism is not defined; and the Party which rejects all known brands of Socialism has no idea what its own Socialism is. In Germany it is therefore practicable, and is indeed necessary, to be pro-Capitalistic and Socialistic at the same time; and no wise man neglects to assert that he is both."[39]

This was true but failed to reach the heart of the matter, which again, was semantic. "Socialism" in its conventional senses was difficult, if not impossible, to locate in Nazi practice.[40] But as an effective concept it had a very real meaning in Nazi attitudes. It was hortatory and defined a state of mind. As such, it was characteristically favored by outgroups in their struggle with ingroups. Thus, as Klönne suggests, it was particularly frequent in the rhetoric of the Hitler Youth in its attempts to establish parity for itself with other groups

[36] Ibid., p. 233.

[37] Das Wichtigste im Arbeitsvorgang ist der Mensch," VB, 15 January 1939.

[38] VB, 1 May 1933. A particularly revealing example of ideological definition can be found in Johannes Büttner, *Der Weg zum nationalsozialistischen Reich,* Berlin, 1943. In a documentary collection intended to show how National Socialism had achieved and fulfilled the twenty-five points of its Party program, Büttner illustrated Point 12, the expropriation of war profiteers, exclusively with examples of legislation having to do with the expropriation of Jews.

[39] "Anti-Socialistic Socialists," *The Economist,* 14 December 1935; cf. "Dr. Schacht and the Nazis," *The Economist,* 7 December 1935, p. 1121.

[40] This will be discussed in later chapters.

in the Nazi establishment.[41] In the same way it tended to be invoked by Party groups in their struggle for control of the economy. Socialism in this context meant Party intervention in the economic process despite the complaints of businessmen. But "secured concentration of capital, a certain 'private initiative,' . . . and modern technology in general" remained fundamentally uncontested.[42]

As examples of socialist achievement Hess told an audience of disgruntled Party leaders at the 1937 Nuremberg congress how, under Party pressure, the Allgemeine Elektrizitäts-Gesellschaft (General Electric Co.) had fired all its Jewish employees, and how the Party's Auslands-Organisation (Foreign Affairs Committee) had organized a consortium for trade with Nationalist Spain. The specifically socialist elements of this arrangement, as Hess enumerated them, included an inversion of the pre-1914 ratio of oranges to industrial raw materials in favor of the latter; guarantees for stability of supply and delivery; exclusion of Jews, Freemasons, and the church from participation on the Spanish side, and the exclusive participation of "aryan" firms on the German side, obliged by contract to restrict their speculative gains.[43] "Socialism" was equally what distinguished Germany from its western neighbors. The new Germany, Hitler told Thuringian Party members shortly after his meetings with Neville Chamberlain, had no place for such "umbrella types" (Regenschirmtypen) who had once peopled German's own political stage.[44] In the same vein, the Nazi press inevitably referred to Wendell Willkie as "General-Direktor."[45]

As an affective word, "socialism" referred principally to a basic social egalitarianism with a streak of social welfare, and a considerable element of militancy. "Our socialism is a socialism of heroes, of manliness," Goebbels told an audience in Königsberg,[46] and Ley declared, "Our socialism has noth-

[41] Arno Klönne, *Die Hitlerjugend,* Hanover–Frankfurt, 1956, p. 76.

[42] Hans Ruban, "Mehr Sozialismus," *Die deutsche Volkswirtschaft,* December 1935, pp. 1108 ff.

[43] National Archives Microcopy T 81, Roll 1, frames 11186 ff.

[44] Domarus, op. cit., p. 963.

[45] William L. Shirer, *Berlin Diary,* London, 1941, p. 349.

[46] VB, 30 July 1933.

ing to do with pity."[47] But in fact the socialist label was often applied to activities that had hitherto been called "sozial," like social work. Thus Hitler described the Winterhilfe (Winter Aid) as a means of educating the German people to socialism,[48] and under the headline "This is National Socialism," the *Völkische Beobachter* described the Hitler-Spende, a foundation endowed with contributions more or less openly extorted from Jewish businessmen to finance paid vacations and recuperation for tired SA and SS men.[49] At Christmas 1933, Party officials erected tables in proletarian North Berlin streets to distribute presents to all, including former Communists. "This is the socialism I was looking for, and which it was an honor to serve with every fiber of my being," wrote Goebbels' adjutant Schaumburg-Lippe.[50] Under the standing headline "Socialism of the Deed," the *Völkische Beobachter* reported that employees of a South German textile plant had volunteered to work extra hours, donating the proceeds to a Nazi-sponsored fund for the victims of industrial accidents; that a Rhenish lawyer had volunteered free counsel for those unable to pay;[51] that farmers had offered the social welfare bureau of the Hitler Youth vacation places for fifty thousand children, and the National Socialist Women's organization of Mannheim had distributed seven hundred more. It told how Dresden municipal employees had created funds to finance a squadron of five airplanes for the Saxon Statthalter, to help SA and SS men out of financial difficulties, and how they had contributed 1 per cent of their salaries—that is, accepted a voluntary cut—for "the promotion of the national effort"

[47] *Der Angriff*, 31 October 1937. More examples: in a party and Labor Front journal produced under his direction, Ley declared, "Socialism is affirmation of life, socialism is community, socialism is struggle, socialism is comradeship and loyalty, socialism is honor. Socialism, my friend, is the blood and the race, the holy, solemn belief in God." The same issue referred to "Georg von Schönerer, a Socialist without Fear or Blame," and to "The German Socialism of the Freiherr vom Stein." *Der Schulungsbrief*, May 1937.

[48] Domarus, op. cit., p. 376.

[49] VB, 23 June 1933.

[50] Schaumburg-Lippe, op. cit., p. 166.

[51] VB, 22 June 1933.

(Förderung der nationalen Arbeit).[52] Other examples in the same series included the completion of a surburban housing project;[53] partial distribution of profits from Erich Koch's *Preussische Zeitung* to employees, with the rest invested in a fund to finance the training of prospective East Prussian candidates for Party offices;[54] and a proposal by a board of directors to distribute a third of their company's dividends to the permanent employees of the firm.[55]

With this went a campaign for egalitarianism intended not so much to change existing class relations, a function of profession and education, as to change status, the self-image, the state of mind. The employer was to remain an employer, and the worker a worker. But these were intended to be occupational designations and nothing more. Under National Socialism the basic determinant of status was common membership in the German people or variously the German "race," not class, education, or occupation. This was expressed in the concept of the Volksgemeinschaft (national community) which transcended all social differences. Thus Nazi social theory denied equality while at the same time asserting it.

In a rather remarkable example, an editorial in the SS journal *Das schwarze Korps* replied to a reader's protest about the inequitable distribution of family allowances. Heretofore, the editorialist began, socialism had come from below, reaction from above. National Socialism had done away with this, enlisting even generals, princes, corporation directors, and high civil servants to fight, where necessary, against the reactionary opposition of workers and petits bourgeois. "We recognized neither 'above' nor 'below' but only differences of attitude (Gesinnung)," he declared, thus bringing himself to the reader's query. The goal of National Socialism, he maintained, was that a child's future chances be solely determined by his genetic material and his physical and intellectual capacities. This, however, was a goal that could not be attained by the distribution of family allowances relative to the income of the recipient, but only through the schools and other edu-

[52] VB, 29 July 1933; 3 August 1933.
[53] VB, 20 January 1934.
[54] VB, 3 January 1934.
[55] VB, 3 July 1934.

cational institutions, of which the Hitler Youth and State-supported Adolf Hitler Schools were already exemplary. Even this was a secondary consideration, he continued. The basic issue was one of achievement (Leistung) and its reward. In this case, it was also a goal of National Socialism that achievement be rewarded not only by the immediate employer but by the State. This included the "achievement" of babies, irrespective of the private circumstances of those who "achieved" them. On the contrary, higher income was presumably a function of greater achievement. The practical result was equality and inequality at once: distribution of family allowances in direct proportion to both indices of achievement—to the number of children *and* to the income of the father. "Does this make us reactionaries?" the editorial asked.[56]

In economic terms, the idea of equality represented a positive threat, leading, as one spokesman said, an estimated three and a half million people to jobs for which they were ill-suited.[57] But in the economic context National Socialism rested on the premise of inequality if not, as Scheuner wrote, of inherited social position or income, still of occupation and achievement. As examples, he cited the inequality, that is, the special rights and obligations of those who practiced medicine or journalism, ran a business, or owned an entailed farm (Erbhof). Equality derived from the community of blood and expressed itself in a community of obligations such as common service in the Army and the Labor Service.[58] What was equal was the right—and obligation—to work as such, something Goering identified as specifically "socialistic."[59] In turn, the right—and obligation—to work at the job for which one was best suited was "socialistic" as well,[60] as was the right to the benefits accruing from the responsibility assumed and the work done. Equality was double: equality of oppor-

[56] "Ist das nun Reaktion?" *Das schwarze Korps*, 7 July 1938.

[57] Wilhelm Mitze, *Die strukturtypologische Gliederung einer westdeutschen Gross-stadt*, Leipzig, 1941, p. 73.

[58] Ulrich Scheuner, "Der Gleichheitsgedanke in der völkischen Verfassungsordnung," *Zeitschrift für die gesamte Staatswissenschaft*, February 1939, pp. 245 f.

[59] VB, 10 April 1933.

[60] VB, 3 March 1935.

tunity and equality of citizenship. The former tended to be an appeal to the worker in the sense of one who worked. The latter was a status appeal to the worker in the conventional sense, the urban industrial laborer, the proletarian who was to become a first-class citizen.

In an interview with Hanns Johst, Hitler redefined the traditional class vocabulary in National Socialist terms.[61]

> J. In 1919 you found Marxist parties on one side and bourgeois indifference on the other. You were counted with the bourgeois on the right.
>
> H. . . . two mistakes. I applied all my energy to overcoming partisan leadership of the state, and second, it has never been possible to think of me as bourgeois. . . . National Socialism derives from each of the two camps the pure idea that characterizes it, national resolution from the bourgeois tradition, vital, creative socialism from the teachings of Marxism. Volksgemeinschaft: this means the community of effective labor, it means the unity of all interests, it means the elimination of private citizenship [Bürgertum] and a mechanical, union-organized mass. . . .
>
> J. To the extent that the Weimar Constitution obliged you to organize on a partisan basis, you called your movement the "National Socialist Workers' Party." In other words, you gave the concept "worker" priority over that of Bürger.
>
> H. I chose the word "worker" because it appealed to me fundamentally and because I wanted to reconquer it for the forces of the nation. I had to grant it citizenship [einbürgern] in the potency of the German language.
>
> J. Thus the National Socialist Weltanschauung is based on the citizen [Staatsbürger] and the worker. And everyone is either both or neither. . . .
>
> H. Exactly. I find this identity fundamental. The German Bürger with the tassel-cap must become a citizen of the State [Staatsbürger] while the comrade with the red cloth cap must become a comrade in the national community [Volksgenosse]. Both must apply their good will to transforming the sociological concept of "worker" into a patent of the nobility of "work." This patent alone is the effective oath of allegiance of soldier and farmer, merchant and scholar, worker and capitalist . . . to the nation.

[61] Domarus, op. cit., p. 349; reprinted in *Frankfurter Volksblatt*, 27 January 1934; Johst, *Standpunkt und Fortschritt*, Oldenburg, 1934.

J. This is to say, you foresee the mythos of a union of worker and Bürger . . . ?

H. I hope this conversation will have an enlightening effect in bourgeois circles. The bourgeois must no longer feel himself a kind of pensioner of either tradition or capital, separated from the worker by the Marxist idea of property, but must aim to accommodate himself as a worker to the welfare of the community. . . .[62]

Translated into practice, this led to an undifferentiated glorification of "the worker," in the form of an almost unlimited appeal to social mobility and in an aggressive emphasis on social egalitarianism. In both of these forms Hitler himself took the lead. "What professions has Adolf Hitler had?" asked a kind of ideological catechism. "Adolf Hitler was a construction worker, an artist, and a student" was the answer.[63] Hitler sat in the front seat next to his chauffeur and set a simple table.[64] One of his first official acts was the rejection of an honorary doctorate.[65] Speaking at the Siemens plant in November 1933 in boots and a Party shirt, he addressed his audience with the intimate plural form "Ihr," telling them, "I was a worker in my youth like you, slowly working my way upward by industry, by study, and I think I can say as well by hunger."[66] The Volkskanzler (People's Chancellor) as he was called, whom Winnig compared with Mussolini and Ramsay MacDonald as a "leader from the ranks" (Führer von unten),[67] described himself to construction workers as "one who went forth from among you,"[68] and prided himself on being a man without estate, stocks, or bank account.[69] "I too am a son of the people," he declared on

[62] It should be pointed out that a large part of the interview is based on a kind of grandiose but untranslatable pun, the double meaning of the German word "Bürger," which means interchangeably "bourgeois" and "citizen."

[63] Alfred Röpke, *Was musst du wissen vom Dritten Reich?*, Berlin, 1935, pp. 4 f.

[64] Rauschning, *Gespräche mit Hitler*, p. 58.

[65] Domarus, op. cit., p. 265.

[66] Ibid., p. 330.

[67] Marr, op. cit., p. 490; August Winnig, *Der Arbeiter im Dritten Reich*, Berlin-Charlottenburg, 1934, p. 44.

[68] Domarus, op. cit., p. 664.

[69] Ibid., p. 613.

1 May 1937.[70] "During the past five years I too have been a worker," he told the Reichstag in 1938.[71] Symbolically, with the completion of the new Chancellery in 1939, he received the building workers first,[72] apologizing for the scale of his new quarters by associating them with his representative functions as head of the German Reich. As a private individual, he continued to live as modestly as before, he emphasized. Four days after receiving the building workers, he received the diplomatic corps.[73,74,75]

Where Hitler led, Party and State followed. Frick appeared at the University of Berlin to enjoin students to forsake the snobbery that separated them from the "uneducated" (ungebildet), reminding them that they, in greater measure than most Volksgenossen, "were in permanent danger of losing contact with the people and thus of disloyalty to socialism."[76] Students were herded into the SA and cultivated the company of "young workers" in discussion groups. Girl students waited on table in university restaurants (mensas) and members of student corps who at first decorated their uniforms

70 Ibid., p. 690.

71 Ibid., p. 793.

72 He also presented all the crew members of the stonemason's firm that had built the new chancellery autographed pictures of himself as well as baskets of groceries, fruit and wine. "Der Führer ehrt und beschenkt Arbeiter," VB, 3 January 1939.

73 VB, 3, 9, and 13 January 1939.

74 Hitler also exploited these themes with ingenuity in interviews with the foreign press. Thus, in an interview with Louis P. Lochner, Berlin bureau chief of the Associated Press, he struck the theme of the self-made man. The first task was to overcome unemployment, then to raise the standard of living, he said. "I agree with the American principle, not equality of income, but the principle of the ladder. But everyone has to be given the same opportunity to climb it." Domarus, op. cit., p. 373.

75 In an interview with Abel Bonnard of *Le Journal* of Paris the theme was égalité. As typical of his characteristic preoccupation, Hitler described how National Socialism had overcome the discrepancy at sea between the comfort of the passengers and the misery of the crews. "Today the crews have decent bunks. They have a deck of their own where they can rest in decent deck-chairs, they have radios and a dining room where they eat with a deck officer. . . ." Domarus, op. cit., p. 693.

76 VB, 31 January 1934.

with the colors of their corps were made to stop doing so.[77] Ley, addressing industrialists, began, "I mean to speak to you exactly as I have just spoken to thousands of workers. In the past a speaker had to accommodate himself to the various classes and professional groups he was addressing."[78] In an interesting case, an instructor at the school of forestry in Eberswalde, a reserve officer, reported a clash with his local representative of the National Socialist University Teachers Organization who refused to grant him credit for a military exercise he had recently completed with the Reichswehr. Not content with this, the functionary had denounced the institution of the reserve officer corps as such, deriding it as the basis of further class distinctions of which there were already enough, and even threatening to see that all instructors with reserve commissions would be discharged from their teaching jobs.[79]

Even more typical was the treatment of civil servants. In a directive of 1937, Frick demanded politeness of all civil servants, reminding them that they were advisors and counselors, not superiors with respect to subordinates, in their relations with the public.[80] Similarly, the head of the Party's Civil Servants Bureau (Amt für Beamte) in Berlin demanded of his members that they avoid professional cliques. "The public official must be the link between the government and the people and not stiffen in professional isolation from his fellow citizens, still less from other comrades in the office (Arbeitskameraden)."[81] The Nazi mayor of Munich publicly invited all municipal employees to the city's Fasching (Mardi Gras) ball and urged private industry to do the same so that the ball would "be what it ought to be: an expression of Volksgemeinschaft."[82]

In Düsseldorf the Party erected counseling offices (Bera-

[77] Wolfgang Höpker, "Studenten und Arbeiter," *Die Tat*, February 1934, pp. 903–5.

[78] VB, 5 September 1935.

[79] Bundesarchiv, R 21/430. The functionary was subsequently reprimanded by the Ministry of Education.

[80] Ministerialblatt des Reichs- und Preussischen Ministerium des Innern, No. 28, Bundesarchiv R 43II/423 14 July 1937.

[81] *Der Angriff*, Bundesarchiv R 43II/423 4 February 1936.

[82] VB, 27 February 1935.

tungsstellen) to which citizens could turn for advice on public services, family affairs, or labor law. A report on its activity cited the example of a domestic servant who had appeared to complain about her working conditions. Her employer, the wife of an industrialist, was called in and instructed in the obligations of Volksgemeinschaft with the result that she raised the girl's wages and personally accompanied her home.[83] With no particular enthusiasm, Schaumburg-Lippe reported that a Christmas show in 1937 had reached a point where a Santa Claus told small children how class hate had been abolished.[84] This, of course, was a statement of intention rather than of fact, but it was striking that Nazi legislation abolished the nominal distinction between blue- and white-collar employees (Arbeiter and Angestellter) and even in certain welfare contexts between commissioned and noncommissioned officers.[85]

All these cases had little to do with fundamental social change. Employers remained employers even when addressed as workers, and it was clear that students continued to have better career prospects on the basis of their studies, however they might be reminded of their "socialist" responsibilities. In Düsseldorf there was no fundamental change in the relationship of the employer to her housemaid, in Munich workers and employers continued to be workers and employers the morning after the Fasching ball. Civil servants were not asked to surrender their offices but only to exercise them differently. In nearly every case, National Socialism intervened in regard to the conduct of free time, "socializing" not the means of economic production but certain aspects of human relations which were visibly subjugated to the directives of Party, community, and State. But the official goal and the actual result was, at least psychologically, a classless society.

Impressively often, the goal was expressed in military images. "Soldier" like "worker" was an honorific, but its application was equally comprehensive and equally abstract. "The

[83] Berlin Document Center, Ordner No. 199b, Gau Düsseldorf.
[84] Schaumburg-Lippe, op. cit., p. 243.
[85] Piper, op. cit., p. 32; VB, "Soldaten aus Berufung," 6 January 1939.

political leader is always a soldier," Hitler declared.[86] The SA were "political soldiers";[87] members of the Labor Service, "Soldiers of Labor." Socialism, Ley explained, was the relationship of men in trenches.[88] As described by a Hitler Youth leader, it meant marching and fighting: "In 1919 Clemenceau declared war on Germany by other means. The fight is hard but a people of socialists will win it."[89] National Socialism aimed to recreate the community of the combat soldier, wrote a spokesman.[90] "The German has always found military leadership the best social organization," declared a high functionary of the Labor Front. "Under our political leadership we stand, as it were, in a marching column whose visible expression is the uniform."[91] The sociologist Pfenning called the industrial manager an "officer of the economy."[92]

To be sure, the Volksgemeinschaft was propagated as a genuine social reality. "We have endeavored," Hitler declared in his first speech in Saarbrücken, "to depart from the external, the superficial, endeavored to forget social origin, class, profession, fortune, education, capital and everything that separates men, in order to reach that which binds them together."[93] He was himself an example, he stated, responsible neither to employer nor to employee, nor to any single class, but the possession of the entire people.[94] What applied to himself he applied to the movement he led, whose foremost representatives included former metalworkers and farm laborers, former bourgeois and former aristocrats.[95]

[86] Domarus, op. cit., p. 762.

[87] Helmut Mehringer, *Die NSDAP als politische Ausleseorganisation*, Munich, 1938, p. 47.

[88] VB, 27 January 1934.

[89] Harro Hagen, "Die Erziehung in der Hitlerjugend," *Süddeutsche Monatshefte*, March 1935, pp. 360–62.

[90] Hans Willi Ziegler, "Erziehung zur Volksgemeinschaft," ibid., p. 338.

[91] Karl Arnhold, *Das Ringen um die Arbeitsidee*, Berlin, 1938, pp. 77 f.

[92] Andreas Pfenning, "Das Eliten-Problem in seiner Bedeutung für den Kulturbereich der Wirtschaft," *Zeitschrift für die gesamte Staatswissenschaft*, July 1936, p. 613.

[93] Domarus, op. cit., p. 486.

[94] Ibid., p. 613.

[95] Ibid., p. 690

"What a difference compared with a certain other country," he claimed at the 1936 Nuremberg congress in a reference to the war in Spain. "There it is class against class, brother against brother. We have chosen the other route: rather than to wrench you apart, we have brought you together."[96] At least as early as 1935, Ley declared uncategorically, "We are the first country in Europe to overcome the class struggle."[97]

But characteristically, the social model found its most perfect propagandistic expression in the military or paramilitary institutions: the Hitler Youth, the Labor Service, the Wehrmacht itself. The Hitler Youth, like the old Prussian Army, was "the school of the nation," one of its leaders told an interviewer, where boys and girls grew up under the laws of a "socialist community."[98] The function of the Labor Service, its leader Konstantin Hierl declared, was the education of the German people in socialism. He could conceive of no better means of overcoming class conflict than to dress "the son of the director and the young worker, the university student and the farmhand, in the same uniform, to set them the same table in common service to Volk and Vaterland."[99] In consistent pursuit of this goal, the Labor Service was declared obligatory for all university students while it remained voluntary for other groups.[100] "Soldiers of honor" they were called, representatives of all classes and professions,[101] and since, for economic reasons, they tended to be employed almost entirely on the land, the "military" and "socialist" motives again intersected conveniently with the anti-urban motif of Blut und Boden.[102]

[96] Ibid., p. 640.
[97] VB, 29 September 1935.
[98] "Die Schule der Nation," VB, 14 September 1935.
[99] VB, 1 May 1933.
[100] "Der Student im neuen Deutschland kennt keinen Standesdünkel," VB, 21 July 1933.
[101] VB, 18 June 1933.
[102] To be sure, the combination was variable as shown by a VB picture page six weeks before the war began. Pictured on one side [were German students departing for rural Labor Service in East] Prussia. This was obviously an example of land-oriented socialism in the service of peace. The other side of the page showed Etonians

In one form or another, the same motifs were also used to characterize the Wehrmacht. A weekend feature for Wehrmacht recruits revolved around the theme "The uniform makes all men equal. The college teacher feels no different from the manual worker, and nothing stands in the way of friendship between the medical student and the gardener's helper."[103] A similar picture story on a farmer recruit proclaimed, "Just as the farmer is unable to develop his full capacity without the aid of the military establishment (Wehrstand), so is the military establishment able to reach its highest level of achievement only when it can derive new strength from the blood source of the nation."[104]

It was typical of National Socialism that a Bavarian official would choose a meeting of the National Socialist Teachers Organization (Lehrerbund), called to commemorate Bavaria's first Nazi Minister of Education, Hans Schemm, who had recently been killed in an air crash, to single out the Labor Service and the Wehrmacht as the two essential German educational institutions. He emphasized particularly the "essential reform" inherent in the new universal conscription system, "that all forms of discrimination according to class or educational qualifications have been dropped."[105]

The reciprocal of this "socialist" world was, correspondingly, a "bourgeois" world whose representatives were defined in consistent opposition to the "workers," "farmers," and

---

being drilled as reserve officer candidates. "Die Erntehilfe der deutschen Studenten," VB, 19 July 1939.

Some idea of the general Labor Service is suggested by the published report of a girl participant who described a working day that began at 4:30 A.M. and included a shift of potato-digging that ran from 7:30 A.M. to 2:30 P.M. with a quarter hour free for breakfast. The day also included a survey of the press, and a talk on Moeller van den Bruck by a student participant. Among other points of interest in the report are the emphasis on the splendor of nature at 4:30 A.M., the spontaneous will of the participants to decorate their quarters with flowers—"you see what a splendid spirit of camaraderie reigns here"—and the characterization of the Labor Service leaders as friendly but "merciless in discipline and order." "Wir sind jung und das ist schön," VB, 3 March 1935.

[103] *Der Angriff*, 2 October 1937.

[104] "Ein Bauernbursch rückt ein," VB, 14 November 1936.

[105] VB, 31 March 1935.

"soldiers" of the new regime. Since the former were, by definition, the supporters, their opposites were, by definition, opponents of the new regime. The Bürger, Kleinbürger, Spiessbürger and often enough the intellectual, collectively the reactionaries: these were the traditional "class enemy" translated into Nazi terms. Thus to Hitler, critics of the anti-Jewish boycott of 1 April 1933 were specimens of "bourgeois cowardice."[106] The enemies of National Socialism, he announced at the 1935 Party congress, included not only the "Jewish Marxists," and the Catholics, but "certain elements of an incorrigible, stupid, reactionary bourgeoisie."[107] Those who begrudged the sacrifices demanded by National Socialism were petits bourgeois, he declared on the third anniversary of his appointment as Chancellor.[108] Spiesser, in the context of Goebbels' New Year Proclamation of 1939, were those few who had voted against the Anschluss;[109] in the context of the *Völkische Beobachter*, those who neglected their contributions to the Winterhilfe;[110] in the context of a Vienna Labor Front pamphlet, those who took offense at the idea of automobiles—the Volkswagen—for the common man.[111] The Bürger was often enough associated with familiar sociological types, and represented in a familiar style of caricature. An SA magazine, *Das neue Deutschland*, rejoiced in cartoons and verse satirizing the monarchists and student corps.[112]

In an official ideological text a question on the behavior of "the reactionaries" led without further definition to a depiction of the "impossible" behavior of two members of a student corps during a Hitler speech, though the answer subsequently led to the circumstances that had necessitated dissolution of the Stahlhelm in Baden.[113] This was not only in the tradi-

[106] Domarus, op. cit., p. 249.
[107] Ibid., p. 525.
[108] Ibid., p. 571.
[109] VB, 2 January 1939.
[110] VB, 23 November 1936.
[111] "Der Spiesser ist empört," *Kraft durch Freude*, NSDAP Gau Wien, 1 October 1938, p. 45.
[112] "Wir wollen unser'n Kaiser wieder" and "Die Herren Korpsstudenten soweit sie feudal sich fühlen," *Das neue Deutschland*, September 1935.
[113] Röpke, op. cit., pp. 46 f.

tional anti-bourgeois style of classical socialism but in the épater le bourgeois style of the prewar *Simplicissimus.* The continuity was underlined by the career of Eduard Thönys, whose cartoons had once appeared in *Simplicissimus* and now appeared in *Das neue Deutschland.* But it was a style that extended beyond sociological types to a general state of mind. In the final analysis, the bourgeois was less what he did than what he thought and how he felt. "He shrieks after security, his capacity for war [Kriegertum] is not a will to attack [Angriffskriegertum] but is exhausted in the will to defense" a Hitler Youth leader said of him.[114] He was an "eternal type," hostile to tragedy, passion, and revolution, vulnerable to humanitarian sentimentality, intellectualism, and routine.[115]

Invoked in these terms, the National Socialist Bürger too was ripe for the rubbish heap of history, and National Socialism consistently fulfilled its self-image in a mythology of its own succession to the bourgeois world. "Unfortunately the architectural elaboration [Ausgestaltung] of public life was neglected during the bourgeois epoch to the advantage of private, capitalistic business interests," Hitler proclaimed in 1935 as he laid the cornerstone of the Party's Kongresshalle in Nuremberg. "The great cultural task of National Socialism consists precisely in reversing this tendency."[116] By definition the bourgeois epoch was over, but both the object of Hitler's remarks and the fact that war appropriations were to prevent the building's completion were clues to the rather special ways in which this, Hitler's socialist revolution, was to be understood.

With the Machtergreifung, National Socialism was faced with the double task of winning the unwon and, with the relatively limited human resources at its disposal, of transforming itself from a spokesman of the "outs" to the exclusive manifestation of the "ins."

[114] Hagen, op. cit., p. 356.

[115] Friedrich Kilian, "Der unsterbliche Bürger," *Die Tat,* December 1933, pp. 729 ff.

[116] Domarus, op. cit., p. 528.

The Party census of 1935, the only one of its kind,[117] was a partial index to its success in achieving the goals it set. Before the Party rolls were closed to further applicants in 1933, the party had grown from roughly 850,000 to nearly 2,500,000. Regional differences tended to be ironed out. Relative to total population, the frequency of Party membership in the Gaue showed little variation. Schleswig-Holstein continued to have the most Party members proportionally, but membership frequency above the Reich average in Catholic Main-Franconia and Cologne-Aachen testified to the effectiveness of the concordat with the Vatican and the disintegration of Catholic resistance.[118] Occupational distribution was as shown in Table 9.[119,120]

TABLE 9

Workers	30.3 %
White collar	19.4
Independent	19.0
Civil servants including teachers	12.4
Farmers	10.2
Miscellaneous	3.23
Pensioners	1.52
Students	1.35
Housewives	2.60

[117] A second census was planned in 1939 but never completed. The questionnaires comprising the census of Gau Berlin repose, still (1965) awaiting tabulation, at the Berlin Document Center.

[118] *Partei-Statistik*, Vol. I, 1935, p. 45.

[119] Ibid., p. 53.

[120] Further subdivided, distribution within the major groups was as follows:

Workers		*White-collar*		*Self-Employed*	
skilled metal	20.4%	sales	59.1%	commercial	39.5%
other skilled	43.0	technical	18.0	handicraft	43.7
mining	2.8	other	22.9	free professions	16.8
farm labor	12.4		100%		100%
unskilled	21.4				
	100%				

Civil Servants	
public officials	72.6%
teachers	27.4
	100%

Relative to the total population, workers were about 30 per cent "underrepresented," and farmers nearly 100 per cent. White-collar employees were "overrepresented" by roughly 65 per cent, the economically independent by 100 per cent, the civil servants by 160 per cent.[121] Compared with Party membership on 30 January 1933, the influx of new members resulted in a relative decline in the proportional representation of all groups except the economically independent, who showed a small gain, and the civil servants, who showed a large one, testifying to Nazi annexation of the German "establishment." The sharp drop in the representation of the "miscellaneous" seemed in turn to testify to the Party's disproportionately great appeal to them—the uprooted existences, career functionaries, and SA men—in the years before 1933.

Roughly two thirds of Party membership as recorded on 1 January 1935 had joined since Hitler's appointment as Chancellor. Given 66 per cent as "normal" growth, the fastest growing occupational groups in the Party were the civil servants (public officials 80%, teachers 85%), followed at some distance by the economically independent (68%) and the school and university students (70%). Gains among both blue- and white-collar workers were roughly "normal" (respectively 65% and 63%) while all other groups (farmers 58%, miscellaneous 60%, pensioners 63%) and particularly housewives (48%) either stagnated or fell behind.[122] Functionaries were specifically encouraged to promote membership among workers, especially in Hamburg, Danzig, Berlin, and Cologne-Aachen, and among housewives in the predominantly Catholic Gaue Main-Franconia, Schwaben (Augsburg), Koblenz-Trier, Württemberg-Hohenzollern, Lower Bavaria, and South Westphalia.[123]

The influx of new membership also made itself felt on the

[121] *Partei-Statistik,* Vol. I, 1935, p. 53.

[122] Ibid., pp. 85 ff.

[123] It is interesting to note that in South Westphalia, where the proportion of housewife members was lowest—under 1.5%—worker membership was highest, nearly 40% of the total, the highest proportion in the Reich. Ibid., pp. 136 f.

age structure of the Party. On 1 January 1935 it was as follows:[124]

TABLE 10

18–20	3.5%
21–30	34.1
31–40	27.9
41–50	19.6
51–60	11.2
61–	3.7

Compared with the membership of 30 January 1933, the 18–21-year-old group had grown significantly, in all probability a by-product of the enormous growth of the Hitler Youth, which had mushroomed from 108,000 members at the end of 1932 to nearly 3,600,000 at the end of 1934.[125] The 21–30-year-old group had meanwhile declined rather sharply in relative representation, a factor obviously related to the increased membership in the over-40 groups. Again given 66 per cent as "normal," the fastest growing groups were the 18–20-year-olds (82.5%), followed by the 41–50-year-olds (70.1%) and the 51–60-year-olds (71.6%). Lagging behind were the 21–30-year-olds (59.7%). But while the age structure approached that of the general population, the Party was still very much a young man's phenomenon.[126]

An interesting testimonial to the appeal of National Socialism was a pamphlet published in 1934 by ten aristocrats, most of them young, most of them in relatively high positions in the new regime. Only two were in traditional aristocratic preserves, one as a diplomat, the other as professor of military science in Berlin. One had become a leader of the Nazi

[124] Ibid., p. 162.

[125] Klönne, op. cit., p. 125.

[126] Cf. Theodor Litt, *Das Verhältnis der Generationen*, Wiesbaden, 1947, p. 46. Describing a train conversation in Austria in 1937, Rebecca West quotes a businessman, "'But all the young people, they are solid for Hitler. For them all is done.' The others said, '*Ja, das ist so!*' and the business woman began, 'Yes, our sons,' and then stopped." Rebecca West, *Black Lamb and Grey Falcon*, New York, 1953, p. 32.

farmer organization in the Rhineland; four were in direct Nazi-patronized positions in the propaganda apparatus; the others had, via the SA, reached police and administrative posts. Uniting all of them was an uneasy awareness of the weaknesses that had brought down the old order and a near-compulsive determination to recognize what they thought to be the handwriting on the wall. One went to the lengths of viewing the Weimar Republic as nothing more than an extension of the moribund imperial order.[127] What all claimed to find in National Socialism was a new social order, an aristocracy of performance (Leistung), an eastward drive like the one that had carried their ancestors in the twelfth century,[128] and a social conscience lacking in the Deutschnationale Volkspartei and Stahlhelm, which several had joined and then left.[129]

"There can be no doubt," wrote Graf Helldorff, before 1933 a Nazi deputy in the Prussian Landtag, and SA leader of Berlin, then chief of Berlin police, "that a new aristocracy is forming under National Socialism. If the old aristocracy stands aside from this great aristocratic popular movement (grosse aristokratische Volksbewegung) fate will overrun it; in that case it would be better if it resolved now to renounce its worthless patents of nobility."[130]

A similar index to the social realignment of National Socialism was the transition in the leadership of the Hitler Youth. If through 1936 Hitler Youth leadership tended to be the monopoly of the "young workers," the apprentices and shop clerks of the pre-1933 days, from 1936 on it tended to become an affair of the academically educated middle class. Klönne estimates that from 1936 on more than 50 per cent of the Hitler Youth leadership was recruited from "respectable middle-class" circles, and that the higher ranks included

[127] *Wo war der Adel?* ed. Schaumburg-Lippe, Berlin, 1934, p. 31.

[128] Ibid., p. 10.

[129] Ibid., p. 33.

[130] W. F. Graf Helldorff, "Adel und Nationalsozialismus," *Das neue Deutschland*, October 1935, p. 11.

up to 25 per cent university students and graduates plus another 50 per cent from the respectable bourgeoisie.[131]

On the other hand, the exaggerated enthusiasm that attended the presence of real proletarians in high places[132] pointed to the limits of the National Socialist appeal, if not to the limit of the social opportunities it offered. These were real enough, for all that they included a place for middle-class youth and sons of the old aristocracy.[133]

But the real triumph of National Socialism, to which even the evidence of its opponents bears witness, was not so much a new society as a new social consciousness expressing itself in the purely affective, "socialist" terms National Socialism preached. It was völkisch provincialism that sustained National Socialism before 1930, economic and political desperation that carried it most of the way to power by 1933. From 1933 on it was supported in no small part by coercion, acquiescence, opportunism, and despair, reflected at least in part in the membership figures of teachers and civil servants, or the fellow-traveling of representatives of the old order. But there is plausible testimony that "National Socialism" as an idea impressed at least some Germans as something more than an invention of their propaganda ministry; that it appealed to a revolutionary spirit which was not *only* that of "the revolution of nihilism." Peter Viereck was impressed by the genuine élan and classless camaraderie of a Labor Service camp;[134] William L. Shirer, by the camaraderie of naval officers and men on the *Gneisenau* and of common soldiers and their officers in France in 1940: "Even the salute has a new meaning. German privates salute each other, thus making the gesture more of a comradely greeting than the mere recognition of superior rank. In cafés, restaurants, dining cars, officers and men off duty sit at the same table and converse as men to men."[135] Even Carl Goerdeler, in 1944, claimed that National Socialism had taught Germans "the lesson that we have to help one another and that social distribution must

[131] Klönne, op. cit., p. 42.
[132] Melita Maschmann, *Fazit*, Stuttgart, 1963, p. 149.
[133] See Chs. VIII and IX.
[134] Peter Viereck, *Metapolitics*, New York, 1941.
[135] Shirer, op. cit., p. 345.

be so arranged that capital no longer distributes excessive profits."[136]

Being (Sein) influences consciousness (Bewusstsein), as Marx maintained. But under National Socialism, the reverse was also true.

[136] Gerhard Ritter, *Carl Goerdeler und die deutsche Widerstandsbewegung,* Stuttgart, 1945, p. 62.

III

The Third Reich and Labor

Generalizations about National Socialist labor policy can only be misleading. The word "policy" presupposes a consistency and an intensive preoccupation with the problems of labor for its own sake. But little evidence of these can be found before 1933 and little more afterward. Individual Nazis, indeed considerable numbers of them, were anti-labor in the sense that the existence of unions and the weight of labor's influence on the legislative process had created what they felt to be a disequilibrium of social benefits and economic opportunity. The small businessman, under pressure to pay labor at union scale wages under tough competitive conditions, to finance insurance and pension funds from which he himself drew no benefit, or to lose business to union-sponsored consumer co-operatives, had reason enough to be anti-labor.[1] Farmers, inclined to identify falling prices with the hostility and pressure of union-organized urban consumer groups, had reason—or at least felt that they had reason—to be anti-labor too, a situation that the traditional anti-agricultural bias of

[1] Senator Claude Pepper's introduction to a U. S. Senate investigation of Nazi treatment of small business is an interesting testimonial to the power of a cautionary example. Pepper, a New Dealer and chairman of the Senate Small Business Committee, exploited the assumption that the neglect of small business at the cost of disproportionate social benefits for wage earners had been one of the major factors in Hitler's success as the very justification for his study. Cf. A. R. L. Gurland, Otto Kirchheimer, and Franz Neumann, *The Fate of Small Business in Nazi Germany* (hereafter *The Fate*), Senate Committee Print No. 14, Washington, 1943.

the SPD scarcely relieved.[2] Between them, as already shown, such small businessmen and farmers represented a powerful block, if not the majority, of Nazi support. They were supplemented, in influence if not in number, by representatives of big business, a group nowhere outstanding for political astuteness, who claimed to see in National Socialism a shield against eventual expropriation, an obstacle to continued union pressures amid universal economic disaster, and —an important consideration where the distribution of campaign funds was concerned—a potential winner.[3]

On the other hand, as the Party's struggle over the expropriation referendum in 1925/26, the considerable personal popularity of Gregor Strasser, and the personal career of Muchow showed, there were real reserves of "socialist," or in any case of anti-capitalist, feeling in the Party, reserves far greater than the trivial response to Otto Strasser's attempted Party-splitting appeal to the "socialists" in 1930 might seem to indicate. Hostile or contemptuous as they may have been either to the labor parties or the unions, the "socialist" Nazis held no brief for private enterprise, or against unions as the expression of organized economic—as opposed to political—interests. Nor did they have any particular objection to a full-employment policy, social services, pensions, insurance, profit-sharing, co-operative ownership, or the institutional apparatus of the welfare state. "For them," as a *Tat* contributor wrote of student demonstrators in early 1934, "nationalization is not necessarily a word that frightens [Schreckenswort]."[4] If workers were a relative scarcity in the Party, there were nonetheless 750,000 of them enrolled by 1933, far too many to stamp the Party as an extended arm of private enterprise, either large or small; and, equally, too many to allow their presence to be neglected, at least as a secondary factor in the direction of Party policy.

Between the two groups was Hitler, neither pro- nor anti-

[2] Cf. Alexander Gerschenkron, *Bread and Democracy in Germany*, Berkeley, 1943, Ch. I.

[3] Cf. L. P. Lochner, *Tycoons and Tyrants*, Chicago, 1954, Ch. I; Norbert Mühlen, *The Incredible Krupps*, New York, 1959; Thyssen, op. cit.

[4] Höpker, op. cit., p. 905

labor but motivated by a combination of pragmatism, resentments, and indifference. The combination, applied before 1933 to the mobilization of support, turned after 1933 to the most efficient mobilization of a war economy in which labor might be employed with a minimum of waste; social benefits might be distributed with a maximum of propagandistic effect; and economic interests—whether of labor or management—might be excluded as far as possible from the political process. In this context, labor policy was at best a subdivision of general economic policy, and, like it, less the product of a unified policy-making process than the result of a largely anarchic combination of momentary political objectives, institutional vested interests, and programmatic slogans. This combination was indeed politically anti-labor in the sense that labor ceased to be an organized political interest. The pressure to Gleichschaltung—the pressure toward political monopoly before which all parties, all interest groups, fraternal organizations, church groups, and even Boy Scouts bowed—necessarily had its effect on labor parties and labor unions. But in the economic sense unquestionably envisaged by large numbers, even by a majority of Party members before 1933, the policy of the Third Reich, at any rate as it might have been felt by the average worker, can scarcely be called anti-labor.

As a supplement, almost as a substitute for a labor policy, the Third Reich offered a labor ideology, combining simultaneous and roughly equal appeals to the pride, patriotism, idealism, enlightened self-interest, and, finally, urge to self-aggrandizement of those exposed to it. The centerpiece was the labor ethos, focusing not so much on the worker as on work itself. "Work ennobles (Arbeit adelt)" was a characteristic slogan,[5] or, in a particularly grotesque form, "Labor Liberates (Arbeit macht frei)," the legend on the front gate at Auschwitz.[6] As in Josef Thorak's colossal design for an auto-

[5] The reply, in a popular joke of the period, was "I prefer to remain bourgeois." Hans-Jochen Gamm, *Der braune Kult*, Hamburg, 1962, p. 91.

[6] Still more grotesque is the possibility that Rudolf Höss, the organiser of the camp, who had himself spent years in prison during the Weimar Republic, was not being cynical when he hung the

bahn monument, three egregiously muscled giants heaving Sisyphus-like at an enormous rock, work was a favored theme of official art.[7] Larger factories even erected chapels whose main aisle led to a Hitler bust beneath the symbol of the Labor Front, flanked by heroic-sized worker figures; in effect, little temples to the National Socialist god of work.[8]

An idealized, generalized image of "the worker" was invoked in turn to achieve the psychological assimilation of the worker into the life of the nation. Sheltered by the common rubric "worker of the head and hand (Arbeiter der Stirn und der Faust)" the rector of the University of Heidelberg and a "worker of the hand" rode through the streets together on 1 May 1934, on a festively decorated beer wagon.[9] The press celebrated the "peerage of hard jobs (Adel der schweren Berufe)" with interviews with garbage collectors,[10] and turned a friendly eye on those who had advanced from humble beginnings, like two miners' sons playing their first concert in Berlin or the son of a Viennese worker who was about to appear in Berlin in a new play.[11] The collapse of a subway tunnel during U-Bahn expansion in Berlin in 1935 was occasion for a grandiose funeral for the nineteen workers killed in the accident and a show trial of the engineers and contractors responsible for the project. Both demonstrations were intended as symbolic expression of the Third Reich's esteem for its working population.[12] With this went

slogan on the Auschwitz gate. Höss, whose war and Freikorps experience, pretentious illiteracy, unquestioning submission to authority of any kind and misty völkisch idealism made him a veritable ideal type of Nazi, wrote in his memoirs: "I talked to many fellow prisoners and then, especially in Dachau, with many of the inmates about work. . . . Work . . . is not only an effective disciplinary method. . . . It is an educational method as well . . . for those who through the blessed effectiveness of work can still be rescued from criminality. . . . Rudolf Höss, *Kommandant in Auschwitz,* ed. Martin Broszat, Munich, 1963, p. 65.

[7] Gamm, op. cit., p. 99.

[8] Ibid., p. 169.

[9] "So zog 1933 der neue Geist ein," *Süddeutsche Zeitung,* 17 March 1964.

[10] VB, 21 November 1936.

[11] VB, 14 March 1935; *Der Angriff,* 15 March 1935.

[12] VB, 1 September 1935 and ff.

a totally humorless hard-sell campaign, whose object was to absorb the worker in the patriotic dedication of a nation in arms, to confer—or impose—on him the political responsibility that from 1933 on was supposed to saturate every sector of national life. "Barbers Face Great Tasks (Friseurhandwerk vor grossen Aufgaben)" declared a typical headline.[13] Propagandistically the worker was to come to the Third Reich, and the Third Reich to the worker, in equal measure. Neither geography nor coincidence dictated the choice of Leipzig as the site of the agreement that absorbed the employers' organizations in the Labor Front, the *Völkische Beobachter* announced, but rather Leipzig's historic significance as a birthplace of the German Labor movement.[14] The subsidized tourism of the Labor Front's "Strength through Joy" organization, a Labor Front functionary declared, was National Socialism's practical fulfillment of a Social Democratic dream, and a Party official told functionaries of the Labor Front that "The demands for liberty, equality, and fraternity, with which the German worker was betrayed by liberal-Marxist demagogues, have become reality, thanks to National Socialism."[15]

Equality was a key word, not economic but, as it were, spiritual equality. In a characteristically ideological treatment of National Socialist labor policy, an instructor in the "Department of German Socialism" of the University of Cologne sketched the example of a white-collar employee at a factory celebration asking a dance of the owner's daughter. "The owner's wife is delighted with the courage and dash of the clerk." Supposing, the writer asks, it had been a worker who requested the dance. How would the wife react? "She would regard it as presumption," is the answer. The snobbery implicit in the answer was the target of the labor ideology. Did the worker resent the discrimination that obliged him but not the foreman or the white-collar worker to punch a clock? The recommended solution: a universal obligation to punch the clock, or, alternatively, the introduction of a morning rally—the so-called Betriebsappell—

[13] VB, 11 July 1939.
[14] VB, 26 March 1935.
[15] *Der illustrierte Beobachter,* 1 May 1935; VB, 1 July 1939.

with mandatory attendance of all employees as a substitute for clock-punching.[16]

Ideally, equality of status was to extend to equality of opportunity, the distinction between employer and employee would disappear in the fluidity of free competition in which all liberated energies were concentrated on the achievement of national goals. Achievement of these goals, in turn, was to reflect back on those who had achieved them, reorganizing society in a hierarchy of merit. "Victory in the battle of labor," wrote another instructor in the "Department of German Socialism," "means a fundamental change in the social, legal, and economic order in Germany." The objective was a new "middle class" formed not of those in what until now had been typical middle-class occupations like civil servants or shopkeepers, but of those whose merit had brought them a common—and relatively high—standard of living.[17] "The worker is ever more aware," a functionary of the Labor Front announced on the sixth anniversary of Hitler's appointment as Chancellor, "that he has the opportunity to reach the highest levels in his plant commensurate with his merit." Asked by a reporter whether National Socialism had already produced perceptible change in labor's status, he produced the example of a recent meeting of skilled industrial workers at which the director of a Realgymnasium (College preparatory high school) had happened to be present. "Can't be distinguished from my Abiturienten [graduating class]," the teacher had declared "with an astonished glance at the young journeymen."[18]

The institutional manifestation of Nazi labor policy was the Labor Service which combined the propagandistic pathos, economic expediency, political dedication, corruption, exploitation, and occasional idealism of Nazi labor policy in general. It was not inappropriately called "symbol of the nation" by the *Völkische Beobachter*.[19] The institution, like its New Deal equivalent, the Civilian Conservation Corps, was

[16] Franz Horsten, *Die nationalsozialistische Leistungsauslese*, Würzburg, 1938, pp. 99–100.

[17] Holtz, op. cit., pp. 34–40.

[18] VB, 30 January 1939.

[19] VB, 27 February 1935.

depression-born, an expedient of the Weimar Republic. Its most urgent purpose was a minimal alleviation of unemployment through public works employing up to 250,000 at the end of 1932 and financed by the unemployment insurance fund.[20] With its seizure of power, National Socialism, which had hitherto boycotted the Labor Service, proceeded to turn it into one of its most intensively cultivated projects. Ideologically the Labor Service became the institutionalized work ethos, the ultimate manifestation of "German Socialism" and Kameradschaft (comradeship), the irresistible solvent of existing class differences. Economically it was used first to create employment, then to block the holes left by the total reintegration of labor in the recovering industrial economy. It was an extended arm of the public sector with maximum propagandistic leverage and a minimum of operational expense. Before the reintroduction of universal conscription and during the preliminary stages of military expansion, the Labor Service also functioned as an agency of pre-military training, a function symbolized in the choice of its chief Konstantin Hierl, a retired Army officer.

Available statistics are a revealing index of official intentions. According to figures of a leading Labor Service functionary shortly before the Labor Service was declared a universal obligation in June 1935, industrial workers were a relatively tiny fraction of the "voluntary" membership, representing only 15 per cent of the total. Agricultural laborers were a still smaller group, only 4 per cent. But those in academic occupations, including Abiturienten, those qualified for university admission, and university students, totaled 7 per cent, a figure vastly greater than their representation in the general population or even in the male population of working age. Since the Labor Service had been declared mandatory for students or as a condition for university admission in 1933, their presence was, of course, far less an expression of spontaneous enthusiasm than of official pressure. This pressure was in turn directed characteristically at both an ideological and a practical goal, the exposure of the student to physical

[20] C. W. Guillebaud, *The Economic Recovery of Germany*, London, 1939, p. 37.

labor on the one hand and the temporary reduction of the university population on the other. The largest single group, however, 50 per cent of the total, was the artisans (Handwerker), up to this point the group least susceptible to the regime's industrial recovery measures.[21] The motives and the mechanism of job creation were sketched in an interview with the father of a young machinist leaving for duty in the Labor Service. The son's job and those of most of his young colleagues were reserved for those leaving the Army for reasons of age, for those of the Party's still-unemployed alte Kämpfer and for older unemployed workers like the machinist's father.[22]

The economic application of the Labor Service was again an index of the regime's objectives and problems. Since "inner colonization," land recovery, and exploitation of all possible arable land for intensified production was one of the government's foremost goals, and since its industrial recovery methods drained all available reserves of agricultural labor, 80 per cent of the male Labor Service in 1938 was employed in various forms of agriculture, forestry, and general work on the land to which the remaining 20 per cent—15 per cent in road construction and 5 per cent in homestead construction—were a supplement. Of the still-voluntary Labor Service for girls, 90 per cent were employed on the land.[23]

The problem of labor organization as such was a far more difficult one to deal with. Neither previous experience nor ideological inclinations were a very satisfactory guide to practical policy, and even the formation of the Factory Cell Organization (NSBO) was at best a makeshift. "Labor policy," wrote a doctoral candidate in 1934, "was an area of only secondary concern in relation to the major goals of the Party."[24] Writing amid the organizational chaos unleashed by Hitler's appointment, he concluded with embarrassment,

[21] *Der illustrierte Beobachter*, 1 May 1935, p. 28.

[22] "Familie Wagner," VB, 15 September 1935; typically, the reintroduction of universal conscription was expected to perform the same function of job distribution.

[23] Müller-Brandenburg, *Die Leistungen des deutschen Arbeitsdienstes*, Stuttgart-Berlin, 1940, p. 29.

[24] Friedrich Käss, "Nationalsozialismus und Gewerkschaftsgedanke," Munich dissertation, 1934, p. 1.

"It is not altogether easy to define the position of National Socialism toward union organization today."[25]

The only universally acceptable premise was hostility to the unions, particularly the socialist unions, in their existing form.[26] But even the problem of the unions was at first handled with gingerly discretion. The efforts of the NSBO to organize revolutionary incursions into the economic life of the nation met Party resistance virtually from the beginning. In March 1933 Goering forbade any initiative from below without explicit permission of the Party's economic authorities. In a Party directive of early April, Hess went further and banned any sort of NSBO, SA, or SS demonstration against any economic enterprise, industrial firm, bank, or union without the Party's permission.[27] Even the dissolution of the socialist unions on May 2, while it brought the Party and the new regime a mass of financial assets and broke up another nucleus of at least potential resistance, was no solution to the organizational problem. It only placed it totally and unavoidably within the Nazi ranks.

Gerhard Starcke, the press secretary of the later Labor Front, divided the institution's history into four periods, the first beginning with the demolition of the unions on May 2.[28] Contrary to the expectations of NSBO functionaries, who had foreseen a future for themselves as a State-sanctioned monopoly, it was a period of successive defeats. In the Labor Front, organized within a week after the dissolution of the unions, NSBO leaders were relegated to a minority position on the pilot committee—the so-called kleiner Konvent—and surrounded by Party functionaries, representatives of management, civil servants, and the agents of the business-interest groups.[29] At the same time, the NSBO was moved from

[25] Ibid., p. 66.

[26] Q: How did the NSDAP demonstrate its total opposition to the idea of class struggle?

A: On 9 August 1928 the leadership of the Party rejected the idea of organizing National Socialist unions.

Röpke, op. cit., p. 16.

[27] Schumann, op. cit., pp. 63–66.

[28] Gerhard Starcke, *Die deutsche Arbeitsfront*, Berlin, 1940, pp. 34 ff.

[29] Schumann, op. cit., p. 77.

Berlin to Munich, and while its staff was increased, it was anchored organizationally in the so-called Political Organization of the Party and prevented from integrating itself in the Labor Front. Self-finance through members' contributions was also ruled out.[30] In a directive in September, Ley again forbade an intervention in economic affairs, defining the NSBO exclusively as a "cadre of German Labor," "the SA of the factories" with purely political propagandistic functions. Before the end of the year, disciplinary actions, triggered in Frankfurt in August by the dissolution of all SA units, had landed impressive numbers of NSBO and Labor Front functionaries in concentration camps as "Marxist gangsters."[31] The NSBO youth organization was at the same time transferred to the Hitler Youth. In November, with the objective of diluting the "leftist" concentrations in the NSBO, Ley announced that all white-collar workers and employers presently in the Party were to be taken into the NSBO as well.

The second phase began in December 1933, with the reorganization of the Labor Front, the reorganization of industrial relations brought about by the law on "The Organization of National Labor" of January 1934, and the dissolution of the still autonomous economic interest organizations. The possibility of a liaison between dissident elements of the NSBO and the industrialists, united in common animosity to further Gleichschaltung by the regime, appeared all the more plausible by summer when a purge of the NSBO followed as a kind of economic aftermath to the purge of the SA.[32] With the announcement of their suspension, Ley declared: "I have established that a small number of persons have tried to sabotage the progress of construction of the Labor Front. These are representatives of the old unions and of the old employer organizations who have tried to prevent this construction at the last minute in the knowledge

[30] Ibid., p. 87.

[31] Ibid., pp. 89 f. ". . . and it can be conceded today without further ado that these organizations, under National Socialist auspices, proceeded to conduct a brisk and cheerful class struggle." Friedrich Völtzer, "Vom Werden des deutschen Sozialismus," *Zeitschrift für die gesamte Staatswissenschaft*, 1936, p. 9. Völtzer was Reich Trustee of Labor in Hamburg.

[32] Schumann, op. cit., pp. 103 f.

that it would abolish for all time their subversive influence in productive circles (schaffende Kreise). A number of functionaries of the Labor Front have offered their services in this effort. I have resolved to act against anyone inside or outside the Party who attempts to sabotage the Führer's objectives."[33] In a later report, Ley identified the NSBO as the cause of all difficulties, and Gregor Strasser, perhaps the most prominent victim of the June putsch, as the scapegoat. "He had intended it to be his personal army (Hausmacht)," Ley said, "and it was to support him in his betrayal. This is why he opposed the membership of employers."[34]

In a subsequent interview Ley added, "the foundation of my ideas was the recognition that the Party was the only source of power in the new Germany. For this reason I placed the Labor Front directly under Party leadership. . . . I thus saw to it that the Labor Front did not turn into a corporatist (ständisch) organization."[35]

By directive of 27 December 1934, with explicit reference to NSBO leaders and the functionaries of the labor departments (Fachschaften) of the Labor Front, intervention in State or municipal affairs was forbidden. On the contrary, those of them employed in public administration were ordered to report any infringement of National Socialist policy by public authorities not through Labor Front channels, but to the relevant minister via his Party liaison staff.[36] By assigning NSBO representatives the ultimate role of Party spies, the measure reflects at least as clearly as Ley's words the status of the NSBO in the Nazi hierarchy.

With the nominal assimilation of the employer groups in March 1935, the Labor Front advanced into a third phase. Carried by the dynamic of a successful, self-generating, self-perpetuating bureaucracy, it left its early competitors behind for good. Advancing beyond its preliminary stages

[33] *Das Archiv*, August 1934, p. 615.

[34] "Rechenschaftsbericht auf der 5. Jahrestagung der DAF zu Nürnberg vom 11. September 1937," *Dokumente der deutschen Politik*, Vol. V, Berlin, 1938, ed. Paul Meier-Benneckenstein, pp. 367 f.

[35] *Der Westdeutsche Beobachter*, 29 January 1938.

[36] Karl Bauer, "Querverbindungen von Partei und Staatsbehörden," Tübingen dissertation, 1936, p. 7.

as a random collection of gleichgeschaltete (co-ordinated) economic interest groups, it claimed a virtual monopoly on all processes of day-to-day economic administration, vocational counseling, legal aid, and social services. The NSBO languished in the middle depths of organizational obscurity. While the Party vegetated in even greater insignificance,[37] the Labor Front grew and prospered. With its thousands of employees[38] and millions in monthly dues, it was one of the most potent organizations in the Third Reich, prepared to contest the Reichsbank, the Ministry of Economics, the Party, or the administrators of the Four Year Plan with a good chance of winning. In a directive to the economic chambers (Wirtschaftskammer), a desperate Schacht enjoined them to file Labor Front memoranda without reading them.[39] Draft legislation in 1937/38 foresaw for the Labor Front a virtual monopoly in economic administration and vocational training in all areas except agriculture, domestic service, and the liberal professions, and direct subordination to Hitler himself. These demands were rejected emphatically by Hess and Goering.[40] But the Labor Front's wealth and numbers, plus the autonomy of Ley's position as Organizational Leader of the Party with control of the so-called Ordensburgen, the training academies for future Party leaders, had created leverage enough by the beginning of the war to allow the Labor Front to carry on almost independently, even conducting its propaganda independent of Party approval.[41] This was Starcke's fourth phase, a phase of virtual parity and autonomy symbolized from 1938 on by the simultaneous conventions of Party and Labor Front in Nuremberg. The institution was carried by its own élan while the traces of its curious sectarian beginnings virtually disappeared. As early as 1935, the majority of the leadership of the NSBO was recruited

[37] This will be handled in greater detail in Ch. VII.

[38] Starcke estimated 36,000. Cf. Starcke, op. cit., p. 144. Reichhardt estimated over 44,000. Cf. Hans Joachim Reichhardt, "Die deutsche Arbeitsfront," Freie Universität Berlin dissertation, 1956, p. 56.

[39] Hjalmar Schacht, *76 Jahre meines Lebens,* Bad Wörishofen, 1953, p. 433.

[40] National Archives Microscopy T 81, Roll 1, frames 10961 ff.

[41] Reichhard, op. cit., p. 84.

from those who had joined the Party since Hitler's seizure of power, while in the so-called trade divisions (Fachämter), newcomers—those who had joined the party since 30 January 1933—totaled 65 per cent of the leadership.[42] Former NSBO leaders were pushed off the main track, side-lined either in the administration of the Labor Front at local levels or, as responsible agents of Ley in his role as Organizational Leader of the Party, as Party functionaries, while their places in the Labor Front at the national level were taken by newcomers from the Party administration.[43]

In its six-year peacetime history, the Labor Front turned from the nucleus of an economic revolution from below, the foundation of the organization of social estates envisioned by earlier Party ideologists, and the embarrassed improvisation of 1933, to a self-perpetuating bureaucracy with relatively little interest in anything but its own further expansion. A characteristic Nazi institution, it combined bureaucracy with a kind of artificial charisma radiating from Hitler and the mobilization of the economy for war. In the ideological scheme of National Socialism, it functioned as a kind of no-interest group, "resolving the class struggle" in a vertical industrial organization, "the gigantic State Prison," as Sebastian Haffner called it, "in which the Nazis, not without sadistic humor, have locked up the former enemies together."[44] It was suspected by State and Party, reluctant to submit its unitary factory council lists to election from 1935 on, contemptuous of the industrialists, who returned its hate;[45] yet the very "objectivity" of its position had a quality of its own. Militant as its very name implied yet inseparably identified with the Nazi status quo, the Labor Front was susceptible to analysis by Parkinson or Rauschning but scarcely by Marx. More conventional formulas, slogans like "pro-labor" or "anti-labor" scarcely did justice to its reality,

[42] Schumann, op. cit., p. 106.
[43] Ibid., p. 101.
[44] Haffner, op. cit., p. 223.
[45] "The expression 'Die Industriellen sind ein Haufen von Frondeuren' [the industrialists are a gang of conspirators] could be heard daily in Ley's headquarters as I know from my own visits there." Lochner, op. cit., p. 179.

describing neither its functions nor its objectives. The Labor Front was a Nazi organization, its functionaries Nazis, its objectives Nazi objectives like "efficient" industrial relations, "efficient" control of the economy, "efficient" prosecution of rearmament and of the war effort, and, where possible, satisfaction of a clientele whose membership necessarily consisted of the vast majority of workers.[46]

The framework of industrial relations was the law on The Organization of National Labor (Gesetz zur Ordnung der nationalen Arbeit) whose superstructure rested explicitly on the basis of contracts previously negotiated with the old unions. Its text bore traces of both ideological and economic pressures more or less directly related to the situation in which it was written. The basic unit of industrial relations was hereafter to be the "shop community" (Betriebsgemeinschaft), based on a monolithic distinction between "leader" (Betriebsführer) and "followers" (Gefolgschaft). This was the economic translation of the Führerprinzip (leader principle) dear to the party's ideologists and a derivative of their antipathy to the divided responsibilities and authority of modern industrial organization. It was a kind of countermanagerial revolution, created in the image of the patriarchal sole proprietor, Ford or Siemens or Thyssen, whom old-fashioned Nazis like Feder admired and who, in the form of countless

[46] A practical example of how this might work is suggested by Krebs' story about how Winnig was called to Hitler in the summer of 1939 to propose measures for guaranteeing labor's loyalty in the event of war. Winnig's suggestion, that the Labor Front find places for loyal and popular leaders from the old unions, was evidently rejected out of hand. Krebs also characterized the majority of Labor Front functionaries as belonging to that group of bourgeois and petit-bourgeois Nazis who tended to see the world from the viewpoint of 1914 and accepted Hitler's version of why the pre-1914 world had collapsed. Krebs, op. cit., p. 47, p. 156. The rejection of the old union leaders, of course, is hard to interpret as pro-labor but equally difficult to view as anti-labor. Hitler opposed them not so much because he was anti-labor as because they had been anti-Hitler. The question of pro or anti was just not an issue, either in Hitler's relationship to labor or that of the functionaries Krebs describes. It is hard to imagine they were particularly friendly to labor but equally difficult to imagine they felt any special sympathy for business, especially big business. Such men had not become Nazis in order to see big business grow bigger.

thousands of Mittelständler (small businessmen), still exerted considerable pressure on the new regime. The weight of these small businessmen could also be felt in the job security provisions of the new law, which were explicitly limited to shops employing ten or more, leaving all the countless thousands of small operations to hire and fire on the same basis as before.[47]

The sections directly affecting the status of the worker dismantled the entire institutional apparatus created by the unions since the birth of the labor movement. The elected factory council (Betriebsrat) gave way under the new law to an advisory body, the Vertrauensrat, with no executive functions whatsoever. Though elected by secret ballot, the new council was to be selected from a single list prepared by the leader of the shop "in agreement with the NSBO functionary in his shop." The leader-follower dichotomy diluted the council yet again in making white-collar and even managerial personnel eligible for election. While the law required that the employer make available to the council member whatever information he might need to perform his duties, the clause guaranteeing him security from sudden loss of his job was capable of broad interpretation to the employer's advantage. The councilman could also be removed for reasons of "objective or personal" incompetence by the Reich Trustee of Labor, presumably at the employer's suggestion. In case of dispute the council could invoke the arbitration of the Reich Trustee. But "repeated, irresponsible and unjustified complaints or demands on the Reich Trustee" were defined as an occasion for prosecution, and the employer was guaranteed the right to apply such measures as he saw fit, even when they provoked a majority of the council to appeal to arbitration, and during the period in which the arbitrator's decision was pending.

The foremost apparent beneficiary of the new law was the employer. The advisory council, according to a sympathetic commentator, was without legal personality, forbidden to express its opinions publicly or to represent any special interest. The employer was under no obligation to accept its decisions.[48] While the creation of the "shop community"

47 Text in Büttner, op. cit., pp. 392–407.
48 Karl Müller-Stork, "Die Überwindung der Klassengegensätze

presupposed the existence of collective contracts, the law resolved and diluted the content and limits of the contractual obligation. Under certain circumstances more could be demanded of the "followers," that is, employees, than "the loyalty required by law and then simply making themselves available" (blosse Zur-Verfügung-Stellung).[49] But the leader, that is, the employer, was apparently freed from pressure from below, answerable only to his own sense of responsibility. Such conflicts as might still occur were automatically dealt with by "courts of social honor," a supplement to the labor courts, composed of a judge delegated by the Ministry of Justice in arrangement with the Ministry of Labor, an employer, and a council member, where possible from the same industry as the defendant.

Riding high above the entire system was the Reich Trustee, directly responsible to the Ministry of Labor and invested with authority to set wages, working conditions, and vacations, to appoint the advisory council in cases where an election failed to produce one, to approve dismissals exceeding certain fixed numbers, and to take part in the "courts of honor." "It must not be overlooked," wrote the Trustee in Hamburg, "that in all questions requiring a decision, the issue of directives on working conditions or on wage scales, the power of decision passes to the Trustee. This is the guarantee that the new self-government (of industry) avoids the risk of reinforcing the interests of any special group."[50]

A high-placed Labor Front functionary was scarcely exaggerating when he admitted "The realization of the shop community, both ideally and materially, places higher demands on the character of the followers than it does on the leader."[51] But available material on the functioning of the new labor institutions produces a more highly nuanced picture of the realities of Nazi labor relations than the legislative paragraphs might suggest.

---

und der Staatseinfluss in der faschistischen und der nationalsozialistischen Arbeitsordnung," Marburg dissertation, 1943, pp. 149 f.

[49] Ibid., pp. 140–44.

[50] Völtzer, op. cit., p. 38.

[51] Willy Müller, *Führertum und soziale Ehre,* Berlin, 1935, p. 34.

The operation of the advisory councils was the cause of one of the earliest crises. Ley rejoiced in April 1935 that "These elections are the freest and most incorruptible in the world. . . . And when, nonetheless, far over 80 per cent of the industrial workers of Germany declare themselves in favor of the idea of community, then this is an unprecedented testimonial to the success of our work."[52] But a letter to Hess's Party staff a week before had warned against undue publicity. Participation in the election in a Hamburg plant had run below 50 per cent and the results had been calculated on the basis of valid ballots only, reducing the level of actual support still more. A similar letter reported 1200 votes from 3125 workers, white-collar workers included. Bormann in turn wrote Hitler's staff urging that Hitler be warned away from repeating Ley's error and misinterpreting the results publicly on May 1.[53] The consequence was a suspension of further elections and indefinite retention of the councilmen elected in 1935. In editorial protest in 1937, the journal *Soziale Praxis* referred pointedly to the unsolved problem of firms that had grown beyond their 1935 size and were therefore entitled to new councilmen. A high-ranking civil servant in the Ministry of Labor was cited by name in favor of new legislation to adjust the discrepancies.[54] New legislation in May 1937 reflected the result of such pressure. While no new elections were ordered, the position of the council members was at least symbolically strengthened by a new directive prohibiting any transfer of the council member against his will without permission of the Trustee of Labor. At the same time, a new institutional apparatus was created, collective councils for multiple-branched enterprises with members drawn from the councils of the respective member plants. A further directive authorized the Trustee to order the presence of the "leader," the chairman of the board of directors, for example, at the new council's meetings.[55]

Court decisions reflected in part the actual power situation

[52] VB, 25 April 1935.

[53] Theodor Eschenburg, "Dokumentation," *Vierteljahrshefte für Zeitgeschichte*, 1955, pp. 314–16.

[54] *Soziale Praxis*, 1937, p. 377 f.

[55] Ibid., p. 574.

within the new institutional framework. In a typical case, an employer had fired the Labor Front representative (Betriebsobmann) in his shop, claiming the man was personally unqualified for his job. A labor court declared the dismissal illegal. "The employer [Betriebsführer] determines the qualifications of his employees [Gefolgschaftsmitglied]," the court decided, "but the responsibility for the qualifications of an employee as Labor Front representative reposes with the Labor Front alone."[56] The decision hardly strengthened the hand of labor in its relations with management. But, on the other hand, neither did it strengthen the hand of management in the unilateral sense the law might have been thought to imply. The real winner was the National Socialist State which used its new authority in revealing ways. In an interesting decision, the Leipzig labor court declared in 1937 that an employer's demands for apology from an employee who had made false statements in good faith were not permissible. This would be tantamount to demanding that the employee admit to having lied, the court decided, and this exceeded the prerogatives of the employer. "The limits of employee loyalty are reached at the point where the employee has to defend his honor," the court said. "The employer must take cognizance of this."[57] The decision was not pro-labor in any conventional sense, but again, scarcely to be viewed as pro-management.

A résumé of proceedings in the "courts of honor" during the last 5 months of 1934 recorded 65 prosecutions, 60 of them against employers, 3 against other managerial personnel. Of prosecutions against 223 persons in 1935, 164 were against employers, 8 against employers' deputies, 33 against other managerial personnel, and 18 against employees. In 9 cases the court revoked the employer's authority as "leader," that is, his right to run his own business.[58]

[56] *Der Angriff*, 17 October, 1937.

[57] *Soziale Praxis*, 1937, p. 231.

[58] Willy Müller, *Das soziale Leben im neuen Deutschland*, Berlin, 1938, pp. 125–26; on the other hand, Guillebaud reported that only twenty-five cases were brought against employers in the Hamburg area between 1933 and 1937 and only one lost his business as a result. Guillebaud, *Economic Recovery*, p. 200.

The effective equalizer, however, was less a factor of judicial decisions or the ideological good will of the regime than the economic situation itself. The new regime took office with 6,000,000 unemployed. But by the end of 1934 there were evidences that certain forms of labor were in short supply. As early as the summer of 1934, the *Völkische Beobachter* reminded the labor exchanges (Arbeitsämter) that jobs alone were not enough, "but that skills and knowledge were to be applied in a way most beneficial to the economy."[59] From then on, the demand for skilled labor became chronic, particularly in the metal and building trades, and later in mining.[60] Even before the war began, the president of the Reich Institute for Labor Exchange and Unemployment Insurance (Reichsanstalt für Arbeitsvermittlung und Arbeitslosenversicherung) estimated the labor shortage, irrespective of skills, at half a million.[61] In 1936/37, the sum of those employed exceeded the total number of those employed and unemployed in 1933.[62] Supporting labor's position were the dynamics of a qualified sellers' market.

What kept labor from making full use of this was the nature of the recovery that brought it about, at first the artificiality of the job-creation program itself, and from roughly 1936 on, the unconventional nature of an economy applied to the non-economic ends of autarky, armament, and war-preparation—objectively reflected in the vocabulary ordinarily used to describe them. "The battle of labor" (Arbeitsschlacht) was the official description of what had previously been called job creation. Einsatz, a word once used to describe the use of things and later of military units, now signified the use of

[59] VB, 22 July 1934.

[60] Cf. "Der ungelernte Arbeiter," VB, 10 September 1935; "Facharbeiter fehlen überall," VB, 14 January 1939. "Unskilled labor must be eliminated in Germany," Ley declared. "There will come a time when the only unskilled workers will and can be those who are absolutely without talent." *Der Angriff*, 3 and 14 November 1937.

[61] "Die Wirtschaftslage in Deutschland," *Vierteljahreshefte zur Wirtschaftsforschung*, Vol. 13, 1938–39, p. 34.

[62] Gustav Stolper, *Deutsche Wirtschaft, 1870–1940*, Stuttgart, 1950, p. 150.

labor.[63] The worker himself was called "soldier of labor," a not inappropriate description of the new status in which he was at once as well-serviced and underpaid, as regimented and as fully employed, as the member of any peacetime Army.

Regimentation began with limits on freedom of movement, applied in May 1934 to movement to Berlin, Hamburg, and Bremen, and subsequently to the Saar, until early 1936. Restriction of further urban unemployment and preservation of farm labor were among the motives behind the measure. A directive of August 1934 authorized the labor exchanges to hire older workers and send younger workers elsewhere, a measure that affected an estimated 130,000 jobs between October 1934 and October 1935.[64] In December 1934 special measures were introduced for skilled metalworkers and later extended to all metalworkers, forbidding them to move without the permission of their local labor exchange.[65] The aircraft industry with support of the Air Ministry had already taken measures to prohibit the manufacturer from hiring without a certificate of release from the potential employee's previous employer.[66] A law of November 1936 obliged employers to report to the labor exchanges any building and metalworkers who were presently employed by them in positions other than those for which they had been trained, and who were thus being held in reserve while unskilled workers were being fired. Similar measures were applied to masons and carpenters in October 1937.[67] A general step toward total labor regimentation was the introduction of labor passes (Arbeitsbücher) in early 1935. The object was total statistical investigation of available labor reserves and then control of them. The employer was explicitly forbidden to withhold the pass or indicate any dissatisfaction or satisfaction with its owner. Twenty-two million were issued in the

[63] Cf. Dolf Sternberger, Gerhard Storz, and W. E. Süskind, *Aus dem Wörterbuch des Unmenschen,* Munich, 1962, pp. 40–45.

[64] Friedrich Syrup, *Hundert Jahre staatliche Sozialpolitik,* ed. Julius Scheuble, Stuttgart, 1957, pp. 415–20.

[65] Ibid., pp. 422 f.

[66] Werner Mansfeld, "Sicherung des Gefolgschaftsbestandes," *Der Vierjahresplan,* March 1937, pp. 154 f.

[67] Syrup, op. cit., pp. 422–28.

first series, covering all public and private workers, both blue- and white-collar. In April 1939 the labor pass was issued to all those who were self-employed, including their families, leaving only civil servants and the members of the liberal professions untouched. All labor pass holders were under compulsory registration at the labor exchanges and catalogued according to age, family status, and skills.

A special problem was the re-employment of older white-collar workers, which was solved in a number of cases by the gordian knot technique of employing them in blue-collar jobs, with credit for their employment granted both to the labor exchanges responsible for finding them jobs and to the employers responsible for making them available.[68]

Under the pressure of the labor shortage in 1937, unmarried textile workers under thirty, still working short-time due to a shortage of raw materials, were denied unemployment relief and thus forced into other occupations.[69] From mid-1933 to mid-1936, about 80 per cent of the total increase in employment, according to Guillebaud, occurred in production goods industries, 48 per cent in the building trades and their subsidiaries. While the increase of employment among workers in industry and handicrafts amounted to 54 per cent, it attained only 17 per cent in trade and transport.[70] From July 1932 to July 1937, employment in production goods industries increased by 150 per cent relative to consumer goods industries, which increased by only 40 per cent.[71] From June 1933 to June 1937, employment in the metal industries increased by over 150 per cent, in the building trades by over 210 per cent.[72] With the construction of the western border fortifications in 1938/39, the last limits on free movement of labor were removed by the "Decree for the guarantee of manpower for tasks of particular political importance" (Verordnung zur Sicherstellung des Kräftebedarfs für Aufgaben von besonderer staatspolitischer Bedeut-

[68] Hans Kühne, "Der Arbeitseinsatz im Vierjahresplan," *Jahrbücher für Nationalökonomie und Statistik*, 1937, pp. 708–10.
[69] Guillebaud, *Economic Recovery*, p. 111.
[70] Ibid., p. 87.
[71] Ibid., p. 136.
[72] Ibid., p. 115.

ung).[73] All men and women in all occupations were hereby ordered to take a new job if required or, where necessary, to undergo special training. The old job and its various pension and insurance claims were to be reserved to them, and the rate of pay in the new job could not be lower than in the old one. In the meantime, the regime took steps to overcome the labor deficit with women and with the marginally self-employed.[74]

With an eye to the future, the regime also began, as early as 1935, to take steps regulating the distribution and development of industrial skills. The president of the Reich Institute assumed responsibility for maintaining a high rate of apprentices to trained labor in important industries, and employers were obliged to register both their employment figures and their apprentice-training capacities with the labor exchanges. From 1938 on, compulsory registration of those leaving school was ordered as well. The labor exchanges assumed the responsibility for vocational counseling in conjunction with the Hitler Youth and the Labor Front. "The foremost goal at the moment is not the enrichment of the individual existence," two Labor Front functionaries declared, "but the increasing prosperity of the nation. Vocational counseling has to serve the interests of all (Gesamtheit) and the wishes of the individual can be respected only to the extent that they do not run contrary to these interests."[75] Official statements thundered against "fashionable occupations" and false vocational choices, and pressure was brought on white-collar occupations and the handicrafts to direct the apprentice supply to industry.[76] Guillebaud reported that the ratio of apprentices to total employment in industry rose from 4.5 per cent to 5.4 per cent between 1934 and 1935; in 1937, in part with the help of Reich subsidies, it had reached 16.5 per cent in the building trades and 24 per cent in the metal trades.[77]

[73] Text in Büttner, op. cit., pp. 435 ff.

[74] This will be treated in more detail in Chs. V and VI.

[75] A. Bremhorst and W. Bachmann, *Ordnung des Berufseinsatzes*, Berlin-Leipzig, 1937, p. 13.

[76] Holtz, *Arbeitspolitik*, p. 75.

[77] Guillebaud, *Economic Recovery*, p. 100.

Vocational schools became the object of critical appraisal, apprenticeships were accelerated and formal requirements eased. In a special course for mining engineers in 1934, for example, twenty-two applicants were accepted though only two met the formal requirements.[78] In a number of technical groups, the secondary school certificate was dropped as a condition of training.[79] An arrangement between the Reichsgruppe Industrie and the professional organization of the handicraftsmen (Reichsstand des deutschen Handwerks) granted skilled labor parity with the master craftsmen, thereby enlarging the available pool of those qualified to train apprentices.[80] The ultimate goal, as the Labor Front's chief of vocational training admitted, was a unitary apprentice program that removed the apprentice from the smaller shop altogether, placing him for the duration of his training in separate, co-operative training shops in bigger plants where he had the advantage of better facilities and where he was in less danger of being exploited as cheap labor.[81]

The preoccupation with skills and efficient application of available labor found its institutional expression in another typically Nazi creation, the annual Reich Vocational Competition (Reichsberufswettkampf) which was invested with all the propagandistic glamor and ideological underpinning at the regime's disposal. "Socialism," wrote a spokesman, "is the characterization of the duty to bring every worker to that position for which he has an inner inclination. . . . The Reich Vocational Competition is a product of this conception of a socialistic selection process."[82] Winners were treated like Olympic athletes or film stars, brought to Berlin, and photographed with Ley and Hitler himself. According to Artur Axmann, the director of the competition, nearly all national winners enjoyed some further form of support; at the regional level, 63 per cent of the male winners and 47 per

[78] Bojunga, *Zur Steigerung der Leistungen in den Berufs- und Fachschulen,* Berlin, 1937, p. 29.

[79] Ibid., p. 81.

[80] Bremhorst and Bachmann, op. cit., p. 27.

[81] Karl Arnhold, "Lehrling—einst und jetzt," *Soziale Praxis,* 23 July 1937, pp. 866–70.

[82] Dr. Hunke, "Gedanken zum Reichsberufswettkampf," *Die deutsche Volkswirtschaft,* February 1935, p. 169.

cent of the girls were honored with some form of promotion, subsidy, or benefit, like shortened apprenticeship, further training, or transfer to another firm with better chance of promotion.[83] Among such cases were a young woodworker sent to a technical school at Labor Front expense, a milk technician sent to an advanced training school and re-employed by her old employer in a white-collar position, a textile worker sent to a technical college, a post office messenger promoted to a higher civil service status.[84] Since more than half the winners came from families of wage earners and up to 80 per cent had never reached secondary school,[85] the regime achieved at least the propagandistic end of conspicuous glorification of its working population. There was also the real possibility of advancement, at least advancement of status, for many who might not otherwise have achieved it.

Introduced on a relatively modest scale in 1933, the competition included virtually all forms of employment by 1938, both industry and handicrafts, white-collar occupations, civil service, and even university students who presented prize essays on such topics as "Planning a Hitler Youth hostel with athletic field and parade ground in Prussian Friedland," or "Political Catholicism in Germany before 1914." In a large number of cases—Axmann claimed 88 per cent in landscape engineering, 83 per cent in textiles and fashion design—suggestions presented by students of technical institutions were passed on for realization in one form or another.[86] A number of ideological papers, discussions of Weltanschaung, were published later in the press or in technical journals.[87]

[83] Artur Axmann, *Der Reichsberufswettkampf*, Berlin, 1938, p. 313.

[84] "Aufstieg durch Förderung," *Der Angriff*, 27 November 1937.

[85] Axmann, op. cit., p. 322.

[86] Ibid., pp. 356–64.

[87] Some sample questions from the commercial competition: "What can you report about the consequences of the government's measures to eliminate unemployment in your area?" "What is the significance of the Leipzig Fair for the German economy?" "Why, in your opinion, should Germany promote exports—or why not?" "What are the tasks of the cartels in National Socialist Germany?" VB, 11 March 1935. Weltanschauung counted 20 of 120 points in the total score. Recalling a train trip through Austria, Rebecca West quoted a fellow passenger's story of the hairdresser's assistant who

In an economy governed by a unique combination of special interests, ideological preoccupations, short-term non-economic objectives, subsidies, and controls, the economic consequences of National Socialism for labor were a peculiar mixture of advantages and disadvantages. In a system elastic enough to absorb the normal effects of Germany's full and overfull employment, the wage scale would ordinarily record the progress of labor's bargaining position. But the closed system of wages and prices, the obsessive fear of inflation, that helped govern economic policy in the Third Reich make the wage scale at best a secondary index. Seen from the wage standpoint alone, labor's position deteriorated. Between 1933 and 1937, wages and salaries increased absolutely by nearly 50 per cent, relatively from 55 to 57.6 per cent of the national product. But profits in the same period increased from 12.9 to 18 per cent of the national product. Compared with 1928, a year of maximum pre-Nazi prosperity, wages and salaries in 1937 claimed a smaller share of the national product, profits in trade and industry a larger share.[88] Income figures, based on withholding tax receipts, revealed that gross income per taxpayer in 1940, that is the ratio of taxpayers to total income in wages and salaries, had declined by 3 per cent relative to 1933.[89] As early as 1935 the increasing lag between employer and employee income was a cause of irritation in Party circles.[90] In response to the labor shortage and its obvious consequences, the trustees of labor, hitherto authorized to fix minimum wages, were authorized in 1938 to fix maximum wages as well, and subsequently to

"was afraid she had failed in the examination which she had to pass for the right to practice her craft. She had said to the girl, 'But I am sure you will pass your examination for you are so very good at your work.' But the girl had answered, 'Yes, I am good at my work! Shampooing can I do, and water waving can I do, and hair-dyeing can I do, but keep from mixing up Goering's and Goebbels' birthdays, that I can not do.'" Rebecca West, op. cit., p. 32.

[88] The figures can be found in Guillebaud, *Economic Recovery*, p. 193.

[89] The figures can be found in *Statistisches Jahrbuch für Deutschland*, Munich, 1949, p. 575.

[90] Cf. "Arbeitseinkommen-Unternehmereinkommen," *Die deutsche Volkswirtschaft*, February 1935, pp. 176 f.

control measures invoked by ingenious employers to offer invisible raises in the form of voluntary overpayments, bogus promotions, bonuses, extra paid vacations, savings funds, and tax and insurance rebates.[91]

The wage model was based on a skill differential. In effect, the job was paid rather than the worker. In each industry, the Trustee fixed basic wages for eight groups according to skill and published catalogues of highly detailed job descriptions. Actual wage policy, in turn, called for further discrimination in favor of the skilled worker by modifying the differential scale of basic wage rates, that is hourly rates without piecework or overtime earnings, relative to skill. The unskilled worker was to draw 75–80 per cent of his income in basic rates, the worker responsible for "highest quality skilled labor" (höchstwertige Facharbeit) drew 133 per cent. The object was to guarantee a fixed income commensurate with his skill to the highly trained worker who was not on piecework and thus unable to increase his earnings accordingly.[92]

The wage pattern was readjusted relative to economic priority, inflationary controls, and the requirements of a national speed-up. It is hardly surprising that National Socialism, with its ideological bias in favor of "elitism," "achievement," and "productivity," had a weakness for piecework.[93] Income figures reflected the combination of general boom with carefully applied incentive premiums. Given 1932=100 as a base, hourly rates in 1938 were set at 97.4, hourly earnings at 108.2, weekly earnings at 126.5.[94] Hourly earnings in production goods industries increased faster than in consumer goods industries. But in the index of weekly earnings the relationship was reversed. This was due to relative dilution of skilled labor in production goods industries caused by the increased employment of women, and to more overtime work in the consumer goods branches caused by the loss of manpower to production goods industries. Highest wages were

[91] Gerhard Bry, *Wages in Germany*, Princeton, 1960, pp. 235–37.

[92] Syrup, op. cit., p. 477.

[93] Cf. Werner Mansfeld, "Drei Lohnthesen," *Der deutsche Volkswirt*, 25 August 1939, pp. 2314–16.

[94] Bry, op. cit., pp. 238–39.

paid in metal trades, machinery, and electrical goods; lowest in brewing, papermaking, and woodworking; with chemicals, hard-coal mining, and rubber in middle positions.[95]

A differential analysis of wage-income distribution[96] between 1932 and 1940 shows that the total number of taxpayers increased by 120 per cent, total income by 115 per cent. The lowest income group, those earning below 1500 marks annually, grew by 167 per cent; a middle-income group, those earning between 2400 and 3600 marks annually, grew by 180 per cent. Those earning between 3600 and 4800 marks a year increased by 122 per cent, roughly the average increase of the total of all groups. All other income groups grew at less than the average rate. The uppermost group, those earning over 7200 marks yearly, 1 per cent of the total in 1932, had declined by 9 per cent absolute by 1940, that is from 87,000 to 79,000. The figures point to a high rate of employment of unskilled labor, a reflection of the boom and the resultant labor shortage, and of the advancing differential between the income of the skilled and the unskilled. They also suggest an impressive rate of upward mobility, presumably a product not only of the boom but of the skilled labor campaign that went with it. The decline in the top income group probably had less to do with official pressure on wages than with the reclassification of those in the top income group in different tax categories.[97] The relatively stagnant groups, for example those earning between 1500 and 1800 marks who increased by only 56 per cent and those earning between 1800 and 2400 marks who increased by only 74 per

[95] Ibid., p. 245.

[96] Based on the figures in *Statistisches Jahrbuch für Deutschland*, p. 575. Data for 1938, undoubtedly a better year for comparison, are unfortunately not given. See Appendix I, pp. 290–91.

[97] German tax law distinguishes between a withholding tax on wages and salaries (Lohnsteuer) and a tax on income (Einkommenssteuer) imposed on the self-employed and those whose salaries exceed a certain level, in this case something over 7200 marks yearly. Considering the extent of the economic recovery and the general economic policies of the Third Reich, it is more plausible to assume the number of those whose salaries exceeded the statutory level, for instance higher managerial personnel, increased and that they were reclassified as income tax payers than that the number fell to a level below that of the worst depression year.

cent, were probably semi-skilled and white-collar workers who benefited less from the economic measures of the regime.

Even though it was estimated that the cost of food absorbed up to 50 per cent of the average worker's income,[98] it would be misleading to assume that the standard of living fell. Given 1932=100 as a base, the average hourly wage in 1938 was 97, the cost of living 104. But weekly real earnings had increased to 121.4 gross, and after tax and insurance deductions and adjustment to the cost of living, 114 compared to an adjusted cost of living index of 109.[99] According to Klein, beer, egg, cheese, wheat, flour, and margarine consumption declined between 1928 and 1938, but meat, lard, butter, fish, potatoes, rice, and coffee consumption increased. A 6 per cent decline in per capita calorie consumption between 1929 and 1933 had been overcome by 1937.[100] According to Guillebaud's figures, consumer goods production, given 1928=100 as a base, was 101.5 by 1937, 107.4 during the first quarter of 1938,[101] and consumer goods prices had been reduced for some products like branded electrical and chemical goods, clocks and watches, and some foods.[102] The cost of clothing rose by 13 per cent.[103] But housing construction in 1937 was only 1 per cent below the 1929 level; in 1938, despite the Four Year Plan, less than 10 per cent below it, according to Klein, creating at least the impression of adequate housing. This was coupled with the advantages of fixed rents and a relative decline in the costs of heating and light.[104]

[98] Hermann Reischle, "Der Weg der nationalsozialistischen Wirtschaft," *Odal*, October 1939, p. 873. Steiner estimated it at 44%, compared with 29% in England. Cf. Steiner, op. cit., p. 97.

[99] Bry, op. cit., p. 263.

[100] Cf. Burton H. Klein, *Germany's Economic Preparations for War*, Cambridge, Massachusetts, 1959, p. 13; Guillebaud, *Economic Recovery*, p. 207. The pattern is mixed in part by the peculiarities of Nazi farm policy, something that will be handled in detail in Ch. V. This might account, for instance, for the rise in rice and potato consumption, and the fall in wheat and flour whose prices were well subsidized. But the trend from margarine to butter, the increased consumption of meat, and the luxury good coffee would seem to point to an over-all rise in living standard.

[101] Guillebaud, *Economic Recovery*, p. 204.

[102] Ibid., p. 178.

[103] Ibid., p. 187.

[104] Loc. cit.

The eight-hour day remained the ideal in industry.[105] Agriculture, fishing, various transportation branches, hotels, and restaurants were however excepted. Ten hours were fixed as the official limit, though the law made provision for exceptional cases. Some of these made a very generous impression like the provision that the ten-hour day could be extended in circumstances where the employer, faced with a shortage of help, could not be asked to accept substitute help from outside. The employer was also granted the concession of thirty days yearly during which he could demand up to two overtime hours, that is a ten-hour day, of his employees. The factory inspectors could also permit extra hours in cases of "urgent need." Overtime pay, in the absence of an alternative ruling either by "the participants" (die Beteiligten), a minister of the Reich, the Minister of Labor, or a Trustee of Labor, amounted to 125 per cent of the normal hourly wage. Seasonal labor was withdrawn from the general regulations on the assumption of an annual equilibrium of work-time, bringing seasonally occasioned short and overtime hours into a balance consistent with the eight-hour model. Despite the pressure of Party officials and the demands of the Four Year Plan, the eight-hour day was maintained with good success according to Syrup, largely on the initiative of employers conscious of the bad effects of extended overtime on productivity.[106]

While the law included ample provision for exploitation, available statistics indicate relatively little of it. A study of selected industries showed only machine construction and paper production operating more than eight hours daily in 1936. Textiles were still working less than seven hours daily, certain branches of the printing industry (Vervielfältigungswesen) and the metal trades were working eight hours, all other major industries between seven and eight. In 1936/37, textiles and clothing had gone up to seven and a half hours. Vehicle construction, the electrical industry, the chemical industry, certain kinds of instrument making (Feinmechanik und Optik), and glass had reached eight hours. In 1937/38,

[105] The text of the 1938 law on working hours can be found in Büttner, op. cit., pp. 414–35.
[106] Syrup, op. cit., p. 486.

ceramics and building materials reached eight hours; textiles, seven and a half. Between 1936 and 1938, ceramics made the greatest gain in working hours, followed by textiles and the production of certain metal goods (Metallwaren). But only machine construction and paper production were working more than eight hours daily, while all other industrial branches, including branches of considerable military importance like the electrical industry, rubber, vehicle construction, chemicals, metal fabrication (Eisen- und Stahlwaren), and non-ferrous metals were still working an average of less than eight hours daily.[107] Klein estimates that the average increase in weekly working hours between 1929 and 1939 was about 3 per cent, reaching 5 per cent in heavy industries vital to the rearmament effort.[108]

As the pressure caused by visibly rising profits and visibly fixed wages increased, the Labor Front intervened to relieve it, not so much in benefits to the individual, which, either in the form of higher wages or the invisible benefits offered by hardpressed employers, were bound to cause inflation, labor mobility, or frustration, but in counterpressure on employers intended to benefit labor in general. This pressure expressed itself in better working conditions, assumed at employer not government expense. "There are already very shrewd employers," Ley remarked with satisfaction in 1937, "who are moving even faster than we."[109]

Employing its characteristic carrot-and-whip method, the regime pressed for technical improvements in the form of better lighting, locker and shower rooms, canteens with subsidized hot meals, athletic fields, parks, kindergartens, and subsidized housing. From 1936 on, employers were included in a competition, which according to official figures included up to 275,000 competitors by 1939, for recognition of their shops as exemplary (Musterbetriebe). Among the by-products were nearly 60,000 new housing units, built at private expense, and more efficient production in the participant plants. Both were obviously considered in the distribution of

[107] "Die Wirtschaftslage in Deutschland," op. cit., p. 35.
[108] Klein, op. cit., pp. 68–70.
[109] *Der Angriff*, 31 October 1937.

prizes.[110] "When the worker knows that the employer is a comrade," Ley told industrialists in 1935, "you can demand anything of him."[111] Depending on his audience, Ley could have said the same of the worker's relationship to the State. Beyond the attraction of physical benefits was a hard-sell appeal to the worker's morale, embracing as broad a spectrum of possibilities as officially sponsored symphony concerts in larger plants[112] and sophisticated appeals to his self-respect. A kind of ideal type of the latter was a scheme introduced at a Cologne motor plant in 1935 which attracted considerable official interest. Confronted with a shortage of supervisory personnel, the plant introduced an honor system, authorizing up to three hundred workers to inspect their own work and another fifty to establish their own piece-work rate. Workers were, of course, reminded that the firm was in a position to examine their work retroactively and uncover any cheating. For the self-inspectors, the honor was purely moral, including a plaque on their work benches. The so-called self-calculators, however, were granted a margin of relative independence and had the chance of increasing their productivity and thus their earnings. Piece-work rates were adjusted, in turn, to the productivity of the self-calculators, thereby, by implication, reducing the general wage rate of the other workers, and incidentally relieving the pressure on supervisory personnel. Basically Darwinian, with tangible advantages for the outstanding worker and obvious disadvantages to the rest, the scheme was advanced in the name of "shop community," the dignity of labor and the career open

[110] *Deutsche Musterbetriebe*, Arbeitswissenschaftliches Institut der deutschen Arbeitsfront, Berlin-Stuttgart, 1940, p. 31.

[111] VB, 5 September 1935.

[112] "In Esslingen, in a machine plant in Württemberg, the radio announcer asked an old grey master craftsman who stood there with tears in his eyes as all around him cheered with enthusiasm, what he had to say to the occasion. 'Who would have dared to think that the Kaiser would send his orchestra to us here in the plant? As our leaders spoke about this recently, how everybody was going to have a chance to enjoy these cultural opportunities, we could hardly believe our ears. Now the Führer himself has sent us his orchestra. We can never thank him enough. . . .'" "Was wir jeden Tag erleben," brochure on the Nationalsozialistisches Reichs-Symphonie-Orchester, Munich, undated but probably 1937, p. 21.

to talent. It could be recommended to personnel departments as an efficient selection of lower grades of managerial talent, to accounting departments as a way of reducing costs. It was, said the SS Journal *Das Schwarze Korps*, socialism.[113] On Sundays, family members were invited to visit the plant and see their fathers' decorated work benches.

The Third Reich's best publicized and best received contribution to industrial relations was without doubt the "Strength through Joy" organization ("Kraft durch Freude," usually abbreviated as KdF). Apparently conceived in a moment of embarrassment as a scheme to win friends and, incidentally, to find use for the confiscated assets of the trade unions, KdF overcame both worker resistance and the gloomy prophecies of Ley's Party colleagues.[114] Its expansive program soon included subsidized theatre performances and concerts, exhibitions, sport and hiking groups, dances, folk-dancing, films, and adult education courses. But its most famous feature was a grandiose system of subsidized tourism whose practical economic by-products included visible benefits to thousands of rural hotelkeepers and the State railroad (Deutsche Reichsbahn).[115]

With its vast subsidies,[116] KdF was itself big business, expanding by 1935, with the construction of two liners, into a shipping company, and by 1937, with the subsidized develop-

[113] "Das ist Sozialismus!," *Das Schwarze Korps*, 5 January 1939; "Persönlichkeitswert des deutschen Arbeiters," *Der Völkische Beobachter*, 15 January 1939; Horsten, op. cit., pp. 102 ff.; H. Stein, "Erziehung," op. cit., and "Arbeiter bestimmen selbst Zeitvorgabe und Stückpreis," *Zeitschrift für Organisation*, Vol. 11, No. 1, 25 January 1937 and No. 4, 25 April 1937.

[114] Cf. Schumann, op. cit., p. 139.

[115] According to a 1938 doctoral candidate, 2,000,000 KdF travelers in 1934 brought 45,000,000 marks into circulation, including 7,000,000 in the form of Reichsbahn tickets. In 1935 3,000,000 travelers brought 68,000,000 marks into circulation. "A considerable part of these contributions benefited emergency areas and represented an important supplement to the general economic recovery." Hans Krapfenbauer, "Die sozialpolitische Bedeutung der nationalsozialistischen Gemeinschaft 'Kraft durch Freude,'" Nuremberg dissertation, 1938, p. 25.

[116] Schumann reports a subsidy of 24,000,000 marks for 1933/34, 17,000,000 for 1935, and 15,000,000 for 1936. Schumann, op. cit., p. 138.

ment of the Volkswagen—known originally as the "KdF Wagen"—into large-scale automobile manufacturing. These KdF activities had their ideological and economic significance and, not surprisingly, their calculated military utility too. With the beginning of the war, the liners became troopships. The Volkswagen, which, in fact, never became available for civilian use but performed the useful function of draining liquidity in the form of weekly installment payments from hopeful owners, found its place as an all-purpose military vehicle.[117] Volkswagen also took the interesting sociological role of making the automobile, heretofore a bourgeois status symbol, at least potentially available to the working classes.[118] Mass tourism, including foreign tourism, performed the same role, something that Ley took every opportunity to emphasize. "The worker sees that we are serious about raising his social position. He sees that it is not the so-called 'educated classes' whom we send out as representatives of the new Germany, but himself, the German worker, whom we show to the world."[119] The impression was intensified with the construction of single-class ships and even, if disingenuously, with the inclusion of employers and white-collar personnel in the tourist groups. "Not only the worker is to be liberated from his feelings of inferiority," Ley declared, "the employer is to experience the same change of view. An employer from West Germany and his wife were on the ship, and it was particularly interesting to hear what they had to say. She said her friends had commiserated with her about traveling with KdF on the false bourgeois assumption that it had been a sacrifice to have to travel with workers. The young woman now announced with pride and satisfaction that she had never before been on such a fine and happy trip."[120]

By comparison, a French correspondent, who had been on

117 Guillebaud, *Economic Recovery,* p. 240; Schumann, op. cit., p. 140.

118 It is of interest that Henry Ford, the first to do this, was something of a Nazi culture hero, not only as the Volkswagen was developed but long before. Cf. Holtz, *Arbeitspolitik,* p. 92; Käss, op. cit., p. 26.

119 VB, 31 March 1935.

120 Ibid.

a KdF cruise to Norway, reported his surprise at the number of Leicas and Rolleiflexes around him. Inquiring about the actual social composition of the groups he was traveling with, he learned that of 939 on board, 217 were workers, 249 clerks and handicraftsmen, 202 women in various forms of employment, 187 housewives, 28 members of the liberal occupations, and 56 men and women with no occupation listed. He also had the impression that the cost of the cruise was beyond the means of most workers unless they happened to be subsidized by their employers.[121] A survey of KdF participation in Mannheim suggests that actually tourism played a relatively minor role in the expanse of KdF activity. Nearly 820,000 had taken part in KdF events there in 1937, but participation sank sharply to 100,000 participants in one- or two-day excursions, 11,000 for two-week trips, and barely 1000 enjoyed the spectacular Norway, Italy, or Madeira cruises.[122]

In its multiple functions and their multiple implications, KdF was again a kind of symbol of Nazi economic and labor policy whose official raison d'être included a broad streak of cynicism. At the KdF convention in Hamburg in 1938, propagandistically expanded into an international conference on the use of leisure time, Ley declared officially, "There are no longer classes in Germany. In the years to come, the worker will lose the last traces of inferiority feelings he may have inherited from the past."[123] But a Dutch correspondent heard him say, "People are children. . . . They have childlike wishes. The state has to care for these and see to it that they get their presents if they are to be happy and stay happy and apply all their enthusiasm and energy to their work."[124] Starcke, the press officer of the Labor Front, announced without inhibition, "We do not send our workers on vacation on our own ships or build them massive bathing facilities at the sea for fun, either for ourselves or for the individual who has the chance to make use of them. We do it only because we are interested in preserving the working

[121] *Le Temps*, 30 August 1937.
[122] *Das Hakenkreuzbanner*, Mannheim, 27 November 1937.
[123] *Der Westdeutsche Beobachter*, 11 June 1938.
[124] *Algemeen Handelsblad*, Amsterdam, 14 June 1938.

capacity (Arbeitskraft) of the individual and in order to send him back to work strengthened and refreshed."[125] Krapfenbauer, reflecting a kind of ideological lag, viewed KdF as the alternative to deindustrialization. "To protect the nation from the harmful consequences of an accelerated work pace, steps have to be taken to guarantee it, during its leisure time, a total relaxation from the pressure of daily life."[126] Perhaps the ultimate argument for KdF was the Total State's total demand on the resources of its citizens, a demand that included total regimentation of time. Only sleep was a private affair, Ley wrote. "There are no more private citizens. The time when anybody could do or not do what he pleased is past."[127]

Like the population to which it applied, social policy was neither advanced nor neglected in the Third Reich; rather, it was manipulated. The unions were destroyed. The social welfare institutions were not, but they were gleichgeschaltet. From 1933 to 1938, the Reich Institute, hitherto an autonomous institution, functioned as an agency of the Ministry of Labor. From 1939 on, its president was an official in the ministry. The hitherto autonomous unemployment insurance fund was tapped to finance the Autobahns, family allowances, and supplemental old-age insurance.[128] "Apart from overcoming unemployment," Syrup wrote, "the product of State-directed social policy during the six peacetime years can only be called minimal."[129] But it was not retrogressive. National Socialism, Syrup wrote, took office with the promise of fast and far-reaching reforms. Virtually nothing came of them, though there were occasional improvements. Between 1935 and 1938, a guaranteed week was introduced in the building trades, ensuring building workers 60 per cent of their weekly wage irrespective of season. Unitary administra-

[125] Starcke, op. cit., p. 10.

[126] Krapfenbauer, op. cit., p. 9. Deindustrialization, according to Krapfenbauer, was not only impossible because the technological clock could no longer be turned back, but "because Chinese and Japanese competition would not permit such a regression anyway."

[127] Ley, *Soldaten der Arbeit*, Munich, 1938, p. 71.

[128] Syrup, op. cit., pp. 407, 460.

[129] Ibid., p. 405.

tion of public employment was introduced in April 1938 with the approximation in a number of branches of working conditions to civil service standards.[130] In 1938 obligatory old-age insurance was introduced for handicraftsmen, in early 1939 obligatory health insurance, for agriculture and related industries.[131] Vacations were extended in certain industries.[132] Marriage loans and baby bonuses benefited labor at least as much as other population groups. Guillebaud reported that a worker with ten children, earning 160 marks monthly, received 140 marks monthly in family allowances, not subject to deduction. Since nearly 20 per cent of his earnings were deducted in taxes, insurance, Labor Front dues, and various other contributions, a worker's family allowance amounted to more than his actual working income.[133] The Ministry of Finance also assisted families with four or more children in having the children attend secondary or technical schools, contributing up to six hundred marks yearly for those in State boarding schools.

One last index to the fate and treatment of labor in the Third Reich is the history of the white-collar worker, who was relatively untouched by the job creation program of the first Nazi years. While industrial employment increased by 54 per cent between 1933 and 1936, employment of salary earners rose by only 14 per cent and, as has been mentioned, the problem of re-employment of older white-collar workers required special measures and the intervention of the labor exchanges.[134] The legal status of the white-collar workers was modified in part by Nazi legislation. The law on The Organization of National Labor made no distinction between blue- and white-collar workers and even included managerial personnel with the blue-collar workers and clerical help in the general Gefolgschaft. In legal status, they were officially the equals of other employees. The 1938 law on hours did not distinguish between blue- and white-collar workers with

[130] Ibid., p. 483.
[131] Ibid., pp. 517, 520.
[132] Guillebaud, *The Social Policy of Nazi Germany*, Cambridge, 1942, pp. 27–29.
[133] Ibid., p. 104.
[134] Syrup, op. cit., pp. 429 f.

the exception of the highest managerial positions, pharmacists, and white-collar employees in agriculture, fishing, and merchant shipping.[135] The committee on labor law of "The Academy of German Law" prepared a draft—which, however, was apparently never turned into law—reducing the distinction between blue- and white-collar worker to certain considerations of job security. The blue-collar worker could be given notice up to two weeks before the fifteenth or end of a given month, the white-collar worker only with a margin of six weeks before the end of the quarter year. This job security in turn was specifically limited to the blue-collar worker with more than a year's employment, while no such limit was foreseen for the white-collar worker.[136] In wage contracts, the difference between blue- and white-collar jobs tended to disappear. But in practical economic status, the historical differences continued to exist. Insurance status and job security, the formal characteristics of the white-collar worker, remained unchanged. The white-collar insurance funds were maintained independently through 1945, the effective income differential continued as it had before, the white-collar worker continued to enjoy more formal job security. The nominal identity of blue- and white-collar jobs in the hours legislation of 1938 was redundant—or demagogic—since working hours had tended to be identical before. The new law made no practical difference.[137] More important was the continued development of new white-collar jobs, a more revealing index to the status of labor in the Third Reich than the statutory definitions of Arbeiter and Angestellter. Between 1933 and 1939, employment in agriculture declined from 29 to 27 per cent, remained constant in crafts and industry at 41 per cent, and rose in services from 30 to 32 per cent. White-collar workers and civil servants, 18 per cent of those employed in 1933 and 19 per cent in 1925, totaled 20 per cent in 1939, while the number of self-employed fell 2 per cent from its 1933 level and 3 per cent from its 1925 level.

[135] Piper, op. cit., p. 32.

[136] Ibid., p. 33.

[137] Interview with Herr Hans Schaumann of the Deutsche Angestellten-Gewerkschaft, Munich, 25 September 1963.

The number of blue-collar workers, 52 per cent in 1933 and 50 per cent in 1925, stood in 1939 at 51 per cent.[138]

The status of labor in the Third Reich was the resultant of all these factors. Institutionally, labor lost its rights. It had lost its right to organize, its freedom of movement, its right of collective bargaining, its right of freedom of vocational choice. To the older worker, the loss must have been perceptible. These rights had been the reward of fifty years of struggle, hope, and sacrifice. For the young worker, as Geiger described him, whose first experience of economic life was unemployment,[139] for which these rights were no relief, the loss may have been less painful.

Economically, labor was again employed. Employment was the touchstone of economic policy from 1933 on, and to many of those who benefited from it, an understandable measure of all things. To many millions, the difference between the years before Hitler and the Third Reich must have been less a matter of lost rights than of regained employment. Employment, in turn, in the quasi-war economy of the Third Reich was not a dead end, but a consciously selective process with genuine opportunities for advancement and a relative minimum of social obstacles. The Third Reich—its apparent ideological principles notwithstanding—removed 700,000 farmworkers and their families from the land, the first stage of the classic mobility pattern in industrial societies.[140] It absorbed thousands in service industries and white-collar jobs, the second stage in the pattern. The campaign against the unskilled worker meant effectively practical chances for thousands. The combination of economic expansion and directed subsidies meant opportunities for the ambitious worker at least as good as his grandfather's in the economic boom preceding World War I.

Politically, the situation was ambiguous. Labor lost its rights of political organization, but so did management, and so did the Catholic church. The loss of liberté, on the other hand, was practically linked with the promotion of égalité,

[138] Croner, op. cit., p. 196.
[139] Geiger, op. cit., p. 96.
[140] Cf. Guillebaud, *Economic Recovery*, p. 115.

an equality exploited propagandistically in every Nazi organization and every Nazi demonstration. Visible State pressure on employers produced visible results in better working conditions, housing, and swimming pools. Visible State intervention in the form of KdF produced symphony concerts, theatre performances, excursions, large-scale tourism. The visible concern of the Head of State for the working population produced post hoc ergo propter hoc a standard of living above that of 1933 if not necessarily above that of 1928. Workers in 1935 comprised only 22.6 per cent of Party leadership;[141] white-collar workers 21 per cent, a proportion that reached 43.1 per cent in Berlin and 38.8 per cent in Hamburg. But this had nothing to do with Party hostility, at least at official policy-making levels. Party workers were encouraged to make particular efforts to bring labor into responsible Party positions in industrial areas "even if they do not at first meet the requirements of political leaders in the desired sense."[142]

Practically, labor was a scarce commodity and treated accordingly. If its legal status was that of a chattel, it should not be forgotten that prudent owners treat their chattels well. Champion cattle are well taken care of, and this, too, was an aspect of labor's status in the Third Reich. It may be a commonplace that status is not only a function of what people are but what they think they are, but the distinction is important if we want to estimate the status of labor in the Third Reich. From our point of view, it may have been slavery, but it was not necessarily slavery from the point of view of a contemporary. Or alternatively, it was a slavery that he shared with former masters and thus, paradoxically, a form of equality or even liberation. The resistance to factory council lists, the reluctance to join the Party, were certainly aspects of labor's picture of itself in the Third Reich. But, as Guillebaud wrote, "The ex-Communist house painter, who described National Socialism as a movement which would enable him to meet his employer outside working hours on an equal

[141] *Partei-Statistik*, Vol. II, p. 164.
[142] Ibid., p. 196.

basis while allowing himself, if he had the ability, to work himself out of the ruck for the benefit of future members of his family, was expressing an attitude towards the regime which is by no means devoid of significance."[143]

[143] Guillebaud, *Social Policy*, p. 60.

IV

The Third Reich and Business

The development of the German economy between 1933 and 1939 is a classic example of the internal contradiction characteristic of the totalitarian state, the discrepancy between its claims and limits of its practice.[1] National Socialism claimed total control of the economy; total command over resources; total direction of wages, prices, production; total organization of credit, manpower, transportation, and planning. But it achieved them—to the extent it ever did—only with and through a total war. Its peacetime practice lagged far behind. Rather than creating a war economy in peacetime, the Nazis in many respects carried a peacetime economy with them into war.

The resulting inconsistency has led to considerable difficulties of interpretation. The claim to total control led contemporary observers to take the Nazis at their word and to assume that they really had created a war economy in peacetime. On the other hand, a postwar review of Nazi practice has led some to a drastic reconstruction of previous hypotheses, as though figures on inefficient manpower mobilization, minimal arms production, and chaotic economic controls somehow required a total reappraisal of Nazi intentions. This conflict of interpretation is the economic equivalent of a revisionist view of Hitler's diplomacy. But the apparent conflict, based on a confusion of style and intentions, exists only in the eye of the beholder. Nazi intentions did lead to war. But Nazi practice, for reasons inseparably connected with the basic inefficiency, heterogeneity, and inherited obligations

[1] Cf. Hans Bucheim, *Das dritte Reich*, Munich, 1958.

of the Nazi State, led not so much to full-scale mobilization as to large-scale disorder.

It should be self-evident that an ideological movement sworn to root out the foundations of industrial society with fire and sword was not the most promising basis of economic organization for modern industrial war. It should also be obvious that a Führer never reluctant to admit his total innocence of economic sophistication[2] was not ideally qualified to be the prime source of policy, including economic policy, in a Führer-state. A generation of Marxist and neo-Marxist mythology notwithstanding, probably never in peacetime has an ostensibly capitalist economy been directed as non- and even anti-capitalistically as the German economy between 1933 and 1939. Little in Germany's peacetime economy, in which a fundamental inability to agree even on priorities of steel allocation is typical, testifies to more than partial planning.[3]

For the anti-economy of the Third Reich, traditional labels, distinctions between "market" and "planned" economies, between "private" and "socialized" ownership, fall short of reality—though it cannot be denied that the old-fashioned expression "political economy" assumed certain dimensions of meaning scarcely anticipated by its inventors. The impact of the Third Reich on the businessman was basically a matter of political rather than economic decisions; hence the appropriate categories for measuring it are political ones; the categories of "regimentation" and "propaganda" against

[2] Cf. Ritter, op. cit., pp. 65 ff.

[3] Cf. Klein, op. cit., p. 80. No less characteristic was the way Wehrmacht orders were carried out, irrespective of the cost this involved in imports and foreign currency reserves. There also seems to have been no investigation of what increased domestic production might mean in terms of increasing raw material imports. Cf. Arthur Schweitzer, "Der ursprüngliche Vierjahresplan," *Jahrbücher für Nationalökonomie und Statistik,* Vol. 168, Stuttgart, 1956. A revealing symptom of the arbitrary administration of the import and foreign currency economy was that Krupp apparently sold better weapons to foreign customers, including Greece, Turkey, and the Soviet Union, than it sold to the Wehrmacht, since higher quality raw materials were reserved for export goods. Cf. Mühlen, op. cit., p. 161.

which business like every other sector of German life must be seen.

The objectives to which this propaganda and regimentation were applied were the series of heterogeneous and even mutually contradictory political goals that dominated German economic policy from January 1933 until the realization of a full war economy in 1941 or 1942. These included full employment, industrial recovery, the rescue of the entrepreneurial middle classes who had been the Nazis' leading political clientele and to whom they were deeply obligated, rearmament, price stability, and conservation of resources, including foreign currency reserves, combined where possible with an expanding export market. The incompatibility of these goals—for instance of rearmament and cultivation of the Mittelstand, of subsidized industrial recovery and price stability on the deflationary basis of the Brüning budgets of 1931/32, of high prices for farmers and low prices for consumers consistent with their low wages, combined again with support for the Mittelstand—these, and not some erroneous estimate of Nazi intentions, account for the curious inefficiency of the German war economy during the peacetime years.

In this system, the businessman—to the extent that he can be considered as a single economic class with coherent outlook and problems—was less the subject than the object, cajoled and coerced in equal measure. The "dual state" of Fraenkel's persuasive and insightful analysis of the years 1933–37[4] with its suggestion of a parity between the new political leadership and the old economic interests, was a reality, but a transitional reality from a Nazi point of view. It was a tactical necessity, but scarcely an affair of the heart.

It was true that ideology tended to stop at the door to the directors' room, the stock exchange, or the bank, true that the courts were prepared to force the State radio to pay royalties to a record manufacturer despite opposition from the official press.[5] They were equally prepared to enforce an ordinance of 1887 denying unmarried workers the right to

[4] Ernst Fraenkel, *The Dual State*, New York, 1941.
[5] Ibid., p. 82.

buy a certain type of knife, thus putting them in a class with beggars, vagrants, gypsies, and the mentally deficient.[6] But Fraenkel himself was at least half aware that the basic motive of the regime—if not of the more conservative judges—had relatively little to do with admiration of the private entrepreneur or of the private entrepreneur's influence on the policy of the Third Reich. The basic goal was far more instrumental than ideological. It was economic efficiency, the sine qua non of all Nazi military and diplomatic goals, that enjoyed priority, not short-term ideological objectives. That many businessmen did well in the Third Reich should not conceal the fact that they did so with the sanction of the regime on which they were dependent, and under controls—fiscal, political, and ideological—that Weimar Socialists even in 1919 had never ventured to introduce. The status of business in the Third Reich was at best the product of a social contract between unequal partners, in which submission was the condition for success, but even then, in the case of thousands of small businessmen, no guarantee of it.

The course of the Nazi economy was already determined in large part by the situation in which Hitler took office, a combination of historical memories, political debts, and pressure for quick and visible economic recovery, as well as longer-range objectives like rearmament. With the inflation a living memory and the depression an inescapable reality, the regime was committed to both pump-priming and stability, a combination whose problematic nature was further complicated by the dubious economic utility of the armament to which the pump-priming was applied. Subsidized recovery began in 1933 in the form of armament credits with the issue by the Reichbank of so-called Mefo (Metallurgische-Forschungs-G.m.b.H.) bills to large plants like Krupp and Siemens. Their volume totaled RM 12,000,000,000 by 1938, a volume equivalent, on the basis of Erbe's figures, to about 62 per cent of total government expenditures, or over 16 per cent of total national income.[7] In December 1933, the regime

[6] Ibid., pp. 85 f.

[7] René Erbe, *Die nationalsozialistische Wirtschaftspolitik im Lichte der modernen Theorie,* Zurich, 1958, p. 34; Bracher, Schulz, and Sauer, op. cit., pp. 662 ff.

concluded a contract for motor fuel with the I. G. Farben, offering ten years of guaranteed demand at fixed prices in return for control of production. The Wehrmacht, according to Erbe's figures, which claimed 23 per cent of a minimal budget of public expenditure in 1933, claimed 49 per cent of a doubled budget in 1934, and 74 per cent of a budget nearly seven times as large in 1938.[8] But the complement to this policy was an assiduous fiscal conservatism perpetuating the deflationary measures of the Brüning government. The tax reductions and deficit spending of a "capitalist" Keynesian theory were never considered. Business recovered, in effect, as an accomplice of the Third Reich, and by the grace of it. But the initiative was the State's and economic recovery a means, not an end.

Business' ambiguous place in the new system was defined and redefined in a series of official and semi-official statements. Full employment, not industrial and business recovery, was declared the foremost goal, and short hours and demechanization were among the measures considered in order to achieve it.[9] At the congress of the co-operatives in Berlin in 1933, Feder, now senior civil servant (Staatssekretär) in the Ministry of Economics, warned under evident pressure that his ideological trademark, the elimination of interest slavery (Brechung der Zinsknechtschaft), did not mean the end of interest. And while adding that "National Socialists reject socialistic experiments in the private productive economy," he emphasized that there were sectors of economic activity where the State had to intervene.[10] A spokesman of the Nazi small business organization (NS-Hago) told his Munich audience that tax reduction could not be introduced in any but gradual stages, and warned them against expecting any immediate revolutionary changes.[11]

According to an editorial in the *Völkische Beobachter*, Nazi economic policy rejected "anarchic individualism but affirmed the creative personality." It aspired to "liberation of the power of the individual as well as protection both of the

[8] Erbe, op. cit., p. 25.
[9] "Der Beschäftigungskoeffizient," VB, 27 July 1933.
[10] VB, 28 July 1933.
[11] Ibid.

individual and the commonwealth from exploitation or incursions of excessive individualism, subordination of the common interest to the selflessly active Führer-personality." The economy (the author) declared, "is part of the national substance [Volkstum]. There is no economic authority as such, no economic freedom, no economic serfdom as such. . . . The economy is a partial expression of the Volksgemeinschaft subordinate to the function of the State."[12] The new regime denied the validity of the Marxist premise that the entrepreneur was a man who lived from the surplus value of other people's labor, an NSBO man declared. "We have always taken the standpoint that the entrepreneur is entitled to his just share of the product of his labor."[13] But a directive on job creation emphasized equally that "profit is to be kept within moderate limits."[14] With the consolidation of the regime, official statements took a progressively sharper tone.

"Any organization that represents the interests of employers," Graf von der Goltz, the deputy commissar, told an audience of businessmen in 1934, "will be regarded as illegal and disbanded, and the guilty parties will be prosecuted."[15] Germany had emancipated itself from capital, an economic spokesman of the Party announced. The Party had nothing against capital in principle, he declared, but "as little as we want to identify the wish for peace with pacifism and the will to military preparedness with militarism, so little do we want to identify the effort to maintain and increase capital with capitalism."[16] A year later, as the regime renewed its efforts to enforce blanket price stabilization, the new commissioner announced in a tone of rhetorical regret that "it is established and confirmed by experience that the economy, left to itself, has neither the inner authority nor the discipline necessary to prevent serious damages that might arise from the exploitation of momentary difficulties. The profit drive is generally stronger than the moral obligation to the general

[12] "Die geistigen Grundlagen der nationalsozialistischen Wirtschaftslehre," VB, 4 April 1933.

[13] "Das gemeinsame Werk," VB, 1 May 1933.

[14] VB, 4 July 1933.

[15] VB, 20 July 1934.

[16] "Kapitalismus und Kapitallenkung," VB, 8 March 1935.

welfare. Again and again the urgent necessity has been revealed for more or less powerful intervention by responsible agencies of the State."[17] With scarcely concelaed cynicism, Goering appealed to business to apply the free initiative it so often spoke of to the new autarkic Four Year Plan, to "think not of profit, but of a strong, independent national German economy."[18] In a theoretical statement on the role of business in the Third Reich, a Nazi sociologist subordinated the business elite to the political–soldierly–belligerent (kriegerisch) elite that had come to the top since 1933.[19] To characterize their relationship, he chose the metaphor of annular rings in which the new political elite had surrounded the old economic leaders.[20] The question, as he saw it, was whether the old economic leadership was capable of the necessary elasticity to adjust itself to the new situation. No elite, he observed, could master every situation, and new economic functions could conceivably "make necessary a new type of leadership and thus alteration of the economic structure."[21]

The voice of business lapsed quickly from a tone of expectation to one of frustration, then to shadowy allusion and finally to effective silence. Business spokesmen read from official scripts. Noisy demands for the elimination of competitors, tax advantages, and public preference, presented in overfilled meetings,[22] were first met with apologies and evasion and then with flat rejection. The Party had no intention of dropping a single point of its program, a spokesman of the retail trade organization declared, "but it must be considered that even unfortunate economic developments can scarcely be re-

17 "Das Aufgabengebiet des Reichskommissars für Preisbildung," VB, 14 November 1936.

18 Goering speech of 28 October 1936, reprinted in *Der Vierjahresplan,* January 1937, pp. 33–35.

19 Pfenning, op. cit., p. 585.

20 Not to be outdone for a mixed metaphor, Pfenning added that the new ring had also "impressed its stamp on the entire system." Ibid., pp. 600 f.

21 Ibid., p. 589.

22 "Der Lebensmitteleinzelhandel im neuen Reich," VB, 23 June 1933.

versed overnight."[23] Overhasty action from above could lead to economic dislocation, another spokesman warned. The Führer would not forget any single branch of the economy, but patience was necessary, declared another.[24] "At the uppermost level of the Reich are the watchmen of the revolution," Goebbels proclaimed in early 1934, in response to evident concern. "They refuse to let themselves be lulled with false phrases. If they look on and seem to do nothing about the reactionaries in the land, it is only because they want to locate them, to make sure first who they are."[25]

By 1936 even the hitherto tolerated hints of dissatisfaction had virtually disappeared. "Retail trade has an important role to play in the German economy," one of its representatives told an audience in Passau, "but it must be appreciated that its struggle for Lebensraum must not be allowed to direct itself against others or that it be directed at the expense of others." The audience replied, according to the report, with a "joyfully received 'Sieg Heil!' and the songs of the new Germany."[26]

Expressions of interest or dissatisfaction were limited to the narrowest of margins—for example, a statement of regret that foreign currency restrictions had made it virtually impossible for the German businessman, salesman, or engineer to go abroad to gain the foreign experience their fathers had enjoyed.[27] But in general the exhortation and the peptalk "joyfully received" dominated public discussion, expressed in demands for more efficiency, better bookkeeping, tasteful window decorations, or good manners. "We need fewer economic bureaucrats," declared a prominent economic functionary, "and more genuine salesmen, salesmen prepared to take risks, able to make their way against a thousand obstacles. We need entrepreneurs to lead our private economy—unimpeachable as private individuals, knowledgeable as business-

[23] "Gewerbe und Handel im nationalsozialistischen Staat," in VB, 7 August 1933.

[24] VB, 13 and 14/15 August 1933.

[25] VB, 15 January 1934.

[26] "Der Einzelhandel in der deutschen Wirtschaft," VB, 22 April 1936.

[27] "Der Wert der Amerika-Studienreisen," *Der Vierjahresplan*, September 1937, p. 546.

men, comradely as colleagues."[28] The monthly journal of the Four Year Plan filled an empty space with the reminder, "Every day the merchant has to guide the various wishes of his customers in such a way that they remain in harmony with the possibilities of German production. . . . The retailer must never be a cold calculator, for he has to prove himself daily the friend, helper, and advisor of customers from every class of the population. The merchant is at the center of economic life and of the Volk as well. He must be the comrade of those in every walk of life."[29]

The development of the corporatist system envisaged in the Party program was characteristic of the way the Third Reich turned its ideological guns on those who had heretofore marched behind them. The key to the corporatist system, a doctoral candidate wrote as early as 1934, was contained in the premise that "the National Socialist ideal State is neither occupational [berufsständisch] nor corporative [ständisch], but power-political [machtstaatlich]. . . . It includes the tendency toward the absolute state."[30] The author of a similar work a year later discovered with the ingenuousness of a Jourdain that the source of initiative was in various organs of Party and State, not in the corporate bodies themselves.[31] "The present situation in National Socialist Germany is characterized by the fact," he concluded, "that real corporate forms have been created in only very limited measure."[32] One could assume with considerable justice, he said, that "a state of clarity just does not exist on the basic organizational principles that are to be pursued, and that society, as well, has not yet developed to the point where it would be able

[28] VB, 23 September 1935.

[29] *Der Vierjahresplan,* January 1937, p. 42.

[30] Ernst Schrewe, "Der Streit um die berufsständische Ordnung," Hamburg dissertation, 1934, p. 147. The author's bibliography alludes silently to the chaos around him in its omission of any title on his subject produced after 30 January 1933. Similarly, his only historical example is the economic parliament foreseen by the Weimar Constitution.

[31] Max Schreiber, "Die nationalsozialistische Ständeentwicklung im Vergleich mit der faschistischen Wirtschaftsverfassung," dissertation of Leipzig Handels-Hochschule, 1935, p. 17.

[32] Ibid., p. 88.

to lead a corporative existence without the far-reaching supervision of the State."[33]

Not surprisingly, State supervision played a major role in official policy statements. Max Frauendorfer, at twenty-four director of the Party's Office of Corporate Organization (Amt für ständischen Aufbau), leaned heavily on negative examples. Corporate organization in the Third Reich, he emphasized, had nothing to do with hypothetical medieval models; it was not autonomous; it had no mandate to represent special interests or restrict competition.[34] Corporate development in Germany was sui generis, without models—including Fascist Italy's Carta del Lavoro.[35] The sociologist Pfenning was still more explicit in his definition of what corporatist organization was not: not "petit-bourgeois sentimental," not "aesthetic-romantic," not "guildist." It was not intended to protect threatened middle-class interests against either "oppressive economic power from above" or "the will to social betterment from below." It had nothing to do with "the notorious good will of those who refuse to appreciate that there is such a thing as social conflict." It was not "pressure group consciousness in disguise."[36] It has "nothing to do with the development of a spiritual-cultural totality, a universal order of human society as such. What it has to do with is the realization of a historically necessitated task by our Volk: the achievement of its unity and the guaranteeing of its völkisch future."[37] The authority of the corporatist organization, declared an official theorist of police law, ended abruptly where the monopolistic police function of the State began.[38]

Behind the hard, if negative, unanimity of the official statements was a real, if muffled, struggle, not about ideological principles, but about the control and direction of the economy.

[33] Ibid., p. 42.

[34] Max Frauendorfer, "Ständischer Aufbau," *Grundlagen, Aufbau und Wirtschaftsordnung des nationalsozialistischen Staates*, Vol. III, No. 47, Berlin-Vienna, 1936, pp. 7 f.

[35] Ibid., p. 19.

[36] Andreas Pfenning, "Gemeinschaft und Staatswissenschaft," *Zeitschrift für die gesamte Staatswissenschaft*, 1936, pp. 300–2.

[37] Ibid., p. 313.

[38] Werner Best, "Neubegründung des Polizeirechts," *Jahrbuch der Akademie für deutsches Recht*, 1937, p. 138.

This was compounded, in turn, with a power struggle inside the Party. On one side were the "populist" Nazis, Gregor Strasser, Feder, and the Party's economic specialist Otto Wilhelm Wagener; on the other, a kind of industrial lobby including Schacht and Walther Funk. Wagener's position, as organizer of a corporatist economy, presupposed, according to Rämisch, that he could make a convincing case for corporatist organization as a means of consolidating power, that he could overcome the hard-bitten resistance of big industry, and that he could get Hitler's support for a direct attack on the problem. None of these proved to be the case.

What followed was a chaotic interim in which, so far as Wagener could be viewed as central, power flowed away[39] from the center, not toward it. SA pressure was deflected away from big business and against the Jews and the unions. Darré organized the farmers in the Reichsnährstand in April, Ley organized the Labor Front in May. Authority in labor relations was delegated to the Reich trustees, authority in industry to Krupp and Thyssen, whose Düsseldorf Institut für Ständewesen, like Frauendorfer's Party office in Munich, was created post facto as a kind of institutional fig leaf for decisions already taken.[40]

In July, Hitler proclaimed the end of the economic revolution before the trustees and Gauleiters in Bad Reichenhall and Wagener was replaced as the Party's economic spokesman by a representative of big business. "If the situation is not yet ready for something, there is nothing to be done about it," Hitler told Rauschning in 1934. "I had to let the Party experiment with the corporate idea. I had to prove

[39] "In practice I have never met two National Socialists with a common view of corporatist organization," Ley later declared. "June and July 1933 were a catastrophe. The corporatist organization proved to me to be a total chaos of opinions. . . . In a word: at that time, between June and August 1933, I was very unhappy." Ley, "Rechenschaftsbericht," op. cit. According to Rauschning, the corporatist organization (ständischer Aufbau) was known in Party circles as "rebellious organization" (aufständischer Bau). Rauschning, *Gespräche*, p. 166.

[40] Cf. Raimund Rämisch, "Der berufsständische Gedanke als Episode in der nationalsozialistischen Politik," *Zeitschrift für Politik*, 1957, pp. 263 ff.

experimentally how far things had gone and whether there was anything to achieve there. You can understand that I had to give the people something to do. They all wanted to help. They were full of fire. I had to offer them something. Well, let them have a crack at it. After all, the corporatist organization is not so important that it could do much damage."[41] In 1936, the offices responsible for corporatist organization were officially dissolved as superfluous.[42]

What arose in its place and in its name was a heterogeneous collection of quasi-autonomous "self-government" organizations, vertically constructed according to industry in a way intended to preclude any effective organization of interest, and subordinate to the shaky hierarchy of economic authorities characteristic of the Third Reich. The effective organizational watershed was size. Small business, partially pacified by emergency measures and buoyed by general recovery, was bullied into Gleichschaltung. Big business was bribed. The result was a differential development of the government's relations with the economy, characterized until 1937 by an uneven double structure oriented on one side around the Party, on the other around the Army and big industry. Exploiting, indeed responsible for, the regime's long-term interests in industrial recovery and rearmament, Schacht used his position to work big business out of the corporate organization and thus out of Party control, and then, according to Schweitzer, to pursue economic mobilization, maintain corporate profit margins, and reinforce the structure of private enterprise.[43]

Crucial issues were the new legislation on the incorporation of business, the struggle over cartelized business organization, and a fight over competition. The corporation, the capitalistic form par excellence, was an obvious target of the Party and the small business interests it represented and led in 1934 to draft legislation offering tax benefits to those willing to turn their corporations (Aktien-Gesellschaften) into the more per-

[41] Rauschning, *Gespräche,* p. 166.

[42] Anordnung des Stellvertreters des Führers No. 27/36 of 18 February 1936, Archive of Institut für Zeitgeschichte 2220/58.

[43] Arthur Schweitzer, "Organisierter Kapitalismus und Parteidiktatur," *Schmollers Jahrbuch,* 1959, pp. 37 ff., 46.

sonal form of sole proprietorship or partnership.[44] The draft law proposed a minimum capitalization of RM 500,000 for corporations, a minimum value of RM 1000 per share, limitation to the directors of executive responsibility and exclusion of the stockholders, and personal identity of the president of the board and the director of the effective operation. On the objections of industry, the draft was revised in 1935, retaining the capitalization and share value provisions, but dropping the rest. The provisions were so drawn that they excluded 58 per cent of the existing corporations, and pressure was effective enough to turn 1860 stock companies and 18,333 limited liability companies into partnerships or sole proprietorships by 1940.[45]

The second phase of the campaign was an attack on the position of the director, beginning with an attack in *Der Angriff* on higher fees.[46] Schacht's special interest pleas and his own and big industry's evident importance to the economy delayed further action until Schacht's own fall. A Justice Ministry draft of January 1937 omitted the Führerprinzip as the basic of business organization, retained the normal form of security ownership and marketing, but restricted shareholders' prerogatives to a discussion of profits, eliminating direct criticism of management. Directors were allowed to grant bonuses only on the condition that they were directly connected to profits and providing that the board had also authorized "voluntary social contributions" to employees, thus granting the Labor Front an indirect share in corporate dividends. This form of Führerprinzip, Schweitzer observes, increased the power of the directors at the expense of the shareholders, introducing a clear distinction between shareholders and management, and institutionalizing government intervention in corporate affairs. Later legislation increased the direct tax on directors' fees from a basic level of 10 per cent in March 1933 to 20 per cent in February 1939.[47]

[44] "Nationalsozialistische Wirtschaftsgestaltung," VB, 12 July 1934.

[45] Schweitzer, "Organisierter Kapitalismus," op. cit., p. 47.

[46] *Der Angriff*, 19 November 1935; cf. *The Economist*, 7 and 14 December 1935.

[47] Statutes quoted in Büttner, op. cit., pp. 492–99.

If the campaign against the corporation had led to a limited victory for big business over its enemies in the Party, the struggle over cartelization and competition led to a proportionally greater setback for the Mittelstand. With reference to the programmatic provision for nationalization of trusts and cartels, legislation of July 1933 authorized the Minister of Economics to create compulsory cartels for the purposes of stabilization.[48] Since big business was, however, already almost totally cartelized, the burden of the new legislation necessarily fell on small business, whose cartels were granted authority to fix prices. Between July 1933 and December 1936 sixteen hundred new cartel agreements were created by the Ministries of Agriculture and Economics,[49] their impact falling with equal weight on outsiders and consumers. If the official motivation was the preservation and maintenance of the Mittelstand and those employed by it,[50] the methods of achieving them were once again Darwinian. They imposed restrictions on what members could sell, in the case of electrical materials splitting the market between small shops and department stores.[51] In the printing industry, they imposed on members the obligation to keep books, controlled their inventories, and prohibited price reductions where they would impair the member's ability to meet his tax obligations. The sale of printing presses was restricted to limit further competition, and investment was forbidden beyond the existing level.[52]

Court decisions consolidated the position of the new cartels. Schweitzer reports that of seventy decisions in 1935, fifty-nine confirmed the exclusion of outsiders.[53] Prices were fixed high and led to a concentration of productive capacity, a cold war between small and large units. The fittest survived. Between 1933 and 1935 court decisions on 54,000 cases

[48] Quoted in Büttner, op. cit.

[49] Schweitzer, "Organisierter Kapitalismus," op. cit., p. 59.

[50] Cf. Claire Russell, "Die Praxis des Zwangskartellgesetzes," *Zeitschrift für die gesamte Staatswissenschaft*, May 1939, p. 508.

[51] Otto Stritzke, "Das Elektro-Abkommen," *Kartell Rundschau*, June 1936, p. 394.

[52] Otto Stritzke, "Die Ordnung des graphischen Gewerbes als Beispiel," *Kartell Rundschau*, December 1936, pp. 829 ff.

[53] Schweitzer, "Organisierter Kapitalismus," op. cit., pp. 61–63.

forced 2000 retailers out of business.[54] The number of radio dealers fell from 60,000 to 37,000, of radio wholesalers from 1500 to 750.[55] In Schweitzer's view, Schacht's decree of 12 November 1936, imposing uniform accounting and bookkeeping regulations on the Mittelstand organizations, was one of big business' triumphs. The cartels were granted the right to adjust their effective territories and their prices in co-operation with the courts.[56] Within three years of the apparent victory of the outraged Mittelstand, the cartel, under Schacht's stewardship, had achieved a magnitude and legitimacy previously unknown even in Germany.

Yet if big business showed a comparatively happy touch in its struggle with small business and its patrons in the Party, the victory was relatively short-lived. It had less luck with tougher opponents. Schacht's position was symbolically and practically the position of big business in toto, and a position whose strength was visibly augmented in successive years by his appointment to the Reichsbank in 1933, to the Economics Ministry in 1934, as Special Commissar for the War Economy in 1935. It was undercut in 1936 and disappeared altogether by the end of 1937.[57] The issue was accelerated rearmament, a wedge that split the hitherto effective alliance of Wehrmacht and big business. The alternative was Schacht's idea, a stepped-up export campaign to reduce inflationary pressure and alleviate the chronic shortage of foreign currency reserves. A new front of Wehrmacht, some Party members and some business interests produced a compromise and a new center of political gravity in September 1936. This was the Four Year Plan, with Goering in charge.[58] Goering's choice of collaborators reflected the shift.[59] The Party in Munich was excluded entirely. Alte Kämpfer, with the exception of

[54] Ibid., p. 67.

[55] According to Neumann and Kirchheimer, the figures showed a decline from 900 in 1935 to 539 in 1939. *The Fate*, op. cit., p. 100.

[56] Schweitzer, "Organisierter Kapitalismus," op. cit., p. 71.

[57] Cf. Amos E. Simpson, "The Struggle for Control of the German Economy," *Journal of Modern History*, March 1959.

[58] Schweitzer, "Der ursprüngliche Vierjahresplan," op. cit., pp. 348–51.

[59] Cf. "Erster Erlass über die Durchführung des Vierjahresplanes," *Der Vierjahresplan*, January 1937.

Gauleiter Wagner, the price commissioner, were left out. The top divisional positions went to nazified civil servants like Mansfeld, the man responsible for labor administration, to nazified representatives of big industry, and to General Staff officers.

The basic objectives of the Four Year Plan—increased iron and steel production, synthetic fuel and rubber development, independence of foreign supplies of such raw materials as industrial fats—divided the business front. The steel industry, reluctant to assume the risk and expense of expanding its capacity while available capacity was still lying unused, resisted, refusing to develop low quality domestic ores. The chemical industry, attracted by the opportunities, collaborated with a will. The steel industry's resistance led to its defeat; the chemical industry's co-operation to winning a special status. The government trumped the steel firms with a major advance into quasi-socialized production, the Reichswerke-Hermann Goering. Of 400,000,000 marks capital, the State claimed nearly 70 per cent—RM 270,000,000—for itself and reserved voting rights to its own shares. The steel industry was made to buy the remaining shares, with a preferred dividend rate of 4½ per cent and the obligation to hold them at least five years. A number of shares were later sold at a loss.[60] Characteristically, while retaining its control, the regime redistributed its burden, imposing the cost of financing the operation on various corporatist organizations, and thus on small business. The artisans' group, the Reichsgruppe Handwerk contributed RM 12,000,000. When, at the end of 1938, the steel industry wanted to expand its capacity, it was told that all available building material and labor were reserved for the Goering-Werke. The industry's effort to retain the decisive place in production planning like its effort to keep the government out of steel production led to a dead end.

The chemical industry, which traveled a different route, had considerably more success. Despite a period of friction, produced in part by Wehrmacht dissatisfaction with quality, in part by the Economics Ministry's dissatisfaction with the price structure, the I. G. Farben succeeded in finding an

[60] Schweitzer, "Der ursprüngliche Vierjahresplan," op. cit., p. 371.

important post for one of its directors Carl Krauch in the Four Year Plan. The secret of its success seems to have been a good relationship with the Air Ministry and thus with Goering, and with Hitler's economic advisor Keppler. Krauch succeeded in forcing his Wehrmacht opponent Loeb out of office and made what was regarded as a brilliant career,[61] personally designing the so-called Karinhall plan for the development of the chemical industry, and cornering unlimited authority to carry it out. With its key positions in both the State planning apparatus and private economy, I. G. Farben succeeded where the steel industry had failed. It revised the planning quotas on its own terms and turned itself into a kind of official government organ, capable of negotiating with the political authorities on an equal basis.

The relationship of the coal industry to State and Wehrmacht formed a third kind of equilibrium. Party pressure resulted in the appointment of a former Labor Front leader as coal commissioner. But as he attempted to expand his authority from the distribution of house fuel to the control of members of the coal cartel, the Ruhr producers joined Director Pleiger of the Goering-Werke and formed a new organization under Goering's auspices. The new organization, the Reichsvereinigung Kohle, granted the continuation of business on the previous private basis and reserved further decisions on the distribution of coal to a combination of private and State-owned coal producers.[62]

Low man in the Nazi economy was small business, whose relative position deteriorated directly and irreversibly from a point of initial strength. Small business was necessarily the Third Reich's first beneficiary. Public orders were reserved for small business, and public authorities were forbidden to deal further with department stores, consumer co-operatives, or chain stores in the distribution of public contracts.[63] The Law for the Protection of Retail Trade of May 1933 prohibited the creation or expansion of chain stores, the addition of new lines of merchandise in existing outlets, the elimination of self-contained craftsmen's shops—i.e., shoemakers, barbers—as well

[61] Ibid., pp. 375 ff.
[62] Ibid., p. 395.
[63] Cf. "Gemeinden und Mittelstand," VB, 5 April 1933.

as any form of restaurant in department stores. An executive decree of July 1933 extended the prohibition to the manufacture of sausage, bread or other forms of bakery, to upholstery and interior decoration, cabinet makers, watch repairs, the repair of bicycles or motor vehicles, furriers, and photographers. A relatively late concession of March 1935 eliminated lending lilbraries from department store premises.[64] A law of November 1933 limited price rebates to 3 per cent, an incursion on the consumer co-operatives. The Länder (States) were authorized to levy a tax on department stores. The building trades, and thus some thousands of carpenters, plumbers, and masons, benefited in September 1933 from the introduction of subsidies and tax benefits for house repairs and reconstruction. The subsidies amounted to RM 500,000,000, distributed in the ratio 4:1 private to Reich for repairs, 1:1 private to Reich for reconstruction.[65]

But the honeymoon was relatively short, as small business proved the most vulnerable to the advancing labor shortage, increased industrial goals, and the consumer needs of a population whose artificially low wages demanded some kind of consideration. By 1935 official support for small business found its modest expression in hortatory but questionably effective appeals to customers to pay their craftsmen in cash.[66] The same year craft apprentices were subordinated to official control. A study by the artisan organization, the Reichsstand des deutschen Handwerks, reported that the number of craft apprentices had risen from 419,000 in 1933 to 618,000 at the end of 1937. But this was still below the figure—633,000—for the depression year 1931.[67] The ratio of craft apprentices to industrial apprentices remained roughly constant,[68] but requirements tightened. In 1931/32, 92.5 per cent of the candidates passed the master's examination, in 1936/37 86 per cent.[69] A report from Baden revealed that the ratio of suc-

64 Quoted in Büttner, op. cit.
65 Erbe, op. cit., p. 29.
66 VB, 19 and 27 September 1935.
67 *Das Handwerk in Staat und Wirtschaft*, Berlin, 1939, pp. 302, 406.
68 Ibid., p. 407.
69 Loc. cit.

cessful candidates had dropped from nearly 80 per cent to nearly 70 per cent.[70] More important, the master's examination, which had hitherto been optional—in 1931 only 31 per cent of the practicing artisans had passed it—in 1935 became compulsory for registration on the official rolls and thus for the right to open a shop.[71] "Henceforth the artisan no longer has a more favorable position than that of other occupational groups," declared an official spokesman. "Achievement alone will determine whether the artisan looks forward to a renascence."[72] Thrust back into the winds of industrial society, the artisan was conceded a role in repair and installation and service industries, particularly in the country. But his chances were linked to his capacity for reducing prices and increasing efficiency.[73] A decree of December 1938 imposed an insurance requirement on the independent artisan. A government contribution was explicitly ruled out and the artisan was left with the choice of public or private insurance at prevailing market rates.[74] "To be sure, many of us are still having a hard time," an official spokesman conceded, "but we again have confidence and courage to face the future."[75]

His words echoed against a decree of March 1939 purging artisans who had accepted public aid for more than three months since September 1937.[76] The decree referred specifically to bakers, butchers, barbers, shoemakers, and men's tailors. It excluded any indemnity through the State, though the Labor Exchanges accepted the responsibility of retraining without pay where it was considered necessary. In fact, the decree was extended only to those genuinely capable of working elsewhere.[77] But there were other indications of pres-

[70] *The Fate,* op. cit., p. 57.

[71] *Das Handwerk,* op. cit., p. 276; *The Fate,* op. cit., p. 57.

[72] Quoted in Oskar Klug, "Möglichkeit und Grenzen des deutschen Handwerks," *Die deutsche Volkswirtschaft,* February 1935, pp. 118 f.

[73] Ibid., pp. 119 f.; cf. W. Kleiner, "Der alte Mittelstand," *Die deutsche Volkswirtschaft,* August 1935, p. 696.

[74] *The Fate,* op. cit., p. 58.

[75] *Das Handwerk,* op. cit., p. 441.

[76] "Erste Anordnung zur Durchführung der Verordnung zur Beseitigung der Übersetzung im Einzelhandel" of 16 March 1939. In Büttner, op. cit.

[77] *The Fate,* p. 59.

sure. On the basis of those employed in the trade per 100,000 of population, the number of smiths fell from 20.7 in 1926 to 16.3 in 1939, of tailors from 70.2 to 59.8, of shoemakers from 35.4 to 26.7, of carpenters from 16.6 to 13.0.[78] The number of artisan enterprises, which had increased by 18.4 per cent between 1931 and 1936, fell again by 11 per cent between 1936 and 1939, though the decline in employed personnel was only 4 per cent. The number of shoemakers' shops declined by 12.4 per cent between 1933 and 1939; the number of masons' shops by 14.8 per cent, of carpenters' by 13.8 per cent, of paperhangers' and upholsterers' by 12.8 per cent, of housepainters' by 11.4 per cent between 1936 and 1939.[79] A number of traditional handicrafts were virtually destroyed by factory competition: violin-making in Mittenwald, basket-making, clock-making in the Black Forest, lens-grinding in Rathenow, file- and lock-making in the Bergisches Land east of Düsseldorf.[80]

A revealing index of the conflict between Mittelstand ideology and practical economic necessity was Nazi Germany's relationship to trade, retail and wholesale. It was characteristic of the German economy, Uhlig observed, that retail trade exerted a more effective pressure than handicraftsmen. The chain and department stores had fewer friends than big industry.[81] They accepted, were forced to accept, discriminatory high taxes on its turnover (Umsatzsteuer). Big industry successfully resisted them. But the victories of small trade were strictly limited. Although the Third Reich began with a full-scale attack on the department stores, this was ambiguous. SA plaques, tokens of commercial acceptability, were officially distributed to acceptable owners, irrespective of size —though independent local actions often overlooked this

[78] On the other hand, it should be said that the number of plumbers rose from 16.6 to 16.9, of electricians from 9.6 to 15.9, of house painters from 30.1 to 33.5, and of barbers from 20.7 to 28.4. *The Fate*, op. cit., p. 140.

[79] Ibid., pp. 30–32.

[80] Syrup, *Hundert Jahre*, pp. 495 f. Exceptions should again be noted, however. A home jewelry industry, specializing in crab shells, enjoyed a comeback on the North Sea coast, and the home manufacture of drinking straws also enjoyed a recovery.

Cf. Uhlig, op. cit., pp. 50 f.

subtlety. The anti-Jewish boycott of 1 April 1933 was conducted against Jewish, not against big, business. While statutory limitations on department and chain store expansion were euphemistically extended in permanence,[82] and a qualified removal of the prohibition on new retail outlets in 1934 created certain new opportunities for small business, the Mittelstand representatives were in trouble almost from the beginning. Neither the banks, industry, nor the civil servants in the Economics and Finance Ministries were prepared or could afford in 1933 to let the department stores go under, in this case to yield to pressure from the Hauptgemeinschaft des deutschen Einzelhandels for punitively progressive taxation on turnover.[83] The result was a mild compromise. The law of 15 July 1933 granted the Länder the right to raise the existing tax rate, as well as to impose it on the municipalities. But only Anhalt and Hamburg introduced a tax on department stores. Bavaria, Wuerttemberg, and Saxony raised rates on retail trade, and Prussia did nothing at all. Neither the corporatist organization nor the State gave retail trade any more benefits. While the corporatist organization brought with it a wave of price increases, two hundred Munich shopkeepers were arrested for raising their prices. In June 1933, Otto Wagener was all but trampled by indignant Munich grocery dealers, crushed between their customers and the Reichsnährstand, the agricultural organization, which had raised its price for butter while the retailers were prohibited from raising theirs. On June 3, the *Frankfurter Zeitung*

[82] The euphemism consisted in the obligation of an official concession from State and local authorities for expansion, as required by the decree of 23 July 1934. Exceptions to the prevailing limit were made contingent on need, proof that the new store would cause no hardship for existing shops, and the personal reliability and professional experience of the applicant, all conditions that made the issue of new concessions unlikely. In communities of 30,000 or fewer, no exceptions were considered at all. Cf. Uhlig, op. cit., p. 94; text in Büttner, op. cit.

[83] The intended schedule was ½% on turnovers of RM 200–500,000, 1% on turnovers from 500,000–1,000,000, 5% on RM 5,000,000, 10% on RM 25,000,000. Rural general stores were to have a taxfree turnover of up to RM 500,000, and the existing tax rate on big specialty shops (Kaufhäuser, Grosse Spezialgeschäfte) was to be lowered. Uhlig, op. cit., pp. 97–99.

printed on its front page a letter from Goering and Hugenberg to von Renteln, the leader of the retail traders, protesting against the pressure of Renteln's Kampfbund on industry and the business organization. On August 7, Ley commandeered and liquidated the Kampfbund, and its successor organizations were ultimately dissolved—like the NSBO—in the Labor Front.[84]

In July, Hess himself intervened in the name of the Party to save the department stores, not only to prevent further unemployment, which was the plausible official explanation,[85] but to defend the Reich's investment. At the end of June, Schmitt, Hugenberg's successor as Minister of Economics, had persuaded Hitler to invest RM 14,500,000 in the Hertie (Hermann Tietz) chain—a Jewish department-store chain—to prevent its collapse and with it, that of its suppliers, financiers, and 14,000 employees. By the end of summer both Tietz chains—H. and L. Tietz—and the Karstadt chain were dependent on banks that were dependent in turn on the Reich whose concern for price stability, its own investment, and the greatest possible employment of labor scarcely permitted the luxury of an anti-department store campaign.[86] "When our economy has recovered," the Minister of Economics told the NSBO in September, "we can put the reins on the further development of the department stores, but we cannot afford to let them break down."[87]

The reins came, but Schmitt's basic proposition was verified by events. The department stores went on. They were excluded from the subsidized business in marriage credits, were taxed in the form of disproportionate contributions to

[84] Ibid., pp. 137–38, 163.

[85] "That their attacks would leave half a million people without their daily bread is something that seems to leave these selfish elements indifferent," Ley declared with fine feeling. Cf. Heiden, op. cit., p. 188.

[86] Cf. Uhlig, op. cit., pp. 115–18. The war on the department store, however, was one of the few Nazi efforts where there was initiative from below, and the Hess decree of July 7 was not observed very consistently. In Gelsenkirchen, police even went so far as to force a store to remove a photocopy of the decree from its window. Ibid., pp. 111 f.

[87] Quoted in Uhlig, op. cit., p. 122.

the Winterhilfe, were crowded out of advertising space in the press and distribution of sales material in the mails, boycotted by various Party organs like the Kampfbund's successor organization, the SA, the Frauenschaft (Women's Organization), and local Party leaders, and kept out of the profitable trade in Party paraphernalia. They continued to be subjected to local pressures and wildcat boycotts as in Celle, where an organization of mechanics demanded the registration of bicycles, typewriters, and sewing machines bought in department stores. Their apprentices had a hard time with examining boards. In 1935, 60 per cent of the department store apprentices in Essen, 66 per cent in Bochum, 50 per cent in Cologne, and 54 per cent in Munich failed. In Berlin 47 per cent passed, 298 of 830 failed outright, and another ninety-two neglected even to appear for the examination.[88] As late as 1937, the Länder were granted an additional raise in the department store tax, and Prussia raised the existing tax on chain stores. The department stores continued to suffer from exorbitant discrepancies in local taxation, and from continued Party discrimination. In 1938 the civil servants organization enforced a department store boycott on its members despite Goering's opposition, and a Party functionary as late as September 1939 classed department store shoppers with tax falsifiers, rowdy SA men, and wearers of unearned medals, in a discussion of those unfit for further promotion.[89]

Even in 1933, on the very edge of bankruptcy as their volume fell, terror intensified, the market for their shares disappeared, and the banks threatened to reclaim their credits, the department stores had held 4.7 per cent of retail turnover compared with 4.0 per cent in 1929. In 1936 after universal price controls had robbed them of their competitive advantage and apparently eliminated the need for differentiated statistics, they still maintained 86 per cent of their 1932 turnover. Large specialty shops (Kaufhäuser) had regained 98 per cent of their 1932 turnover.[90] During Goebbels' 1938 pogrom, the Reichskristallnacht, twenty-nine de-

[88] Ibid., pp. 159–60.
[89] Rudolf Schultz, "Erziehung oder Auslese," *Der Hoheitsträger*, September 1939, p. 6.
[90] Uhlig, op. cit., p. 218.

partment stores were burned, but it was significant that even the boiling folk-soul, as the Ministry of Propaganda called it, had distinguished successfully between Jewish and non-Jewish department store property.

From the low point of 1933/34, the department stores enjoyed a discreet but perceptible official rehabilitation. Renteln, the most active of the Mittelständler, lost his organization and was not named chairman of its successor, the Gesamtverband des deutschen Einzelhandels whose membership, unlike that of the old Kampfbund, was extended irrespective of size of business. From 1935 on, there were no more official statements on the department store as such. A pact concluded in February 1934 between industry and wholesalers, whose official purpose was aid for the Mittelstand, continued to extend rebates to consumer co-operatives and department stores,[91] and official criticism of boycott efforts in September and October 1935 led to a reorganization of retail trade. The Labor Front awarded diplomas for "exemplary social welfare arrangements" to department stores. An official statement of the Adolf-Hitler-Spende in November 1938 declared the maintenance of the standard of living as the most important economic objective, pointed out the inadequacy of the small shopkeeper, and indicated the willingness of important Party officials to see some of his number disappear rather than discriminate against retail outlets where the working population could buy cheaply.[92] The economics editor of the *Völkische Beobachter* declared early in 1939 that "Mittelstand ideology is an inadequate basis for building a popular economy (Wirtschaft des Volkes). It presupposes first that the Volk is itself incapable of becoming Mittelstand, and creates a barrier against all those who want to reach it. And second, the representatives of a Mittelstand ideology have no intention of putting the Mittelstand at the service of the Volk. On the contrary, the Volk is to be put at the service of the Mittelstand."[93]

Nazi Germany's schizoid relationship to its Mittelstand was reflected as vividly in its relationship to the consumer co-

[91] Ibid., p. 144.
[92] Ibid., p. 173.
[93] Ibid., p. 189.

operatives. On 27 April 1933 the Hitler government discontinued the subsidies to the co-operatives which Papen had introduced; 24,000,000 marks had already been spent on them, another 8,000,000 were blocked.[94] But although the co-ops were gleichgeschaltet, and local initiatives went still further—as in Thuringia where municipalities and counties were ordered to give up their memberships and in Baden where the creation of new co-operatives was officially banned—Berlin was not prepared to see them go under. Ley threatened the exclusion of any Party member who laid a finger on them and was supported by Economics Minister Schmitt. The co-operatives were accordingly absorbed in the Labor Front, though as a subsidiary of the banking organization. Their top offices were meanwhile occupied almost entirely by deserving Alte Kämpfer, creating an additional, non-economic vested interest in the co-operatives' further survival.[95] The ostensible goal was an integration of the existing twelve hundred co-operatives under common direction; their outlets were then to be leased to private operators. But little was ever to come of the transfer.[96]

[94] Paul Hertz, "Das Ende der deutschen Konsumgenossenschaftsbewegung," *Zeitschrift für Sozialismus,* May–June 1935, p. 663.

[95] Ibid., p. 664.

[96] Politically and economically fatuous but ideologically interesting reasons for this can be found in a contemporary dissertation. How, the author asked, could the central organization control its merchant-tenants? This was one of the basic obstacles. "A direct takeover of the shops by private proprietors without direct control of the central organization meant the sacrifice of the fundamental justification of the consumer co-op, regulation and competitive stimulation of private retail trade. On the other hand, control of the retailer as tenant was equivalent to the sacrifice of his independence, and reduced his function practically to that of an employee." Fritz Alvermann, "Die Verbrauchergenossenschaften im Dritten Reich," Cologne dissertation, 1938, p. 24.

Neumann and Kirchheimer report that the Fröhling AG. of Frankfurt, not a co-op but a grocery chain, actually tried such a transfer and sold its stores to its branch managers. Though the new system was intended to conserve the advantages of collective buying for the new independent proprietors, the experiment nonetheless ended after three years in bankruptcy court. Neither the new buying co-op nor the independent managers had been able to overcome initial credit problems. *The Fate,* p. 52.

In March 1934 a pact between the retail trade organization and the co-operatives guaranteed the suspension of further action on the condition that the co-operatives ceased to campaign for new members. Indirect pressure had nonetheless had its effect. In May 1935 the government chose to liquidate weakened co-operatives rather than resume subsidies for their support. The new law appropriated 6,000,000 marks to finance liquidation. The remaining co-operatives were ordered to liquidate their savings accounts—and thus the basis of their capitalization—by 1940. While subsequent legislation removed their tax privileges,[97] and introduced new discriminatory forms of taxation, the competitive position of the co-operatives was at the same time bolstered by Party initiative. Before the end of 1934, Hess had succeeded in bringing about a repeal of legislation forbidding co-operative membership to State and local civil servants. In 1938, membership was theoretically open to all comers, though only former co-operative members could be actively recruited. The general limits on retail expansion inhibited the creation of new outlets, but "in cases where the authorities are of the opinion that consumer co-operatives are better capable of meeting available demand than private retail trade, nothing stands in the way."[98]

The law of 1935 succeeded in breaking up 72 of 1187 co-operatives, about 6 per cent, but the 72 controlled about 24 per cent of total turnover.[99] The liquidated co-operatives owned 372 bakeries, 111 butcher shops, 80 department stores, 496 warehouses, about 3000 outlets in all. They employed some 50,000, of whom about half lost their jobs.[100] The fate of the liquidated outlets turned into a bone of contention, picked with questionable success by space-hungry shop owners. In March 1937, nearly two years after passage of the liquidation law, a spokesman of small business reported that only about 1000 of the outlets had passed into private hands, while 300 had already been closed down altogether. Transfer of the remainder, despite serious efforts, was too dif-

[97] Cf. Alvermann, op. cit., pp. 32 f.
[98] Ibid., p. 30.
[99] Ibid., p. 36.
[100] Hertz, op. cit., pp. 668 f.

ficult to master, he said. Further return to private ownership was not to be expected.[101] His report was echoed in the files of the Party's economic advisor in Coburg, who reported how negotiations, begun in 1936, were still in progress in summer 1937 on the sale of a local co-operative to private interests. Inadequate offers by the local buyer were matched by the reluctance of the Reich to sell unless losses incurred in the liquidation were covered. In this case, the buying initiative came from a group of local wholesalers, supported by the Gauleiter, who offered 24,000 marks, the practical value of the mortgage. The co-operative had itself estimated its assets at 482,000 marks, and losses due to liquidation were estimated at 600,000 marks. Resistance to the sale came from Schacht.[102]

The anti-co-operative campaign succeeded between 1933 and 1936 in reducing the number of co-operative outlets from about 12,500 to under 9000, and co-operative membership from about 3,500,000 to 2,000,000. Turnover had dropped from an estimated 4.5 per cent of total retail volume to 1.8 per cent. But co-operatives continued to exist, and, at least ideologically, the future was presumably theirs. It was not, in any case, on the side of small business. By 1938, Party theoreticians were speaking openly of vending machines and the introduction of concessions in certain areas, like tobacco sales, both to reduce welfare expenditure—the concessions were to be granted only to those on public assistance—and to make available additional supplies of labor.[103] Even the Mittelstand spokesmen talked about "rationalization" as they contemplated the declining number of retail sales apprentices and foresaw a bright future for the retailer precisely because Darwinistic selective principles had reduced his numbers and with them competitive pressure, thus increasing chances.[104] A spokesman of the retail trade organization of the Labor Front told the *Berliner Tageblatt* that it was the labor re-

[101] *Kölnische Zeitung* of 2 March 1937, quoted in Alvermann, op. cit., p. 25.

[102] Bundesarchiv, File NS 22/209.

[103] Cf. Holtz, *Arbeitspolitik*, pp. 68 f.

[104] "Aussichten für den jungen Kaufmann," *Der Angriff*, 24 November 1937.

serves of retail trade that could be expected to solve the general labor shortage. His spirited defense of the wholesaler made it clear that this sector of the economy, too, was being submitted to reappraisal along lines other than those envisaged by its spokesmen in 1933.[105]

The economic reports, particularly from rural areas, were a continual series of complaints: loss of labor in retail trade and crafts, ostensible discrimination in favor of sugar and tobacco imports against fruits and other farm products,[106] and apparent support for chain and department stores.[107] A Party functionary remarked pointedly that the expropriation of Jewish businesses "would have had still better results in relieving the pressure on retail trade if the chain stores had not used the opportunity to rent evacuated Jewish shop space in the main business areas, and thus to move their affiliates from unfavorable areas into better locations."[108]

That the Third Reich, its own economic logic notwithstanding, produced no radical reorganization of retail trade had less to do with public opinion, let alone the organized pressure of the Mittelstand, then with the bizarre but characteristically Nazi fragmentation of interests that prevented the development of systematic alternatives. Mittelstand pressure survived, as has been seen, at the local level. At higher levels, where economic decisions were taken, Mittelstand influence declined from 1933 on. But rather than leading to alternatives, it seems to have led to a polarization of interests whose effective mutual opposition led to deadlock. At a meeting in

105 *Das Berliner Tageblatt*, 27 January 1938.

106 ". . . even if it means that the chain smoker has to smoke domestic weeds instead of Oriental tobacco." Kreis Hof, March 1939, Bundesarchiv, File NS 22/208.

107 "Apparently the same old principle is still valid. What matters is low prices and not the trained counsel of the sales personnel." Kreisleitung Amberg-Sulzbach, February 1939. "Retail trade is complaining about the retention and further expansion of the chain stores. Considering the present shortage of skilled labor, the two or three single women employed in such a shop could easily be employed elsewhere and the existence of countless families dependent on retail trade would not be in danger." Kreisleitung Dingolfing-Landau, April 1939, Bundesarchiv, ibid.

108 "Die Praxis der Arisierung," *Der Hoheitsträger*, July 1939, p. 15.

Cologne in 1934, the local Gauleiter distinguished between department stores, which, in his opinion, sold bad merchandise for good money, and co-operatives, which did not. He was immediately corrected by Hayler, the Reich Commissioner for Retail Trade, who declared that the only relevant difference was between private and collective forms of organization, whereby it was understood that the former were good, the latter bad.[109] These seem to have been the basic lines of policy. Organized retail trade, to the extent that it had an official voice, favored private ownership regardless of size. Its policy, as such, was not prejudicial to the department store. The Party favored the co-operative, particularly under private auspices, and was apparently supported by the Labor Front. The result seems to have been a virtual stalemate of Party and Labor Front on one side, of retail trade and—improbable as it may seem—SS on the other.[110] "It was my opinion that National Socialism had as its mission the dissolution of collectivization, the latter SS General Ohlendorf told a French psychiatrist during his war crimes trial in the American Zone in 1947, "but without proletarianizing the middle classes or causing the disappearance of independent factories. . . . In the Security Service, I was given political and economic tasks and combatted the socialist and collectivist tendencies of the people around Speer and Bormann."[111] His efforts were honored after the war by Hayler who wrote "In the interest of trade in general, and thus of the department and large specialty stores (Grossbetriebe), Ohlendorf's activity as managing director of the Reich Retail Trade organization proved useful. Ohlendorf had, at the same time, a position in the Reich leadership of the SS and made use of his power to the advantage of the Trade Organization against the tendencies of Ley, Bormann, and Darré

[109] Cf. Uhlig, op. cit., p. 150.

[110] Yet it is questionable how clear the lines might have been in the absence of any official policy. Holtz, for example, the advocate of vending machines and little old ladies was, as lecturer in the Institute for German Socialism of the University of Cologne, responsible to an autodidact former sailor and Alter Kämpfer who was also for a short time Trustee of Labor. But Holtz, like his colleague Horsten, was also an SS man.

[111] Bayle, op. cit., pp. 39 f.

to limit and disparage trade. Among other things, he managed successfully to resist Ley's later State-socialistic plans for turning trade into a mechanical distribution apparatus run entirely by functionaries."[112]

The statistically visible results of this policy or combination of policies were relatively small, but unambiguously unfavorable to the Mittelstand. In 1925, 16.2 per cent of the working population was employed in transport, communications, and trade; in 1933, 18.4 per cent; in 1939, 17.5 per cent.[113] In absolute figures, 2,781,022 were employed in commercial establishments in 1933; 2,750,063 in 1939. The increased employment of family members, from 311,911 to 345,828, pointed to the real loss of labor.[114] A survey of soap and brush shops in early 1939 revealed that 43.5 per cent were run by women. Of the male owners, 51.2 per cent were over fifty and 25 per cent between sixty and seventy. In 25 per cent, the male owner's working capacity was impaired, while 38 per cent also had other sources of income.[115] More revealing still was an analysis according to business status. Given 1933=100 as a base, the number of owners and managers in trade, communications, and transport declined to 93.1 in 1939, pointing to evident concentration and elimination of small firms. Unpaid family employees meanwhile increased to 105.4, an index of the pressure on small operators, while salary earners fell to 98.1.[116] An analysis of persons employed in commercial establishments between 1933 and 1939 revealed an 11 per cent gain in the absolute number of unpaid employed family members, and a loss of 9 per cent in salary earners—a figure all the more impressive considering that some 7,000,000 had been employed and re-employed during the same period.[117]

An indirect index of the economic consequences of the Third Reich was the volume of retail trade as such. The department stores, as has been seen, genuinely suffered, and

[112] Quoted in Uhlig, op. cit., p. 204.
[113] *The Fate*, op. cit., pp. 13 f.
[114] Ibid., pp. 34 f.
[115] Ibid., p. 67.
[116] Ibid., p. 132.
[117] Ibid., p. 143.

other retail trade made only relatively small gains. In 1938, only furniture and household goods—both subsidized in the form of loans to newly married couples—were beyond their 1928 level. Neither food nor textiles reached the maximum level of pre-depression volume, however impressive the economic gain since 1933.[118] The combined result, relative discrimination against the consumer economy but relatively little discrimination against its biggest units, consolidation of large units and elimination of small ones, plus the labor shortage and fixed prices, was, for the Mittelstand, at best a pyrrhic victory. If it won its—in itself meaningless—fight against the Jews, it was still far from victory in its fight against big business. If it had achieved the desired official support, this had taken undesired forms in an economy in which consumption tended to be regarded more as a necessary evil than as a positive good. The tradesman was en route to becoming a kind of concessionary, an indirect functionary of the State whose endlessly invoked "personal integrity and professional experience" qualified him to sell what the regime put at his disposal, at prices the regime had set, and irrespective of falling standards of quality, indefinite delivery dates, and unyielding pressure on his labor supply. The craftsman at the same time was being hustled into the industrial age. "Of course National Socialism has been in favor of Handwork from the beginning," wrote the *Völkische Beobachter*, "but this does not mean that the State is obliged to help the artisan with subsidies, etc. The best help is always self-help, achieved through greater efficiency. The strong side of the Reichsstand des Handwerks was that it succeeded in resolving misunderstood traditional ideas, and understood how to adjust to advancing technological developments."[119]

But even the comparative advantage of big business was relativized by an economic policy in which business paid the piper and the State called the tune. Between 1933 and 1938

[118] *The Fate*, op. cit., p. 144. Compared with 1932, however, total retail turnover had increased to 122, food to 117, clothing and textiles to 127, and—obviously a by-product of the marriage loan policy—household goods and furniture to 151.5. Uhlig, op. cit., p. 218.

[119] "Das deutsche Handwerk im Aufschwung," VB, 1 July 1939.

public investment increased from 6.8 to 25.6 per cent of the national income, according to Erbe's figures.[120] Military spending increased by about 2000 per cent, transportation expenditure—including the Autobahns—by over 170 per cent. Public spending in 1938 totaled 35 per cent of the national income, compared with 30 per cent in France, 23.8 per cent in the United Kingdom, and 10.7 per cent in the United States.[121] This public domination was the tune the economy danced to, and Nazi fiscal policy alone is a revealing indication of the price business paid for it. Maintenance of Brüning's high deflationary tax rates, prohibitions on the issues of new securities, blocked dividends, "organic"—which is to say discriminatory—interest policy, foreign currency controls, variable exchange rates restricting imports: these all appeared on the bill that industry was prepared to pay. Tax receipts totaled 21.6 per cent of the national income, compared with 12.9 per cent in 1933.[122] The only way to see the Nazi fiscal economy, Erbe observes, is to realize that public inflation was matched and financed by private deflation;[123] in other words, that business was prepared—and obliged—to pay and sacrifice for the war economy from which it hoped to profit.

Profits came under control virtually from the date of their reappearance. In 1934, dividends were restricted to 6 per cent. Additional profits were to be turned into Reich bonds, which in turn were made non-negotiable. In 1935 there was a grand-scale conversion as interest on mortgages, municipal, and Reich bonds was reduced from 6 to 4½ per cent.[124] Bond holders were given no notice, and effectively, no choice. What was offered was either 4½ per cent with a unique bonus of 2 per cent in the year of issue, or rejection. In case of rejection, the holder theoretically had the right to claim continued payment at the old rate, but non-converted papers were excluded from the securities market and from transac-

120 Erbe, op. cit., p. 25.
121 Ibid., p. 35.
122 Ibid., pp. 180 f.
123 Ibid., p. 143.
124 Securities sold abroad were of course excepted. Cf. Büttner, op. cit., p. 481.

tions of the Reichsbank. Not surprisingly, only 1 per cent rejected the conversion offer.[125] The ostensible economic object was encouraged investment; the ostensible ideological object, the profit-sharing and Brechung der Zinsknechtschaft of the Party program.[126] But the real object was obviously a government loan at bargain prices and a better competitive position for Reich issues. During the years 1933–39, private issues declined to a total value of RM 2,262,000, more than 10 per cent of it in shares in the Reichswerke-Hermann Goering. This compared with RM 7,336,000 in private issues in the period 1926–32, a period that included three years of intense depression.[127] At the same time, corporation taxes were increased from 20 per cent in 1934 to 25 per cent in 1936, 30 per cent in 1937, 35 per cent in 1938, and 40 per cent in 1939/40.[128]

The one area of the economy where private initiative was positively encouraged was, characteristically, housing, an area where the State was anxious to be rid of its burden. Increased private participation in the housing market was another by-product of the reduction of the mortgage rates in 1935. Public spending on housing declined meanwhile from 5.8 per cent of total public expenditures in 1933 to less than 1.2 per cent in 1938. The State share of the housing market declined to

[125] Cf. Erbe, op. cit., p. 58; Rudolf Stucken, *Deutsche Geld- und Kreditpolitik,* Tübingen, 1953, p. 145. Legislation quoted in Büttner, op. cit.

[126] Cf. Büttner, op. cit., pp. 534–37.

[127] L. Hamburger, *How Nazi Germany Has Controlled Business,* Washington, 1943, p. 26.

[128] The 4% discount rate of 1933/34 is an indication of the dubious validity of the argument about increased investment. Cf. Erbe, op. cit., p. 60. On the other hand, according to Hamburger, investment did increase, but as a form of resistance to the Reich bonds rather than a happy intended by-product of them. He reports that only 175 corporations had bought Reich bonds through the end of 1937, and that bond sales totaled only 90,000,000 marks, 12,000,000 of them paid by the Reichsbank itself. Profits were obviously reinvested instead of being distributed as dividends. But this too was a Nazi objective. This form of self-finance meant reduced liquidity and thus reduced inflationary pressure. It also meant that now private issues would not compete with those of the Reich. Cf. Hamburger, op. cit., p. 74.

13 per cent of the total.[129] Reich participation was concentrated in rural homesteads, where it was hoped this might keep labor on the farm, and in cities, particularly those with rapidly growing industrial concentrations, where it was hoped this might keep factory labor in the plant.[130] In 1936, according to Schweitzer, big industry was investing 50,000,000 marks annually—almost 28 per cent of the total amount of Reich expenditure—in housing for its workers, and in subsequent years still more. And with this went the redistributed burden of welfare expenditure.[131]

In the meanwhile, the State itself had actively invaded the domain of private industry, becoming itself, or in its various forms, a new and public sector of big business, in areas as diversified as the Goering-Werke, Volkswagen, and airplane manufacture, ocean tourism, bicycle pedals, and mineral water.[132]

But inconsistent as Nazi practice might have been, Nazi theory meanwhile systematically undermined the legal premises of private property. Theodor Maunz demonstrated the disappearance of the heretofore practical distinction between expropriation and limitation of property, in which the latter had required compensation. The distinction was based, he wrote, on a presumed distinction between State and society. Since in the Third Reich this distinction had ceased to exist,

[129] Cf. Erbe, op. cit., pp. 25–27.

[130] Cf. Schweitzer, "Der ursprüngliche Vierjahresplan," op. cit., pp. 382–84. This will be handled in greater detail in Ch. V.

[131] According to Labor Front figures, private industry invested RM 60,000,000 in housing in 1938/39. *Deutsche Musterbetriebe*, op. cit., p. 31.

[132] Cf. Enno George, *Die wirtschaftlichen Unternehmungen der* SS, Stuttgart, 1963. Yet there seems to have been nothing dogmatic about this. Between 1935 and 1937, the Reich transferred all 50,000,000 marks in shares of the Deutsche Bank and Diskontogesellschaft back to its original owners, and did the same in 1936/37 with the Commerz und Privat Bank. In 1937 it sold the Dresdner Bank for an estimated 200,000,000 marks. In March 1936, it sold out its controlling interest in Deschmag (German Shipbuilding and Engineering Co.) to Bremen merchants, and in September, 8,200,000 shares in the Hamburg-South America Shipping Co. In early 1936, it sold out its controlling share of the Vereinigte Stahlwerke, which it had acquired under Brüning.

property was thus no longer a private affair but a kind of State concession, limited by the condition that property be put to "correct" use. National Socialist law therefore authorized the Führer—if only the Führer—as the effective agent not only of the State but of society to limit or expropriate property at will where this limitation or expropriation was consonant with the "tasks of the community."[133] E. R. Huber produced practical examples, all of them anchored in the legislative paragraphs. They included Autobahn rights of way, land for Wehrmacht installations and exercises, canals on the Weser, and several dams. "Should the property of a Volksgenosse be put in the service of a public task," Huber wrote, "an expropriation has taken place even where the formal deed of ownership remains."[134] Compensation could be considered in cases where the gesundes Volksempfinden (public sense of justice), in the form of the Minister of the Interior, concluded that more was demanded of the expropriated individual than could legitimately be expected of him.[135] But in no case was the compensation initiative to come from the expropriated individual. The corporatist organization had brought with it large numbers of cases of what, according to previous legal usage, would have been regarded as expropriation. This included limitations on the right of individuals in various groups, like journalists, to practice their professions, the merger of farms, the statutory limitations on imports and exports, or the control of various commodities.[136] The citizen's capacity for sacrifice was theoretically unlimited.[137]

Any meaningful assessment of the status of business in the Third Reich, like the assessment of the status of labor requires a distinction between the status of business as an institution in its legal and administrative framework, and that of the businessman as a functional social and economic entity.

[133] Theodor Maunz, "Zur Neugestaltung des Enteignungsrechtes," *Deutsche Juristen-Zeitung*, 1935, p. 101.

[134] Huber, op. cit., p. 464.

[135] Ibid., p. 470.

[136] Cf. Annemarie Vocke, "Grundrechte und Nationalsozialismus," Heidelberg dissertation, 1938, p. 98.

[137] Ibid., p. 101.

Where the businessman himself was concerned, it cannot be denied that he did well, the big businessman better than the small businessman. Between 1934 and 1938, the number of income tax payers—in effect, of businessmen—increased by 70 per cent, their gross taxable income by 148 per cent.[138] But the tax volume itself increased by 232 per cent. In 1934, the 63 per cent in the lowest income categories earned 24 per cent of the total income and paid 9 per cent of the taxes; those in the top two categories comprised 0.4 per cent, earned 10 per cent of all income, and paid 26 per cent of the total taxes. In 1938, those in the bottom categories had declined to 49 per cent with 14 per cent of the income and 4.7 per cent of the tax burden. The uppermost groups had increased to 1 per cent of the total, with 21 per cent of the income and 45 per cent of the tax burden. The number of taxpayers in all categories had increased, the gain expressing itself in more or less direct proportion to income: the higher the tax bracket, the greater the relative increase in earnings. The increase in even the lowest category—those earning under RM 1500 yearly—was 5 per cent; in the top category—those earning more than RM 100,000 yearly—445 per cent. In the two lowest categories, the tax rate increased slightly faster than income; in the middle categories it was virtually parallel; in the top category again faster.

The intended impression was one favorable to small business whose total share of income increased, while its total share of the tax burden declined. In 1934, 79 per cent earned 39 per cent of all taxable income, and paid 18 per cent of the taxes. In 1938, 83 per cent earned 41 per cent and paid 17.7 per cent of the total taxes. But an analysis of comparative growth gives a different picture. Given 70 per cent as average growth of all income groups, all categories grew faster than the average, except the two lowest income groups (under RM 1500, RM 1500–3000). But given 148 per cent as the average rate of income growth in all groups since 1934, this was exceeded in only the top four income groups (over

[138] Figures can be found in the *Statistisches Jahrbuch für das deutsche Reich*, 1937, p. 511, and 1941/42, p. 579. See Appendix II, pp. 306–8. The analysis is the author's and limited by slide rule accuracy.

RM 25,000 yearly). Both the number of big earners and, still more, their income, increased considerably faster than the rate of increase in the lower categories. While the uppermost group in 1938 (over RM 100,000 yearly) earned 13 per cent of all taxable income and paid 31 per cent of all income tax, the increased tax rate ran parallel to increased income, and increased income, in turn, grew faster (560 per cent) than the number of taxpayers in this category (445 per cent). Seen from this standpoint, the Third Reich brought about nothing revolutionary in income distribution. It created opportunities, shown by the growth in the number of income tax payers. It also discriminated in favor of the businessman. While wages remained static, and even fell slightly between 1934 and 1940, the average net income of income tax payers, and thus of managerial and entrepreneurial business, rose by 46 per cent, from roughly RM 3700 in 1934 to about RM 5420 in 1938.[139] But the opportunities were scaled: small for the small businessman, middle for the middle businessman, big for the big businessman, though the big businessman appears to have paid the price in heavier taxation.[140]

The quantitative demonstration of these opportunities should not be allowed to disguise their implications. If the businessman did well, the same can be said in only a very limited sense of business. The businessman's victory was a pyrrhic victory. With the demolition of the unions and the introduction of the law on "The Organization of National Labor," business exchanged the pressure of the unions for the pressure of the State. With the ascent of Schacht, big business won a relative victory over small business. But with his defeat, it exchanged the relatively minor pressure of the Mittelstand lobby for the pressure of the Four Year Plan. That

[139] An interesting aspect of Nazi income policy was a liberalization of the inheritance tax. In October 1934, the limit on taxfree inheritance was raised from RM 5000 to RM 30,000 for spouse and children, and RM 15,000 for grandchildren and great-grandchildren. *Statistisches Jahrbuch,* 1937, p. 519, 1941/42, p. 592.

[140] Between 1934 and 1938, the average tax rate on incomes of more than RM 100,000 rose from 37.4 to 38.2%. For comparison, the current rate in the Federal Republic is about 44%.

the I. G. Farben made a home for itself in the Third Reich like few other firms can be viewed only by the willful as a victory for big business. It was a victory for the I. G. Farben. The creation and capitalization of the Reichswerke-Hermann Goering—or the flight of Fritz Thyssen—tells at least as much about the status of big business in Nazi Germany.

More important than the relative conservation of ownership in its traditional hands was its control in a thoroughly, if inefficiently, regimented economy. The Third Reich was notable for the far-reaching transfer of managerial decisions from the managers. Wages, prices, working conditions, allocation of materials: none of these was left to managerial decision, let alone to the market. It was expedience, not ideological bias, that left property in the hands of its owners, something made evident by the regime's own free-wheeling entrepreneurial activity, its tax and credit policy, and its theoretical treatment of the right to property. Nazi economic policy was remarkably free of dogma, or perhaps more accurately, of principle. But if no one was sure at any moment of just what policy might be,[141] there was at least negative certainty of its premises. Investment was controlled, occupational freedom was dead,[142] prices were fixed, every major sector of the economy was, at worst, a victim, at best, an accomplice of the regime.[143]

As a general rule, business, particularly big business, declined or flourished in direct proportion to its willingness to collaborate. If it recovered, it recovered on Nazi terms. Like a variation of Gompers' theory of the labor movement, Nazi

[141] "We cannot yet speak of a 'National Socialist economic theory' in the same way we speak of a liberal economic theory. The philosophical revolution of National Socialism is still too new to have had already such an effect on economic theory that a complete National Socialist substitute can be offered for problems hitherto treated according to liberal theory. Much work remains to be done." Theodor Kuhr, "Begriff und Problem der Marktordnung in der liberalistischen und in der nationalsozialistischen Wirtschaftstheorie," *Kartell-Rundschau*, November 1936, p. 760.

[142] For an extensive discussion, cf. Werner Hyllus, "Die Neuordnung der Berufszulassung und Berufsausübung seit der nationalsozialistischen Revolution," Göttingen dissertation, 1935.

[143] Cf. Leonhard Miksch, "Wo herrscht noch freier Wettbewerb?" *Die Wirtschaftskurve*, December 1936.

policy sought to reward the Third Reich's friends and punish its enemies. Business survived and succeeded in the same way as the Army and the civil service.[144] Exploiting its image of its own indispensability, it made its dispensability superfluous by collaboration. But there can be no question of the price it paid. Business no more succeeded in "engaging" the Third Reich than Papen succeeded in "engaging" Hitler. To identify the success of German business with the successes of the Third Reich is to neglect in the crassest way Lenin's famous distinction between "who" and "whom."

144 This will be discussed in more detail in Ch. VII.

V

The Third Reich and Agriculture

Since farm policy was one of relatively few social issues on which there was something like a consistent Nazi attitude, if not a program, it stands in retrospect as a kind of guidepost to the direction and consequences of the Third Reich.

Only Mittelstandspolitik might have played a similar role in mobilizing decisive support for the Nazis en route to power. But one wonders how many active Nazis genuinely identified themselves with the goals—stuffy, bourgeois, undynamic—of their petit-bourgeois supporters. The animus against the department store had a certain negative dynamism. Anti-Semitic, anti-urban, anti-commercial, it found its "capitalist" target in an object incomparably more tangible than a steel cartel or a bond issue. But one can scarcely believe that its conscious purpose was to make the world safer for the corner shopkeeper. Nazi economic logic in fact precluded it. Characteristically, the Mittelstand ideology had practically vanished by 1936. Those who still advanced it—isolated SA groups and local Party leaders—were representing only their own vested interests. They had themselves become a rear guard, victims of a kind of culture-lag, old-fashioned Nazis, representatives of institutions whose stars had been on the wane since Hitler's triumph. Feder, the spokesman of "shopkeeper socialism" par excellence, was an outsider from the beginning, a man with as little place in Hitler's New Deal as William Jennings Bryan might have had in Roosevelt's. Ohlendorf's SS lobby represented business as such. It was no more than a shadow of Renteln's old Kampfbund. But Blut und Boden went on.

Of course this had its practical side. Farm recovery was as crucial to the Third Reich as business recovery, and farm productivity was still crucial after the recovery of small business had lost urgency. Farm morale was a constant factor in the political calculation of public opinion as the morale of the half-satiated, half-intimidated Mittelständler was not. The very pressures the Nazi economy imposed on agriculture and particularly on farm labor required propagandistic redress. There was no inevitable contradiction in the apparent lunacy of the *Völkische Beobachter* which demanded more industrial labor and deplored the loss of farm labor in the same week.[1] That there might be a connection between the demand for the former and the shortage of the latter was a fact that can scarcely have escaped the editors' attention. That there was a shortage of labor, both on the farm and in the factory, was nonetheless a fact and worth publication if only to remind farmers that official agencies were aware of it.

What was not a fact was the ideological thesis that accompanied such publication. That the farmer was the ideological darling of official Germany in 1939 as he was in 1933 had a certain logic, however the economic situation of the farmer and the economic situation of the Reich had changed in the meanwhile. But that the language in which this affection was declared, and that the official goals to which it was applied, remained fixed as the situation changed—this was a matter not of logic but of faith. The tenaciously maintained discrepancy between ideology and real life was not cynicism in this case, as it was in the about-faces that accompanied the anti-Mittelstand campaign or the reintegration of women in the economy.[2] It was largely sincere. That the Third Reich, or important elements of it, wanted an agrarian State while, at the same time, accelerating industrialization, was not a misunderstanding or a feat of propaganda. Like anti-Semitism, it was one of the few consistent premises of Nazi life. It could be rationalized strategically as a means of resisting Polish encroachment, sociologically as the basis of certain egalitarian virtues and a kind of social stability, economically as an al-

[1] VB, 8 and 14 January 1939.
[2] This will be discussed in Ch. VI.

ternative to imports and loss of foreign currency reserves. But for the true believer such rationalizations were unnecessary. For him, Blut und Boden, the East German homestead, the superior virtue of rural life, were ends in themselves and approximations—if not the realization—of a state of nature. They appealed like little else to a certain kind of Nazi imagination, and like little else they were maintained from the beginning of the Third Reich to the end.

Hitler's cultivation of the farm vote was opportunistic. But there is no reason to doubt that the agrarian fantasies of Darré were anything but sincere. Systematic dispersal of both bourgeoisie and working class—i.e., of urban society—the encouragement of illiteracy, and war on Christianity as well as Judaism, all had their places in a grand design that was to embrace the continent. Historical status was to yield to biological status, "the new peerage of blood and soil."[3] Stripped of social-Darwinist and plain megalomaniac elements, this was a social revolutionary program, a cross between neo-feudalism and a kind of perverse jacobinism whose central figure was the "bourgeois" farmer.[4] Its premises, virtually invulnerable to empirical criticism, were liberal and conservative alike. They were anti-money and anti-bourgeois, anti-aristocratic and anti-Western, ineradicably rooted in the conviction that the practicing German farmer was a superior individual and that the city with all it represented was a moral swamp. Rooted in pre-Nazi and non-Nazi attitudes alike, the agrarian ideology survived its various proponents with a rare durability, borne on a current of real social emotion. If National Socialism had a program and a goal, this was it. Embedded in the romantic soul of Heinrich Himmler and carried by the irresistible institutional ascent of the SS, this —if anything—was the "National Socialist idea."

A battery of theoreticians working out a "German Monroe doctrine" to house the new society,[5] Ferdinand Fried tire-

[3] Rauschning, *gespräche*, p. 40.

[4] Or, if one chose to see it that way, the kulak. Cf. G. W. F. Hallgarten, *Why Dictators?* New York, 1954, p. 232.

[5] Cf. Lothar Gruchmann, *Nationalsozialistische Grossraumordnung*, Stuttgart, 1962. This presupposed a self-contained and inviolate "Europe for the Europeans," analogous to the Americas of

lessly propagating the end of traditional capitalism,[6] SS chieftains whose eyes brightened and voices caught as they contemplated a life on the land,[7] Himmler, like Darré, tinkering with deep inner satisfaction with grandiose plans for vast social and land reforms,[8] a South German female Party member struggling manfully in 1944 to find evidence that Stauffenberg's ancestors had played a shabby role in the repression of the peasants in 1525,[9] a KdF functionary railing against the inclusion of dance bands, chorus girls, and dirty jokes in rural entertainments,[10] a Frankfurt sociologist anticipating genuine tension between the "urban principle" of Italian fascism and the "peasant principle" of Germany and claiming to see genuine if limited evidence of anti-urban population movement,[11] the mayor of Stuttgart in 1939 protesting weakly that the urban birth rate made unnecessary the nonetheless continued migration to the city[12]—all of these were expressions of the "idea," irrespective of social developments, competing ideological goals, or economic necessity.

The idea had little direct foundation in either economic or political interests. The East Elbian estates, despite their difficulties, had a genuine economic justification. They had not been invented by conspiring "economic royalists," and the homestead movement launched against them had never found many participants, despite its ideological appeal.[13] It was prices, not land hunger, that precipitated Nazi support in rural areas from 1928 on; and despite all official efforts, en-

---

the Monroe Doctrine. It was to be based politically on German hegemony and economically on the quasi-colonial relationship of German industry and its satellites' agriculture and raw materials.

[6] Cf. Ferdinand Fried, *Die soziale Revolution*, Leipzig, 1942.

[7] Felix Kersten, *Totenkopf und Treue*, Hamburg, 1952, p. 89.

[8] Ibid., pp. 82–87.

[9] But without success. National Archives Microcopy T 175, Roll 49, frame 2562712.

[10] "Feierabend des deutschen Bauern," VB, 8 January 1939. On the other hand, chamber music enjoyed an unqualified endorsement, particularly the quartets of Mozart and Haydn "in denen der Geist der Volksmusik naiv und lebhaft sprudelt." Also military bands.

[11] Marr, op. cit., p. 552.

[12] "Gross-stadt mit Geburtenüberschuss," VB, 26 January 1939.

[13] Cf. Borcke-Stargordt, op. cit., pp. 55 ff.

thusiasm for the Nazis in rural areas of Schleswig-Holstein and Pomerania was the exception, not the rule. The frequency of Party membership among farmers chronically lagged behind the frequency of farmers in the working population. "A number of Gaue must set themselves the goal of attracting a particularly large increase in farmer membership," was one of the recommendations of the Party census commission.[14] The membership lag was even more conspicuous in the SS, whose farmer ideology stood out against the under representation of farmers in its ranks. While SS statisticians estimated that farmers comprised 22 per cent of the population in 1937, farmers comprised only 9 per cent of SS membership.[15] A year later, farmer membership had increased by 1 per cent.[16]

What was involved here was not facts but faith. Against this quasi-religious background, farm policy made its complicated way, guided less by considerations of ideology than of practice. Against the reiteration of the ideological theme, actual policy developed in two divergent phases. The first, deriving from the uneasy equilibrium of Feder, Darré, and Schacht, from ideology, farm pressure, and business interests, still had some similarity to the ideological slogans. But the second, based on the Four Year Plan with its pressure on labor and resources, tended to reverse the slogans altogether.

The legislative substructure of the Nazi farm program was based on three premises: total control of markets and prices; the stabilization of land ownership in the form of entailed property (Reichserbhofgesetz) and credit provisions to bail farmers out of their debt; and a land-planning scheme intended to redistribute population. Only the first was applied with consistency. The second, though exploited to its full propagandistic advantage, was far more conservative than it appeared.[17] It applied to perhaps 35 per cent of the units in agricultural production in 1933, and the proportion seems to

[14] *Partei-Statistik*, I, 1935, p. 137.
[15] *Statistisches Jahrbuch der Schutzstaffel der NSDAP*, 1937, p. 74.
[16] Ibid., 1938, p. 106.
[17] The text can be found in Büttner, op. cit., pp. 642 ff.

have been unaffected by both the passage of time and the annexation of Austria and the Sudetenland.[18]

Theoretically the kulak farm of 7.5 to 10 hectares was declared a norm and bestowed—or imposed—on its owner in perpetuo. It was, by definition, "that area of land necessary to support a family and maintain itself as a productive unit independent of the market and the general economic situation." Larger properties, like the East Elbian estates, were specifically excluded, though their owners were granted the right to subdivide their property, providing the volume of debt did not exceed 30 per cent of the current tax value of the estate. A subsequent paragraph included spacious provision for exceptions, for instance "in recognition of a German distinguished by particular service to the common welfare of the German Volk." An ideological provision preserved the honorific Bauer (peasant) for the proprietor of the entailed farm, the Erbhof. All other farmers, whether of suburban allotments or of East Prussian estates, were relegated to the status of Landwirt, agriculturist.[19] More significantly, the Erbhof was withdrawn from normal commerce. It could neither be sold nor mortgaged, a short-term advantage in the depression economy of 1933 but a potential millstone around the neck of the beneficiary in the recovery that followed. For the moment the farm was attached to the farmer; for the future, however, the farmer was attached to the land. This was indeed, an official spokesman declared, a realization of "German socialism,"[20] and "a revolutionary advance into the very heart of the historic concept of civil law," as another com-

[18] According to statistics of the West German Ministry of Agriculture only 1,394,597 of 3,075,454 farms in 1933 fell within 5 to 100 ha. in 1933, and 1,712,373 of 3,748,624 in the first quarter of 1939. The statutory requirement for an entailed farm was 7.5 to 125 ha. Even assuming that half the farms of 5 to 10 ha.—which continued in 1939 to be the basis of statistical tabulation as it was in 1933, irrespective of the Erbhofgesetz—were of 7.5 ha. or more, it is likely that 35% is still a generous estimate.

[19] Cf. "Wer ist Bauer und wer ist Landwirt" in VB, 8 January 1939. On the other hand, the academically trained farmer continued to be a Diplom-Landwirt, and Heinrich Himmler was chief of the Reichsbund Deutscher Diplomlandwirte.

[20] "Der Sozialismus im Reichsnährstandsgesetz," VB, 31 July 1934.

mentator remarked,[21] adding with some justice, "a fully unromantic piece of legislation."

Subsequent revision made the Erbhof harder not easier to establish,[22] since its creation presupposed a level of solvency that the practical farm policy of the Third Reich made increasingly difficult to attain. While inheritance provisions were loosened, credit provisions were tightened, as were controls on the efficiency of operation.[23] The farmer who failed to meet his obligations, whether financial or managerial, could be disqualified altogether and his property turned over to a trustee. While the creation of further Erbhöfe was officially endorsed, no further legislation was introduced for the purpose. On the basis of available figures, under 40 per cent of the active farm population was directly affected. The inclusion of unpaid family dependents in the total[24] would have reduced the figure still more.

The limited applicability of the Erbhofgesetz, which was the Third Reich's outstanding affirmation of its ideological goal, had its counterpart in the continued dissolution of family entails (Fideikommisse) according to the law of July 1938.[25] This was as close as Nazi legislation came to institutionalizing its support for the homestead and its opposition to the eastern estates. The net effect was all but nil. The legislation itself was an extension of the policy of the Weimar Assembly, which had started to break up the family entails in 1919. According to Borcke-Stargordt,[26] 1400 of 2114 entails had already been dissolved before the passage of the Nazi law. The rest were dissolved in 1939. But neither the

[21] Harald Eckert, "Erbhofrecht und Kapitalismus," *Die Tat,* June 1934, p. 169.

[22] Cf. Karl Blomeyer, "Neuerungen im Erbhofrecht," *Jahrbücher für Nationalökonomie und Statistik,* Vol. 146, October 1937, pp. 453–54. The text of the 1936 amendments can be found in Büttner, op. cit., pp. 658 ff.

[23] Blomeyer, op. cit., p. 459.

[24] The total included small farmers, tenants, day labor, hired help, estate owners, and the owners of Erbhöfe, all minus their families. Cf. Eckert, op. cit., p. 185.

[25] Text in Büttner, op. cit., pp. 691 ff.

[26] Correspondence with author of 31 October, 1963. Photocopy in Institut für Zeitgeschichte, Munich.

estates as economic units nor their ownership changed appreciably as a result, and since most consisted in large part of forest, whatever might have been gained ideologically in breaking the Junker grip on East Elbian land, there was no visible gain in the creation of homesteads.

Land planning, the third premise of Nazi farm policy, produced as little effect, even before the characteristic confusion of competences rendered it inoperable. The law on the New Formation of German Peasantry of 14 June 1933 left the big estates untouched and applied only to land already purchased or reclaimed. Priority of settlement was granted not to city dwellers but to young farmers ineligible for the family inheritance. Business and the military collaborated with the Junkers to frustrate the homestead program, while the divergent interests of the military, business, and the Party frustrated comprehensive planning. By 1934, the Ministries of Economics, Labor, and Agriculture all had planning prerogatives and were later joined by the SS, whose ideological interests were institutionalized in the Office of Race and Settlement (Rasse- und Siedlungshauptamt) which was responsible for certain occupied areas after 1939.[27]

Planning legislation systematically eliminated direct private interests, but the control of public land thus achieved was reserved with deliberate ambiguity to "utilization of land in ways consistent with the needs of Volk and State."[28] Public authorities, the Party, and autobahn construction were all granted the right to unhampered commerce in real estate.[29] But the direction this traffic was to take had already been determined by Schacht's exclusion of the Bank for Land Settlement (Siedlungsbank) from the bond market. The low priority of homestead development was confirmed in the general reduction of interest rates of 1935,[30] which undercut the remaining private settlement companies, whose last vestiges

[27] Bracher, Schulz, and Sauer, op. cit., pp. 577 f.

[28] Gesetz über die Regelung des Landbedarfs der öffentlichen Hand of 29 March 1935, in Büttner, op. cit., p. 754.

[29] Bekanntmachung des Wortlauts der Bekanntmachung über den Verkehr mit landwirtschaftlichen oder forstwirtschaftlichen Grundstücken of 26 January 1937, Büttner, op. cit., pp. 748 ff.

[30] Gesetz über die Durchführung einer Zinsermässigung bei Kreditanstalten of 24 January 1935, in Büttner, op. cit., p. 471.

of autonomy were in any case reserved to the will of public or Party authorities by the Law on Land and Water Companies (Gesetz über Wasser- und Bodenverbände) of February 1937.[31] Meanwhile, while investment planning deliberately reduced the volume of credit available to agriculture, soaring land prices did the rest. The price per acre, 643 marks in 1932, rose by 1938 to 1457 marks.[32]

The net result was the contrary of all ideological fantasies. The State had imposed its control on real estate and the agricultural economy. But social experiments were increasingly far from its official purpose. The Third Reich created 20,748 new farms of 325,611 hectares total area. The Weimar Republic had created nearly twice as many–38,771 with a total area of 429,934 hectares. While the number of new farms created annually by the Republic increased from year to year, it fell steadily through the Third Reich. Only in 1934, a depression year, did the Third Reich exceed Weimar's figure for 1928, a year of maximum prosperity.[33] An interesting, depression-induced alternative to the homestead program was a program of "rurban" settlement around bigger cities, something introduced by the Republic against Nazi opposition. In the Third Reich, this program came under fire from the farm organization, the Reichsnährstand, from the beginning and finally led to Feder's dismissal from the Ministry of Economics in December 1934.[34] A decree of February 1935, intended to "reunite the German worker with the land," made legal provision for further settlements of this sort, but withdrew their subsidies, reduced the volume of credit available to them, and made them contingent on the applicant's job security and private means. Between 1934 and 1936, the

[31] Text in Büttner, op. cit., pp. 757 ff.

[32] Arthur Schweitzer, "Depression and War: Nazi Phase," *Political Science Quarterly*, September 1947, p. 325.

[33] Ibid., p. 327. At the dedication of a new settlement in July 1939, a retired official of the Ministry of Agriculture explained the decline in the homestead program with admirable candor. "At the moment we have more urgent tasks which take precedence over the homestead program. Particularly the defense effort, with its considerable land demands, takes direct priority over settlement projects." "800 neue Bauerndörfer in 6 Jahren," VB, 21 July 1939.

[34] Schweitzer, "Depression and War," p. 332.

number of such settlement units declined from 30,000 to 14,000.[35]

Another index of the status of agriculture in the Third Reich was the budget of the Ministry of Agriculture which rose by about 620 per cent between 1934 and 1939, compared with an average increase of 170 per cent for all ministries during the same period. But this was still far behind the enormous growth of the Ministries of War, Interior, Aviation, and Justice. While the Ministry of Agriculture advanced from the Reich's eighth to its fourth biggest spender, the Ministry of War continued to be first, and the Ministry of the Interior advanced from ninth place to second.[36]

Despite budgetary gains, the basic tendency was against agricultural expansion. Only in 1934 did Nazi Germany's land reclamation figure exceed that of Weimar's bumper year, 1930.[37] Steiner estimated in 1938 that land reclamation projects, including North Sea dikes, represented a potential gain of 536,000 hectares. But current requirements for military, residential, industrial, and autobahn construction ran to 650,000 hectares, a net loss, despite intensive and expensive efforts since 1933, of some 70,000 farms on the basis of the average homestead allotment of 1933–37.[38] Reflecting general investment policy, Bavarian land improvement—drainage, irrigation, rural roads, etc.—amounted to RM 13,589,100 in 1937 compared with RM 18,559,003 in 1928.[39]

For the career farmer, as Geiger described him, who voted Nazi so that the city would have to buy his bread at any price,[40] the fruits of Nazi farm policy were mixed. What could be done for the grain economy was done. More enthusiastic theorists even considered hitching the wage and

[35] Ibid., p. 333. Text of Verordnung über die weitere Førderung der Kleinsiedlung insbesondere durch Übernahme von Reichsburgschaften of 19 February 1935, in Büttner, op. cit., pp. 705 ff.

[36] Figures in Paul Seabury, *The Wilhelmstrasse*, Berkeley, California, 1954, p. 63.

[37] Borcke-Stargordt, op. cit., p. 63.

[38] Steiner, op. cit., pp. 15 f.

[39] *Zeitschrift des bayerischen statistischen Landesamtes*, 1929, p. 509, and 1939, p. 352.

[40] Geiger, op. cit., p. 117.

price structure to the price of grain,[41] an ironic reminiscence, considering the anti-Junker ideology, of the "Roggenmark" campaign of 1923 when the Junkers had tried to hitch the mark to the price of rye.[42] According to Erbe, German grain imports declined from 6,178,000 metric tons in the single year 1928 to 1,681,000 metric tons in the four years 1933–37.[43] According to Guillebaud, the price index on cereals (October 1909–13=100) rose from 96 in October 1932 to 109 in October 1937. The gain, to be sure, reflected not only official price and production policy, but a combination of other factors like weather, a labor shortage, and resultant short supplies.[44] Only wheat production seems to have maintained some constancy. The annual average, 4,800,000 metric tons between 1930 and 1935 was still held at 4,600,000 metric tons in 1937. During the same period rye had fallen from 7,800,000 to 6,900,000 metric tons.[45] Total grain production fell from 22,500,000 to 21,100,000 metric tons. This seems to have been related as well to a planning failure that discriminated against rye to the advantage of wheat, against feed grains to the advantage of bread grains,[46] and subsequently against grain to the advantage of livestock.[47] For the Nährstand, whose basic goal was increased production, this was no cause for rejoicing. But for the grain producer, it was an improvement on the pre-1933 situation. The Third Reich may not have produced more grain for Germans, but it produced fixed prices and a domestic monopoly for German farmers.

The prices of virtually all other commodities were also fixed and placed under control. The emergency measures of early 1933 were subsumed in September in the Law on the Reichs-

[41] Cf. Reischle, op. cit., pp. 875 f.; Holtz, *Arbeitspolitik*, p. 10.

[42] Cf. Gerschenkron, op. cit.

[43] Erbe, op. cit., p. 79.

[44] Guillebaud, *Economic Recovery*, p. 156.

[45] Hermann Bente, *Deutsche Bauernpolitik*, Berlin-Stuttgart, 1940, p. 21. By comparison, annual average rye production in 1910–14 was 11,200,000 m.t., wheat production 4,600,000 m.t., and total grain production 27,600,000 m.t. The territorial losses of 1918/19 however account for a large part of the difference.

[46] Cf. Preiss, op. cit., p. 673; Steiner, op. cit., p. 60.

[47] Preiss, op. cit., p. 677.

nährstand, and extended in the course of 1934 to all other agricultural products.[48] The short-term results were visible in the price index. Given 1909–13=100, potatoes rose from 67 in October 1932 to 111 in October 1935, livestock from 68 to 95, and butter from 84 to 96. Eggs were maintained at their previous high level of 128. Subsequent price development through October 1937 showed a slight decline, potatoes falling back to 108, and livestock to 92.[49] Seen absolutely, farm income nonetheless rose visibly from RM 4,200,000 in agriculture and forestry in 1933 to RM 5,600,000 in 1937.[50]

Seen relatively, the picture was less favorable. Farm income amounted to 8.7 per cent of the national income in 1933, but only 8.3 per cent in 1937. While wages and salaries had increased in volume by 49 per cent and profits in trade and industry by 88 per cent, farm income had increased by only 33 per cent. Steiner estimated that the sale of farm products increased between 1932/33 and 1937/38 by about 38 per cent, while the national income during the same period had risen by 50 per cent.[51] After an accelerated period of growth between 1933 and 1935, when it had increased annually by about 17 per cent, farm income virtually stagnated, while the national income continued to increase in yearly increments of 6 to 12 per cent.[52] Estimation of income relative to working hours was still more unfavorable. Between 1933 and 1938, working hours in agriculture fell from about 30 to 24 per cent of the total. But farm income, relative to working hours, lagged behind non-farm income by a constant factor of 7 to 10 per cent, just as it had during the Weimar Republic.[53] While the work-year, according to Mül-

48 Cf. Hyllus, op. cit., § IV.

49 Guillebaud, *Economic Recovery*, p. 156.

50 Ibid., p. 193.

51 Steiner, op. cit., p. 99.

52 Wilhelm Bauer und Peter Dehem, "Landwirtschaft und Volkseinkommen," *Vierteljahreshefte zur Konjunkturforschung*, 1938–39, p. 427. "The decision about how income ought to be distributed is ultimately a political and weltanschaulich matter," the authors wrote. "The true value and the significance of an economic sector with respect to the whole cannot be measured statistically." But one wonders if the authors were really convinced of this, and if so, if they would have written their article.

53 Ibid., p. 430.

ler's estimate, ran to 2400 to 2700 hours in industry, on large and middle-sized farms it ran from 2800 to 2900 hours and on small farms to more than 3000 hours.[54] The farm workday totaled ten to twelve hours compared with the normal eight-hour day in industry.[55] Müller estimated the annual gross income of a farmer in Main-Franconia with a five-hectare farm and four children at RM 1090. Minus RM 718 in operating expenses, this represented a net annual income of 372 marks.[56] About half of Germany's farms were under five hectares.[57] The index of wholesale prices (1909–13=100), in 1938 105.9 for agricultural products and 125.8 for finished industrial goods, reflected the general development of farm and non-farm income.[58]

The Third Reich imposed a burden on the farmer in return for the benefits, in the form of subsidized prices, that it brought. Subsidized prices, as well as the general economic policy, necessitated autarky. But autarky created a new circle contrary to the apparently beneficial circle of subsidized prices, cheaper credits, and reduced farm debt. If Germany was to be agriculturally self-sufficient; if, for a variety of reasons, agricultural expansion was out of the question, further intensification was the only alternative, and the farmers had to pay the price. The law governing German agriculture was not so much the Law on the Reichsnährstand as the law of diminishing returns. According to Stolper, tax reductions and interest benefits to agriculture between 1934 and 1938

[54] Josef Müller, *Deutsches Bauerntum zwischen gestern und morgen*, Würzburg, 1940, pp. 10 f.

[55] Hans von der Decken, "Die Mechanisierung in der Landwirtschaft," *Vierteljahreshefte zur Konjunkturforschung*, 1938–39, p. 354.

[56] Josef Müller, *Ein deutsches Bauerndorf in Umbruch der Zeit*, Würzburg, 1939, p. 12.

[57] To be sure, in thousands of cases their owners had other occupations or regarded the farm only as a supplementary source of income. Müller's specimen farmer, for example, earned an additional RM 360 yearly in a second occupation, bringing his net annual income to 732 marks. Nonetheless it is doubtful that the Third Reich did much to correct Geiger's estimate that 60% of the farm population—in any case, of independent proprietors—was living on a proletarian income.

[58] Josef Müller, *Deutsches Bauerntum*, p. 30.

amounted to RM 60,000,000 and RM 280,000,000, respectively.[59] But farm debt rose, particularly on small and middle-sized farms. "If the emergency situation has been relieved since 1933," Müller wrote, "the consequences for the farmer have been very limited indeed."[60] He reported that debt per hectare on small units had risen from 569 to 574 marks between 1932 and 1935, from 48 to 49 per cent of the estimated value of the average small farm. On middle-sized farms it had fallen from 44 to 41 per cent, on large farms from 68 to 63 per cent; in both cases to the level of the first major crisis year 1929.[61] In 1937/38, the burden of debt equaled the value of total farm production, and was estimated at RM 1,500,000 more than the value of total farm sales. Röpke observed how limited fodder imports resulted in limited livestock—and thus natural fertilizer—production. The result was less the development of oleaginous fodder plants and of ensilage, despite tentative efforts, than increased demand on the chemical industries.[62] According to Steiner, per hectare consumption of nitrates increased by 350 per cent and of potash by 250 per cent between 1913/14 and 1936/37.[63] But the gain in productivity per hectare during the same period was 26 per cent.[64] While further compensating price increases were made virtually impossible by the official price policy—not to mention consideration for a population already spending half its income on food—farm production costs continued to rise and profit margins to fall.

This situation, in turn, created a secondary circle. Rising costs and falling returns inhibited, even precluded, the mechanization that might have increased efficiency. As it was, German agriculture, like Alice and the Red Queen, found itself running faster and faster to stay in the same place. Rationalization of ownership might have increased the size of

[59] Stolper, op. cit., p. 53.
[60] Josef Müller, *Deutsches Bauerntum,* p. 28.
[61] Ibid., p. 27.
[62] Wilhelm Röpke, *International Economic Disintegration,* London, 1942, p. 147.
[63] Steiner, op. cit., p. 22.
[64] Ibid., p. 18.

productive units and thus the efficiency of machinery.[65] Co-operative ownership of machines might have had the same effect. But neither seems to have been encouraged. Land rationalization legislation was first introduced in 1936 and 1937. According to a 1938 estimate, 7,000,000 hectares awaited rationalization, but rationalization measures in 1937 had affected only 70,000 hectares.[66] "Until now nothing has been done to do away with dispersed ownership (Feldzersplitterung) or to take other measures that would only then make rational gains possible," wrote Müller of the village in Main-Franconia he had studied in 1938.[67] In a village of 147 farms, he counted nine electric motors and seven sewing machines. There were no co-operatives at all. According to von der Decken, Germany in 1938 had one tractor to every 338 hectares, compared to Britain's ratio of one to 130,[68] and this after five years of intensified investment. Between 1933/34 and 1937/38, farm machine purchases had risen by 156 per cent.[69]

The alternative was intensified application of human labor. But this was becoming less and less realistic with the recovery of the industrial economy and the simultaneous worsening of farm conditions. To stay on the farm meant working ever longer hours for ever less return. Not surprisingly, German farm studies of the late '30s read like *Tobacco Road*. Müller

[65] As examples of West German farm structure, Müller cited two farms in Main-Franconia of 9.078 and 5.57 ha. respectively. The first was divided in 66 separate parcels whose total distance from the farmer's house amounted to 135 km., the second into 28 parcels, whose total distance from the house amounted to 97.3 km. [one kilometer=.6 miles] Josef Müller, *Ein deutsches Bauerndorf*, p. 7.

[66] Steiner, op. cit., pp. 8–9. Müller estimated that the yearly rate of rationalization since 1933 amounted to 95,000 ha. Josef Müller, *Deutsches Bauerntum*, p. 88. By comparison, Hessen, one of the smaller of the present West German Länder, rationalized 50,000 ha. in 1960.

[67] Josef Müller, *Ein deutsches Bauerndorf*, p. 16.

[68] Von der Decken, op. cit., p. 355.

[69] And were to go up further. Müller reported that an annual turnover of 50,000 tractors was planned from 1940 on. If von der Decken's figures were reliable, however, this would have meant an annual increase of 100%.

reported that 65 per cent of all farms were without running water.[70] Given radio ownership as an index of living standard, the residents of the village Müller studied owned 38 radios per 1000 of population, compared with 71 in nearby Würzburg, the Reich average of 129, and 224 in Berlin.[71] The farmer, as Bohn described him, was poor, coarse, dirty, and overworked. The folkloristic elements, the idyllic extra-economic rewards that might have appealed to the Nazi imagination, had disappeared years before the arrival of his village's first modest factory in 1914.[72] Rumpf reported bad sanitation and evidences of malnutrition within commuting distance of Nuremberg. Seasonally his villagers visited a local barber to be bled.[73] It can scarcely be a coincidence that a poll of children leaving school in spring 1939 revealed that only seven, four boys and three girls, intended to stay on the farm. Three girls wanted to find household jobs in the city and one planned to work in a factory. Of twenty children from non-farm families, none had any interest in making a career on the farm.[74] A similar poll of 1388 Silesian vocational school pupils revealed that only a little more than half wanted to work in agriculture. It was apparently a common occurrence for whole Labor Service camps to declare their unwillingness to return to the land.[75] A Labor Exchange study of a Silesian district in 1937 revealed that of 1499 vocational school graduates between 1933 and 1936, only 36.3 per cent were still in the villages they came from, though the total was expected to reach 50 per cent when military and Labor Service conscripts returned. Of the 36.3 per cent, nearly a third were Erbhofbauer and virtually obliged to return. Another 13 per cent were craftsmen and thus, strictly speaking, not in agriculture at all. A rapporteur at a congress in Dresden in 1939 reported that a survey in 1936 had re-

[70] Josef Müller, *Deutsches Bauerntum,* p. 92.
[71] Josef Müller, *Ein deutsches Bauerndorf,* p. 121.
[72] Hans Bohn, *Schwäbische Kleinbauern und Arbeiter der Gemeinde Frommern,* Stuttgart, 1940, pp. 14 f.
[73] Max Rumpf and Hans Behringer, *Bauerndorf am Grossstadtrand,* Stuttgart and Berlin, 1940, pp. 390 f.
[74] Ibid., p. 399.
[75] Cf. Friedrich Carl von Hellermann, *Landmaschinen gegen Landflucht,* Berlin, 1939, pp. 23 f.

vealed that 66.8 per cent of all independent farmers in Wuerttemberg were over fifty compared with 30–36 per cent of all workers employed in crafts or industry.[76] In a single district, Birkenfeld near Siegburg, 4000 small farms were put up for sale between August and November 1938. "The worst thing we District Farm Leaders (Ortsbauernführer) have to fight against," wrote one in 1939, "is the feeling of inferiority that makes itself felt here and there. . . . I know many farmers who haven't bought themselves a new Sunday suit for ten years. In my district I know scarcely two who have radios, and those are the ones whose sons or daughters work in factories. . . ."[77]

That misery produced more misery seemed self-evident. ". . . [T]o get our people to keep accounts of what they spend on their farms is something neither the tax officials nor the Reichsnährstand have succeeded in doing," Rumpf wrote.[78] Müller reported nods of approval from countless village meetings, but noted that nothing—for instance, the construction of a silo—had ever come of his suggestions.[79] Preiss was impressed with the inefficient use of fertilizer and the nearly total absence of bookkeeping among the farmers he studied.[80] The generally low standard of agricultural education was registered by all observers, but apparently produced minimal reform. "Most" of the winter vocational schools in Upper Franconia, the Upper Palatinate, and Lower Bavaria agreed to admit needy farm children tuition-free in 1935/36, the *Völkische Beobachter* reported.[81] A new program offered an accelerated diploma course from the ninth school year on, including a two-year practical course and three additional years at an agricultural college.[82] In November 1937, the Reichsnährstand introduced a new four-year program for

[76] Quoted in Josef Müller, *Deutsches Bauerntum,* p. 55.
[77] Ibid., p. 41.
[78] Rumpf, op. cit., p. 383.
[79] Josef Müller, *Ein deutsches Bauerndorf,* p. 10.
[80] Preiss, op. cit., pp. 638 and 670.
[81] VB, 27 September 1935.
[82] A. Hergenröder, "Ausbildung der Diplomlandwirte," VB, 13 September 1935. "Candidates must bear with them a profound awareness of the völkisch and cultural mission of the German peasant," the author emphasized.

farmhands, Guillebaud noted with interest, and speculated whether the rise in status it promised would appeal to the general German weakness for titles and diplomas.[83] Steiner provided the answer. In 1937, 41,000 such agricultural apprenticeships were offered, she reported. Only 7000 of them were taken.[84] At the university level, the number of students of agriculture fell from 1039 to 821 between 1932 and 1939, and of students of veterinary medicine from 2004 to 1377, declines of 20 per cent and 22 per cent respectively.[85]

The consequences of this deterioration, both direct and indirect, on productivity were recorded. Preiss noted the preference for wheat-raising at the cost of rye, irrespective of price. Wheat required less labor.[86] This was equally true for the production of grain at the expense of fiber plants like flax, Steiner reported. Between 1937 and 1938 alone, the area in flax production declined by 20 per cent.[87] More and more cases were reported of farmers selling their cows for lack of labor, or machines, to tend them. "In a single Saxon district it was reported that the number of dairy cows was cut from 95 to 65, in another from 60 to 45, in a third from 14 to 7, in a fourth from 34 to 25. . . ."[88] Dissatisfaction with the milk price, which was connected to fat content and thus, in turn, to the variability of available fodder supplies, was included among the motives that led to such sales. The farmers felt that they were penalized for a situation they were unable to control.[89]

In the single area of rural social policy where the Third Reich seems to have produced visible results, the improvement of working conditions for farm labor, the cure had the

[83] Guillebaud, *Economic Recovery*, p. 117.

[84] Steiner, op. cit., pp. 27 f.

[85] Charlotte Lorenz, *Zehnjahres-Statistik des Hochschulbesuchs und der Abschlussprüfungen*, Berlin, 1943, p. 42.

[86] Preiss, op. cit., p. 673.

[87] Steiner, op. cit., p. 50.

[88] Gustav Behrens, "Stillstand in der Erzeugungsschlacht," *Odal*, 1939, p. 152.

[89] Cf. Joseph Drassen, "Chronistische Beschreibung der Orts-, Schul- und Zeitgeschichte in Kraftisried, Krs. Markt Obersdorf," unpublished manuscript, Bundesarchiv, NS/12, Box 2 and 3, Bundle 7, p. 52.

same effect as the disease. In 1937, at a time when the requirements of the Four Year Plan had taken the government almost entirely out of housing, Goering introduced an expansive program of credits for farm workers. The owners of houses valued at RM 5000 to 6000 could apply for credits as high as RM 4200 to 4500 at 4 per cent interest, payable over sixty-five years, in effect at RM 12 to 16 monthly. The farm worker could also apply for a supplementary RM 1500 credit at 3 per cent.[90] The Decree on the Welfare of the Rural Population (Erlass zur Förderung der Landbevölkerung) of July 1938 extended equally generous credits in the form of marriage loans to applicants employed in agriculture or forestry, providing one of the partners had been employed in agriculture or forestry for five years prior to marriage. Ten additional years of farm work sufficed to liquidate the loan altogether. Another RM 400 subsidy was offered to set up housekeeping. It could be renewed every five years. For employers, new farm housing was declared tax free and could be written off for tax exemption.[91] Farm wages rose 20 per cent between 1932/33 and 1936/37.[92] According to Müller, they doubled in certain areas, reaching industrial levels or even exceeding them.[93] But each aspect of this program, increased housing construction, wage-paying capacity, and the financial security necessary to secure or underwrite credits, discriminated against the small or middle-sized farmer. For him, the new program only increased his already rising expenses and made it still more difficult for him to hold his labor in competition with large farms. Between 1935 and 1937, all farmers lost labor, according to Müller's survey, but the loss was in inverse proportion to the size of the farm under study. Given 1935=100, hired male labor over eighteen years of age on farms of 5 to 20 hectares declined by 1937 to 62, on farms over 200 hectares to 91.[94]

The loss of hired labor also showed interesting regional

[90] Schweitzer, "Der ursprüngliche Vierjahresplan," p. 382.
[91] Cf. Steiner, op. cit., pp. 28 f.
[92] Guillebaud, *Economic Recovery,* p. 117.
[93] Josef Müller, *Deutsches Bauerntum,* p. 33.
[94] Ibid., p. 9.

variations. Given 1935=100, hired farm labor over eighteen on farms up to 50 ha had declined in 1938 to 69 in the south, 72 in West and Central Germany, and 76 in Northwest and East Germany. On farms over 100 hectares, it declined to 93 in East Germany, 89 in Central Germany, and an average of 86 in all other regions.[95]

The figures testified to the relative stability of the East Elbian estates, despite the grandiose visions of the ideologists. Darré speculated in 1933 on the strong-willed but heavily indebted estate owner throwing in his lot—and 90 per cent of his property—with the new Germany, re-establishing himself on the remaining 10 per cent as the protector of a new generation of homesteaders as his ancestors had done during the great eastward migration of the twelfth and thirteenth centuries.[96] Enthusiastic commentators even predicted that the East German population would increase by anywhere from 1,000,000—about 8 per cent—to 4,300,000.[97] "The present creation of a peasantry must consciously achieve a fundamental reorientation of East German property and farm structure," wrote a professor at the University of Rostock in 1934.[98] But this turned out to be the stuff of dreams, though the eastern Gauleiters, Karpenstein in Pomerania, Hildebrandt in Mecklenburg, Koch in East Prussia, and Brückner in Silesia, enjoyed playing the role of social revolutionaries. In January 1934, a detachment of SA men broke up a Kaiser's Birthday celebration of East Elbian aristocrats in Berlin, and there were cases of arrest in connection with alleged irregularities in the administration of the Republican subsidies (Osthilfe).[99] If only for reasons of economic rationality, the Junkers nevertheless held their own. As early as 1935, a refugee commentator was even prepared to declare that "fifteen months after the ascension of National Socialism

[95] Ibid., p. 8.

[96] Interview of 27 April 1933, quoted in Haas, op. cit., p. 121.

[97] Ibid., p. 94.

[98] Hans-Jürgen Seraphim, "Neuschaffung deutschen Bauerntums," *Zeitschrift für die gesamte Staatswissenschaft,* November 1934, p. 146.

[99] Walter Görlitz, *Die Junker,* Glücksburg, 1956, pp. 385–91.

to power, the Junkers had regained real control."[100] But this, too, was a considerable overstatement.

The strength of the Junker position was at best relative.[101] Economically, he had avoided expropriation. "There, where the individual estate owner uses his property to maintain an efficient operation, this property will be maintained," Darré told a Pomeranian audience. "On the other hand, economically inefficient units must give way to a vital economic structure. The East Elbian estate can maintain itself, but only if its owners recognize the spirit of the times."[102] This could be interpreted as a threat, but also, in its way, as a discreet offer of compromise. The Junker could go on as before, said Darré in effect, but at his own risk and not the State's. The practical result of Nazi policy was a relative advantage for the Junkers, but this was the product of the Junkers' better competitive position rather than any deliberate discrimination in their favor. In certain respects, policy actually discriminated against them. Grain price policy was more likely to benefit the Lower Saxon or Bavarian wheat producer than the East Elbian rye grower. Pure agronomic circumstances made wheat production more expensive for the East Elbian producer than for his West German competitor. The regional differentiation of prices discriminated against East Germany too. Guillebaud noted that the price of wheat varied by as much as RM 20 per metric ton from West to East.[103] The Palatinate and Baden enjoyed the highest prices, East Germany and the grain-raising areas of Central Germany the lowest. The Reichsnährstand justified its price discrimination in terms of simple economic rationality. The East German producer and the West German consumer were far apart. Transport expenses sustained in supplying the urban markets were compensated with correspondingly low prices for the producer.[104]

[100] Karl Brandt, "Junkers to the Fore Again," *Foreign Affairs,* October 1935, pp. 127 f.

[101] The social aspects of the Junker situation will be discussed in Ch. IX.

[102] Rühle, *Das dritte Reich,* p. 111.

[103] Guillebaud, *Economic Recovery,* p. 160.

[104] Cf. Steiner, op. cit., p. 10.

Drescher's study of East German farm finances illustrated both the relative security and the absolute difficulties of the Junker position. The absolute volume of Junker debt combined with the Junkers' relatively high assets brought them the lion's share of Osthilfe (government subsidies). By 1938, Junker debt had been reduced by 18.6 per cent compared with 15.5 per cent for Erbhöfe and only 9.8 per cent on farms under 7.5 hectares.[105] The estates were also in the best position to get credit. Absolute size, liquid assets, and rising land prices made it possible for the estates to put up about 85 per cent of their assets as loan security, compared to 74 per cent for Erbhöfe and only 59 per cent for small farms.[106] But average reduction of debt nonetheless ran to only 16.5 per cent. The rest of the debt burden was not cleared but consolidated by long-term loans and price controls. The absence of comparable controls on expenses meant rising production costs in terms of wages and housing obligations. In this situation, the estates obviously had a relative advantage over smaller units, but were still forced to accept higher costs.[107] Drescher estimated that 63 per cent of the estates had assumed new debts since 1933 compared with 81 per cent of the Erbhöfe.[108] But on the estates the debts took the form of new investment, while for the Erbhöfe it tended to represent an absolute loss. For the Erbhöfe, new debt had in fact reached a point where it was expected that 25 per cent of them would have to start over where they had begun in 1933. The Junkers' situation was tolerable relative only to the near desperation of their smaller competitors.

"When one now considers the five years of National Socialist farm policy," Hellermann observed—presumably with satisfaction—"it can be seen that, according to the present view, a comprehensive volume of land has been surrendered and a corresponding number of homesteads have been established with the help of the Reich. From now on, existing size and ownership relationships, particularly in the East where the homestead program was envisaged, will no longer

105 Drescher, op. cit., p. 45.
106 Ibid., p. 46.
107 Ibid., pp. 72 ff.
108 Ibid., p. 77.

be changed appreciably."[109] Given available supplies of labor and credit, and the government's evident reluctance to maintain the homestead program at the expense of the Junkers, they scarcely could. Left to pure economic forces, without the artificial stabilization of the Erbhofgesetz, the development would presumably have led to still bigger units than before. With the continuous loss of farm labor, Drescher noted, the smaller farms were inexorably losing their only competitive advantage, the relatively high intensity of labor per unit of land. Rationality, both in the use of land and in investment, was all on the side of the big estates, while efficient mechanization, the only alternative to human labor, was increasingly beyond the reach of the small farmer.[110]

What meanwhile went on was a mass migration comparable only to that of the late nineteenth century.[111] According to Syrup's conservative estimates, the number of farm workers had declined between 1933 and 1938 by 8.9 per cent in Brandenburg, 10.5 per cent in the Rhineland, 9.9 per cent in Lower Saxony, 12.7 per cent in East Prussia, 13.2 per cent in Central Germany, 15 per cent in Pomerania, 17.6 per cent in Bavaria, 17.7 per cent in Westphalia, 23.8 per cent in Southwest Germany, and 29.9 in Hesse. Silesia showed a slight gain of 2.5 per cent, but according to Hellermann's figures, there were in 1938 more than three jobs waiting there for every male and five for every female applicant.[112] Syrup estimated the net loss, in absolute figures, at about 250,000. Röpke estimated it at 400,000 during the same period, and quoted a Reichsnährstand survey of early 1939 that placed the figure at 650,000.[113] Müller estimated the loss at 800,000 or, with the inclusion of family members, at a million.[114]

This corresponded to steady and even spectacular urban growth, directly proportional to industrial recovery and the vast exertion of the Four Year Plan. Even during 1932–34, the end of the depression and the Feder period of National

[109] Hellermann, op. cit., p. 27.
[110] Drescher, op. cit., p. 75.
[111] Cf. Gerschenkron, op. cit., p. 13.
[112] Friedrich Syrup, "Arbeitseinsatz gegen Landflucht," *Odal*, July 1939, pp. 525 f.; Hellermann, op. cit., p. 21.
[113] Röpke, op. cit., pp. 145 f.
[114] Josef Müller, *Deutsches Bauerntum*, p. 8.

Socialism, the only period when the Third Reich dared to experiment at home with its agrarian dreams, the university towns of Bonn, Heidelberg, and Münster were the only cities in Germany to show a net loss of population mobility.[115] "The political objectives of the great economic reorientation of the Four Year Plan are clearly revealed in our building and homestead development," the *Völkische Beobachter* reported in 1939. "We have left the stage of workers settlements, suburban developments and rural communities for a comprehensive industrial development with the consequent need for industrial settlements. Today this phase is already becoming obsolete due to the expansion of our newer middle-sized and big cities."[116] This was amply confirmed by the growth of the chemical towns of Central Germany.[117]

TABLE 11

	1933	1938
Magdeburg	102,000	233,000
Halle	98,000	202,000
Halberstadt	41,000	87,000
Dessau	33,000	81,000
Bitterfeld	38,000	80,000
Bernburg	34,000	74,000

It was no less true of the metropolises.[118]

TABLE 12

	1933	1939
Berlin	4,242,501	4,332,242
Hamburg	1,675,703	1,682,220
Munich	773,095	828,355
Cologne	756,705	768,426

[115] Rudolf Heberle and Fritz Meyer, *Die Grossstädte im Strome der Binnenwanderung*, Leipzig, 1937, p. 169. Heidelberg's loss might have been at least a partial reaction to its enormous growth in the decade before. In 1926, Heidelberg was the fastest growing city in Germany. Ibid., p. 163.

[116] "Neue Grosssiedlungen wollen versorgt sein," VB, 26 July 1939.

[117] Schweitzer, "Der ursprüngliche Vierjahresplan," p. 381.

[118] Encyclopaedia Britannica, 1950, Vol. 10, p. 238.

Berlin, the city that Albert Speer was appointed to replan in January 1937 in terms commensurate with its future role as capital city of Europe, was expected to grow to 10,000,000,[119] and thus the biggest and most densely populated city in the world.

All this was an index to the status of the farmer in the Third Reich. If National Socialism had set itself the goal of turning the clock back, the clock of social development continued nonetheless to run forward, and Nazi policy, if anything, accelerated the pace. Between 1933 and 1939, the agricultural population of the German Reich (boundaries of 1937) declined from 20.8 to 18 per cent of the total, and the proportion of workers engaged in agriculture and forestry decreased from 28.9 to 26.0 per cent of the total number employed.[120]

Efficiency, not ideology, was the guide of policy, and both the relative stringency of homestead qualifications and the relative tightness of credit provisions showed how little risk National Socialism was prepared to take in the name of its own ideological program.[121]

On the other hand, Nazi policy virtually precluded the efficiency to which it aspired. Official spokesmen thundered against rationalization.[122] "This new relationship to agriculture and agricultural policy can be evaluated and understood only in the context of general economic policy and only according to political, and thus to foreign trade and irrational considerations," Steiner wrote.[123] But this was less an argu-

[119] Brenner, op. cit., pp. 125 f.

[120] Hedwig Wachenheim, "Hitler's Transfers of Population in Eastern Europe," *Foreign Affairs*, July 1942, p. 710.

[121] This became still more apparent in the course of the war. A vast homestead program under Himmler's aegis continued to be the ideological goal in the occupied eastern territories. But the example of the Romanian Volksdeutsch homesteaders in western Poland, the so-called Warthe-Gau, showed how little National Socialism could afford to carry out its own program. The Volksdeutsche, as backward and inefficient a farm population as could be found in Europe, were settled in 1940. By 1942 they had been removed in toto and replaced with tractors. Cf. Wachenheim, op. cit.

[122] Cf. "Ausbildung der Diplomlandwirte," VB, 13 September 1935.

[123] Steiner, op. cit., p. 3.

ment for irrationality as such than for production regardless of the expense. Yet the application of Nazi policy was an obstacle even to this. The marginal gains of further intensification bore no relationship to the expense involved in achieving them. Mechanization, rationalization of ownership, organization of subsidized co-operatives—all measures that might have increased productivity—were beyond the means of an economy already approaching the bursting point due to its own inflationary pressures. Agriculture's position in the budget hierarchy bore no relation to its ideological status.

What this meant for the individual farmer was a life little different than before. In return for some security of land tenure and the flattery of official rhetoric, the farmer was expected to work harder and longer for increasingly little return. The difficulties of his position were in inverse relationship to his size; desperate for the small farmer, hard for the middle-sized farmer, only a little less hard for the estate owner. Only the farm worker, under the pressure of circumstances, showed a relative gain. The farmer, Rumpf noted, was overworked, technically inefficient, and ignorant. These were problems the Reichsnährstand did little to change,[124] whatever its intentions.

The history of Nazi farm—and economic—policy could be read in the Munich edition of the *Völkische Beobachter* of 8 January 1939. While the editorial on the front page discussed the introduction of a universal service obligation for girls, an inside page reported an interview with the Labor Exchange in Rosenheim on the desperate farm labor situation. Between 1925 and 1938, the number of agriculturally employed persons in Rosenheim had declined from 38,222 to 35,800. A boot factory which had employed 380 in 1933 employed 1335 in 1938. The town itself had grown from 19,000 to 20,850. The Third Reich had begun with the promise of fixed prices, new homesteads, and farm security. But its practical results could be deduced from the question of an anxious and overworked farm woman who wanted to know whether there was any way her family could avoid selling its cow.

[124] Rumpf, op. cit., pp. 489 ff.

VI

The Third Reich and Women

In the days before 1933, Nazis thought relatively little about the place of women in the Third Reich they hoped to create. But what they thought tended to be conservative. The entire complex of attitudes National Socialism represented drove it inevitably to anti-feminism, distinguished as it may have been with patriarchal deference, moral self-righteousness, and the noisy glorification of motherhood. Here, if anywhere, National Socialism was crabbed, provincial, spiessbürgerlich.

In anti-feminism, the most heterogeneous elements had their common denominator. "Woman's place is in the home"—or in the family shop—was the natural corollary of the Mittelstand ideology. The war on the department store or the chain store was at once a war on the economic liberation of thousands of women sales clerks; the war on the university, a campaign against an ever increasing contingent of women doctors, lawyers, judges, and social workers. The campaign against the big city, industrial society, the twentieth century, was at the same time a campaign against social forces that had brought—or forced—thousands of women into shops, offices, and professions in competition with men. The campaign against the democratic republic was a repudiation of the equality of women.

Anti-feminism functioned as a kind of secondary racism. The natural inferiority of women was an obvious if implicit corollary of the inferiority of non-Germans, non-Christians, non-Caucasians. Though Hitler had little to say on the subject in *Mein Kampf,* one can assume his attitude toward professionally trained women paralleled his attitude toward professionally trained Negroes: It was ". . . a sin against the will of the Almighty that hundreds upon thousands of his most gifted creatures should be made to sink in the proletarian swamp while Kaffirs and Hottentots are trained for the liberal professions."[1] Parliamentary democracy, Křenek's jazz opera *Jonny spielt auf*,[2] and emancipated women were interchangeable manifestations of the world that National Socialism was sworn to destroy.

In this spirit, women were excluded from membership in the Party executive as early as January 1921.[3] On the other hand, motherhood—legitimate motherhood understood—was placed in the front rank of patriotic as well as moral virtues. Not only did Point 21 of the Party program envisage maternal protection as a major goal of social policy. Gregor Strasser was prepared to see motherhood rewarded with political privileges—in the form of a multiple vote—according to a formula that equated it with military service for men.[4]

The alternative to motherhood was the nebulously defined art- und naturgemässe Frauenarbeit, work consistent with women's natural inclinations like domestic service, sales help —the indispensable buttress of countless thousands of Mittelstand existences—and farm work. Under the electoral pressure of a working population consisting in 1932 of one third women, Strasser was prepared to concede recognition to the working woman, too, at least to the extent her work was art- und naturgemäss. "The working woman has equality of status in the National Socialist state," he declared, "and has the same right to security as the married woman and mother. A reduction of female labor in the present situation can be undertaken only pragmatically and with guarantees of economic security."[5] Under the circumstances, Strasser was prepared to see women as teachers, nurses, in secretarial positions, social welfare institutions, administration of sport and recreation, and as judges in labor courts, even in public ad-

[1] Hitler, *Mein Kampf*, p. 423.
[2] Cf. Hitler, *Zweites Buch*, Stuttgart, 1961, pp. 198–200.
[3] Franz-Willing, op. cit., p. 82.
[4] Speech of 15 June 1926, in Gregor Strasser, op. cit., pp. 133 f.
[5] Undated speech of early 1932, ibid., p. 339.

ministration where women's welfare measures or the administration of women's affairs were involved.[6]

Where, in any case, they did not belong was in politics. "In contrast with other political women's organizations," wrote an official commentator, "the NS-Frauenschaften are determined to lead the women under their direction out of the depths of the day-to-day political struggle and back to the particularly feminine tasks that millions of Germans regrettably underestimate."[7] This was Hitler's view. "We National Socialists have struggled for years," he told the Frauenschaft in 1934 during its first official appearance at a Nuremberg congress, "to keep women from a political engagement we felt to be unworthy of them. A woman once said to me: 'You must see to it that women are elected to Parliament, for only they can ennoble it.' 'I am unable to believe,' I told her, 'that a human being can ennoble that which is itself ignoble, and that women who mix in parliamentary affairs will ennoble them and not be degraded by them.'"[8]

But like Strasser's qualified concession of economic equality, this did not exclude a qualified concession of political equality. "We have made a place for women in the struggle for the völkisch community," Hitler continued, a place for "women who turn their gaze not at the rights offered them by a Jewish intellectualism, but at the duties which nature imposes on us." This, Hitler added in 1935, did not mean military service. "Equal rights for women means that they experience the esteem that they deserve in the areas for which nature has intended them."[9] This presumably meant motherhood, but its practical definition was the basic problem of Nazi policy.

Of the three officially sanctioned areas of feminine activity —reproduction, the home, and "womanly work"—the last was the most susceptible to restriction. Removal of women from the labor market was one of the basic considerations of the

[6] Ibid., pp. 339 f.

[7] Emil Stürtz, "Die Organisation als Verwirklichung der Idee," Josef Wagner, *Hochschule für Politik: Ein Leitfaden*, Munich, 1934, p. 162.

[8] Domarus, op. cit., p. 451.

[9] Ibid., p. 531.

social program of 1933. At the beginning of 1933, eleven and a half million women were still employed, about twice as many as in the United States in a population half the size. Male unemployment ran to 29 per cent, female unemployment to only 11 per cent.[10] It was hoped that the marriage loan program would remove eight hundred thousand women from their jobs within the coming four years, while complementary subsidies were expected to employ an additional two hundred thousand men in the production of household goods. "The women's movement of yesterday led thirty-six parliamentarians and hundreds of thousands of German women out onto the streets of the great cities," wrote a feminine supporter. "It made one woman a ranking civil servant and hundreds of thousands wage slaves of a capitalist economic order. The right to work is taken from almost six million men. Only women, as cheap and readily available objects of exploitation, can still find work."[11]

But even here there was a feminist countermovement. The National Socialist State excluded women only from politics, the Army, and the administration of justice, Frau Goebbels told the *Daily Mail*,[12] and a Nazified feminist literature of 1933/34 argued ingeniously that back-to-the-home notions were a vestige of Jewish patriarchalism.[13] The feminists particularly criticized male domination of the Frauenschaft. The leading Nazi feminist, Sophie Rogge-Börner, was nonetheless officially silenced in 1937.[14] But Frau Scholz-Klinck, the leader of the Frauenschaft, daughter of a small-town surveyor and herself mother of a stately brood, was evidently given reasonable latitude to express the interests of her members. "It is an error to assume that the German woman finds esteem only as a mother," she declared in an interview. "Women

[10] Kirkpatrick, op. cit., pp. 204–6. According to Meister's figures, 42.1% of male workers were unemployed, 26.7% of female workers. Cf. Angela Meister, "Die deutsche Industriearbeiterin," Munich dissertation, 1938, p. 164.

[11] Paula Siber in *Lichterfelder Lokal-Anzeiger*, 18 April 1934, quoted in Kirkpatrick, op. cit., p. 207.

[12] Quoted in *Vossische Zeitung* of 6 July 1933; cf. Kirkpatrick, op. cit., p. 117.

[13] Kirkpatrick, op. cit., pp. 120 f.

[14] Ibid., p. 297.

find recognition in all activities for which they are suited. The working woman must take her place in her way and according to her capacity and her essential nature in the environment of the Volksgemeinschaft. One-sided maternal training is undesirable."[15]

The Frauenschaft nonetheless tended to confine its influence within domestic limits. Prenatal instruction was inevitably among its major tasks. Then came the important function of consumer guidance in the use of leftovers, butter substitutes, and the various by-products of autarky, the organization of home economics courses for schoolgirls (the so-called "Home Economics Year"), and excursions into foreign propaganda. Yet despite its numbers, the organization showed no sign of overt political ambition. In number of functionaries it was exceeded only by the Labor Front and the Organization of Civil Servants (Amt für Beamte, Beamtenbund) but its share of non-Party member functionaries, nearly 70 per cent, was second only to that of the Labor Front.[16]

But while the institutional limits on women remained more or less constant, the range of economic possibilities widened spectacularly under the impact of full employment. Frau Scholz-Klinck indicated interest in seeing women outside domestic employment, in stores and offices, as teachers, doctors, and lawyers, as before.[17] With the tightening labor market, she had no trouble finding support. "We owe to National Socialism the recovery of the realization of earlier times that motherhood is a woman's real vocation," began a male doctoral candidate in 1937. But there were more women than there were men, he noted, and all could not be expected to marry. The unmarried women, too, had a right to earn a living. "Should a woman practice a profession to which she feels herself 'called,' she deserves the same respect, protection and encouragement as every German man who exercises his abilities for the good of the Volksgemeinschaft," he de-

[15] VB, 27 September 1935.

[16] *Partei-Statistik*, III, p. 145; by comparison the non-Party member ratio in the Labor Front was 80%.

[17] Cf. Kirkpatrick, op. cit., pp. 114 f.

clared.[18] The feminine role, he suggested, was not exhausted in guided consumption or indulgence of a taste for home-made furniture, nor even in department store boycotts.[19] Women, he maintained, had an important part to play in the production of butter and dairy goods, the management of grocery shops, and in both crafts and light industry like textile and clothing. It was not Point 21 of the Party program, the provision for maternal assistance, that he saw as National Socialism's covenant with its feminine population, but Point 16, the provision for a stronger Mittelstand.[20]

A more direct index of women's place in the Nazi economy was the Labor Service for girls, created on a voluntary basis in 1936. Its modest membership, roughly 1000 in 1936, was itself a reflection of the consistently high rate of female employment and the relative conservatism of Nazi ideology, and perhaps of German parents as well. But the application of even this modest force was revealing. In 1938, 90 per cent were employed as farm help, only 7 per cent in urban social work and 3 per cent in urban kindergartens.[21] This relative state of female grace ended abruptly in January 1939 with the introduction of a year's service obligation for all girls under twenty-five.[22] By 1940, the Labor Service for girls had grown to 200,000. It was to "reinforce the farm and the household economy, particularly the farm women and the mother of large families." In a long editorial defense, the *Völkische Beobachter* concealed its embarrassment behind the distinction between the new measure—a short-term emergency measure—and the principle of the Labor Service itself, which was eternally valid. "The transformation of the Labor Service for girls into a universal service obligation must not be allowed to be made dependent on momentary difficulties in finding labor. That would mean the end of the Labor

[18] Richard Peikow, "Die soziale und wirtschaftliche Stellung der deutschen Frau in der Gegenwart," Berlin dissertation, 1937, p. 5.

[19] Ibid., p. 42.

[20] Ibid., p. 74.

[21] Müller-Brandenburg, op. cit., p. 29.

[22] VB, 3 January 1939. Its front page was divided that day beneath twin headlines. One read "Soviet Union Without Labor and Social Security Legislation," the other, "Service Obligation for Every German Girl under 25."

Service obligation in the National Socialist sense. On the other hand, we are in no position to wait until the Labor Service obligation for girls, which is not organized on the basis of immediate necessity, has been reorganized. For this reason, the distinction between the Labor Service year and the universal service obligation is only an apparent one. At the moment, they exist side by side because the extension of the Idea and the relief of momentary needs move at different speeds."[23]

The sheepishness of the editorialist found its ideological echo in Horsten's high-handed reservations about the reemployment of women. Technical rationalization was the appropriate way to fill the gap, he declared, "but this does not mean, at a moment when the Volk finds itself in the gravest state of emergency, that the last woman, any more than the last man, is duty-free, absolved of the duty to serve in defence of the Volk."[24] But this was to be understood as support and not as competition. Nonetheless, "in the present situation, in which it is necessary to exert all available capacity in order to reach the great political goals, military independence, agricultural independence, and independence in raw materials, women, too, will, for the moment, have to accept a larger share of the burden."[25]

In its practical consequences, this meant that women's employment was again on the increase. According to the *Frankfurter Zeitung*, the total share of women in the working force had declined from 29.3 per cent of the total to 24.7 per cent between 1933 and 1936, and risen again to 25 per cent

[23] "Weiblicher Arbeitsdienst und Pflichtjahr," VB, 8 January 1939.

[24] Horsten, op. cit., p. 43.

[25] Holtz, *Arbeitspolitik*, p. 88. "In their attempts to reconcile the new policies with their basic ideology," Bry notes, "the leaders of National Socialist women's organizations may well have established a record in free interpretation of terms. They had previously declared that women's place was in the home, but now women were needed in industry. Hence 'home' was redefined as whatever can be 'encompassed by the spirit of motherhood' and thus they could state that 'our home is Germany, wherever she may need us.' See Ruth Kohler-Irrgang, *Die Sendung der Frau in der deutschen Geschichte*, Leipzig, 1940, p. 235," cited in Bry, op. cit., p. 247, footnote.

in 1938. In the white-collar population, women's share had declined from 35.2 per cent.[26] But relative figures were misleading, since they concealed the spectacular growth in the absolute number employed. Seen absolutely, the number of working women had risen between 1933 and 1936 from 4.24 to 4.52 million and between 1936 and 1938 to 5.2 million.[27] The distribution was equally interesting. Even in production goods industries, women's share in the labor force had dropped from 11.4 per cent in 1933 to a low point of only 9.2 per cent in 1936, and had risen again to 9.9 per cent in 1938. In consumer goods, the comparable development was 50.1 per cent–49.2 per cent–50.8 per cent. The number of women employed in industry rose from year to year. In absolute figures, there were more than half again as many women in industry in 1938 as there had been in 1933. In production-goods industries, the number of women employed rose in the same period by 82.9 per cent, in consumer goods by only 35.8 per cent.[28] Female labor attracted the special attention of production planners who found women qualified for virtually anything—so long, as one observed, as it excluded chances of advancement that might have undermined the morale of male colleagues.[29] Women, it was found, could be efficiently employed in chemical, electrical, and rubber plants, as well as in the production of toys, food, and clothing. Employers were urged to work out a kind of mobilization plan for power-driven machinery, additional vehicles for heavy loads and security devices, to increase the efficiency and capacity of their female staff. It was conscientiously demonstrated that employment of women need not reduce the birthrate, that women were neither weaker nor less intelligent than men. The advancing pace of women's employment was

[26] "Die Frauenarbeit," *Die Frankfurter Zeitung*, 6 June 1939.

[27] This based on Stolper's figures compared with the *Frankfurter Zeitung* ratios. Stolper, op. cit., p. 150. According to Bry's estimates, based on insurance figures, employment of women rose between 1932 and 1937 from 4.8 to 5.9 million, but fell from 37 to 31% of the total. From 1937 to 1939, it rose from 5.9 to 6.9 million and from 31 to 33%. Bry, op. cit., p. 246.

[28] *Die Frankfurter Zeitung*, op. cit.

[29] E. Bramesfeld, "Frauenarbeit in der Industrie" *Werkstattstechnik und Werksleiter*, 1937, pp. 333–35.

marked by a corresponding increase in women's wages. Given 1935=100, hourly earnings for skilled and semi-skilled women workers increased between 1936 and 1938 from 107 to 118.2, compared to a rate of 105.6 to 116.5 for men. For unskilled women, the rate of increase was virtually the same, from 103.9 to 115.5 compared to 102.9 to 111.9 for men.[30] The differential nonetheless remained. Given 100 as the male industrial wage, the average wage for skilled women workers, 62.9 in 1928 and 62.5 in 1930, advanced to 65.9 in 1935, and for unskilled women workers from 65.9 to 66.3 to 69.7. Skilled women's work was less well paid than that of unskilled men,[31] though in what was apparently an exceptional case, a Trustee's order of 17 December 1936, decreed that women in men's jobs in the hat industry were to be paid at men's rates.

Meister reported wide dissatisfaction with general working conditions, though she registered a slight improvement since 1933.[32] Both the Nazi labor situation and the official concern for efficient motherhood were thrust into an unexpected perspective by the fact that pregnant women tended to stay at their jobs virtually until the moment of delivery. The alternative to this practice—which meant 100 per cent in wages plus 50 per cent in hospital insurance and thus an effective short-term income of 150 per cent—was wage reduction to 75 per cent for women who left work four to six weeks before the expected birth. This was evidently a loss few women were prepared, or could afford, to take.[33] No less interesting was the implication that neither the Labor Front, the Frauenschaft, nor any other agency was prepared or in a position to take steps that might have relieved such a situation and eased the worker-mother's decision. Voluntary participation of idealistic girl students as short-term replacements for tired and pregnant women was enthusiastically propagandized but exceedingly limited in its realization, the skeptical Kirkpatrick observed. The yearly number of women's working hours ran into the hundreds of millions, the yearly number of student

[30] Bry, op. cit., p. 242.
[31] Meister, op. cit., p. 95.
[32] Ibid., pp. 62–64.
[33] Ibid., p. 75.

replacement hours ran at best, according to his estimate, to fifteen thousand.[34]

But industrial labor, despite eventual discrimination in wages and social service, continued to attract women from agriculture as, at the same time, it attracted men. On farms up to fifty hectares, given 1935=100, the number of hired women workers over eighteen had declined by 1938 to 78 in southern Germany, 72 in Central Germany, 71 in West Germany, 70 in East Germany, and 67 in Northwest Germany. The losses were compensated particularly in Northwest Germany, West Germany and South Germany by the employment of fourteen- to eighteen-year-olds, whose employment rate rose respectively to 109, 113, and 115. As usual, labor loss was in inverse proportion to size. Measured against the 1935 base, hired women farm laborers on farms of 5 to 20 ha. declined to 73, on farms of 20–50 ha. to 71, of 50–100 ha. to 80, 100 to 200 ha. to 83, and over 200 ha. to 84.[35] While women were the object of visible discrimination in the Erbhofgesetz—the order of succession in inheritance was (*a*) son, (*b*) father, (*c*) brother, (*d*) daughter,[36] though the revised Erbhofgesetz of 1937 included slight improvements in the wife's position in the event of the husband's incapacity[37]—women were of crucial importance to German agriculture, where they totaled nearly 50 per cent of the available work force.[38] Of the total, 75 per cent were not hired, but family members. The intensity of female labor was again in inverse proportion to the size of the unit. On units of 0.5 to 2 ha., women constituted 70.4 per cent of the labor force; 2 to 5 ha. 65.6 per cent; 5 to 10 ha. 63.7 per cent; 10 to 20 ha. 59.8 per cent. On units of over 200 ha., women's share fell to 25.5 per cent.[39] According to a 1939 study, the women's work-year in agriculture ran to 3933 hours—10¾ hours a day 365 days a year—compared to 3554 for men, and 2400–2700 hours in industry.[40]

[34] Kirkpatrick, op. cit., p. 224.
[35] Josef Müller, *Deutsches Bauerntum,* pp. 8 f.
[36] Cf. Büttner, op. cit., p. 642.
[37] Blomeyer, op. cit., p. 455.
[38] Josef Müller, *Deutsches Bauerntum,* p. 12.
[39] Ibid., p. 13.
[40] Ibid., p. 14.

According to Rumpf, a poll of 10 to 14-year-old girls revealed not surprisingly, that, with the exception of a single respondent, all wanted to go to the city.[41]

That the move was worth their interest, that new careers were opening to female talent, was officially confirmed and even emphasized by a functionary of the Frauenschaft who reminded her readers that the "commercial economy, under the pressure of circumstances, is reaching even further into the untapped resources of female labor, and there is evidence that whole job categories, until now men's domain, are to be declared open to women. What dimensions this might take is hard to foresee but this much is certain: whoever fails to give his daughter a complete and consciously directed education is committing a sin against her future."[42]

This was a full about-face of the position of 1933 that had imposed quotas on university enrollment and fixed the ratio of girl students at 10 per cent of the total. In 1934, 10,000 girls had left secondary school with the Abitur, the traditional qualification for university study. But only 1500 were explicitly qualified for university entrance. To stall both university enrollment and female pressure on the labor market, the Home Economics Year (Hauswirtschaftliches Jahr) had been introduced. The participant was engaged in domestic service without pay. Her employer was obliged to pay, beyond providing room and board, only health insurance, and was granted an additional tax benefit for making the position available. In February 1938, a similar year of compulsory service was introduced for unmarried girls as condition for a job in the textile, clothing, or tobacco industries.[43] But by 1939, while the qualification conditions remained virtually unchanged, the general universities admission policy had been substantially relaxed. Of 2033 girl students who entered the university in the winter semester of 1938/39 and the summer

[41] Rumpf, op. cit., p. 398. According to the Hitler Youth leader who conducted the survey, this testified only to the attraction of "cinemas, fashionable clothes and the other attractions of the big city."

[42] Dr. Ilse Buresch-Riebe, "Hier sollen Frauen arbeiten," VB, 22 January 1939.

[43] Syrup, *Hundert Jahre,* pp. 446 ff.

semester of 1939, 1522 had been in the Labor Service.[44] But by 1939, the ratio of girl students had increased from the official 10 per cent ratio to 11.2 per cent of the total. No less striking was the reorientation this enrollment took. In medicine and dentistry, the ratio of girl students declined between 1932 and 1939 from 15.8 to 11.2 per cent, in law and political science from 10.2 to 8.3 per cent, in the liberal arts from 33.4 to 31.7 per cent, in the natural sciences from 18.8 to 9.4 per cent. At the same time, the ratio in pharmacy increased from 28.1 to 38.5 per cent, in physical education from 22.8 to 52.2 per cent and in journalism (Zeitungswissenschaft) from 20.7 to 27.9 per cent.[45] But despite the apparent limitations on medical study, Kirkpatrick reported that the number of women doctors had increased, from 3405 in 1932 to 3675 in 1935.[46] During the same period, however, the number of women teachers in girls' secondary schools had declined from 11,370 to 9941, and of university teachers from 59 to 46.[47]

A special category of female employment was the civil service. A decree of the Prussian Ministry of the Interior of 27 April 1934 had dismissed women public employees who could be supported at home.[48] As a matter of policy, only men were to be appointed to the upper categories of the civil service. Nonetheless, as early as 1936, Freisler appealed for the appointment of women to administrative positions in the judiciary as an alternative to the positions—as judges and attorneys—from which they were excluded.[49] In a letter to Hess of 8 June 1937, Lammers indicated that Hitler himself was prepared to make exceptions in the civil service appointment policy, particularly where administrative positions in the

[44] Lorenz, op. cit., p. 95.
[45] Ibid., p. 48.
[46] Kirkpatrick, op. cit., p. 249. The target of policy was apparently admission to study, not admission to practice. Doctors admitted to practice between 1932 and 1935 had, presumably, begun their studies between 1926 and 1929.
[47] Ibid., p. 43.
[48] Ibid., p. 232.
[49] Bundesarchiv R 43II/427, correspondence of 16 January 1936.

social services were concerned.[50] His letter was invoked in 1938 in an indignant letter to Bormann from Frau Scholz-Klinck in a case arising from the rejection of a woman observatory assistant in Berlin for the position of Oberassistent (head assistant) despite her qualifications. Lammers informed Bormann that there would be no objections to the promotion, thus overruling the Ministry of Education.[51]

A revealing fact, though probably one of limited applicability, of women's civil service status in the Third Reich was job security regardless of illegitimate motherhood. Hess in 1939, as part of his campaign for more party authority in civil service affairs,[52] requested the prerogative of consultation in cases where women civil servants were liable to disciplinary measures because of illegitimate motherhood. Extramarital motherhood was never itself occasion for disciplinary measures, Lammers declared in an answering memorandum.[53] The same held, despite a ruling to the contrary by the Prussian Oberverwaltungsgericht (Administrative Court) of 14 December 1936, for adultery. "The Führer," Lammers wrote, "considers a general line of policy impracticable in this question which affects the private sphere of the civil servant concerned."[54]

In general, the Third Reich did little to change the status of German women. The intended conservative revolution failed here as it had failed in small business, agriculture, and the attempt to stop urban growth. The retention of women's suffrage is a quiet indication of the reversal of the front. The blue-stocking ideal, like the Alter Kämpfer ideals of the pre-1933 generation of Nazis, disappeared from view, surviving

[50] Ibid.

[51] Ibid., correspondence of 24 January, 21 February 1938.

[52] This will be handled in Ch. VII.

[53] Bundesarchiv R 43II/444, memorandum of 14 July 1939.

[54] Ibid., memorandum of 10 February 1937. Affairs are the least dangerous of scandals because the most natural, Goebbels told Schaumburg-Lippe and presumably knew whereof he spoke. Schaumburg-Lippe, *Zwischen Krone und Kerker*, pp. 185 ff. In the course of the conversation, Goebbels also expressed sympathy for the remarriage of proletarian Gauleiters with more attractive wives and the desirability of propagandizing a more appealing female type than that hitherto favored by the party.

as a theoretical norm but never as legislative statutes.[55] The older model, pious, passive, and invulnerable to tobacco and cosmetics, gave way to a new ideal, the Mädel, institutionalized in the girls' organization of the Hitler Youth, the Bund der Mädel. The Mädel, pink-scrubbed non-smoker though she might have been, was the product of a different historical tradition. Comradely, up to date, anti-bourgeois, a hiker and reader of Rilke, she had her origins in the prewar Youth Movement.[56] For the general public, the traditional heroines, the film star and the operetta singer, continued as before to be cut to prevailing standards.

Economically, the status of the German woman, if anything, improved. "In any case," Hitler told a French woman interviewer, "an unmarried woman has the same right to earn a living as a man. I remind you, by the way, that it was a woman who made the party congress film, and it is a woman who will make the film about the Olympic games."[57] This was less a statement of overt policy than a confirmation of facts. Pressure on the labor market at all points—including the professions—was bound to better the competitive position of all women, excepting perhaps the farmer's wife. "There is no evidence," wrote Borkenau, "that women have been driven out of any positions they held before (except high political positions) and there is every evidence that the percentage of women in full-time and half-time work is considerably increased."[58] The loss of political status was shared no less by men, for all that they continued to hold office. Any loss of status was also compensated for in job opportunities, access to the professions, and rising wage rates, as well as such aspects of specifically feminine social policy as improved maternal clinics and services.

Measured against the historic status of women in German

[55] Cf. Kirkpatrick, op. cit., p. 108.

[56] Cf. Gerhard Storz, "Mädel," *Aus dem Wörterbuch des Unmenschen*, pp. 78–82.

[57] Domarus, op. cit., p. 567. Interview with Mme. Titayna of *Paris Soir*. In both cases, the woman mentioned is Leni Riefenstahl.

[58] Franz Borkenau, *The Totalitarian Enemy*, London, 1940, p. 56.

society, the pressures of the totalitarian state combined with those of an industrializing and industrial society to produce for women, as they had produced for labor in general, a new status of relative if unconventional equality.

VII

The Third Reich and the State

Though Hitler and his movement had never had any goal other than final capture of the State that had tolerated them, the victory itself posed problems few Nazis had even considered. As usual, the Party program was no guide. What it proposed, "the creation of a strong central authority," "unconditional authority of the central political parliament," and "the formation of corporatist and professional bodies for the execution of general legislation in the respective States," had a certain appeal for the völkisch and Great German imagination (Point 25). But it was scarcely an adequate map through the constitutional no man's land of 1933, quite apart from the fundamental implausibility of the suggestion that the NSDAP, the elitist Party par excellence, should climax its war against parliamentary government with the reform and recreation of parliamentarism. The only other programmatic guidepost was a disingenuous statement of opposition to "filling civil service posts according to political convenience without consideration of character and qualification." (Point 6.) Beyond this was little more than a negative consensus of opposition to the Weimar State, not—despite laborious distinctions between State and Volk[1]—against the State as such. For the majority of Hitler's followers, the object of the reform was nostalgic, the recreation of the authoritarian Beamtenstaat of happier days when, in Friedrich Stampfer's phrase, "Germany had the strongest economy, the best administration, and the worst government in Europe."[2] For a

[1] Cf. Hitler, *Mein Kampf*, pp. 377 ff.

[2] Friedrich Stampfer, *Die vierzehn Jahre der ersten deutschen Republik*, Karlsbad, 1936, p. 7.

minority, the goal was power, patronage in the form of public office, and revenge—in effect, the existing State with new faces. For a still smaller minority, those like Röhm, with his dreams of a levée en masse, it was something like a conventional revolution, not only a circulation des élites but of institutions. The SA was to be the new Reichswehr. But a general institutional reconstruction, a constitutional reform, considerations of the future relations of Party and State, of Party and corporatist organizations, or corporatist organizations and State, these were unanswered and even unanswerable questions for a political movement whose common denominator was opposition and whose leader aspired to legal succession to the status quo. The result was a "legal" revolution. Its premises were derived from the extension, not the reversal, of the status quo, and its direction defined less by ideology than by tactical judgment.

The institutional basis of this revolution was the executive function of the Reich President as prescribed in the famous Article 48 of the Weimar Constitution, combined with the political initiative of the Chancellor and manifest in the special organs—Reichskommissare—appointed to perform special tasks of short duration. These three elements, in combination, had been the basis of German government since 1930. Hitler's appointment—whatever may have motivated it—was not a reversal of this policy but its extension.[3] What followed was a paradoxical kind of normal extraconstitutionality, not a matter of barricades, of soviets or special assemblies, of military juntas or provisional governments, but of existing precedents, an extension of Brüning's prerogatives and a multiplication of Papen's special executive organs. All of this was institutionalized by the fiction of legality as represented in the Reich President's Decree on the Protection of People and State of 27 February 1933, and specifically transferred to Hitler by the Enabling Act of March 24.[4]

[3] To be sure, Hitler's parliamentary support played a role. He had it, as Schleicher and Papen did not. But the efforts to confine Hitler to a minority role in the government that was presumably based on his parliamentary plurality make it difficult to recognize his appointment as a democratic legitimation. What was intended was government as before but minus parliamentary obstruction.

[4] Cf. Bracher, in Bracher, Schulz, and Sauer, op. cit., Ch. II.

The "revolutionary" union of state and party followed in the institutional form of the Reichsstatthalter, all of them Party Gauleiters, who were authorized as representatives of the Reich in the respective German states. With this went the prerogatives of appointing new governments, dissolving parliamentary assemblies, and the proclamation of law, as well as the appointment of civil servants and the issue of amnesties. Hitler himself relieved Papen as Statthalter in Prussia.

At the same time, the Nazis invaded the central administration via the Ministry of the Interior. The traditional distinction between service to the State—the legitimate function of the public official—and Party politics—which he was to avoid—eased the way. "Legality," "Christianity"—in part in the form of the new Concordat with the Vatican—unemployment, and a general reluctance to take a political stand also played a part. Civil servants were dismissed. But the civil service as such went on theoretically as before. Rather than the affairs of State becoming an affair of the Party, National Socialism became an affair of State. As early as July 1933, a Silesian attorney general declared to his staff that "National Socialism is no longer a Party affair, but the exclusive German Weltanschauung."[5] Frick meanwhile appealed to the conservatively disposed civil service as a "second pillar of State," second only to the Reichswehr.

The effect, in terms both of personnel policy and constitutional development, was that the Party as such was not integrated in the affairs of State. In part it was superimposed on them, in part excluded from them altogether. Considerations of expediency limited the possibilities of a purge from the start. Even after all patronage debts were paid, political enemies eliminated, and ideological goals—such as the elimination of Jewish officials—achieved, the loss in Prussia, the hardest-hit of the states, was only 25 per cent, in the rest of Germany 10 per cent. Nazification followed rather than preceded the ascent to power. In 1937, 81 per cent of all Prussian civil servants were Party members, but only 48 per cent

[5] Quoted by Schulz, in Bracher, Schulz, and Sauer, op. cit., p. 488.

of them had joined the Party before 1933. In the rest of the Reich, the comparable ratio was 63 per cent and 11 per cent.[6] Considerations of public opinion, the necessary good will or reliability of the incumbent civil service, and the limited supply of qualified material, otherwise limited the Nazi incursion on key positions. The remaining civil service was first intimidated and then gleichgeschaltet. The Law on the Re-Establishment of the Career Civil Service of 7 April 1933,[7] dissolved all existing distinctions between federal, State, and local administration, excluded so-called "Party book" civil servants—those who had entered the civil service without either the required or "the usual" qualifications since 1918—as well as Communists, those considered to be less than 110 per cent loyal to "the national State," and those from Jewish families. All barriers against geographical or departmental transfer were removed within the same rank and income bracket. Retirement was offered as an alternative to transfer.

Like the parties, the unions, and every other form of interest representation, the civil service organizations were eager to offer their co-operation. Like them, they proceeded into the ranks of the gleichgeschaltet, in this case as members of the National Socialist Beamtenbund (civil service league), whose functions, however, were kept purely ideological. Almost from the beginning, local and regional Party officers were kept out of personnel positions, though a fully centralized statute had to wait until 1937. Nazification of the city and provincial administrations proceeded fastest. Nazis also took command of the uppermost ministerial bureaucracy, most conspicuously in the Ministries of the Interior, Justice, Education, and Agriculture. But at no point, as Schulz observes,[8] was there a centralized hierarchy of Party authorities comparable and parallel to the state civil service. Non-civil service administration was left to improvisation or a process of institutional Darwinism or to political pressure. Thus functions were invented for the SA in late 1933 in regional and provincial administrations, and even on an advisory basis in

[6] Ibid., p. 509.
[7] Text in Büttner, op. cit., pp. 182 ff.
[8] Schulz, in Bracher, Schulz, and Sauer, op. cit., p. 512.

the Prussian ministries. A characteristic early Nazi institution was Popitz' invention—despite the opposition of Goering—of a representative if non-functional Prussian State council from industry, the churches, and the universities, whose good will was considered worth having, and who, in turn, helped legitimize the new State with their names.

Having got control of the State, the Nazis in State positions then applied themselves to asserting them, with total centralization as the ultimate goal. The short-term result was rather the contrary, a wild growth of new institutions, jurisdictional disputes, and personal conflicts, arising not only out of the conflict between State and Party but between Nazi and Nazi. Schulz identifies three distinct nuclei of formal organization: the totalitarian executive deriving from the authorities of the Reich President, the system of corporatist organizations, and finally the autonomous, self-perpetuating Police State.[9] Hitler's functions were organized around two chancelleries, Lammers' State chancellery which soon gained priority, and a Party chancellery. Party authority was delegated to Hess who was absorbed, in turn, in a cabinet that soon lost any collective responsibility it might have had.[10] At the beginning, the Ministry of the Interior played a key role, exploiting the executive functions of the Republic to eliminate the functions of its constituent states, centralizing the administration, and repulsing the encroachments of Party and SA.

But its new role was more complicated than eased by the operative premise of the union of Party and State, as institutionalized in the laws of 1 December 1933 and 29 March 1935. The old conflicts between Prussia and the Reich, the State and the Party, continued to exist despite Röhm's and Hess's accession to the government. Helmut Nicolai, a former civil servant and the Party's foremost theoretician of such problems, notified Frick in April 1933 that giving jobs to

[9] Ibid., p. 582.

[10] "The Reich cabinet, though it existed in theory, had no significance in fact and never met. Lammers, the Nazi constitutional pundit, stated at Nuremberg that he had once tried to get the members to meet each other informally, to drink beer; but Hitler had forbidden such a dangerous experiment." H. R. Trevor-Roper, *The Last Days of Hitler*, London, 1958, p. 1, footnote.

Nazis was as dangerous as letting them interfere with the administration of the State from outside. His solution was subordination of the Party to the Ministry of Propaganda since "Propaganda is its main task anyway." It was a solution that understandably found little echo in Party circles, but impressed Frick enough to bring Nicolai, whose fortunes had brought him a Nazi seat in the Prussian Landtag and a minor administrative post in Magdeburg, to the Ministry of Interior in Berlin. Nicolai's solution to the administrative problems of the Reich was equally clear and simple. Party and civil service were to be separated, and the functions of the Länder, Prussia included, were to be taken over by the Reich. In the organizational system of his colleague Medicus, the Party was reserved a middle status between the Chancellor and the Cabinet—now called Reich Council—at the top, and the local government unit at the bottom. But the route to such a solution was anything but direct, and lay over the bodies of both regional and institutional vested interests.

In fact, the destination was never reached. What was attained was not so much centralism as a kind of polycentrism, resulting from the successful elimination of some factors combined with the growth and development of new ones. Thus the Enabling Act of 24 March eliminated parliamentary competition, the law of 14 July eliminated the competition of other parties, and the law of 30 January 1934, which granted the Reich the prerogative of de facto constitutional change, eliminated the competition of the Länder, placing them under the jurisdiction of Frick's Ministry of the Interior. The Local Government Act of December 1933 transferred local government to the Reich; the historic conflict between Prussia and the Reich came to an end with the union of both Ministries of Interior under Frick. In February 1934, Frick took over the legislative prerogatives of the Reichsstatthalter, who continued henceforth to exist only in a shadowy executive form, according to the law of 30 January 1935, he took over the remaining provincial executive prerogatives.[11] Since the Statthalter were first and foremost Party officials, this represented an approximation of Medicus' model administra-

[11] Schulz, in Bracher, Schulz, and Sauer, op. cit., p. 583.

tive hierarchy. But the traditional, as it were vertical, tensions of Reich, State, and local government were not eliminated but only redistributed. They were now recreated horizontally, concentrated in Berlin in the form of the Reich ministries, corporatist institutions, and Party organs, separated at the top but merging, intersecting, and colliding at all other levels on down.

All this affected the role and the function of the civil servant. Theoretically, the supercentralization of the State was an appreciation of the value of the State, and with it of the civil servant who tended it. With the elimination of all possible forms of competition, of structural limits, parliamentary control, and even, to a large extent, of Party patronage, this was, presumably, as pure a form of the Beamtenstaat as Germany had known since 1918, conceivably since 1848. The very claim of the State to totality, an innovation of the twentieth century, was an innovation that presumably strengthened the hand of the civil servant who represented it. In this point, Nazi reality topped even Frederician nostalgia. The total Beamtenstaat: this was something new under the sun, and certainly the goal of at least Helmut Nicolai's dreams.

Yet reality was far more complex and evidently far less satisfying. The charisma and bureaucracy of Max Weber's famous typology[12] were mutually exclusive. But in the Third Reich they were indissolubly merged. The Third Reich was a state of bureaucratized charisma, and no less a state of permanent improvisation.[13] The compulsive dynamism, so characteristic of Nazi foreign policy, was no less characteristic of the Nazi State. The consequences of its operative principle, "stability through movement" in Wolfgang Sauer's phrase,[14] overgrew the historic institutions of German civil life like a jungle. The favored biological metaphor of the "organic" State must have seemed to the contemporary civil servant to take on new dimensions of meaning as new institu-

[12] Max Weber, *Wirtschaft und Gesellschaft,* Tübingen, 1956, p. 122.

[13] Cf. Hans Gerth, "The Nazi Party, Its Composition and Leadership," *American Journal of Sociology,* January 1940, p. 537.

[14] Sauer, in Bracher, Schulz, and Sauer, op. cit., p. 689.

tions grew, flourished or died, spawned mutations, struggled for survival, and thrust their offshoots under the very doors of the established ministries. Positive law, the gardener's hand, was gone. The process was a kind of bureaucratic state of nature.

The Weimar Constitution was neither in effect nor out of existence, but no Code Hitler followed. An Academy of German Law was created, but no new German law followed. The regime assumed the prerogative of proclaiming constitutional law, but no constitution followed. Carl Schmitt declared the Third Reich a state of law, but of Führer law,[15] a situation acknowledged with dismay by some, with a certain pride by others. But only the naïve could question it. "Antiquated models and formal legality are no guide to anyone seeking to comprehend the relationship of party and state," wrote one doctoral candidate;[16] "The National Socialist constitution is legally neither completely explicable nor comprehensible," wrote another.[17] It would not have occurred to their examiners to question their conclusions.

The consequence of this process was a kind of cancerous growth and deterioration, visible in budgetary figures alone. Between 1934 and 1939, total ministerial expenditures increased by 170 per cent but at wildly dissimilar rates. Expenditures of the Interior Ministry increased by 2400 per cent, of the Justice Ministry by 3650 per cent, and of the military ministries, including the Oberkommando der Wehrmacht (Army High Command) by 1550 per cent. The Foreign Ministry budget grew by less than 100 per cent.[18]

Since the Foreign Ministry was, by its nature, an inevitable target for Nazi encroachment, its experience after 1933 is a special case of the relations of Third Reich and civil service. What happened to the Foreign Ministry tended to befall all

[15] Carl Schmitt, "Was bedeutet der Streit um den Rechtsstaat," *Zeitschrift für die gesamte Staatswissenschaft*, Vol. 195, pp. 189–201; cf. Ernst von Salomon, *Der Fragebogen*, Hamburg, 1951, pp. 450 ff.; Otto Strasser found the institutionalized state of lawlessness the most characteristic single element of the Third Reich. Interview with author, op. cit.

[16] Karl Bauer, op. cit., p. 9.

[17] Vocke, op. cit., p. 106.

[18] Figures quoted in Seabury, op. cit.

ministries. But it befell the Foreign Ministry harder and less ambiguously. Like all Foreign Ministries, the German Foreign Ministry enjoyed a strong esprit de corps, relatively impervious to the encroachments of political change. The consequences of the 1918 revolution were minimal: abolition of the distinction between consular and diplomatic service, and a diploma in law as a fundamental qualification for admission. Of eight department heads (Ministerialdirektoren) in 1922, all had entered the Foreign Ministry between 1896 and 1906. Of six listed in the German Who's Who in 1928 and 1935, five were career civil servants of the prewar era. Of Germany's fifteen most important foreign missions in 1929, ten were led by prewar diplomats and three by career civil servants whose prewar careers had begun in other ministries. Only two posts were in the hands of republican "amateurs."[19] This was a situation the Third Reich initially made little effort to change. The Foreign Office staff remained intact. Not a single Nazi became chief of a foreign mission. A single socially respectable Nazi, the Prince of Waldeck and Pyrmont, an ex-Stahlhelmer and Freikorps veteran, now an Obergruppenführer (general) in the SS, was grudgingly accorded a Foreign Office post. He then resigned a few months later.[20]

In its initial contacts with its diplomats, the Third Reich seems to have been guided only by a discretion, that reflected its concern for good foreign public relations. A Foreign Office complaint of 23 August 1933 about the irregular invitations of various party organs to foreign diplomats was dealt with within a week. Henceforth, invitations were to issue only from the Reichsparteileitung, and the government press secretary was enjoined to see that the names of the invited appeared in the next day's papers.[21] A letter of Meissner's of December 1934 reminded von Neurath that, while Hitler had cancelled his traditional New Year's receptions for the government, the Reichstag, the directors of the Reichsbank, and the

[19] Seabury, op. cit., pp. 13–20.
[20] Ibid., p. 30.
[21] Bundesarchiv R 43II/463, correspondence of Staatssekretär Bülow of 23 August 1933, and of Staatssekretär Lammers of 29 August 1933.

Reichsbahn, the traditional reception for the diplomats would continue as before. A comparable honor was reserved only to representatives of the Wehrmacht.[22] Foreign office indignation about discrimination at Hindenburg's funeral—in the form of priority of access to cars leaving the ceremony—was cooled with a new traffic order reserving top priority after Hitler himself to foreign diplomats. Then came the Cabinet, the top Party leaders, civil servants, and the military.[23] A new version of June 1938 rearranged priority as follows: (1) Hitler, (2) foreign ambassadors, (3) Goering, (4) Hess, (5) Foreign Minister Ribbentrop.[24] With at least a vestige of its old sovereignty, the Foreign Office in 1938 cold-shouldered a Party complaint about non-notification of the arrival of distinguished foreign visitors. Official State visits were received by Party representatives in any case, declared an official spokesman, and outside Berlin the Gauleiters were officially notified of the presence of official visitors. But unofficial visits were to continue to be handled by the Foreign Ministry chief of protocol. In cases where other agencies invited foreign guests without the official participation of the Foreign Office, the Foreign Office was in no position to notify the Party, the spokesman concluded.[25]

The real threat to the Foreign Office came not so much in the form of direct attack as in partisan action. The Foreign Office was at first not occupied but undermined. An initial threat, the encroachment of Rosenberg's Party agency, the Aussenpolitisches Amt (the foreign policy office), was stifled by Rosenberg's conspicuous failure to win royal friends and influence British opinion on a mission to London in 1933. But a new threat arose simultaneously in the form of the so-called Dienststelle (Bureau) Ribbentrop created in 1933 and attached to Hess's staff. Endowed with RM 20,000,000 from the Adolf-Hitler-Spende, ostensibly a charitable foundation, the Ribbentrop agency grew from a staff of fifteen

[22] Ibid., Meissner letter of 1 December 1934.

[23] Ibid., decree of Reichsministerium des Innern of 21 February 1935.

[24] Ibid., decree of Reichsführer SS und Chef der deutschen Polizei im Reichsministerium des Innern of 27 June 1938.

[25] Ibid., statement of 11 January 1938.

in 1934 to three hundred in 1937.[26] Arbitrary and non-bureaucratic, it was staffed with young amateurs, a sprinkling of aristocratic names, deserving Party functionaries, and Ribbentrop's personal friends and protégés. As it turned out, this and not the Foreign Office was to be the incubator of Nazi diplomacy.

At the same time, Rosenberg organized a new competitor, a six-month diplomatic school under Party auspices with the objective of making good the revolution that the Republic had never achieved. Candidates were to be drawn from the ranks of the Party, editors, and economists included. Only age —twenty-five to twenty-nine—and language qualifications were specified. The ultimate aim was monopoly claim on diplomatic posterity.[27] But monopolies, here as in many other areas, ran contrary to Nazi practice. It was characteristic that one of the organizers of the Rosenberg school should remark that "there are many Party schools at which politics is taught or political training is offered, but the graduates of these schools are out on the street at the end of the course. No question that they have learned something—but they have no job."[28] In the end, the Rosenberg school tended to be no great exception, though some of its organizers, and a few of its graduates, were later to make unconventional foreign service careers in the occupation of Russia and Scandinavia.[29]

But well before this point, the diplomatic channels had been rerouted. Ribbentrop's negotiation of the anti-Comintern pact fifteen months before he was appointed Foreign Minister was an example among many of how the increasingly self-confident Third Reich conducted its formal diplomatic relations. It was consistent that within a year of Ribbentrop's appointment, Ulrich von Hassell noted in his diary that "even the highest officials, with the possible limited

[26] Seabury, op. cit., p. 52.

[27] Cf. H. W. Scheidt, "Aussenpolitischer Nachwuchs aus den Reihen der Partei," *Der Hoheitsträger*, June 1939, pp. 19–21.

[28] National Archives Microcopy T 81, Roll 11, Reel No. 282, Dahlem conference of Aussenpolitisches Schulungshaus, 17 June 1938.

[29] Seabury, op. cit., p. 116.

exception of Weizsäcker, knew nothing whatsoever about political goals or policies."[30]

It was also characteristic of the Third Reich that Ribbentrop's influence on foreign policy was greatest before his appointment as Foreign Minister. His appointment represented no redirection of policy but formal occupation of the Foreign Office. A Party membership roster of the higher diplomatic ranks shortly before his accession had already shown the deterioration of Foreign Ministry sovereignty since 1933. As of 1 December 1937 seven of ninety-two staff members had joined the party before entering the diplomatic service, twenty-six had joined since, thirty-seven were non-members, one had been formally rejected, on twenty-one there was no information.[31] From February 1938 on, the pressure understandably intensified, in spite of the fact that Ribbentrop dropped large numbers of his Dienststelle staff and turned for the moment to career foreign officers like Weizsäcker. Great plans were nonetheless afoot. Ribbentrop planned a full-scale renovation of the German diplomatic corps and fundamental changes in the recruitment system, his secretary subsequently testified at Nuremberg. It was only because of the war, she said, that little came of it.[32] "The Führer has commissioned me to undertake a full-scale renovation of the entire Foreign Service according to definite new considerations," Ribbentrop wrote Frick in January 1939. "Insofar as my new appointments require the approval of your ministry, I ask that this approval be granted without further delay."[33]

"I have given instructions," Frick replied testily after a two-week delay, "that in cases where general considerations give occasion for doubt, decision is to be reserved to my exclusive judgment."[34] A test case was already in process. In late 1938, Ribbentrop appointed one of his old Party hands, Kriebel, once Consul General in Shanghai and a Party

[30] Ulrich von Hassell, *Vom anderen Deutschland* (1946), Frankfurt, 1964, pp. 31 f.

[31] Quoted in Seabury, op. cit., p. 63.

[32] International Military Tribunal, Vol. X, pp. 211 ff., German edition, pp. 189–90, English edition.

[33] Bundesarchiv R 43II/452, letter of 18 January 1939.

[34] Ibid., Frick letter of 3 February 1939.

member since 1928, as chief of the personnel section. Manfred von Killinger, a veteran of the Ehrhardt Freikorps and the SA, later wartime emissary to Romania, was commissioned to organize a diplomatic school which was then, in February 1939, placed under supervision of the SS.[35] It was at the appointment to a senior civil service position of Paul Karl Schmidt that Frick hesitated. Schmidt, Ribbentrop's press secretary, had been a Party member since 1931, had reached the rank of SS Hauptsturmführer (captain) in 1934, and after a brief academic career at the University of Kiel, had joined Ribbentrop. The issue was not his record but his age. Schmidt was, at this point, twenty-eight, well below the official promotion age, and thus an affront to Frick's bureaucratic sense of order. The case was finally referred to Hitler who, despite contrary precedents, confirmed the promotion.[36] In 1941, again despite Frick's objections, Schmidt was again promoted, five years ahead of the statutory minimum age for the position to which he now advanced.[37]

The deterioration of the Foreign Service meanwhile took other forms, some symbolic, some practical. In 1938, the Foreign Service was issued new uniforms. The complete outfit, including both a single and double-breasted coat, three hats, white trousers and accessories, cost RM 1141.50,[38] a figure approximating the annual income of perhaps 30 per cent of the working population. In August 1940, of 120 high-ranking foreign service officers, seventy-one were Party members and of these, fifty were career officials who had entered the Service before 1933. At the same time, the influence of the Foreign Service continued to decline in roughly direct proportion to the increasing Nazification. Balkan posts were to go to old SA leaders, eastern posts to an extraordinary collection of party functionaries, Rosenberg alumni and Labor

[35] Seabury, op. cit., pp. 70 f.

[36] Bundesarchiv R 43II/458, memo of Reichsministerium des Innern of 8 February 1939. Pfundtner's memo of 14 April nonetheless declared that Hitler had "in the recent past repeatedly refused to pass applications of persons who, like Schmidt, had not reached the minimum age but were nonetheless older than Schmidt and had been in the party longer."

[37] Ibid.

[38] Bundesarchiv R 43II/465, tailor bill of 6 April 1938.

Front officials, whose only qualification was their momentary accessibility.[39] In response to military manpower requirements, the screws on the Foreign Office were also tightened, with the consequence that the Ribbentrop infiltration campaign came to an end. His Foreign Service training center was cut back sharply and its director returned to his duties with the SS.[40]

A parallel case was that of the Army, an institution no less self-confident, no less sacrosanct, no less indispensable than the Foreign Service, and in possession of a superior initial bargaining position as well. Neither its prestige, its momentarily irreplaceable experience, nor the understandable concern of the new regime for a good foreign image, could hide the fact that the Foreign Office was playing with a thin hand. It was not only experience and prestige—and at that, the enormous advantage of domestic prestige, something the Foreign Office could scarcely match—that the Army brought with it, but guns. These, plus a commanding position in a recovering economy,[41] could be played for their full worth in institutional sovereignty. Few, if any, officers seem to have been aware between 1933 and 1938 that they were playing anything less than an even game in accepting the visible signs of Nazi authority, at first in the form of the swastika, far more significantly in August 1934 in the form of a personal oath to Hitler. Nor does there seem to have been any considerable opposition to far-reaching institutional changes such as the loss of the counter-intelligence monopoly to Goering in 1933/34, or the reorganization of the air force under the Ministry of Aviation.

The fee seemed well worth the price. It included good will (Wehrfreudigkeit), growing budgets, evident diplomatic strength, and resources of popular support for the realization of the Army's long-term aims, rearmament, military parity with the West, and the reintroduction of universal conscription. With this came the government's seeming will to self-

[39] Cf. Alexander Dallin, *German Rule in Russia,* London, 1957, pp. 101 f.

[40] Seabury, op. cit., p. 109.

[41] Cf. Schweitzer, "Organisierter Kapitalismus," op. cit.; Sauer, in Bracher, Schulz, and Sauer, op. cit., Ch. II.

sacrifice, most evident in the decimation of the SA in June 1934. With no apparent insight into Hitler's motives, few officers seem to have thought of this, the voluntary elimination of their major rival, as anything other than victory. The personal oath to Hitler that followed a few weeks later, the appearance of the Wehrmacht at the Nuremberg Party congress in September, seemed a modest enough price for the apparent restoration of the military monopoly and the apparent institutional sovereignty that went with it. According to a decree of Blomberg's of 3 July 1934, neither officials nor employees of the War Ministry were allowed to join the SA, SS, or the Hitler Youth. A decree of 10 September 1935 prohibited acceptance of any Party office, though Party membership as such was conceded in an arrangement with Hitler a few weeks later.[42] In October 1935, Hossbach notified Blomberg that the recently instituted participation of Hess in the appointment of civil servants did not apply to the War Ministry, though this too was modified in June 1936 to apply only to those who had applied for positions or were promoted from within the Wehrmacht. Hess was conceded a share in the appointment of those coming from outside.[43] Hess himself decreed that Party membership was to be suspended during the tenure of a member's military service.[44] For the Army's benefit, the military rather than the Hitler salute was introduced in the new Air Force, and it was ordered that the new Waffen-SS was to be subordinate to the Army in case of war.[45] Even after the evident Gleichschaltung of the Army in February 1938, the Army leadership felt no inhibitions about forbidding officers in a West German garrison to hear a series of ideological lectures by a local civil servant and SA officer. The order was reported to Lammers, the chief of Hitler's Chancellery of State, by a skeptical Army paymaster, who suspected he might be privy

[42] Bundesarchiv R 43II/426, decrees of 3 July 1934, 10 September 1935, and 24 September 1935.

[43] Ibid., correspondence of 25 October 1935, memorandum of 9 June 1936.

[44] *Anordnungen des Stellvertreters des Führers*, 92/36 of 29 July 1936.

[45] Hermann Foertsch, *Schuld und Verhängnis*, Stuttgart, 1951, p. 72.

to activities hostile to the state. Lammers passed the memorandum on to Hitler, who passed it on in turn to the Army High Command which upheld the order.[46] As late as February 1939, the War Ministry rejected a decree requiring Party membership or its equivalent of all civil service applicants. The Army politely indicated its determination to continue hiring as before.[47]

After 1938, such assertions of independence were nonetheless submitted to a new and symptomatic drumfire of plebeian propaganda reminiscent of Röhm's "revolutionary" oratory of 1933/34.[48] Since the beginning the sovereignty of the generals had been subverted. Institutional forms and symbols remained more or less intact. But practical influence had already been undermined. A major military decision, like the remilitarization of the Rhineland in 1936, taken against the professional advice of the generals, was characteristic. In February 1938, the shell of institutional independence was smashed as well. It was, as the French Ambassador François-Poncet said, "a dry June 30."[49] Advancing behind a smokescreen of affected moral outrage, Hitler eliminated the mediating instance of the War Ministry and took over the Army as its supreme commander. The generals, scarcely trained for this kind of warfare, gave up without a fight. In their preoccupation with a secondary issue—the rehabilitation of the cynically and illegitimately discredited Fritsch—many failed even to realize that there had been more than a skirmish.[50] From here on the routes divided. Some went the way of rebellion, most went the way of acquiescence. In any case, the monopoly was gone. In August 1938, authority over the police and SS in case of war was transferred directly to Hitler.[51] The first weeks of war confirmed that the Army's authority was gone for good. Charges brought by field com-

[46] Bundesarchiv R 43II/427b, correspondence of 18 March 1938, memo of 19 April 1938.

[47] Bundesarchiv R 43II/450a, decree of 28 February 1939.

[48] Hassell, op. cit., p. 44.

[49] André François-Poncet, *Souvenirs d'une Ambassade à Berlin*, Paris, 1946, p. 290.

[50] The causes and consequences of the army command crisis of 1938 have been treated at length by Foertsch, op. cit.

[51] Ibid., p. 164.

manders against SS men for murder and plundering were dismissed or resolved in an amnesty.[52] In successive stages, the Army had deteriorated by 1939 from "sole carrier of arms" to "primus inter pares." It was now, at best, according to an epigram attributed to Gottfried Benn, "the gentlemanly form of emigration."

The deterioration of the historic civil service could be observed in contrary motion in the new ministries created since 1933. While the old organs fought, negotiated and compromised to hold their ground, the new ministries, well equipped with money, competences, and empty places, fought hard to gain it. The promotion lists reflected the pace of expansion. Goering's Ministry of Air, founded in the summer of 1933, promoted all its newly promoted Oberregierungsträte of August 1933 to Ministerialräte (i.e., from the third to the fourth civil service rank) in January 1934, achieving in four months a process that ordinarily ran to more than four years.[53] What in Goering's Ministry was still related to considerations of technical and administrative experience went on in Goebbels' Ministry of Propaganda on the basis of patronage. With evident efficiency, Goebbels raided the other ministries to staff his administrative positions and continued to do so to the understandable indignation of his colleagues.[54] The rest of the staff was composed of bright young Nazis.[55] As early as June 1934, the Ministry of Finance was begging for more reserve in personnel policy with at least a year between promotions.[56]

An interministerial memorandum limiting family bonuses

[52] Hassell, op. cit., p. 81.

[53] Bundesarchiv R 55/45–46.

[54] Bundesarchiv R 55/24, correspondence of 14 November 1935 to 16 December 1935 on raid on Finance Ministry; Protest from Ministry of Posts and Telegraph of 20 June 1938. R 55/45–46 on initial appointments of 25 July 1933. Of three initial Ministerialräte hired to organize the new ministry, one came from the Ministry of Interior, one from the Finance Office in Berlin, the third from the Reich Insurance Office.

[55] Cf. Bundesarchiv R 55/19, a four-page list of Goebbels' staff dated 21 February 1934, with indications of party and NSBO activity.

[56] Bundesarchiv R 55/45–46, correspondence from Ministry of Finance of 12 June 1934.

to civil servants over twenty-eight, produced an indignant protest in January 1935 from the Ministry of Propaganda, fifty-five of whose employees, including three in high positions, were discriminated against by the age limit.[57] Characteristic of Goebbels' personnel policy was a list of six higher civil service ranks, employed between 1933 and 1935, promoted to the provisional civil service list in 1935, and presented in October 1936 for transfer from the provisional to the career list. The eldest had been born in 1890, the youngest in 1910. All were Party members, five with membership numbers under one million, two with numbers below one hundred thousand. Of these two, one had been born in 1907, the other in 1910. Both the Ministry of Interior and the Ministry of Finance indicated disapproval, but granted the promotions.[58] A second list of five, born between 1906 and 1910 and including four Party numbers below one million, was submitted for career status in November 1937, seven to twenty-two months after provisional appointment to the civil service.[59] A third list of sixteen upper ranks—from Regierungsrat (second civil service rank) to Ministerialrat—on provisional status in September 1939 included only two membership numbers over one million. Of the sixteen, twelve were forty or under, seven were thirty-five or under.[60]

This was accompanied by a notable amount of un-Prussian corruption. An intraministerial survey in April 1934 revealed that Goebbels' staff had found jobs for 192 of their relatives in the Reich radio alone; a survey of the Ministry's other ancillary agencies, publishing houses, and the Reichsmusikkammer (Reich Chamber of Music) was ordered to follow. In a memorandum to his staff, Goebbels—obviously under pressure from outside—indicated no basic objection to the practice, but forbade it in the future.[61] A 1935 report revealed that ministerial staff were accepting fees for radio talks, various services in the various Kulturkammer (culture

[57] Bundesarchiv R 43II/436, memorandum of Ministry of Propaganda of 12 January 1935.

[58] Bundesarchiv R 55/29, Vol. 1, list of 28 October 1936.

[59] Ibid., list of 27 November 1937.

[60] Ibid., list of 4 September 1939.

[61] Bundesarchiv R 55/24, report of 17 April 1934.

chambers), and the film censorship. Some took honorary directorships in a company producing loudspeakers.[62] An index of the highly non-traditional relationship of Party, State, and private business, was the extended case of the propaganda director of the Reichsfilmkammer (Reich Chamber of Film) who had been charged by the executive secretary—unjustly as it appeared—with commissioning a film without official approval. The propaganda leader, born in 1905, a former sales clerk and a Party member since 1930, left to direct public relations for a radio manufacturing firm. The executive secretary, whose charges had apparently been motivated by a desire to cover his own somewhat irregular employment practices, subsequently resigned.[63]

Despite the ostensible merger of State and Party, the outstanding loser in the institutional struggle for survival was the Party. Advantages to Alte Kämpfer were kept to a minimum; direct party interference in the traditional civil service sectors was eliminated almost immediately. The files of the Ministry of the Interior could be read as a series of jurisdictional conflicts in which, almost without exception, the civil service won and the Party lost.

The only possible exception was at the local level. To the extent a union of Party and State took place, it took place in city and county offices. According to the Party census of 1935, Party members occupied 60 per cent of all State and local offices. Of these, a third were occupied by pre-1933 members. Of city positions, 47.1 per cent were occupied by pre-1933 members, 78.2 per cent by Party members. Of the mayors of incorporated cities, 22.1 per cent had been Party members before 1930. Of the county executives (Landräte) 28.2 per cent had been pre-1933 members, of rural mayors 19.3 per cent, leading Schäfer to the thesis that there was a conscious effort in the distribution of offices to balance urban resistance with rural support. Of 256 party Kreisleiter (county unit leader), 58.6 per cent were lord mayors or mayors. Of 3968 Ortsgruppenleiter and Stützpunktleiter (local unit leader), 98.9 per cent were mayors of their rural communi-

[62] Bundesarchiv R 55/46, report of 1 February 1935.
[63] Bundesarchiv R 55/173, final report of 25 June 1938.

ties.[64] In a symbolic order of March 1936, Hess granted Nazi mayors the right to wear their chains of office with their Party uniforms.[65] But even here, after available Party resources had been stretched to their limits the distribution was relatively thin. Lower Party leaders—Kreisleiter, Ortsgruppenleiter, Blockleiter—occupied only 20.7 per cent of the rural, 24.0 per cent of the urban mayors' offices. Of Landräte, only 11.3 per cent were Party leaders.[66]

At the ministerial level, the union of State and Party can scarcely be said to have existed. Aside from Hitler himself, only Rust, as Minister of Education and Gauleiter in Brunswick, and Goebbels, as Minister of Propaganda and Gauleiter in Berlin, combined State and Party offices. Hess' position in the Cabinet was, to the extent the Cabinet as such ceased to have meaning, a dead end. Theo Habicht, between 1934 and 1938 a prominent Austrian Nazi, became State Secretary (permanent undersecretary) in the Foreign Office in 1939. A few more prominent Party officials—Ley as leader of the Labor Front, Gauleiter of Silesia Josef Wagner as Commissar for Price Stabilization—found non-Party positions outside the classical field of political gravitation. But this marked the limit. Of the twelve top executive officers of the Party (Oberbefehlsleiter), with ranks approximating the civil service rank of State Secretary or Ministerialdirektor, none held an important civil office. Twenty Gauleiters were confined effectively to their local Party posts.[67] "The distribution of State positions after 1933 was by no means a matter of Party policy alone," wrote a former Gauleiter. "Technical qualifications almost always had priority. Not even the much maligned Alter Kämpfer had a monopoly."[68]

[64] Schäfer, op. cit., pp. 26–30.

[65] *Anordnungen des Stellvertreters des Führers,* 41/36 of 16 March 1936.

[66] Schäfer, op. cit., p. 30.

[67] It should be added that during the war a number of Gauleiters took important posts in the occupied territories, particularly in Russia and Scandinavia. Cf. Dallin, op. cit.; Alfred Rosenberg, *Das politische Tagebuch,* ed. Hans-Günther Seraphim, Munich, 1964, pp. 137 ff.

[68] Karl Wahl, . . . *es ist das deutsche Herz,* Augsburg, 1954, p. 96.

The whole ambiguous relationship of Party and State was recorded in a series of administrative orders. A Party decree of January 1936 established unequivocally that a Party membership card had no official validity in dealings with public officials.[69] A Frick decree in early 1935, introducing the so-called Hitler salute for uniformed civil servants and employees—i.e. the police—produced friction enough to be brought to Hitler's attention; a resultant ruling modified it to the point of cancellation.[70] The question of the civil servant's relationship to the Party also remained unanswered. Bormann demanded notification in July 1935 of dropped Party membership and was supported by a memorandum from a member of the Ministry of Education indicating that staff members who left the party sacrificed their priority on the promotion list. But this was diluted again by Hess's order of 1937, which also called for leniency in parallel cases on the part of private employers.[71] A letter from the Ministry of the Interior to the civil administration in Koblenz in 1939 left the situation still more ambiguous. "No consequences are to be taken in the case of rejection of a civil servant's Party application in such cases where the competent Party office has not indicated the grounds for the rejection," wrote Pfundtner, Frick's permanent undersecretary, appending nonetheless, "Publication of this order, which is supported by the Führer's Deputy [Hess], is to be avoided."[72]

Personnel policy reflected the Party's difficulties. A common memo of the Ministries of the Interior and of Finance in July 1933 indicated the possibility of civil service status for

[69] *Anordnungen des Stellvertreters des Führers*, 8/36 of 23 January 1936. A memorandum from the SS Hauptamt at the same time indicated that the SS card was subject to the same limits. National Archives Microcopy, T 175, Roll 31, frame 2538640.

[70] The issue was a common salute for Wehrmacht, SA, SS, and police that would have symbolized parity. The order was evidently withdrawn under Wehrmacht pressure. Bundesarchiv R 43II/422, Frick decree of 22 January 1935, memo of 9 January 1936, Lammers report of 18 January 1936.

[71] Institut für Zeitgeschichte Film 103/1, Deutsches Zentralarchiv, Potsdam, 49:01, folder labeled "Partei" with penciled catalogue number ZIIa.

[72] National Archives Microcopy, T 81, Roll 54, frame 157660.

public employees with a record of "particular services to the national cause." But even here there was evidence of a conservative reaction. It was inhibition of such promotions, not their encouragement, that was evidently on Frick's and Schwerin-Krosigk's minds. Thus age and educational qualifications were to be maintained and promotions to follow at official statutory intervals.[73] A statement of the Ministry of the Interior of February 1934 granted priority to candidates with a record of activity in organizations well-disposed toward the Volksgemeinschaft, but the priority was confined to candidates for the middle service, that requiring only a secondary school certificate without university study.[74] A supplementary decree of November 1934 granted a comparable priority to Werkabiturienten, those who had earned their secondary school certificates at their own expense. This was personnel policy in the interests of Volksgemeinschaft. The requirement of Hitler Youth membership of civil service candidates in November 1935 was a concession limited by its universality—by this time the Hitler Youth could scarcely be avoided by a university aspirant anyway—and by the implied distinction between Hitler Youth and Party. It was qualified still further by the protests of Reichenau and Keitel who demanded and got parity, irrespective of Hitler Youth membership, for pensioned veterans of the Wehrmacht.[75] "It repeatedly strikes the attention of Party offices," Hess protested in 1937, "that the directors of provincial agencies are concerned almost exclusively with professional qualifications. The question of political reliability is considered only to the extent to which it can be established that the political position of the civil servant in question is not explicitly antagonistic."[76] Only with a decree of February 1939 did Party membership become an official condition of application. It was then issued in the form: "The applicant must belong or have belonged to the Party or an affiliated organization."[77] This was tailored not only to meet the protests of the Wehrmacht, but also of

[73] Bundesarchiv R 43II/451, memo of 26 July 1933.
[74] Bundesarchiv R 43II/451, decree of 6 February 1934.
[75] Bundesarchiv R 43II/452, decree of 1 November 1935.
[76] Ibid., letter of Hess to Frick, 29 November 1937.
[77] Bundesarchiv R 43II/450a, decree of 28 February 1939.

the Labor Ministry, which complained of any further obstacles in what had already become an intolerable shortage of staff. Hans Frank too objected, perhaps disingenuously, that since the Party was to be an order (Führerorden), and Party membership therefore a status of some exaltation, it was inappropriate to demand such exaltation of all public officials.[78]

Promotion was a key issue. In a memo to the directors of the Reichsbahn and Reichsbank of July 1935, Frick declared that appointments and promotions were to remain the prerogative of the agency or department concerned.[79] In an interesting case in 1939, Hess protested the promotion of a non-Party member in the Ministry of Finance, and asked the Ministry of Interior to forbid the appointment of non-Party members to high administrative positions. "I have presented the matter to the Führer," Lammers replied. "The Führer has ruled (a) that until a further decision is taken, Party membership of civil servants eligible for promotion to important positions is only to be considered 'desirable,' and (b) that in a few years the matter is to be reconsidered."[80]

With evident confidence in Hitler's ultimate decision, this kind of sovereignty could be asserted at virtually every point. As early as summer 1933, Frick threatened to arrest Nazis. In December 1934, he announced with similar impunity that neither the corporatist organizations nor the Labor Front had any place in either State or municipal administration.[81] An apparent concession, Hitler's decree of 24 September 1935 made Hess a participant in the appointment of those civil servants Hitler himself appointed.[82] But an administrative decision of March 1938 pointed to the limits of the concession. In a memorandum of December 1937, Frick had declared political reliability a condition of promotion, but made it clear that the Minister was to be the judge. If in doubt,

[78] Ibid., Frank memo of 29 May 1938.

[79] Bundesarchiv R 43II/423, memo of 10 July 1935.

[80] Bundesarchiv R 43II/421a, Hess letter to Ministry of Finance of 21 March 1939, to Ministry of Interior of 10 March 1939, Lammers reply of 7 June 1939.

[81] Bundesarchiv R 43II/421.

[82] Cf. *Anordnungen des Stellvertreters des Führers*, 52/36 of 30 March 1936.

Frick said, he could consult the Party. The ruling was immediately challenged by Bormann and almost as quickly supported by Lammers with Hitler's implicit approval. Since it was the Führer who appointed officials, and not his Deputy, Lammers declared, it followed that the Führer's Deputy was not qualified to assume responsibility for promotion.[83] His position was firmly anchored in the Civil Service Act of January 1937,[84] which declared the civil servant directly responsible to Hitler as "executor (Vollstrecker) of the will of the NSDAP-supported State." This, plus the provision that appointment was to be declared invalid in cases where it only subsequently became known that the appointee had at the time of his apointment been excluded or rejected from the Party, exhausted the civil service role of the Party. The civil service disciplinary law at the same time institutionalized another aspect of the Party's impotence. The Party, Frick declared in a commentary to the new law, was to be informed of action against Party members and of the outcome of the case. The Führer's Deputy was to have the right to send a representative to the trial. But the participation in the constitution of the court was to be governed by the Ministry of the Interior and the Ministry of Justice "in co-operation with the Führer's Deputy." This meant, in effect, that the Party was to be represented in the form of officials who were incidentally Party members.[85] Any doubt of civil service mastery in its own house is resolved by State Secretary Pfundtner's remarkable memorandum of a few weeks later:

> "In a memorandum of 8 November 1933, I asked that any case of untruthful reply to the question of earlier Party affiliation in the questionnaires distributed in connection with the introduction of the Law on the Restoration of the Career Civil Service was to be pursued with the aim of dismissal from the service . . .
>
> "According to my request, the high administrative courts in

[83] Bundesarchiv R 43II/421, Frick memo of 18 December 1937, Bormann protest of 8 January 1938, Lammers reply of 28 March 1938.

[84] Text in Büttner, op. cit., pp. 189 ff.

[85] Bundesarchiv R 43II/444, Frick commentary of 30 January 1937 to law of 26 January 1937.

> the Reich and in the Länder have taken severe measures in the prosecution of such cases. . . . Among them are the cases of several civil servants who were members of the NSDAP before 30 January 1933.
>
> "Like the Führer's Deputy, I am of the opinion that the fundamental policy of the memorandum of 8 November 1933 must be maintained but that in the execution of the decision of the administrative court, the particular circumstances of the respective cases and the motivations that led to them must be considered.
>
> ". . . Thus in the cases of civil servants who demonstrably and actively supported National Socialism before 30 January 1933, in other words, of those who were not intended as targets of the laws named above, it remains to be seen whether the action resulting from this falsification of the questionnaire is to be prosecuted further with the ultimate goal of dismissal, or whether a lesser penalty is to be recommended.[86]

The unstated premise of this kind of sovereignty was, of course, the loyalty of the civil administration. The Ausschaltung (exclusion) of the Party was not an alternative to the Gleichschaltung (co-ordination) of the civil service but its complement. It was not for reasons of resistance that Party intervention failed, but for reasons of its own superfluousness. In part for reasons of fear and self-preservation, in part for reasons of sympathy, in part for reasons of stupidity, in part for reasons of "preventing the worst" like those Foreign Service officers who stayed at their desks in 1933 as they had stayed at their desks in 1918,[87] the civil service saw to its own Gleichschaltung. Since it commanded incomparably greater reserves of experience, discipline, and esprit than the Party, there was no reason, from an official point of view, why it should not. But the civil service paid for its external sovereignty in internal pressure, beginning with the purge of 1933. The bill was immediately presented in the form of the questionnaires on earlier political activity that Pfundtner mentioned, as well as reports on professional organizations.[88] Civil servants, who had enjoyed the illusion of serving the eternal State as distinguished from its ephemeral partisan rep-

[86] Bundesarchiv R 43II/422, Pfundtner memo of 19 March 1937.
[87] Cf. Seabury, op. cit., pp. 20–30.
[88] Bundesarchiv R 43II/422, Frick decree of 17 August 1935.

resentatives, then found themselves saying "Heil Hitler,"[89] and, in the law of 1937, swearing an oath to Hitler, the representative of the Party State. Paragraph 42 of the 1937 law made the civil servant responsible for reporting activities hostile to the State not to the Party but to his permanent undersecretary or to Lammers, a testimonial both to the apparent sovereignty of the civil service and to the price at which it was bought. Before the year was over, Lammers was advertising in the civil service journal in an effort to stop the flood of correspondence Paragraph 42 had brought him.[90]

If a Frick memo of January 1938 emphasized that church membership was to bring with it no professional disadvantages,[91] a supplementary decree of October 1938 forbade membership in confessional professional organizations.[92] Declarations of earlier Masonic activity were demanded in 1935,[93] and in 1939 written into personnel policy: Masons were no longer eligible for civil service jobs.[94] A decree of September 1937 ordered civil servants to remove their children from private schools. A boycott organized and enforced by the Beamtenbund required civil servants not to patronize department stores.[95] The regimentation of the civil service took symbolic form with the introduction of a civil service uniform on the foreign service model.[96] It took a practical

[89] Ibid., decree of 22 January 1935.

[90] Bundesarchiv R 43II/427b, Lammers' notice of August 1937 in "Der deutsche Verwaltungsbeamte" of 17 October 1937.

[91] Bundesarchiv R 43II/422a, Frick memo of 3 January 1938. In its apparent tolerance, the memo nonetheless, of course, made one exception.

[92] Ibid., decree of 4 October 1938.

[93] Bundesarchiv R 43II/423.

[94] Ibid., decree of 6 June 1939. It was, to be sure, very mild personnel policy. Higher degree Masons were to be kept out of personnel departments and still-active members of the third degree or higher were either ineligible for employment, or, if already employed, for promotion. Cf. Hess-Frick correspondence of 19 July 1937 and 26 August 1937 in the same file.

[95] Bundesarchiv R 43II/423, decree of 9 September 1937, correspondence of January 1938. Cf. Uhlig, op. cit., p. 178.

[96] Bundesarchiv R 43II/465a, Lammers' memo of 1 August 1938. A Hitler decree of 30 March 1939 exempted those who already wore the uniform of the party or an affiliated organization.

form of unique severity in 1939 in Goebbels' intervention in his capacity as Minister to prevent the marriage of one of his higher ministerial officials to an Italian.[97]

Other symptoms pointed directly at falling standards and declining morale, among them symbolic protocol complaints, easier application requirements, and loss of personnel. Senior Prussian civil servants were enraged to be seated with the public at the Reich harvest festival in October 1934 while certain Reich colleagues, Army officers, and Party officials occupied a private stand.[98] The presiding judge of the high court of the Reich acknowledged receipt "finally" of a good seat at the Berlin Olympics. In a letter from the Minister of Justice to Frick, it was reported that at the recent Heidelberg University anniversary celebration the judge had been excluded from Hitler's reception and finally got a ticket only through the intervention of Hans Frank.[99]

After an extended interministerial discussion, a decree from the Minister of Finance in conjunction with the Reich Chancellery in June 1938 reduced the candidacy for the higher civil service from four to two years, and included further concessions for time already spent in professional activity outside the public administration, as well as for good Party records. With the proper qualifications, candidacy could be cut from four years to one.[100] A subsequent decree of the Ministry of Interior extended certain advantages to winners of the Reich Vocational Competitions, not only for entrance to the middle service, but for entry into the higher service without the statutory educational requirements.[101] At the same time, Frick saw himself obliged to protest the employment of too many municipal employees to high municipal civil service positions

[97] Bundesarchiv R 55/aus No. 50 of 26 October 1939.

[98] Bundesarchiv R 43II/463, memo of Staatssekretär Körner of 13 October 1934.

[99] Ibid., letter of Minister of Justice to Minister of Interior of 3 August, 1936.

[100] Bundesarchiv R 43II/451, Frick memo of 3 February 1936, memos of Ministry of Propaganda of 15 March 1937, Hess of 16 April 1937, Lammers of 1 July 1937, Hess staff of 1 July 1937, Frick of 6 September 1937, and decree of 7 June 1938.

[101] Ibid., decree of 21 April 1939.

without the necessary qualifications.[102] An interesting index of the relationship of Nazi State and civil service was a memo of Frick's to his staff in February 1937 protesting the continuation of the traditional practice of sending incompetent staff members to virtual exile in Silesia and East Prussia. A second memo on the subject, a week before the beginning of the war, indicated clearly that the practice went on nonetheless.[103]

The salary situation was perhaps the most revealing. In 1939, the civil servant, like the rest of the employed population, was still living on the scale of Brüning's deflationary budget. Budget increases were going into staff, not salaries. Frick underlined the civil administration's worsening competitive position in a memo to Lammers. Two young municipal officials in Düsseldorf, both from traditional civil service families, had resigned, complaining they were unable to live on RM 204 a month.[104] In his own Ministry the net monthly income of a Regierungsrat with wife and two children, RM 471.72, left him with a net monthly deficit of RM 44.43, Frick reported. A Regierungssekretär—the junior rank in the national civil service scale—with one child, earned RM 218.38 net.[105]

Carried out under fire from Hess, the wage debate was another symptom of the tortuous relationship of State and Party. In a memo to Hitler, Hess suggested the alternatives of a tough selection with higher salaries for those who survived it, direct connection of the civil service scale with the general wage scale, or restriction of salary increases to the lower categories. In their reply, Frick and Schwerin-Krosigk indignantly pointed out that the Party had already anticipated any civil service increase by paying its own officials a thirteen-month salary (with the thirteenth month in the form of a Christmas bonus), and this despite a general salary level al-

[102] Ibid., decree of 22 May 1939.

[103] Bundesarchiv R 43II/423, Frick memos of 5 February 1937 and 21 July 1939.

[104] Bundesarchiv R 43II/433a, Frick memo to Lammers of 29 July 1938, citation of letter from Landrat von Werder to Regierungspräsident in Düsseldorf of 18 July 1938.

[105] Bundesarchiv R 43II/432, report of 1 December 1937.

ready above that of the civil service.[106] The result was an interesting compromise. Rather than granting a visible increase, Hitler conceded a 3 per cent tax cut in 1939. Released in the form of a decree of the Ministry of Finance, the measure was labeled "top secret," excluded from publication in the ministerial journals, and kept from the press.[107]

The complement of this budgetary pressure was status pressure, an effort to compensate income with prestige. Symptomatic was a kind of revolt of the engineers, characterized by the demands of a Bavarian civil servant for reorganization, direction of technical departments by technical personnel instead of lawyers, and parity of status for technical civil servants with their administrative counterparts.[108] Though presented not to the Ministry of Interior at all but to Hitler's adjutant Brückner, the demand turned up in a conspicuous position in a memo from Pfundtner a few months later. A structural reform was as urgent as a salary reform, Pfundtner declared to Lammers, though he indicated his own reluctance to integrate "foreign bodies in the administrative apparatus" and implied that the idea had in fact come from Todt, the Autobahn commissioner. In any case, he recommended formation of a committee to study the matter. Pfundtner's list of candidates indicated the center of administrative-political gravity of the Third Reich after six years of "national revolution": himself, Lammers, the Minister of Finance, the Plenipotentiary for the Four-Year Plan, Hess, and "perhaps" the Prussian Minister of Finance. Lammers' reply indicated basic approval and no initiative.[109]

In the absence of a systematic reform, the ad hoc activity so characteristic of the Third Reich was reflected in a correspondence of April 1938 dealing with an upward revaluation of official titles. The Ministries of the Interior, Finance, Posts and Telegraph, and Church Affairs went on record in

106 Bundesarchiv R 43II/432b, Hess memo of 21 June 1939; Frick-Schwerin-Krosigk reply of 30 June 1939.

107 Bundesarchiv R 21/430, decree of Ministry of Finance, 12 July 1939.

108 Bundesarchiv R 43II/422a, letter of 30 November 1938.

109 Ibid., Pfundtner memo of 13 February 1939, Lammers' reply of 4 March 1939.

favor of it, Lammers on record against. "There are already indications," he declared, "that the sons of higher civil servants have opted against legal study because they said to themselves that such positions as they might previously have reached as jurists can be attained today by a more comfortable route." But, as he added, his was a minority position.[110] The majority was conscious, as the Minister of Church Affairs wrote, that "since the civil service pay scale has not followed the development of the general economy, it has become extremely difficult and in many cases impossible to find qualified civil servants or even to attract potentially qualified candidates."[111] If a higher title was any compensation for a higher salary, they were apparently prepared to offer it. With the inflation of titles came a parallel upward adjustment of the retirement age, again typical of the effects of the Third Reich on the civil service. It was no less typical that the retirement age was raised despite Party opposition.[112]

If the civil service survived the institutional struggle, weakened but still functional, the Party came out only somewhat more effective than the SA. The uncertainty of its constitutional function, in the absence of stable prerogatives, tended to provoke a kind of embarrassed mysticism from its commentators,[113] in which it could only be defined as "movement," intermediary between "State," "Führer," and "Volk," as a Volkskirche (People's Church), or as an "order."[114] The terminology covered a two-front struggle in which the Party was obliged not only to assert itself against outside competitors, but against its own centrifugal forces. If Hess failed to assert the Party's authority outside, he succeeded at least in asserting his own within the Party, an authority that covered a huge organization with a vast bureaucracy and a kind of

[110] Bundesarchiv R 43II/442, memo of 23 April 1938.

[111] Bundesarchiv R 43II/423a, memo of Minister of Church Affairs of 11 November 1938.

[112] Lower retirement age was one of the first reforms the party wanted to impose on the civil service. Cf. Bundesarchiv R 43II/447; R 43II/423a, Frick memo of 26 October 1938, amendment of civil service act of 25 March 1939.

[113] Cf. Bauer, op. cit., pp. 1, 9; Bracher, in Bracher, Schulz, and Sauer, op. cit., pp. 217 ff.

[114] Cf. Schulz, in Bracher, Schulz, and Sauer, op. cit., pp. 583 ff.

influence on public opinion. The continued maintenance of Party headquarters in Munich after 1933 was indicative enough of the Party's distance from the center of things. It managed nonetheless, according to an interview with its treasurer, to fill forty-four Munich houses with 1600 employees. This structure was filled out in the rest of the country by an administrative staff of 25,000.[115]

But a collection of executive orders from Party headquarters reveals how curiously intangible was the substance on which this administrative structure was built. Party staffs were requested to maintain reliable files,[116] to look after—or alternatively to avoid—patronage,[117] to set a good example in the consumption of scarce commodities like meat,[118] and to make a good public appearance.[119] In this case, white shirt and white collar were recommended as well as an "avoidance of excess." Occasionally benefits were announced.[120]

A series of administrative orders was a commentary on general discipline and perhaps on morale. A Gauleiter was dismissed for originating the rumor that a colleague's wife was not 100 per cent "aryan,"[121] Party officials were reproached for granting their chauffeurs political rank,[122] respective bureaus of the Party administration were called upon to initial orders originating in other bureaus that infringed on their areas of competence,[123] Party officers were forbidden to undertake any statistical survey without approval from Munich and required to prevent circulation of existing Party statistics outside the Party.[124] An order of 1935 reserved the appoint-

[115] Interview with Reichsschatzmeister Schwarz in VB, 27 February 1935.

[116] *Anordnungen des Stellvertreters des Führers,* 52/36 of 30 March 1936.

[117] Ibid., 63/36 of 27 April 1936.

[118] Ibid., 129/36 of 6 October 1936.

[119] Ibid., 116/36 of 4 September 1936.

[120] Ibid., 26/36 of 19 February 1936. Bormann let it be known that the Ministry of Labor had been notified by the Reichsbahn that disabled Alte Kämpfer were to be treated the same way as disabled war veterans.

[121] Ibid., 99/36 of 8 August 1936.

[122] Ibid., 109/36 of 15 August 1936.

[123] Ibid., 126/36 of 5 October 1936.

[124] Ibid., 114/36 of 4 September 1936.

ment of all higher Party officials to the personal judgment of Hess.[125] At the same time, the Party tended to give up its competences or potential competences without a fight—a Division for Cultural Peace intended to deal with church affairs in 1934, an Office of Racial Affairs (Nationalsozialistische Auskunft) and the Office for Corporatist Organizations in 1935, a Division for the Maintenance of Professional Morality in 1936. The Party intelligence service was absorbed by the SS.[126]

For the Alte Kämpfer as such, the benefits of victory were sparse. A priority list to be used in the employment of postal messenger boys put the sons of dead or severely disabled Alte Kämpfer first, followed by the sons of disabled Alte Kämpfer, war orphans, sons of dead or disabled postal employees, sons of disabled war veterans, sons of families of four or more children, and finally, sons of active postal employees.[127] A Hitler order of 29 March 1935 asking places in the lower and lower-middle ranks of the civil service for publicly employed and unemployed (pre-1930) Alte Kämpfer was still under active consideration in November 1937. Since the order had been issued, there had been indications of employers who had refused to hire them. The Ministry of the Interior ordered that those employed by State or municipal agencies should be granted civil service status effective 1 April 1938, a decision that meant that thirty-six Alte Kämpfer engaged as technicians on the stages of opera houses in Berlin and Wiesbaden advanced from monthly incomes of RM 124–178 to RM 140–289. In its practical consequences, the transfer to civil service status meant a loss of net income for some younger employees. They nonetheless accepted, though a request for compensation for the loss involved in the honor was turned down.[128]

For a majority of Alte Kämpfer, the Third Reich soon

[125] Ibid., 79/35 of 18 April 1935.

[126] Cf. Schäfer, op. cit., p. 48.

[127] VB, 20 September 1935.

[128] Bundesarchiv R 55/aus No. 50, memo of Interior Ministry of 19 November 1937, survey of Ministry of Propaganda of 23 February 1938, rejection of application for compensation of 14 April 1938.

turned from the promised land to yet another in the long line of betrayed revolutions. By the beginning of 1935, nearly 20 per cent of the functionary staff with pre-1933 membership, over half of them local Party leaders,[129] had again left the Party. Not surprisingly, the withdrawal of former Strasser functionaries proceeded about half again as fast as the withdrawal of what had been Ley's staff.[130] Necessarily, the growing Party machine absorbed increasingly large concentrations of younger functionaries who, in turn, engendered a generation conflict that weakened the Party once again. While the Gau offices continued to be in the hands of the Alte Kämpfer, post-1933 functionaries took over at the respective sublevels of Kreis and Ort, and thus, in the complicated hierarchical command structure, at more effective positions. The dilemma of the Alte Kämpfer—transfer to the Kreis or Ort level meant more effective power but also loss of status and influence at higher Party levels—was neatly expressed in a directive indicating that measures taken at the Kreis level were to be passed down only in cases where "it is absolutely necessary that the political leaders of the Ort and Stützpunkt groups be aware of them."[131] While older Party functionaries stuck to higher Party levels in the interest of their prestige and security at the cost of effective power, Party-appointed mayors, forced to choose between their civil and their Party duties, tended to leave the Party altogether for the same reason. Nearly 40 per cent of the Party-appointed mayors and over half of the Landräte were inactive in the Party by 1935, a trend recognized in the municipal code of 1935 that dissolved the so-called "personal union" of local Party and civil functions.[132] The passage of time obviously made Party careers less rather than more attractive. By 1938, Kreisleitun-

[129] Schäfer, op. cit., p. 41.
[130] Ibid., p. 42.
[131] Ibid., p. 46.
[132] By 1944 municipal appointment seemed to be entirely a matter of luck, recommendations, and technical qualifications. Only in the biggest cities, it seems, did direct Party sponsorship of mayors continue and even here, as in Frankfurt, Party offices protested without any evident result that the mayor refused to co-operate with the Party but went his own administrative way. Bundesarchiv R 18/2030.

gen, relatively high Party organs, were reporting unfilled administrative jobs.[133] Ley's staff in 1937 noted an impressive scarcity of suitable and interested candidates for Party administration even in East Prussia.[134]

Meanwhile university graduates, the traditional source of civil service recruitment, continued as before to go into the civil administration, not the Party.[135] What was new was Party recommendation supplementary to academic training, a frequent record of Party activity, and an understandable tendency to gravitate to the centers of speedy promotion and growing influence like the Propaganda and Interior Ministries, rather than the more traditional administrative centers.[136]

[133] This might have had something to do with the salary scale. The director of a department in the Kreisleitung in Rothenburg was offered RM 190 monthly, a chauffeur RM 150. Bundesarchiv Gau Franken/2, *Personalstatistik,* Report of Kreisleiter Rothenburg o. Tauber of 27 May 1939, Kreisleiter Erlangen of 11 July 1938.

[134] Bundesarchiv NS 22/565, letter to Ley from Gauleitung Ostpreussen of 4 May 1937.

[135] Bundesarchiv R 55/62, applications to Propaganda Ministry of 1937–39. An interesting commentary on the striking conservatism of even the "revolutionary" cadres was the application in 1937 of a young lawyer, born in 1910, for a job in the Propaganda Ministry. It indicated that he was prepared to sacrifice his present position with the Newspaper Publishers Association at RM 800 monthly for the security of a civil service position at RM 293.

[136] Bundesarchiv R 43II/458a. An example was the recommended promotion on 29 September 1938, of a Regierungsassessor in the Ministry of the Interior who was born in 1906 and a Party member since 1928. Between 1927 and 1930 he had been active in the Nazi student organization. The candidate had passed his second State bar examination, the condition for employment in the higher civil service, in 1936, and been employed in Hitler's Führer Chancellery before coming to the Ministry of the Interior. Although it was pointed out that the candidate had not held his present rank the mandatory four years, and had no experience in the provincial administration as ordinarily required, his promotion was nonetheless confirmed. Of nine candidates presented for promotion to Ministerialrat at the same time in 1941, that is, to the third higher civil service rank, all had been born between 1909 and 1910, joined the Party between 1928 and 1931, passed their second State examinations between 1936 and 1938, and entered the Ministry of the Interior, where they won their first promotions in 1938/39.

The alternative to the civil service, in part its complement, in part in competition with it, was the SS. With the possible exception of the Labor Front, it was the Third Reich's outstanding example of a successful institutional innovation. Confining itself initially to infiltration rather than direct challenge, and to quasi-conservative elite ideology in sharp and conscious distinction to the populist egalitarianism of SA and party, the SS succeeded where its competitors failed. By 1939, when the SA had long ceased to have any meaning at all and the functions of the Party, despite its huge numbers and vast administrative machine, stagnated in a kind of querulous Moral Rearmament combined with patronage, the SS had become a real organ of State, ultimately responsible only to Hitler. If Himmler's status as Chief of German Police according to a statute of 1937 ambiguously subordinated him to the Ministry of the Interior—he was called "autonomous deputy"—the extension of his police prerogatives in the form of the Waffen-SS gave him, in effect, parity with the Wehrmacht.

The separate but equal status granted the Waffen-SS in 1938 and then transferred to other SS detachments like the so-called Disposal Forces (Verfügungs-Verbände) responsible for the concentration camps, created an institutional priority for the SS in the occupied areas superior to those of State and Party. Himmler's ideological prerogatives in his capacity as Commissar for the Consolidation of the German Race (Reichskommissar für die Festigung deutschen Volkstums) were institutionalized, in turn, in the so-called Office for Race and Settlement (Rasse- und Siedlungshauptamt), the basis of a new authority over certain of the occupied territories that reduced the Foreign Office, by comparison, to a minor diplomatic auxiliary.[137]

If it was the war itself that brought the potentialities of the SS to their full realization,[138] the structural and, above

[137] Cf. Hans Buchheim, "Die SS in der Verfassung des dritten Reiches," *Vierteljahrshefte für Zeitgeschichte*, 1955, pp. 130 ff.; Seabury, op. cit., p. 112.

[138] Symptomatic indications of this can be found in the relatively modest dimensions of the SS—it numbered only 146,000 at the end of 1937 and 162,000 at the end of 1938—and the stagnation

all, the sociological nucleus of its growth was organized at the very beginning. From 1933 on, the SS exploited its status as *the* Nazi elite to attract members of the old social elites into an institutional identification with the new regime incomparably more attractive than the unwashed Volksgemeinschaft of Party or SA.[139] With its ideological predilections and expansive capacities, the SS also offered new careers and promotion possibilities for university graduates—particularly in law and medicine—that could scarcely be matched by any other institution. Its attraction for the young could be seen in the average age—29.2 in 1938;[140] for the sons of aristocratic families, in the relatively high concentration of aristocrats in its leadership—9 per cent, or 58 of 648 with the rank of colonel or higher in 1938,[141] and for those in liberal professions, in its absolute membership figures. At the end of 1938, nearly 12,000 of these were SS members, including roughly 3000 lawyers and 3000 doctors.[142]

Behind the façade of social respectability was the comparable attraction of equal career opportunities despite what in

---

of membership in years immediately before the war. Even the apparent growth of membership between 1937 and 1938 tended to be an optical illusion caused by the organizational annexation of a number of police organs. In the meanwhile, the SS admitted the resistance of skeptical fathers who urged their sons to join the Wehrmacht instead, and the loss of active functionaries to better paying jobs in industry. Cf. *Statistische Jahrbücher der Schutzstaffel der NSDAP,* and National Archives Microcopy T 175, Roll 17, frames 2520662 ff. Yearly Report of SS of 31 December 1938.

[139] Ermenhild Neusüss-Hunkel, *Die SS,* Hanover and Frankfurt, 1956, pp. 15 f.; Eugen Kogon, *Der SS-Staat,* Munich, 1946, p. 288. Characteristic elements of the recruitment campaign included even the black uniform, which was not distributed but tailored like a military officer's uniform at the owner's expense, or the absorption of aristocratic names by the device of making participation in riding competitions dependent on SS membership, and thus the organizational annexation of riding clubs. These, in the form of SS-Reiterstürmen, had the distinction of being the only SS group to be acquitted of criminal activity at Nuremberg. Neusüss-Hunkel, op. cit., p. 16; Kogon, op. cit., p. 288.

[140] *Statistisches Jahrbuch der Schutzstaffel der NSDAP,* op. cit., 1938, p. 62.

[141] Neusüss-Hunkel, op. cit., p. 16.

[142] *Statistisches Jahrbuch der Schutzstaffel der NSDAP,* op. cit., 1938, p. 103.

the regular civil service would have been unequal qualifications. The SS officer candidate schools organized at Bad Tölz in 1934 and Brunswick in 1935 were commanded, characteristically, by a former lieutenant general of the Reichswehr but required no academic preparation of their candidates.[143] In 1938, a decree of the Ministry of Education granted the SS Administration School parity with similar Party institutions. Candidates could apply without secondary school certificates and had the opportunity to go on subsequently to study economics at a university.[144] The military possibilities of the SS exercised a comparable attraction for frustrated younger officers like the later SS Generals Wolff and von dem Bach-Zelewski without in any way reducing the chances of genuine specimens of the Volk like Sepp Dietrich, the illegitimate son of a Bavarian farm girl.[145]

The product of this combination of opportunity and snob appeal, mixed with elements of bizarre idealism, was a unique mixture of open society and secret society, whose prerogatives extended to virtually every province of public life. In one form or another, the SS made foreign policy, military policy, and agricultural policy. It administered occupied territories as a kind of self-contained Ministry of the Interior and maintained itself economically with autonomous enterprises. Unlike other Nazi institutions, which aspired to one or another of the State functions, the SS potentially superseded the State, reproducing it within its own ranks and even endowing it with administrative novelties hitherto unknown in more conventional practice. An interesting example was the policy of holding ranks in the so-called Security Service, the nucleus of the political police, artificially low so that rank and authority no longer coincided. It was thus not only theoretically but practically possible that an officer of the Security Service could be superior to an SS officer who outranked him.[146] But it

[143] Cf. Neusüss-Hunkel, op. cit., pp. 23, 36.

[144] Bundesarchiv R 21/446, memo of the Ministry of Education of 10 December 1940.

[145] Cf. Gerald Reitlinger, *The SS*, London, 1956, pp. 76 ff.

[146] Cf. Neusüss-Hunkel, op. cit., p. 21. An exemplary case was of course Adolf Eichmann who, with the rank of lieutenant colonel (Obersturmbannführer), was invited to the so-called Wannsee

should be remembered that this all took place in wartime and, equally important, for the most part outside the boundaries of the prewar Reich. While the expansive potential of the SS existed long before, the Third Reich was full of expansive potentials—not to mention the ruins of what had once been expansive potentials. Even the informed observer, surrounded as he was by the formidable dynamism of the Third Reich in which he lived, although he might have been aware of where the race would lead, had no more than betting certainty of who would be the first to arrive there. His standpoint in 1939, after six peacetime years of Nazi rule, was something like the mid-point in a steeplechase.[147]

The difficulties involved in defining the quality of the State in which he lived were implied in its very salary schedules. Effective in 1937, the permanent undersecretaries, the presiding judges of the Reich courts, the presiding officer of the budget bureau (Reichsfinanzhof), the Reichsführer SS, the leader of the Hitler Youth, and the General Inspector of Highway Construction were a single group. According to Hitler's option, the chiefs of police responsible for security (Sicherheitspolizei) and civil order (Ordnungspolizei) were to be classed either in the same group, or with the ambassadors, a group lower.[148]

While this was symptomatic enough of the "revolution of destruction" that was unquestionably in progress, it was by

conference of 20 January 1942 in the company, among others, of four permanent undersecretaries and three SS generals, to discuss the "final solution of the Jewish problem," before being sent to various European capitals to help arrange it.

[147] An early wartime memo from a high-ranking SS officer points to the variety of possibilities, and no less the uncertainties, of even those who were running. In a letter of 26 February 1940 an SS general reported that the Wehrmacht had introduced an accelerated program to train Party functionaries as commissioned and non-commissioned officers. This, he concluded, represented an effort to buy off the Party from its previous support for the SS. He accordingly suggested that the SS appeal to the Party by instituting a comparable program. National Archives Microcopy, T 175, Roll 127, frames 2652401–2.

[148] Bundesarchiv R 43II/430c, undated salary schedule of 1937. The salary of the first group was fixed at RM 24,000 yearly, of the second at RM 19,000.

no means clear to the contemporary observer. Rauschning, it need scarcely be said, was the exception and not the rule. The very anarchy of Nazi manifestations itself led to error, euphemism, and recourse to the familiar static models of normal historical experience. This was as understandable as it was disastrous, when what was required to appreciate the reality of National Socialism, its "stability through movement," was a kind of social-historical calculus. In the absence of such a calculus, capable of integrating all the dynamic components of National Socialism, the contemporary observer saw instead the single aspects that he wanted to see or had been trained to see, like the last stage of monopoly capitalism, or the triumph of the efficiency experts,[149] or the spirit of Prussian militarism.[150] All of these were certainly there to see, but even in 1939 more reassuring elements would have seemed at least to balance the scales, at least for the German observer—providing he was not Jewish, not locked up, and not excessively interested in pogroms or the disappearance of neighbors. He, after all, had to continue to live in the Third Reich. For him, the demonic elements could still be dismissed as the circus half of "bread and circuses," and even the undeniable terror as a transitory phenomenon. The State continued to be the State. The voluptuous growth and disorganization of its institutions was no occasion for confidence—but equally, considering the risks, no occasion for action. The eternal conflicts of Economics Ministry, Reichsbank, Labor

[149] Cf. Robert A. Brady, *The Spirit and Structure of German Fascism*, London, 1937.

[150] Cf. Sumner Welles, *The Time for Decision*, Cleveland and New York, 1944, pp. 336 ff. "Throughout the past one hundred years, whether the rallying point for German patriotism was the venerable figure of William I, Bismarck, the superficial and spectacular William II, the Marshal President Hindenburg, or, in most recent times, Hitler himself, public opinion in this country (the United States) has always been prone to take the figurehead as the reality. It has overlooked the fact that German policy during the past eighty years has been inspired and directed, not by the Chief of State, but by the German General Staff." The irony of such a proposition in the mouth of a U. S. Undersecretary of State in the year 1944 can only be the object of awe and respect for human fallibility.

Front, and the General Plenipotentiary for the Four Year Plan, the existence of up to three foreign ministries, the potential existence of two armies and an air force, could be rationalized both juridically and practically. They were legal and they would, in one way or another, take care of themselves. The true believer was prepared to accept them as given, the non-Nazi or anti-Nazi, as an object for resignation or even a kind of optimism. "These people have no idea what a state is like," von Hassell, a particularly perceptive anti-Nazi, noted in his diary. "Such an apparatus is incapable of surviving the test of war."[151] From here it was only a step to the conclusion that war was impossible, that Hitler's divided house could not stand. None of these ways led of itself to revolutionary conclusions.

For the average citizen, the Third Reich, in its 1939 form, was not the product of Hitler's "legality" tactics of pre-1933, now extended to the civil administration, but legality itself.[152] By and large, the development of the Nazi State had reinforced this belief as often as it had shaken it. The "revolutionary" situation of 1933/34 was already giving way to "revolutionary legality" by the summer of 1933. The purge of 30 June 1934 had, in fact, wiped out the "revolution" with one blow. What followed might offend good taste and even good sense, but it was still within the realm of the familiar. The civil service went on as before, the familiar names of its most prominent representatives—Meissner, Papen, von Neurath, Syrup, or Schacht as examples—still figured prominently enough in its public representation to guarantee a semblance both of respectability and of continuity. Young men continued to make their careers in the civil service after the regular completion of the regular studies. As Hitler, the profligate Prince Hal, became King Henry, the Alte Kämpfer had, by and large, been repulsed from the bastions of the State like so many old Falstaffs. Their continued drone of contempt for Bonzen (big wheels), civil servants, Akademiker, teachers,

[151] Hassell, op. cit., p. 87.

[152] This is not to say it was legality, but only that it was felt to be legality. Cf. Bracher, in Bracher, Schulz, and Sauer, op. cit., Ch. III.

lawyers, could be interpreted as the expression of frustration.[153]

For the civil servant himself, the situation seemed far from hopeless. The purge had been confined to relatively modest limits; the new masters like Frick and later Ribbentrop were no less concerned with the traditional prerogatives than their predecessors. The disadvantages of public employment—first the salary level, then declining prestige—were in any case long-term trends. They had not begun in 1933.[154] To balance them, the Third Reich was capable of symbolic rewards to civil servants like the appointment of the permanent Undersecretaries in the Reich and Presidential Chancelleries, Lammers and Meissner, to ministerial rank.[155]

Confident of their indispensability and, equally, intimidated by the prospects of rebellion, trained in the tradition of positivist legality and susceptible to the argument of "the lesser evil," the civil servants in effect held their offices by virtue of their own capitulation. Carried into the abyss on an escalator that had required of them only the first step, they realized much later, if ever, that they had surrendered the State they thought they were serving.

153 Cf. Walter Tiessler, "Klassenkampf," *Der Hoheitsträger*, June 1939, pp. 10 f. According to Tiessler, even this was to stop. "We have to stop holding the old sins of all professional groups under the noses of all other professional groups," Tiessler wrote in a party organ. In fact, the elimination of this practice, as he saw it, was the party functionary's foremost task.

154 Otto Most, *Zur Wirtschafts- und Sozialstatistik der höheren Beamten in Preussen*, Munich-Leipzig, 1916. Most traced the decline in salary and status back to at least 1866.

155 Bundesarchiv R 43II/430c, decree of November 1937.

VIII

The Third Reich and Social Opportunity

While there was never any doubt that National Socialism was a social revolutionary movement, the problem of a social revolutionary ideology was one it never solved. Point 20 of the Party program endorsed the career open to talent, but this had been a commonplace of every movement with popular ambitions since 1789. Point 4, on the other hand, imposed an exclusion principle. Citizenship henceforth was to be a matter not of birth or wealth or aptitudes, but of "race." Point 9, in turn, proclaimed the goal of equal rights and obligations for all citizens. Since Point 20 presupposed a Leistungsgemeinschaft (a community of achievement) while Points 4 and 9 presupposed a Volksgemeinschaft (a community of national affiliation), the result was a potential dilemma. Points 4 and 9 led by logical extension to a classless society; Point 20, to a new set of classes. Equal opportunity derived from equal rights had been, since at least 1789, the classical European solution of this dilemma. But for Nazis with serious feelings about "race," it was not so easy to solve. If it was true that all Germans—in either a national or a "racial" sense—were superior to all non-Germans, it was also true that some Germans were superior to other Germans. If the natural superiority of all Germans was the premise of the Volksgemeinschaft, the natural superiority of some Germans was the premise of the Leistungsgemeinschaft, and, more important, of the Führerprinzip. But how reconcile this Führerprinzip with equal rights and obligations? In its practical implications, the attempt to square an elite principle with an equality principle was an attempt to square the circle.

Not surprisingly, Nazi theorists, rather than trying to solve the problem, tended to deny its existence. "We hold no brief for equality," Goebbels declared in an early editorial. "We want classes, high and low, up and down."[1] But only the bravest or the foolhardiest were prepared to say how and where they ought to come about. Gregor Strasser, in a speech to the Bavarian Landtag in 1926, presented a grandiose plan for the new society, in which military service was to be voluntary, but everyone who did not serve was to learn a manual trade. Since, however, military service demanded more time, involved more danger, and produced less practical advantage, it could be assumed that those who accepted it were by definition superior and entitled to commensurate rewards in the form of multiple suffrage. For women, motherhood was to be the equivalent of military service.[2] Privately —according to Rauschning[3]—Darré and Hitler also enjoyed social revolutionary day dreams in which the old class structure fell prey to the vitality of a new elite whose (assumed) biological superiority was to be the basis of a new society. But considerations of expediency alone, quite apart from considerations of logic, reduced such speculations to a minimum.

For a movement that aspired to mass popularity, elitism was practical only to the extent that anybody could identify

[1] Goebbels, *Angriff*, p. 224, editorial of 23 July 1928.

[2] Strasser admitted that "at first glance, this might appear utopian." Gregor Strasser, op. cit., pp. 133 f.; cf. Ch. VI.

[3] "Let me tell you how the new social order will look," Rauschning quoted Hitler. "There will be a ruling class (Herrenschicht), historically rooted, composed of the most divergent elements and born in struggle. There will be the mass of hierarchically organised Party members. This will be the new middle class. And then there will be the anonymous mass of those who serve (Kollektiv der Dienenden), who never achieve their majority (ewig Unmündige), irrespective of what they were before, representatives of the old bourgeoisie, estate owners, or manual workers. . . . Then there will be the class of subjugated foreigners; we can call them the modern slave class. And above all, there will be a new high nobility of particularly deserving and particularly responsible Führer-personalities. . . . The East will be our field of experimentation. This is where the new European social order will be created. And this is the great significance of our Eastern policy." Rauschning, *Gespräche*, p. 44.

himself with the future elite. The practical definition of this elite had therefore to be as expansive as possible, a mixture of biological hocus-pocus—since nearly everybody could be Germanic but very few gebildet (educated) or aristocratic—and appeals to traditional social antagonisms. In practical application, this scarcely looked like elitism at all, but just another form of populism with side appeals to the general national weakness for the Fachmann (the apolitical expert)[4] and the strong man. Condemnation of democracy[5] was part of the Zeitgeist, an appeal to nostalgia for the prewar world, a way of opposing the status quo. But mixed with rhetorical contempt for a degenerate aristocracy or a decadent bourgeoisie, for wealth or diplomas, there was nothing intrinsically elitist, no direct element of Männerbund or knightly order, about it.[6] The appeal was, rather, egalitarian with a platitudinous commitment to equal opportunity. This, if anything, was the social program that appealed to simple souls like Drexler[7] and that formed the main stuff of *Mein Kampf*.[8] Since, officially, no one was himself elite but only the movement itself, every individual was potentially as elite as he chose to see himself. Further differentiation would only have led to trouble. Reflecting more than thirty years later on his Party experience, Otto Strasser recalled that Party, SA, and

[4] Cf. Heuss, op. cit., pp. 65 f. "It was characteristic that the first critique of German parliamentarism was based on the professional training of the new ministers. So strong, despite all disappointment, was the faith in the capacity—including political capacity—of a trained civil service."

[5] "It is the double curse of the present democratic-parliamentary system that it is not only incapable itself of producing genuinely creative achievements but that it also prevents the rise and thus the achievements of such men who somehow stand out above the average." Hitler, *Zweites Buch*, p. 67.

[6] Symptomatically, despite apparent similarities of style and ideology, elitist youth groups were in fact indifferent if not hostile. Hitler converts from this direction, like Baldur von Schirach, were the exception. Cf. Walter Laqueur, *Young Germany*, London, 1962.

[7] Drexler, op. cit., p. 38.

[8] Hitler called this "Germanische Demokratie." *Mein Kampf*, p. 344. "It is not the task of the völkisch state to maintain the predominant influence of an existing class, but to find the most capable of all its Volksgenossen and bring them to office and honor." Ibid., p. 424.

SS alike enjoyed feelings of superiority with respect both to the world and to one another, all of them equally indulged by Hitler who was their only positive common denominator.[9]

Even at this early stage, however, there were visible sociological differentiations, ranging from the inner circle of Hitler's petit bourgeois Party cronies like Streicher, Amann, and Esser, to the young bearers of old aristocratic names already being cultivated by Himmler. In contrast, ex-officers and career soldiers in general tended to gravitate to the SA, according to Strasser, and rather less to the SS where Himmler had reason to suspect that their previous autonomy and traditional commitments might cause personal or ideological conflicts. But where all this was to lead was left to private speculation. Some, like Nicolai, dreamed of a Beamtenstaat,[10] some, like Himmler, of a Praetorian Guard.[11] Hans Schwarz van Berk, a Party publicist, wanted to see the future elite in an exclusive party, reorganized on the basis of a knightly order. In place of an obsolete bourgeoisie and a bankrupt labor movement, a new civil leadership was to arise,

[9] Interview with author, op. cit. This is not to say that there were no negative common denominators. Strasser himself referred to the common anti-Communism, anti-Semitism, anti-capitalism (however this might be understood), and anti-clericalism of all Nazi groups. They were also in favor of a better deal for the common man, and the priority of the common good over private gain—but who was not? What both united all Nazi groups and differentiated them from all non-Nazi groups was not a program but attraction to Hitler.

[10] "Mediary between the highest civil authority and the Volk in a National Socialist State is, as today, the civil official (Beamte). . . . The human material adequate to the tasks facing the public official must be chosen according to rigid requirements of character and intellect. For Party patronage officials (Parteibuchbeamte) . . . the National Socialist State has no room." Rudolf Roebling, "Staat und Volk," in Wagner, op. cit., pp. 101 f. While this presumably referred to SPD officials, Nicolai's memoranda make it clear that only SPD officials were referred to. Cf. Ch. VII.

[11] Cf. Heiden, op. cit., pp. 27–29. "There has always been such a guard," Himmler declared in a speech of 1931. "The Persians had one, the Greeks had one, Caesar had one, Napoleon had one, der alte Fritz had one and so on to the war, and the guard of the new Germany will be the SS. This guard will be the cream (Auslese) of a particularly careful selection."

"born in years of struggle in the smallest communities and professional groups; this is the present Party leadership, which has maintained the knightly virtues: poverty, honor, obedience, courage, and finally, renunciation of a quiet life within the clan (Sippe)."[12] This would be a victory of no single class but of all classes, "the greatest, most magnanimous socialism there is: from the simplest farm worker to the general with his medals and pension, all have the opportunity to take their place as representatives of the authority of the State."[13]

Hitler's appointment, bringing with it the obligation of reconciling the ideological mishmash with the more prosaic requirements of economic and military mobilization, social rapprochement, and holding the ship of state on course, only increased this eclecticism. While Darré protégés prattled portentously about a peasant nobility (Adelbauerntum) and biological predestination,[14] and Himmler combed the backwoods in search of Nordic Herrentypen[15] Hitler continued to pursue the quasi-Jacobin line of equal opportunity. Adjusting himself as always to his audience, pleasing everybody and offending nobody, he kept to the broadest of generalizations—"opportunity for every individual to develop his creative capacities,"[16] "our greatest pride that in this Reich we have opened the way for every qualified individual—whatever his origins—to reach the top if he is qualified, dynamic, industrious, and resolute."[17] Nothing could be more splendid than "such a selection as that which the Leibstandarte (guards regiment) represents," he was reported as saying after review-

[12] Hans Schwarz van Berk, *Die Sozialistische Auslese*, Breslau, 1934, p. 16.

[13] Ibid., p. 22.

[14] Cf. Hans F. K. Günther, *Führeradel durch Sippenpflege*, Berlin, 1941. Günther was also a protégé of Frick, who had appointed him professor at the University of Jena. He was subsequently professor of physical ethnology (Rassenkunde), anthropological biology (Völkerbiologie) and rural sociology at the universities of Berlin and Freiburg.

[15] Cf. Kersten, op. cit. But Himmler continued nonetheless to cultivate his public relations and distribute honorary SS commissions where they might do some good. Cf. Neusüss-Hunkel, op. cit.

[16] Domarus, op. cit., p. 206, speech of 2 February 1933.

[17] Ibid., p. 702, speech to Autobahn workers, 23 June 1937.

ing the SS Leibstandarte Adolf Hitler.[18] "In National Socialism, the German people has received that leadership which, as a Party, has not only mobilized, but above all organized, the nation, and organized it in such a way that the most natural selective principles, from the ground up, guarantee continuity in political leadership for all times," he told a Reichstag of Party leaders.[19] This—like "my SA,"[20] or the Hitler Youth as "School of the Nation,"[21] or the ceremonial reception of Berufswettkampf (professional competition) winners, or the Blutorden (Order of Blood) for old Party members, or the creation of new and mutually competitive academies, colleges, schools, scholarships, selection programs —was in the multiple elite tradition of the period before 1933. Such declarations, references, foundations were guided by no exclusive principle of social selection, but by considerations of vanity, expediency, institutional morale, or social necessity. Given the heterogeneity of the Nazi system and the endless dynamism of its goals, it was evident to all but the most dedicated SS man that a single exclusive selective principle did not and could not exist.

The ideal of "racial selection," of a "new nobility of Blut und Boden," was, in any case, a chimera, albeit a chimera capable of pursuit by a regime foolhardy enough to accept its consequences. There was, in principle, no reason why a Nazi regime could not have experimented with a small farmer elite, with a Party state, with the expropriation of Junkers and the incarceration of intellectuals, with the erection of neo-feudalism or a corporatist society, with the dissolution of universities and urban communities, with any of the racist phantasms or populist aspirations of the Party program. But to do so was to accept consequences the new regime was not prepared to face. It would have meant, in the first place, the sacrifice of that social rapprochement without which effective social mobilization was out of the question. It also meant the sacrifice of those long-term imperialist goals to which the regime was dedicated and of which such a social mobilization

[18] Ibid., p. 560, quoted in VB, 17 December 1935.
[19] Ibid., p. 796, speech of 20 February 1938.
[20] Ibid., p. 447, Nuremberg congress of 1934.
[21] VB, 14 September 1935.

was the first premise. Willy-nilly, the option for industrial rearmament in 1933 and against Feder in 1934 was an option against the new aristocracy of Blut und Boden and in favor of the long-term dynamics of industrial society as they had been working in Germany and all other industrial countries since the beginning of the nineteenth century.

The basic tendencies of social development had been visible to German observers as dissimilar as Marx, Lassalle, and Lorenz von Stein since the mid-nineteenth century and had been examined with considerable empirical precision before World War I. The mobility of German society was axiomatic, affecting even those whose personal misery led them to deny it, like the textile workers Marie Bernays investigated in 1909.[22] The basic course of development, migration to the cities, the development of a white-collar class, the decline of small farmers and, later, of small businessmen, affected every social institution, including even such buttresses of the ancien régime as the Army, the university, and the civil service.[23] The fact of social mobility was reflected in the attention paid it as a favored theme of a strikingly vigorous sociology. The classical pattern of social mobility[24] was identified by P. Mombert as early as 1920 and treated theoretically by J. A. Schumpeter as early as 1926.[25] This was a development by stages: from farmer to worker to skilled labor or economic independence, to middle civil service to university.[26]

[22] Cf. Marie Bernays, *Auslese und Anpassung der Arbeiterschaft der geschlossenen Grossindustrie*, Leipzig, 1910, p. 231. Bernays established that nearly 40% of the sons of male workers, as skilled workers, artisans, white-collar workers, civil servants, and elementary school teachers, were upwardly mobile.

[23] Cf. *Führungsschicht und Eliteproblem*, Jahrbuch III der Ranke Gesellschaft, Frankfurt-Berlin-Bonn, 1957.

[24] Cf. S. M. Lipset und Reinhard Bendix, *Social Mobility in Industrial Society*, Berkeley and Los Angeles, 1960.

[25] Cf. P. Mombert, "Die Tatsachen der Klassenbildung," *Schmollers Jahrbuch*, Vol. 44, 1920, pp. 1048 ff.; Joseph A. Schumpeter, "Social Classes in an Ethnically Homogeneous Environment," *"Imperialism" and "Social Classes,"* ed. Paul Sweezy, tr. Heinz Norden, Oxford, 1951.

[26] The civil service stage, it should be added, is more characteristic of Europe, where the civil service enjoys prestige, than it is of

With the political revolution of 1918, this development continued with uninterrupted consistency through the Weimar years.[27] The farm population continued to decline, the number of self-employed to fall, and the white-collar population to grow. The Bavarian statistician Nothaas noted that the working class continued to maintain itself with rural emigrants, while the white-collar population recruited itself, in turn, among the working class.[28] The way to the top, particularly where it lay via the university, continued to be peopled by the children of this white-collar class, particularly of teachers and middle civil servants.[29] The direct consequences and distortions of the crisis years were nonetheless visible. It was significant enough that the university population grew, and that its distribution shifted. While previous career opportunities like paternal businesses and the military closed, a new generation gravitated to the anticipated centers of gravity of a maturing industrial society. The number of law, economics, and engineering students grew conspicuously. The number of medical, veterinary medical, and Protestant theological students declined.[30] At the same time, the relatively high prewar frequency of students from small business and farm families fell, reflecting economic pressure.[31] But the frequency of students from working-class families remained low—roughly 2 per cent—despite indications of an even greater rate of upward mobility than that of the prewar era.[32]

The gravitation of the middle classes, particularly of the "new middle class," to the universities contrasted with the

America. Mombert, in turn, identified a characteristic German development, the graduation of the son of the artisan or small shopkeeper to non-commissioned officer, and then to the middle civil service or a teaching position in a Volksschule. His son then attended the Gymnasium, graduating in turn to the university or a military commission. Mombert, op. cit.

[27] Cf. Ch. I.

[28] J. Nothaas, "Sozialer Auf- und Abstieg im deutschen Volke," *Kölner Vierteljahreshefte für Soziologie*, Vol. 9, pp. 70–73.

[29] Ibid., p. 65.

[30] Ibid.

[31] Ibid., p. 66.

[32] Ibid., pp. 68, 77.

gravitation of the industrial working class to politics. While little more than 5 per cent of the Prussian Gymnasium enrollment came from working-class families as the Republic began, 29 per cent of the elected Reichstag deputies identified themselves as workers,[33] and Nothaas estimated that 70 per cent of all politicians in 1925 came from "middle and lower" classes. The professionals and bourgeois who had once dominated German politics, but who had increasingly withdrawn from political life even before the war, continued their decline.[34] Nevertheless, of the eighty Weimar ministers between 1918 and 1930, forty-nine had doctoral degrees, and another fifteen diplomas or comparable upper civil service qualifications, a total of 80 per cent. Only 12 had been blue-collar or white-collar workers, one (Erzberger) had been a teacher, one a middle civil servant; 9 per cent came from the nobility.[35]

The differential rates of political and social change were still more conspicuous in other sectors. While the domestic civil service in the course of the nineteenth century had turned into a bourgeois institution,[36] both political decisions and the general conservation of formal qualifications limited further social movement in government offices. This was particularly true of the diplomatic service[37] which continued to be a preserve of the aristocracy. It was equally true of the Army despite the massive prewar incursion of bourgeois sons into the reserve officer corps and the increasing number of bourgeois career officers in unfashionable technical branches

[33] Ibid., pp. 74, 77.
[34] Cf. Günther Franz, "Der Parliamentarismus," *Führungsschicht*, op. cit., pp. 87 ff.
[35] Ibid., p. 92.
[36] In 1911 78% of the undersecretaries of state and 82% of the civil service departmental chiefs were bourgeois. Cf. Nikolaus von Preradovich, "Die politisch-militärischen Führungsschichten in Österreich and Preussen während des 19. Jahrhunderts," *Führungsschicht*, op. cit., pp. 63 f.
[37] Cf. Ch. VII. A *Simplicissimus* cartoon of the period shows a wing-collared gentleman telling his monocled colleagues ". . . no, not to be considered as an ambassador. A bourgeois name damages the reputation of the Republic." Reproduced in *Magnum*, April 1960, p. 33.

like artillery and transport.[38] While the Republic undertook a tentative shake-up of its armed forces,[39] the 100,000-man Army of the Versailles Treaty in fact perpetuated the status quo. While exclusiveness, Zeitgeist, and war experience all contributed to a relative revolution of attitudes—a decline in social snobbery, a respect for technical education, and an interest in what were called "social problems"—there was little comparable revolution in social origins. Of newly commissioned lieutenants in 1922/23, over 21 per cent were aristocrats, in 1931/32 36 per cent.[40] Between 35 and 50 per cent of all officers were sons of officers, a higher frequency than that of the prewar years. The sons of upper civil servants, clergymen, lawyers, doctors, and professors continued to represent about 35 to 40 per cent, roughly the level of the prewar years. The most generous estimate of the representation of non-commissioned officers' sons ran at 8 per cent, the most modest at under 1 per cent.[41] Aristocrats in 1932 still held nearly 20 per cent of staff positions, a modest decline from a share of 26.4 per cent in 1920. Their representation, true to the prewar pattern, continued to range from 47.3 per cent in cavalry units to 5.1 per cent in transport.[42] At high-command levels, the predominance of the ancien régime was, of course, still more conspicuous. In 1920, all three generals, eight of fourteen lieutenant generals, and nine of twenty-seven major generals were aristocrats.[43]

[38] Cf. Franz Carl Endres, "Soziologische Struktur des deutschen Offizierkorps vor dem Weltkrieg," in Archiv für Sozialwissenschaft und Sozialpolitik, October 1927, pp. 287 ff.; Karl Demeter, *Das deutsche Offizierkorps*, Berlin, 1930.

[39] In 1919 Noske informed the Weimar Assembly that half of the future officer corps was to be reserved for former non-commissioned officers. In 1920, however, former non-commissioned officers comprised only 10% of the naval officer corps. Demeter, *Das deutsche Offizierkorps*, (second edition) Frankfurt, 1962, p. 51. Of the 4000-man Army officer corps in 1920, 200 were former non-commissioned officers. Hans Mundt, *Führungsschicht*, op. cit., p. 117.

[40] Demeter, 1962 edition, p. 55.

[41] Ibid., p. 53.

[42] Ibid., p. 56.

[43] This, however, represented some change compared with the wartime ratio. At the end of World War I, 6 of 7 marshals, 11 of 15 generals, 20 of 29 infantry generals, 53 of 97 lieutenant generals,

Even with a generation of hindsight, causes and effects are hard to distinguish, but this was all symptomatic of the Weimar predicament. To what extent Hitler's rise can be directly identified with status anxiety is hard to establish. To what extent this status anxiety can be identified in turn with real loss of status is no easier.[44] What happened in German society also happened in other countries without comparable consequences. But the discrepancy between political and social revolution and the differential effect of a continuing social revolution on such different sectors of public life as politics, civil service, Army, and university, unquestionably complicated the solution of political problems in Germany in a way that can scarcely be compared either with other industrial countries or with the revolutionary and industrializing Soviet Union. These social conflicts need not have led to Hitler. Despite exceptions, nothing indicates that either students, civil servants, or Army officers were, as a rule, inclined to be pro-Nazi. Tradition, conservatism, snobbery, all led in other directions: to elitism, youth movements (Jugendbewegung), monarchist nostalgia, and all the other phantoms and utopias that bedeviled Weimar society. But in toto these conflicts reflected and perpetuated the fateful lack of consensus that haunted and finally undermined the Republic.

The success of the Third Reich was a reflection of the extent to which this consensus was restored. In part ideologically, in part pragmatically, Hitler succeeded, where the Weimar Republic had failed, in desociologizing politics. Neither patronage for his followers, rapprochement with the old economic, military, or civil service elites, nor economic recovery was the single key to his success, although all of them were factors. All of them had had their equivalents in the Weimar Republic. But the unique climate of the Third Reich, its ideological euphoria, expanding opportunities, distribution of both advantages and disadvantages among all social groups, created an unstable but unmistakable social equilibrium. Since the Third Reich involved all classes, since

---

and 160 of 300 major generals were aristocrats. Mundt, *Führungsschicht*, p. 115.

[44] Cf. Lipset and Bendix, op. cit., p. 36.

it brought both benefits and disadvantages to all classes, both loyalty and hostility largely ceased to be matters of class, and, perhaps for the first time, Germany achieved a certain identity between leaders—or Leader—and followers. Unlike 1919–33, the political revolution coincided with the inherited social revolution.

The sociologists Croner and Bolte both indicate how consistently, the counter-revolutionary dreams of Hitler's voters notwithstanding, the revolution went on.

TABLE 13

Occupational Distribution	*1907*	*1925*	*1933*	*1939*
Agriculture	34%	30%	29%	27%
Industry and crafts	40	42	41	41
Services	26	28	30	32

TABLE 14

Occupational Status	*1907*	*1925*	*1933*	*1939*
Self-employed	27%	21%	20%	18%
Employed dependents	8	10	11	11
White collar and civil service	14	19	18	20
Workers	51	50	52	51[45]

Not a single clock was turned back. Agriculture continued a decline visible since the nineteenth century, and the service industries recorded their regular 2 per cent census-to-census growth in six years, compared with the 18 years needed between that of 1907 and that of 1925. The proportion of the self-employed declined faster between 1933 and 1939 than it had between 1925 and 1933 when the self-employed had contributed so much to the rise of National Socialism. The proportion of employed family dependents, employed to some extent in 1925 and a greater extent in 1933 because the small shopkeeper had had nothing to pay the unemployed, was at the same level in 1939, because

[45] Croner, op. cit., p. 196. The apparent retrograde motion of 1933 is presumably a reflection of the differential effects of unemployment.

there were no unemployed to hire. The growth of white-collar employment continued as before. Croner's figures, which reflect uninterrupted industrialization, also point to the environment of social opportunity that uninterrupted industrialization produced, and whose effects Bolte confirms.

Analyzing mobility within and between occupational groups, Bolte establishes a movement from hired agricultural labor to unskilled industrial labor, or skilled craftsmen to semi-skilled and skilled industrial labor, and of unskilled to semi-skilled and skilled industrial craftsmen. Self-employed agriculture maintained remarkable stability. Public and private white-collar employment showed gains.[46] In terms of occupational status mobility, Bolte estimated upward movement between 1934 and 1939 at almost 20 per cent in East Germany and almost 30 per cent in West Germany, compared with a universal rate of about 12 per cent in the years 1927–34.[47] Upward class movement characterized all age and regional groups, although young West Germans tended to be the most mobile. Most striking was the movement from lower to lower middle class.

While National Socialism maintained and accelerated the rate of movement in society, it produced comparable, if differential, results in the social composition of the State. A contemporary study of the technical civil service, post office (Reichspost) and transport (Reichsbahn), revealed relatively little change, or, more accurately, continued change in pre-Nazi patterns at lower and middle levels. After 1933 as before, lower and middle technical civil servants tended to be the sons of artisans and farmers, and to a lesser extent of workers and lower civil servants.[48] The same ratios applied with little variation to elementary school (Volksschule) teachers.[49] At higher levels, the picture was more complex.[50] Since civil service qualifications remained virtually

[46] Karl Martin Bolte, *Sozialer Aufstieg und Abstieg*, Stuttgart, 1959, pp. 130–33.

[47] Ibid., p. 139.

[48] Heinrich Tisch, "Das Problem des sozialen Auf- und Abstieges im deutschen Volk," Heidelberg dissertation, 1937, pp. 19–31.

[49] Ibid., p. 48.

[50] Cf. Ch. VII.

unchanged, and the social composition of the university population also showed little change, it can be assumed that there was relatively little change in the social composition of the civil service. In diplomacy, traditional social snobbery—or concern for foreign opinion—seems to have played a role even after the disintegration of the foreign service was almost complete. Even in wartime, the Third Reich was represented in Bucharest and Budapest by the aristocrats von Killinger and von Jagow—aristocrats, to be sure, from the SA—as it was represented by the more orthodox aristocrat von Weizsäcker at the Vatican.[51] Even at the ministerial level, there was little direct indication of a social revolution. Of thirty-one Reich ministers between 1933 and 1945, nine of ten bourgeois ministers were university graduates and high civil servants—with Seldte as the only exception. The list also included five aristocrats, most of them taken over from the Papen government. But of the twenty-one Nazi ministers, only two, Hitler himself and Kerrl, were of petit bourgeois origins. Of the rest, sixteen were also professional men or high civil servants.[52]

In the Army and the universities, as in the civil service, change tended to be more a matter of subversion than of radical reorganization. In the Army it was not direct but indirect; in part psychological, in part the result of increased opportunities.[53] By all accounts, the Army remained the most conservative of the services. But even here, the rate of expansion and promotion accelerated a quiet social revolution in progress since the end of World War I. The 100,000-man Reichswehr of 1920 included 44 generals, 27 (61%) of them aristocrats; the Wehrmacht of January 1939 included 261 generals, 72 (27%) of them aristocrats, with the promise of greater changes to come. All three colonel generals, the

[51] Even the anti-aristocratic Rosenberg school, which aspired to turn out the diplomatic establishment altogether, took exception to the everyday Saxon accent of one of its candidates; this despite qualifications that included a law degree and command of six languages. National Archives Microcopy T 81, Roll 11, Reel 282.

[52] Franz, op. cit., p. 93.

[53] "I have a Prussian Army, an Imperial Navy, and a National Socialist Air Force," Hitler is supposed to have said. Quoted in Demeter, 1962 edition, op. cit., p. 191. Cf. Erich von Manstein, *Aus einem Soldatenleben*, Bonn, 1958, pp. 268 f.

highest military rank, had been promoted within the previous years, as had 17 of 31 generals, 58 of 87 lieutenant generals, and 90 of 140 major generals.[54] Hitler expanded the number of yearly peacetime officer candidates from 120/180 to 2000, found places for 300 legal clerks for whom there were no available positions in the civil administration, arranged the reintegration in the Army of 2500 former Army officers currently serving in the police, saw to the promotion of 1500 noncommissioned officers and the reinstatement of 1800 retired career and reserve officers of the old Army as well as 1600 Austrians in 1938.[55] From 1935 on military reorganization accelerated anti-traditional tendencies by breaking up such units as cavalry and guards regiments that had tried after 1933 to continue recruiting on the basis of personal acquaintance. But this, according to at least one who experienced it, was a cause of regret only in the most conservative, and older, officer groups.[56] There were no sweeping purges, and seniority continued to be the criterion of promotion. But both recruitment and promotion were dictated and accelerated by increasing need, and absolute standards gave way to more pragmatic considerations. Mundt's words, the moderate premise of careers open to talent, already increasingly accepted before 1933, took the extreme form of "recherche de la paternité interdite" afterward.[57] The Wehrmacht officer corps was en route to becoming the least snobbish in German history. The Abitur nonetheless continued to be required of officer candidates.[58] The difference, relative to the old Army,

[54] H. H. Podzun, (ed.), *Das deutsche Heer*, Bad Nauheim, 1953. Seniority list of 3 January 1939. By comparison, the generals and staff officers down to the rank of lieutenant colonel in 1931 had been promoted on an average of two ranks since 1923, i.e., once every four years. During these eight years, however, most majors had advanced only one rank and nearly 20% of the captains had not been promoted at all. *Untersuchungen zur Geschichte des Offizierkorps, Anciennität und Beförderung nach Leistung*, Militärgeschichtliches Forschungsamt, Stuttgart, 1962, p. 173.

[55] Cf. Mundt, op. cit., p. 118.

[56] Interview with Lt. Gen. Hermann Boehme, former director of the Franco-German armistice commission, 8 November 1963.

[57] Mundt, op. cit., p. 118.

[58] During wartime this too was changed but before 1939 effective recruitment plus obstacles to university enrollment produced

was rather one of attitude, general sympathy for the idea of Volksgemeinschaft, general sympathy for a new officer generation of Hitler Youth graduates who were expected to act like gentlemen, not necessarily to be born such. In a personal letter to Beck in 1935, the commander of an infantry division expressed serious doubts about the intellectual capacity of the new officer corps "despite all good will."[59] In a letter to Brauchitsch of October 1939, the commander of an Army Group expressed doubts about its professional capabilities.[60] But this was, presumably, a minority position. In World War I, the bourgeois technician Ludendorff had been an exception. With the coming of the mechanized army and World War II, Ludendorffs tended to become the rule. Of World War II marshals, 7 of 16 were bourgeois, compared with a ratio of 1 to 7 in World War I; 21 of 26 colonel generals were bourgeois compared with 4 of 15 in World War I, 140 of 166 infantry generals were bourgeois compared with 9 of 29 in World War I.[61]

The fate of the professors like that of the generals is an index of subversion rather than social revolution in the traditional high-status occupations. While the Army grew, the universities declined. Between 1933 and 1938, the list of ac-

---

the desired results. An official spokesman of the Reichswehr reported in 1937 that of 18,200 male Abiturienten in 1936, 10,000 had enlisted as officer candidates. Cited in Karl Obermann, "Studienbedingungen und Möglichkeiten im Dritten Reich," *Zeitschrift für freie deutsche Forschung*, Paris, July 1938, p. 157.

[59] Quoted in Demeter, 1962 edition, p. 106. But in principle this was nothing new. Bernhardi reports similar worries even before World War I when "the sons of old officer families preferred making money to service. The sons of rich parvenus wanted to be officers. The spirit was still high, but with time it could be expected that the level of performance would sink." Friedrich von Bernhardi, *Denkwürdigkeiten aus meinem Leben*, Berlin, 1927, p. 263.

[60] "The sword lacks the sharpness that the Führer assumes it to have. The blunt edges, particularly the dilution of the officer corps, are thus bound to take their revenge and produce still greater consequences than was the case in the last war. . . . An artillery unit has just been reported to me that represents a greater threat to our own troops than it does to the enemy." Letter from Col. Gen. W. Ritter von Leeb of 31 October 1939, quoted in Hans-Adolf Jacobsen, *1939–1945*, Darmstadt, 1961, p. 604.

[61] Mundt, op. cit., pp. 115–19.

tive professors (Ordinarien) fell to 71 per cent of its 1931/32 level, the list of non-professorial university teachers to 67 per cent.[62] The economic and social sciences, mathematics and geography, the humanities and law faculties, were hit hardest. Compared with the total, the list of those purged—including both political and "racial" groups—shows a high representation of university teachers' sons, sons of lawyers, industrialists, merchants and rentiers, and a correspondingly low frequency of sons of schoolteachers, high and middle civil servants, judges, clergymen, white-collar workers, and farmers; in general, outwardly at least, a purge of the bourgeoisie.[63] But the dubiousness of this as the expression of anything more profound than the ideological elimination of Jews and the practical elimination of political opponents, is expressed in its lack of consequences. Quantitatively, the university shrank, but its shrinkage was more or less equally distributed, with the exception of the law faculties whose total teaching staff by 1938 declined to 68 per cent of the 1931 level. In other faculties, the decline ranged between 4 and 15 per cent, averaging 9 per cent in all faculties, including law. In an exceptional case, social sciences, the decline was about 6 per cent, from 118 to 111, but the limited statistical decline concealed a mass turnover.[64] Three groups, veterinary

[62] Christian von Ferber, *Die Entwicklung des Lehrkörpers der deutschen Universitäten und Hochschulen, 1864–1954*, Göttingen, 1956, p. 144.

[63] This impression is probably an optical illusion as long as the causes of dismissal are unknown. It is at least conceivable that academic and commercial-industrial occupations were "Jewish" to a greater extent than civil service, judiciary, and white-collar employment.

[64] The fate of the German sociologists is a particularly interesting aspect of academic life in the Third Reich, revealing in this case not by its representativeness but its uniqueness. Notwithstanding the basic anti-intellectualism of the Third Reich and Hitler's animus against law and lawyers, sociology was probably the only discipline objectionable to the Third Reich in itself. Other academics were dismissed as individuals. The sociologists—for all that they tended for historical reasons to Jewish origins and Marxist sympathies—were presumably objectionable per se. The self-defense of compromise-inclined "aryan" sociologists, prepared to bid for a place as architects of "Gemeinschaft" and students of its institutions, still makes interesting reading but understandably fell on deaf ears. *The*

medicine, forestry, and certain unenumerated technical specialities even showed gains. But aside from its apparent confirmation of official animosity toward law—there being no reason to doubt the readiness of German lawyers to take the places of their dismissed colleagues, and thus no reason to assume that the decline in teaching lawyers represents any absolute shortage of material—the policy and its consequences seem to show no great hostility to universities as such. For reasons of expediency and general consideration for public opinion—including foreign public opinion—universities underwent a deterioration like that of the civil service, becoming the object of pressure, purge, Gleichschaltung in part imposed, in part voluntary, *and* some patronage. Younger staff members were herded into the SA, those sympathetic to the National Socialist cause advanced into positions vacated by Jews and political opponents, and occasional Party protégés and charlatans like Hans Günther, the racist, or Willy Börger, the Cologne Trustee of Labor, were given professorial rank. But that this was limited can be seen by comparing the professorial losses with the active staff of 1938. Rather than distributing professorships, the Third Reich tended to leave the holes unfilled or filled them from below. The Gestapo filled out reports on older instructors—between the ages of 48 and 65—who celebrated the Kaiser's birthday,

---

bourgeois social science can scarcely have had much appeal for a group sworn to destroy bourgeois society, and practical considerations alone made investigations of their own past or present the last possible thing leading Nazis can have been interested in. Such sociology as survived in the Third Reich survived in the form of philosophical or historical speculation, as physical anthropology, or as limited statistical tabulations—like the Party census—marked "secret." For some historical observations on German sociology, see René König, "Judentum und Soziologie," *Der Monat,* August 1961. For contemporary apologetics, see Ernst-Wilhelm Eschmann, "Die Stunde der Soziologie," *Die Tat,* March 1934, pp. 957 ff.; Reinhard Höhn, "Die Wandlung in der Soziologie," *Süddeutsche Monatshefte,* August 1934, pp. 643 ff.; Hans Freyer, "Gegenwartsaufgaben der deutschen Soziologie," *Zeitschrift für die gesamte Staatswissenschaft,* 1935, pp. 118 ff. For the fate of German sociologists at home and in exile respectively, see articles by Heinz Maus and René König in *Kölner Zeitschrift für Soziologie und Sozialpsychologie,* 1959.

interrogated and subsequently locked up a Greifswald lecturer for telling anti-Nazi jokes, and subsequently took away his teaching qualification. After concluding a treaty with Poland in 1934, the regime let it be known at the University of Berlin that a professorship in Polish history would be desirable. But in Innsbruck in 1938, it gave way to local pressure against the appointment of an Italian.[65] Even one of the dismissed professors reported that the older generation was generally left undisturbed by the Nazis, providing, of course, that it was not active against them.[66]

But there were visible changes in the younger generation. The rate of professorial appointment accelerated, and the length of service as Privatdozent—traditionally the purgatorial period of a German academic's life[67]—fell in the medical, natural science, law, and even theological faculties.[68] The greatest single downward changes were in the law faculty, which had suffered the greatest losses. The Third Reich's law professors were, at an average age of thirty-seven, by a margin of a year and a half on the next group the Protestant theologians, Germany's youngest professors.[69] At the same time, the rate of appointment in the humanities, mathematics, and the social and economic sciences showed slight declines.[70]

More interesting was a visible shift in the social origins of those qualified (Habilitiert) for university teaching positions. But it is difficult to establish to what extent this was con-

[65] Bundesarchiv R 21/366.

[66] Paul Kahle, *Bonn University in Pre-Nazi and Nazi Times*, London, 1945.

[67] Cf. Max Weber, "Wissenschaft als Beruf," Munich and Leipzig, 1919.

[68] Ferber, op. cit., pp. 155 f.

[69] In the years 1923–32, they had been, on the average, the second youngest group, led only by the mathematicians. But the average appointment age was roughly 38½, a year and a half older than in the Third Reich.

[70] The average age of professorial appointees in mathematics increased from 37.5 to 40.0, by far the greatest change in either direction of any single group. Nonetheless professors of medicine, despite an average reduction of appointment age of over a year to their advantage, continued to be the oldest of all appointees between 1933 and 1944, averaging 43.5.

scious policy, and to what extent a reflection of the changed university enrollment of the 1920s, the period when many of the professorial appointees of 1933–44 had begun their studies. The absolute numbers declined by 34 per cent.[71] But compared with those from the same group who qualified between 1922 and 1933, the number of sons of the self-employed, the academically trained white-collar class, and military officers declined between 1933 and 1944 by 43 per cent. The proportion of sons of university graduates—including university and gymnasium teachers, higher civil servants, judges, lawyers, doctors, clergymen, artists, publicists, architects, pharmacists, etc.—declined by 49 per cent. The proportion of sons of those neither self-employed nor with academic degrees declined by only 2 per cent. Of the absolute total of those who qualified, the proportion of those in the first group fell from 35.8 to 30.7 per cent, of those in the second from 47.8 to 44.0 per cent.[72] The third group, on the other hand, grew from 16.4 to 25.3 per cent. Within the first group, the disproportionate tenacity of the sons of artisans and small businessmen, whose numbers declined by only 10 per cent compared with the average of 43 per cent, and of white-collar employees in managerial positions who declined by only 19 per cent is striking. Together, the two subgroups accounted for about 25 per cent of the total number of such bourgeois sons who qualified for academic careers.

In the second group, the sons of university graduates, only the sons of the academic proletariat—pharmacists, architects, veterinarians—maintained themselves with comparable success, declining by only 19 per cent, compared with an overall decline of 39 per cent. The sons of higher civil servants and university teachers continued to be the biggest subgroups in this category. In the third group, the sons of the non-academic, non-self-employed and the sons of white-collar workers showed the greatest gain, an absolute gain of 28 per

[71] The number of Habilitationen fell from 2333 in the years 1920–33 to 1534 in the years 1933–44. Unfortunately, Ferber's figures give no indication of the extent to which this decline was concentrated in the years 1940–44 or distributed equally over the entire period.

[72] Analysis is based on figures in Ferber, op. cit., pp. 177 f.

cent compared with the group average loss of 2 per cent. They remained, however, of little consequence, only 11 per cent of their group total. But the sons of middle and lower civil servants showed a 9 per cent gain, and grew at the same time from 41 to 47 per cent of the total. Seen absolutely, they were, with 179, the largest single group of all, followed by 152 sons of small businessmen and 135 sons of non-graduate teachers. This was followed by the first academic group, 133 sons of university teachers.[73] Working-class representatives, the sons of workers or industrial foremen, showed no absolute change, though a slight relative gain, from 8.2 to 8.7 per cent of their group total, from 0.14 to 0.21 per cent of the absolute total of all groups.

But the real source of social revolutionary impulse was not to be found primarily in the distribution of places in the traditional status order. This too was a factor. The fact of Hitler's accession as head of State would have been significant enough even if it had been the only comparable precedent—which it was not. A social revolution is not only a matter of who holds office, however, but of how he holds it. Frick, for example, ran the Ministry of the Interior in ways that would not have occurred to his predecessors, regardless of their common sociological background.

The outstanding characteristic of the Third Reich was the infiltration of the entire traditional order—whether by the superimposition of the Party or of ad hoc technical administration—that revolutionized the State as it revolutionized society. Daniel Lerner's analysis of the 1934 *Führerlexikon,*[74] and the

[73] The 1920–33 figures, for comparison, show the 278 sons of small businessmen to be far and away the biggest group, followed by 210 sons of university teachers and 196 sons of doctors. Only then come 164 sons of middle and lower civil servants, 150 sons of non-graduate teachers and 148 sons of higher civil servants.

[74] A second edition of the *Führerlexikon,* like a second edition of the party census, was apparently contemplated but never appeared. Like all Who's Whos, the *Führerlexikon* was no guaranteed guide to who was who, to who was a Führer, but only to those it was thought expedient or desirable to call a Führer—a revealing and interesting point of view, particularly considering that it had no sequel, but not necessarily the same thing. Thus, as Lerner observes, such later military luminaries as Rommel, Jodl, Model, Dietrich, Guderian, and Ramcke were not included. Nor were the various

1935 Party census reflect not so much the creation of a new Nazi leadership as its encroachment on the old pre-Nazi one. Thus certain middle-class elements showed an impressive durability, particularly industrial managers, lawyers, civil servants, and technologists.[75] Middle-class elements also tended to dominate the group Lerner called the "propagandists." In contrast with the "administrators"—Party functionaries or former Party functionaries now holding positions in the civil service or the new corporate organizations—the "propagandists" tended to come from military, clerical, or professional families. They tended to have been trained in non-technical and non-scientific university faculties, and to enjoy foreign contacts, in the form of birth, travel, education, or marriage, to a greater extent than other groups, and in a manner commensurate with their bourgeois origins. Compared to other groups, the "propagandists" were outstandingly young—93 per cent under 50 compared with 79.2 per cent of the administrators and 56.3 per cent of a random sample of the total[76]—and well educated—50 per cent of the "propagandists" had been to universities compared with 25 per cent of the "administrators." They had also done the least military service of all groups.

"Administrators" frequently had rural or small-town origins, came from the lowest educational levels and the lowest military ranks, published least and married latest. Most plebeian of all were what Lerner called the "coercers," the policeman whose homely origins were emphasized by comparison with the professional soldiers many of them would once have hoped to become. Fewer than half the "coercers"—SA and SS officers—had begun their careers in police service. Many had had extended Freikorps service in the first postwar years and gone through periods of unemployment disproportionately longer than those of the other groups. Among their number the frequency of aristocratic names was under 9 per

victims of the June 30 purge who appeared, to the extent their inclusion had been planned at all, as empty space.

[75] Daniel Lerner, *The Nazi Elite,* Stanford University Press, 1951, p. 6.

[76] Ibid., pp. 9–26.

cent compared with 36 per cent among the soldiers.[77] Common to all Nazi groups were certain deviations from statistical norms[78] ranging to 80 per cent compared to 50 per cent in non-Nazi groups, including both the soldiers and a random sample of all entries. Also common to Nazi groups was relative youth.

"The differences spotlighted by our data are sufficient evidence that the *Führerlexikon* is not really a handbook of 'the Nazi *élite*' in any strict sense," Lerner writes. "From this we infer that there was in fact no Nazi *élite* that spanned and integrated the whole German society. There was rather a more limited set of changes in 'the composition of the ruling few' which produced a Nazi variant of the German *élite*."[79]

Though Lerner's generalization is based specifically on the premises of a Nazi "elite" in the years 1933–35, its validity was confirmed and intensified by subsequent Nazi experience. The personnel changed as did the premises of selection, but the characteristic eclecticism remained. "For the duration of its collective life, of the time during which its identity may be assumed," Schumpeter wrote, "each class resembles a hotel or an omnibus, always full, but always of different people."[80] This was no less true of the Nazi "elite," such as it was, but it included the additional characteristic of growth. The Nazi elite was, in this case, a chain of hotels, a fleet of buses, some new, some old, united only by common management.

Even the ranks of the Party "and affiliated organizations" showed an impressive heterogeneity, varying according to age and function. On the basis of their personnel records, the Gauleiters[81] showed the greatest relative consistency. They included ten white-collar workers, both private and civil

[77] Ibid., p. 63.

[78] These included place of birth, religion, occupation, father's occupation, education, marriage age, father-in-law's occupation, military rank, date of Party membership, foreign birth, foreign parentage, higher education abroad, occupation abroad. Ibid., p. 86.

[79] Ibid., p. 84.

[80] Schumpeter, "Social Classes," op. cit., p. 130.

[81] Listed in *Anschriftenverzeichnis der NSDAP*, 3d ed., undated, c. 1940/41. The personal records cited here and on the following pages are in the Berlin Document Center.

service, three blue-collar workers including a farm laborer and six Volksschule teachers. Only five seem to have attended universities, only three to have completed their studies—as a dentist, a lawyer, and a student of literature (Goebbels) respectively. Beyond these, only two had attended the Gymnasium, the rest having either stopped at elementary school or gone on to commercial institutions. Ten listed Party office as their first occupation, another six as a secondary occupation. Common denominators seemed to be small-town origin—only three coming from relatively large cities (e.g. Fürth and Saarbrücken)—war service, early Party membership—all had joined before 1930—and petit bourgeois origins as sons of farmers, lower civil servants, and artisans. A major common denominator was age. In 1933, sixteen of thirty were under forty.

By comparison, of eleven top party administrators (Oberbefehlsleiter),[82] three were doctors, including a doctor of medicine, another was a former university student, another a non-academic engineer (Techniker). Five listed white-collar occupations, two blue-collar. The common denominators were again age and a certain community of experience. Only one was forty in 1933, the rest younger. One—one of the two listing blue-collar occupations—was twenty-three in 1933 and had joined the party in 1930. Only two seem to have come from big cities, in both cases Munich. The impression of relative youth was reinforced by the next administrative ranks. Of a list of twenty department heads (Hauptstellenleiter) compiled in 1939, all had been born between 1901 and 1912.

Both the heterogeneity and the fluidity of Nazi leadership was visible in the composition and metamorphosis of the SA leadership. Among the nineteen Obergruppenführer and Gruppenführer in 1933,[83] were seven aristocratic names and one doctor. By far the biggest occupational classification was the military: twelve had been officers or cadets. Only one seems to have come from a working-class family, another was son of a farmer. The rest had bourgeois or aristocratic occu-

[82] Listed in *Anschriftenverzeichnis der NSDAP*, 4th ed., undated, c. 1941/42. Oberbefehlsleiter were considered equal in rank to Staatssekretäre in the State administration.

[83] Listed in Institut für Zeitgeschichte archive F 107, 120–21.

pations: a merchant, a career officer, an estate owner. Age distribution in this case was more diffuse: ten were born between 1883 and 1893, eight between 1893 and 1903. With the 1934 purge, this group broke up entirely, its members either disappearing altogether or reappearing elsewhere, in the SS, in State office, or in the diplomatic corps.[84] Only the plebeian Lutze remained, the vacancies being refilled this time from the lower ranks. A list of regional SA leaders of equivalent rank in 1943[85] showed no aristocratic names at all and a single one-time cadet officer. Only four, a dentist and an engineer included, had academic degrees, three were Volksschule teachers, six technicians of one sort or another, twelve white-collar workers. Common denominators were again war experience—about half had been in World War I and a third in postwar Freikorps—and small-town origins, as well as a certain concentration of age: nineteen of twenty-seven had been born between 1897 and 1907, and over half had joined the Party before 1930. This, like the Gauleiter list it resembled, was now a kind of honorary elite, a representational group rewarded for its loyalty and kept around for parades, Party schools, laying cornerstones, and meeting trains.

In the SS, which aspired to more demanding duties and called for more tangible qualifications, a sprinkling of aristocratic names survived. Four appeared in a 1941 list of thirty-five generals, three of them among the nine Obergruppenführer, the top rank.[86] Of twenty-seven with establishable occupations, twelve had been cadets and officers, one, in fact, a career lieutenant general. At the other end of the occupational scale were a former electrician, a former truck driver, three former mechanics, and two transient day laborers, both of whom had been prevented by war and inflation from resuming their university studies. Another seven claimed experience in agriculture, but among them were a prince and a baron. Despite the SS farm mystique, only one, and he a

[84] Beside Killinger and Jagow, examples include Kasche, Nazi emissary in Zagreb, the Freiherr von Eberstein, a wartime general of the SS, and Graf Helldorff, Chief of Police in Berlin, later executed in connection with the July 20 plot.

[85] Institut für Zeitgeschichte archive F 107, 175–86, 260–345.

[86] Listed in *Anschriftenverzeichnis der NSDAP*, 3d edition.

one-time student of agriculture at Göttingen, listed agriculture as his first occupation. He was, in turn, one of only six who listed any civilian occupation as first occupation. Again the group was relatively youthful: twenty of thirty-one were born between 1894 and 1903, though the eldest had been born in 1874. The characteristic thoroughness of SS documents offers in addition a relatively differentiated view of family background which, in its breadth, if not in its proportions, transcribes German society. Among the SS generality were the sons of princes and estate owners, of professional officers and civil servants, of a tavern keeper, a china dealer, an otherwise undefined worker, and a farmhand. Only a fairly high frequency, perhaps two to one, of small-town origin, and of birth in peripheral areas like Alsace, Lorraine, Vienna, Danzig, and the Prussian territories lost in 1919 seem to be common denominators. Marriage records document yet another aspect of SS—and thus of Nazi—society, indications at least of connubium, of social intermarriage, in this case of a customs official's son with the daughter of an aristocratic Landrat and of the farmhand's son with the daughter of an industrial director. In both cases, a second marriage was involved; in the first case that of the wife, who had previously been married to a baron; in the second, that of the husband who had previously been married to a plebeian.[87]

If the SS leadership, united by certain communities of experience despite differences of social origin, casts a certain light on the sources and process of recruitment of Himmler's organizational nucleus, the staff of the SS mobile unit Einsatzgruppe D, as tried at Nuremberg in 1947/48, is a revealing

[87] Another Nazi romance was the marriage of August Heissmeyer, an SS general and head of the National Political Training Institutions, with Frau Scholz-Klinck, head of the Nazi women's organization. But the marriage, that of a farmer's son with the daughter of a small-town bookkeeper and district surveyor, was not so striking that it might not theoretically have come about anyway. In fact, Nazi connubium seems to have been relatively limited, though affairs—to judge from the *Gauleiter* documents—were common enough. Schaumburg-Lippe reports that Goebbels thought it a fine idea that proletarian Gauleiters should remarry. Schaumburg-Lippe, *Zwischen Krone und Kerker*, p. 185. But it was evidently seldom that they did.

cross section of the SS as an institution in the establishment of the Third Reich.[88] The twenty-three defendants ranged in rank from general to lieutenant. With one exception, their ages at the beginning of the war, from twenty-four to thirty-eight. Impressive in this case was the high frequency of academic titles: seven doctors and a total of seventeen Akademiker, not counting a dentist, an engineer, and an opera singer. One had, in fact, been a professor at Königsberg and, for a period, directed the cultural department of the Foreign Office with ambassadorial rank. Without exception, the doctors—including Ohlendorf[89]—had studied economics and law, and virtually the entire group had made its way through administrative posts in the civil service, the Sicherheitsdienst (Security Service), or the internal administration of the SS before being brought together in Russia to organize murder.

To these groups may be added a functional economic elite in the form of the Trustees of Labor and the regional executives of the Labor Front. The Trustees[90] also tended to span society. In their case, age distribution approximated a normal curve, birth ranging from 1881 to 1904 with no particular concentration. Of fourteen, only four had joined the Party before 1930, seven joined before 1933, two after 1933, and the last had not joined at all. Occupations ranged from a former admiral and an industrial lobbyist who had been a General Staff Officer to a cashier, a boatmaker, and a mechanic (Monteur). Not surprisingly, the proletarian Trustees had come to the Party first, the bourgeois—including a factory director, a wholesaler in paper, and three corporation lawyers—latest. Social common denominators seemed lacking altogether.

Among the Labor Front functionaries[91] common denominators were largely those elements that had led to Party membership before 1930, and that characterized the group Lerner called "administrators." Of twenty-eight whose occupations can be established, twenty-five had joined the Party before 1930. Educational qualifications were low. Only one,

[88] Biographical data in Bayle, op. cit.
[89] Cf. Ch. IV.
[90] Listed in *Anschriftenverzeichnis der NSDAP*, 3d edition.
[91] Listed in Schumann, op. cit.

an engineer, was a university graduate. A second had interrupted his studies to enlist in World War I, and never returned to them, going on instead to a career in the Völkisch movement and, from 1930 on, in the NSDAP. The rest divided almost equally into blue- and white-collar workers, though the blue-collor group was relatively heterogeneous, including various artisans, a former window washer, a former quarry worker, and a former farm hand. Age distribution was concentrated: twenty-seven of a total of thirty-three were born between 1897 and 1906.

It was consistent that this eclecticism tended to reproduce itself in its own image. Neither the traditional social incubators of school and university nor the various academies of the new regime approached any new homogeneity, but only perpetuated the multiple elite that had created or maintained them.

An instructive example was university admission policy. Neither ideology nor long-term interests seem to have guided policy, but the characteristic ad hoc considerations of the immediate situation. Massive reduction of university enrollment was the academic equivalent of price-fixing or Erbhofgesetz. It was a measure understandable only with respect to immediate pressure in the form of apparent oversupply of university graduates. In the summer semester of 1933, 12,966 students matriculated at German universities; in the summer semester of 1939, 7303, a decline of 44 per cent.[92] But the basic premise was not social revolution; it was ideologized practical relief. The student himself was manipulated, not, in any fundamental sense, the collective student body. Theoretical discussion confined itself to change of heart, not of social structure.[93] The university student was expected to hold his own as a member of the Hitler Youth, the SA, or SS, to have done his duty in the Labor Service, but also presumably to have learned his Latin, his Goethe, and his algebra, to have made his Abitur at the classical Gymnasium

[92] Lorenz, op. cit., p. 21. The decline of newly matriculated males however was only 36%.

[93] Cf. Höpker, op. cit.; Frick's remarks to students of the University of Berlin, op. cit.; E. R. Jaensch, *Zur Neugestaltung des deutschen Studententums und der Hochschule,* Leipzig, 1937.

or the Realgymnasium just as before. Only under the pressure of anticipated needs[94] did the subject again become a matter of discussion. Beginning in 1935, the Nazi student organization, the Hitler Youth, and the Ministry of Education organized a university admission program for non-Abiturienten with good records in either the Hitler Youth or Labor Service.[95] This relaxation of formal requirements, which had certain Weimar precedents,[96] was unified on a Reich-wide basis by the Ministry of Education in 1938,[97] then reinstitutionalized in 1938 in the Langemarck scholarship for deserving young Nazis, age 17–24.[98] But in practice the results were scarcely visible. In the summer of 1939, Langemarck scholars comprised 0.14 per cent of the newly matriculated at all German higher institutions. The sum of those who had entered by qualifying examinations or by accelerated secondary-school programs represented another 0.93 per cent; with the Langemarck scholars a total of 1.07 per cent. Though new university enrollment as such had declined between 1933 and 1939 by 57 per cent, and new technical college enrollment had increased by 170 per cent,[99] there was no ap-

[94] "Whereas, before the *Machtübernahme*, public opinion continued to be influenced by the impression of academic oversupply, in recent years, before the beginning of the war, this gave way to the conviction that the future academic supply scarcely even approximated future demands." Lorenz, op. cit., p. 20.

[95] F. A. Six, "Nachwuchs und Auslese auf den deutschen Hochschulen," *Der deutsche Student*, March 1935, pp. 188 ff.

[96] On the basis of special examinations about 800 of 3000 non-Abiturient applicants were accepted for university admission in the Weimar Republic. Cf. Hans Huber, *Die Begabtenprüfung als Mittel der Begabtenauslese und Begabtenförderung*, Reichsministerium für Wissenschaft, Erziehung und Volksbildung, April 1940, Archive of Institut für Zeitgeschichte 2626/60.

[97] Bundesarchiv R 21/446, decree of 8 August 1938.

[98] This involved, after what was evidently a careful, or at any rate restricted, selection, a year and a half of special training including two more examinations, before final university admission. Cf. *Merkblatt für das Langemarck-Studium der Reichsstudentenführung*, Büttner, op. cit., pp. 872 f.; "Der vierte Lehrgang des Langemarck Studiums eröffnet," VB, 10 December 1938.

[99] This indicates a genuine if belated reversal of Nazi policy. Between 1933 and 1938, total enrollment of universities had declined by 55%, at technical institutions by 42%. *Statistisches Jahrbuch für Deutschland*, Munich, 1949, p. 622.

preciable relative difference between the universities and the technical institutions. The special entrants, including Langemarck scholars, represented 0.81 per cent of new university enrollment, compared with 1.76 per cent at the technical institutions. The Langemarck scholars alone, who represented 0.15 per cent of new university enrollment, represented 0.10 per cent of new technical enrollment.

Correspondingly, change in social origins was minimal. Children of higher civil servants, including teachers, rose from 15.5 to 17.42 per cent of the newly matriculated; children of middle civil servants fell from 26.55 to 22.95 per cent. The children of white-collar workers rose from 6.89 to 11.43 per cent, of those in liberal professions from 6.87 to 10.32 per cent. The proportion of children of white-collar employees in managerial positions fell from 5.96 to 3.70 per cent, of workers from 3.87 to 3.24 per cent, of farmers from 7.00 to 4.96 per cent, of small businessmen from 20.88 to 18.81 per cent. As before, the children of civil servants, both high and middle, of white-collar workers and of small businessmen continued to be the largest single groups, about 75 per cent of the total both in 1933 and 1939.[100] Regrouped in the categories Ferber applied to their teachers, the representation of the children of the self-employed, of managerial employees, and of officers, declined from roughly 35 to 29 per cent of the total, while that of the children of university graduates rose from roughly 24 to over 31 per cent. The last group, children of those neither self-employed nor academically trained, remained at roughly 40 per cent. The pattern consistently reproduced tendencies visible in German university life since the nineteenth century.[101]

[100] Analysis based on Lorenz, op. cit., p. 21. Cf. Wilfried Altstädter, "Sippe und berufliche Herkunft der Studierenden an der Universität München im Winterhalbjahr 1935/36." *Zeitschrift des bayerischen statistischen Landesamtes,* 1937, pp. 239 ff. On the basis of a random sample of newly matriculated Munich students, Altstädter comes to virtually the same conclusions, notes however that the representation of children of university graduates and higher civil servants reflects the disproportionately low birth rate in these groups rather than any deliberate selection policy. Ibid., p. 242.

[101] Cf. Tisch, op. cit., p. 9.

University policy had its counterpart in school policy. While official statements referred piously to "selection" (Auslese) and at least one official spokesman noted disapprovingly that 40 per cent of the 1938 Abiturienten were sons of civil servants and only 9 per cent the sons of workers,[102] policy was confined almost entirely to rhetoric. School fees continued to exist. "Selection," in the context of the Ministry of Education's decree of 27 March 1935 on the subject meant only that financial aid to Jews was to stop.[103] With the restriction of university entrance in 1933/34, the Saxon Minister of Education, anxious to do his part to reduce Bildungsinflation (excess of college graduates), introduced comparable restrictions for entrance to the upper secondary school classes,[104] but these, like the university restrictions, were repealed in 1935.[105] Prussian school fees were, in fact, increased by a third in 1935 with compensatory benefits for families with more than three children. As of 1938, an additional 10 per cent of the remainder, after such benefits had been distributed, was to be reserved for exceptionally bright children from poorer families.[106] In general, school fees continued to be levied on the basis of legislation issued in 1930.[107] Unchanged selective principles can be assumed to have been reflected in unchanged social representation in the secondary school, an assumption apparently confirmed by the records of a classical Gymnasium in Aachen which show relatively minimal—perhaps 5 per cent—variation in the frequency of sons of university graduates, of the self-employed, and of clerical and working-class fathers between 1926/27 and 1938/39.[108] Unlike the number of university students, the number of male Abiturienten also showed little variation, declining 3 per cent between 1931 and 1938.[109]

[102] Quoted in Büttner, op. cit., p. 850.
[103] Büttner, op. cit., pp. 866 f.
[104] Rolf Eilers, *Die nationalsozialistische Schulpolitik*, Cologne, 1963, p. 19.
[105] Alfred Homeyer, *Die Neuordnung des höheren Schulwesens im Dritten Reich*, Berlin, 1943, B 10a.
[106] Ibid., F 7.
[107] Ibid., F 1.
[108] *350 Jahre Humanistisches Gymnasium in Aachen*, Festschrift des Kaiser-Karls-Gymnasium, Aachen, 1951, p. 66.
[109] *Statistisches Jahrbuch für Deutschland*, 1949, p. 622.

Outside the normal school system was a new system of Nazi schools, variously intended as the incubators of future Party, SA, or SS men, but neither co-ordinated nor in any way mutually complementary, but rather, like their creators, Ley, Hess, Röhm, and Himmler, in competition. The oldest of these were the National-Political Training Institutions (Nationalpolitische Erziehungsanstalten, usually abbreviated to Napola) created in April 1933 as successors to the old Prussian cadet academies. The schools were ranked as the equivalent of Gymnasien, with initial priority for officers' sons and the sons of "proven" National Socialists, and intended as the academy of a future elite. Jointly steered at first by the SA and SS with the nominal co-operation of the Ministry of Education, the Hitler Youth, and the Army, the institutions drifted by 1936 under the direct control of the SS, which was prepared, theoretically, to extend them without limit. Their director, August Heissmeyer, made no reference to Party, Hitler Youth, or any other institutional limits on prospective applicants in an undated article of the late 1930s.[110] Any Volksschule teacher was eligible, in fact encouraged, to recommend candidates in 1937, and Napola staff were authorized to review Gymnasium applicants. In a reply to the puzzled queries of a regional Party functionary, unable to unscramble the institutional confusion of 1936, Heissmeyer emphasized that the Napolas were the perpetuation of the cadet academies and that their immediate competitor, the National Socialist German Secondary School (Nationalsozialistische Deutsche Oberschule) at Feldafing on the Starnberger See, in implied contrast to the Napolas, recruited its pupils from the ranks of "proven" Party members with the limited aim of supplying future leadership for the Nazi "State and movement."[111] In a supplementary policy statement of December 1936, he made Party membership desirable, adding that the Napolas were intended to benefit the rural and economically weaker sections of the population, with the sup-

[110] August Heissmeyer, "Die nationalpolitischen-Erziehungsanstalten," Schriften der Hochschule für Politik, Berlin Document Center, Ordner 270II.

[111] Heissmeyer letter of 12 May 1936 in Berlin Document Center, ibid.

plementary objective of penetrating Catholic areas "in which the Church has previously recruited a large part of its future leadership requirements on the basis of the boarding schools it erected there."[112]

Fees varied from full scholarships to RM 1200, though Heissmeyer estimated the average at about RM 50, an indirect indication that recruitment might have succeeded among the groups he hoped to reach. By the end of 1938, the number of Napolas had increased from three to twenty-one, including four in Austria and one in the Sudetenland. At the end of 1940, one hundred were planned at the rate of fifteen yearly, and another eighteen were in fact created in 1941/42 at a time when school expenditure was otherwise in a state of stagnation.[113] Graduates of the Napolas tended, as a rule, to military careers, at first in the Wehrmacht, later in the Waffen-SS, where there were indications that they were heartily despised.[114] The Waffen-SS nonetheless enjoyed increasing popularity among wartime pupils, rising from 11 per cent in 1942 to 53.9 per cent in 1944 of pupils' first choice of military branch.[115] Heissmeyer's report to Himmler in early 1944, referring to the heroism of his graduates, 1226 of whom were already dead or missing in action, was an ironic commentary on the successes of his enterprise.[116]

Feldafing was created in 1933 as Röhm's cadet academy and remained under SA control until 1936. Qualifying conditions in January 1934 gave first priority to the sons of "Dedi-

[112] Memo of 8 December 1936, ibid.

[113] Eilers, op. cit., p. 41.

[114] National Archives Microcopy T 175, Roll 127, frames 2–652240 ff., letters of November 6 and 12 1940. A Napola teacher reported to an SS general that his old pupils had written him not only of general hostility to Abiturienten as such in their Waffen-SS units but of being beaten up and in one case of nearly being left to drown in a training exercise.

[115] This compared with 17.6% opting for the Air Force, 13.1% for the Army and 5.6% for the Navy. Only 18% however indicated the intention of making a military career. Over 25% wanted to be engineers, about 15% teachers, about 12% doctors and another 10% farmers or foresters. Heissmeyer report of 10 January 1944, Berlin Document Center, op. cit.

[116] Report of 9 March 1944, ibid.

cated National Socialists, above all the sons of old and deserving fighters for the National Socialist movement," second priority to the sons of combat veterans of the war, third to the sons of Germans living abroad and those from territories lost in World War I, and last to "other" pupils.[117] In March 1936, the school passed under the direct authority of Hess,[118] and finally of the Nazi teacher organization, with the apparent co-operation of Heissmeyer. Of thirty-five graduates in 1939, fifteen went into Party work.[119] Theoretically, only health, good athletic performance, attractive personal appearance, character, and "good family" were required of applicants. "If sons of proven fighters for the movement are to be given preferential treatment," Heissmeyer wrote irritably to the director of the school in 1939, "they should nonetheless be considered only if they represent the very best material."[120] Not without evidence of Schadenfreude, he wrote to Munich Party officials in 1942, "Unfortunately I have to inform you that the selection for Feldafing in 1942 has taken a negative course for your Gau."[121]

The last of the Nazi academies was the so-called Adolf-Hitler-Schule, created in 1936 by Schirach and Ley as a successor to the Hitler Youth, in which membership had meanwhile become universal. The Hitler schools were exclusively Party institutions—exclusive even of the Ministry of Education—and, in the original prospectus, declared within the supervisory prerogatives of the Gauleiter in whose territory they happened to be built. Entrance was reserved to outstanding graduates of the Jungvolk, the junior division of the Hitler Youth, and selection was reserved to local Party and Hitler Youth leaders. Theoretically, all State and Party careers were to be open to graduates, but only in 1942 was the Hitler

117 Berlin Document Center, op. cit.

118 *Anordnungen des Stellvertreters des Führers* 35/36 of 3 March 1936, Archive of Institut für Zeitgeschichte, op. cit.

119 Eilers, op. cit., pp. 48 f.

120 Heissmeyer letter to Reichsschule Feldafing and Gauleitung Munich-Upper Bavaria of 28 September 1939. Berlin Document Center, op. cit.

121 Heissmeyer letter to Personalamt Gau Munich-Upper Bavaria of 4 May 1942, ibid.

school diploma accepted for university entrance.[122] "Satisfactory school records," like Party membership of parents, were declared desirable, but not essential. As in other cases, good athletic performance and leadership qualities could be considered as alternatives. In the tradition of the Volksgemeinschaft, illegitimate applicants were granted parity with the legitimate, Volksschüler with those from secondary schools.[123] But from the beginning the Hitler School was plagued by problems and at times even had difficulties meeting its relatively modest quota of six hundred pupils. Reflecting their difficulties, a decree of 1939 declared the Hitler schools off-limits for doctoral studies,[124] and an ambiguous memo of February 1941 reported that the past year's performance had been even worse than that of the year before.[125]

While no indication of quality, a 1940 survey indicates the social origin of Hitler pupils compared with Napola pupils and the general population:

TABLE 15
FATHERS' OCCUPATIONS[126]

	Napola	Hitler Schools	Reich
Officers	5.6%	3.0%	0.3%
Farmers	7.2	5.0	10.0
Civil Servants	26.0	12.0	5.0
White Collar	22.0	21.0	10.7
Blue Collar	13.1	11.0	45.0
Small Business	16.3	33.0	20.0
Other	9.8	9.0	9.0

[122] Cf. Eilers, op. cit., p. 46; *Erklärung der Reichsleiter Dr. Ley und von Schirach über die Adolf-Hitler-Schulen,* Büttner, op. cit., p. 871.

[123] *Volksgemeinschaft* was also built into the curriculum. The Hitler Youth leadership in 1938 advertised for "particularly qualified and pedagogically gifted journeymen" to teach the Hitler pupils wood and metal work. *Vorschriftenhandbuch der Hitler-Jugend,* 18VD/RB/RJF/24/III, memo of 22 July 1938.

[124] Ibid., RB/RJF/13/IV of 5 April 1939, p. 1881.

[125] Ibid., RJF/6/41 of 14 February 1941.

[126] *Statistische Monatshefte* of SS Erfassungsamt, November

One last institution lay outside the school system altogether. This was the Ordensburg (the castle of a knightly order). "The loss of leading Party members for purposes of promoting National Socialist policies in State positions and taking over numerous tasks within the Party, has led since 1933 to an ever more perceptible shortage of Party members capable of taking over Party positions from the rank of Kreisleiter on up," Hess noted in a memo of early 1936. "But the necessary reserves of future leadership material—despite my various suggestions—have not been systematically trained and developed."[127] This the Ordensburg was to correct, but to correct in the grand manner, as its name implied. Not only a kind of Party university, it was to be the institutional core of a band of brothers, united in mystic union and remote from the more prosaic world to which they were to return.

Three were built, all in locations at once striking and inaccessible, in Pomerania, Upper Bavaria, and the Eifel. Each was to house one thousand members plus an impressively inflated corps of five hundred instructors, cooks, porters, grooms, and various service personnel, befitting the "elite" the Ordensburgers were intended to be. Consistent with such a style, Ley introduced recruitment in 1936 with drumrolls and Napoleonic associations.[128] Formal qualifications were reduced again to a minimum: age 25–30, good health, service

---

1940, National Archives Microcopy T 74, Roll 15, frame 386828. Unfortunately the second column totals only 94%. A similar survey by the Hitler schools themselves, effective 1 October 1940, reported 21.3% civil servants' sons, respectively 2.7% upper, 13.0% middle and 5.6% lower, plus 3.5% sons of full-time Party functionaries. Sons of professionals total 15.0%, of those in academic occupations 5.5%, of self-employed artisans 10.5%, of non-self-employed artisans 9.0%, of industrial workers 7.0%, of farm workers 2.0%, of farmers 3.9%, and of officers 2.6%. It was also reported that 28.2% came from big cities, 51.6% from middle and small communities, and 20.2% from the country; 39% from the Volksschule, 17.5% from middle secondary schools, and 43.5% from Gymnasien. *Die Adolf-Hitler-Schule*, 1941, Archive of Institut für Zeitgeschichte 1720/55.

[127] *Anordnungen des Stellvertreters des Führers* 22/36 of 17 February 1936, op. cit.

[128] Cf. "Der Marschallstab im Tornister," *Der Völkische Beobachter*, 25 April 1936.

in Hitler Youth, Labor Service and Wehrmacht, and practical experience as Party functionary, SA, or SS man. This system, Ley announced, "represents an entirely new basis of selection. It opens the door to political leadership to the man on the street. The question is no longer 'Are you a graduate lawyer?' but 'What kind of a chap are you?' [Was für ein Kerl sind Sie?]"[129] All social considerations, education, occupation, and income, were explicitly excluded, as was an entrance examination. Selection was reserved to a hierarchy of party functionaries: the Kreisleiter, the Gauleiter, and finally to Ley himself. The Ordensburg candidate was to be maintained at public expense.[130]

While the Ordensburg administration seemed to show an even greater reluctance to submit to statistical investigation than its fellow institutions,[131] all indications point to the same difficulties that beset the Hitler schools. An East Prussian functionary wrote to Ley's office in 1937 that he had succeeded in finding seven candidates to meet his quota of twenty,[132] and a letter from Ley's office to a functionary in Bochum suggests that he was not invited but ordered to attend the Ordensburg.[133] Schwarz van Berk, who lectured at the Ordensburg Vogelsang in the Eifel shortly before the war, had the impression that Ley had succeeded in filling only 50 to 60 per cent of his three thousand places. He estimated that perhaps 10 per cent of these had made the Abitur, and perhaps 1 per cent had been at universities. The majority

[129] "Die Musterung des Führernachwuchses," VB, 7 April 1936.

[130] "Der Weg zur Ordensburg," Berlin undated, Archive of Institut für Zeitgeschichte 1783/55. An interesting consideration was nonetheless the following: "It is of no importance whether the candidate is married or unmarried. Should he be 26 or over, however, and still unmarried, this is a questionable indication of his capacity for decision, his courage, and his view of life."

[131] It is striking, for instance, that even the newspaper reports of Ley's initial inspection of the Ordensburg candidates, while emphasizing their social comprehensiveness, were loathe to give this comprehensiveness concrete meaning.

[132] Bundesarchiv NS 22/565, letter from Gauleitung Ostpreussen of 4 May 1937.

[133] Bundesarchiv NS 22/568, letter from Amt Führernachwuchs of 31 May 1937.

were either the sons of Party or Labor Front functionaries, or of those small-town artisans or farmers who might at one time have sent their sons, for similar reasons, to theological seminaries.[134] Such analysis as is possible[135] seems to confirm his impression. Of a random group of twenty-four, one listed his occupation as Abiturient, two—one of them an Austrian—as university students. The rest tended to be artisans, unskilled laborers and white-collar workers, including a teacher. Virtually all came from small towns. Fathers' occupations, in the few cases where they could be established, included a mason, a printer, a carpenter, a farmer, and an Austrian forester. Subsequent careers also reflected the dubious success of the enterprise. Some graduates found places in the administration of conquered eastern territories.[136] A number—seven of the twenty-four in the group referred to above—went to the SS. A large number seem to have gone into the Army, where they seem to have suffered a high number of casualties, and, more interesting perhaps, where an impressively high number—considering their ostensible "elite" status—seem not to have been given commissions. Only one of the random list had advanced by 1943 as high as captain. Unable to resolve the conflict between the popularity, necessary to bring it to power, and the expertise necessary to

[134] Interview with author of 15 November 1963. Schwarz van Berk recalled having tried to organize a seminar in foreign relations and letting an English acquaintance, now a London solicitor, address his audience. The results he described as "katastrophal." He estimated that perhaps 15 of his 500 listeners had some comprehension of what they were hearing. He added that he later complained to Ley, not only about the quality of the material but about its physical accommodation—there was in the entire structure, Schwarz recalled, not a single room for the future "elite" that housed fewer than 8–12 persons. Ley dismissed his critique with the observation, "Sie sind doch ein Intellektueller."

[135] Compiled on the basis of announcement of marriages, promotions, decorations, casualties, etc., in "Die Burggemeinschaft," Ordensburg Krössinsee (Pomerania), 1934, No. 11/12, pp. 16–17, Archive of Institut für Zeitgeschichte 1720/55, compared with available personnel records at Berlin Document Center.

[136] Here they were known as "golden pheasants," Schwarz reports, and again heartily despised by all including the Waffen-SS. Cf. Dallin, op. cit.

maintain it there, National Socialism itself precluded the exclusive elite of which it never ceased to speak. Only age,[137] a tendency to some sort of social marginality, an inclination to active dissatisfaction in the postwar years, and a common attraction to Hitler, united the Nazi leadership at all.

Franz Neumann's thesis that "National Socialist social policy consists in the acceptance and strengthening of the prevailing class character of German society,"[138] that the Third Reich represented, as before, the domination of the generals, the Junkers, and the industrialists with an admixture of Nazis, is a generally accurate reflection of the basic social situation, but doubly misleading. It is misleading in its suggestion of conscious purpose, its confusion of expediency with moral approval. It is still more misleading in its neglect of the dynamism characteristic of all Nazi policy, which revolutionized the role and influence of institutions and individuals with little reference to their size or titles.[139] What was involved was a revolution of class and a revolution of status at the same time. Two tendencies again interacted. On the one hand, the imperialist dynamics of the Third Reich, its eugenics and anti-intellectualism notwithstanding, sustained the position of the

[137] "With respect to age . . . the Nazi elite may be considered 'marginal' in the sense that it is dominated by a generation which took power in the state a decade or so younger than was the rule for German and other elites in western societies." Lerner, op. cit., p. 86.

[138] Franz Neumann, *Behemoth*, New York, 1942, p. 367.

[139] Irrespective of their striking similarities, a striking difference between Hitlerism and Stalinism is the near absence of purges in the former. The purge of June 1934 is remarkable as an exception. Failure or differences of opinion with Hitler led not to show trials, exile or execution, but at worst to private life in the case of Schacht or the Nazi version of an old Bolshevik like Feder; in the case of others, Frank, Rosenberg or Goering, it led to continued or even augmented titles and honors. At the same time, it seemed a characteristic of both states that actual influence could well be in inverse proportion to size—though the Labor Front might again be an exception. Thus, in the Third Reich, Party influence declined as the Party increased, and in the SS, as total membership grew, power was continually concentrated in one subdivision after another. Cf. Hannah Arendt, *The Origins of Totalitarianism*, New York, 1958, p. 403; Karl O. Paetel, "Geschichte und Soziologie der SS," *Vierteljahreshefte für Zeitgeschichte*, 1954, pp. 1 ff.

intellectual and the technician. National Socialism accelerated the already considerable mobility of German industrial society, creating at least an atmosphere of opportunity, and often enough, real evidence of it. Actual opportunity was limited in school and university, but neither of these was exactly a key institution in Nazi society. But it was real enough in the military, the economy, and even the civil service, the institutions that held Nazi society together.[140]

The status revolution, that accompanied this, was not a matter of elitism, even in the form of technocracy, but the triumph of egalitarianism, the reward and consummation of the Volksbewegung that had brought Hitler to power. The triumph of the down-and-out's, of the "armed Bohemians," did not necessarily mean that they ruled the state, or in the special case of the SS, committed murder in a Volksgemeinschaft with princes and graduate lawyers. What it did mean was that they represented it, that a man without diploma, family, or independent economic position laid cornerstones, greeted foreign visitors at the station, shook the hands of graduates, and claimed the royal box at the theatre. This symbolic role represented real social opportunity for those who enjoyed it, opportunity that neither Weimar nor the Empire had offered them. Like a super Elks Club, the Third Reich pampered the familiar human weakness for distinction on a scale probably without precedent. As early as 1935, the party listed over 200,000 "representatives of authority" (Hoheitsträger). Functionaries of various satellites like the

[140] Cf. Shirer, op. cit., p. 218. "Did a mike interview with General Ernst Udet tonight. . . . Udet . . . is something of a phenomenon. A professional pilot, who only a few years ago was so broke he toured America as a stunt flier, performing often in a full-dress suit and a top hat, he is now responsible for the designing and production of Germany's war planes. Though he never had any business experience, he has proved a genius at his job, . . . I could not help thinking tonight that a man like Udet would never be entrusted with such a job in America. He would be considered 'lacking in business experience.' Also, businessmen, if they knew of his somewhat bohemian life, would hesitate to trust him with responsibility. And yet in this crazy Nazi system he has done a phenomenal job." Udet, the hero of Carl Zuckmayer's 1946 play *"Des Teufels General,"* later committed suicide in despair with Hitler's policies.

corporatist groups, professional and welfare organizations, totaled nearly 1½ million, not including the representatives of still embryonic institutions like the Hitler Youth or the SS.[141] This, in the form of jobs, medals, uniforms, irrespective of authority, was status distribution in the grand manner, personal identification for thousands with the brave new world Hitler offered them. If it produced no elite, if it, in fact, precluded one, it nonetheless contributed to the general image of an open society.

The parents of a former pupil who had recently fallen in action expressed thanks to the commander of an Adolf Hitler School "for the splendid hours that our Hellmut was allowed to spend at the highest school of the Reich as a simple miner's son, something we could not have afforded to offer him ourselves."[142] Their letter tells at least as much about the Party academies, and by extension about opportunity in Nazi society, as any number of demonstrations of their practical failures.

[141] *Partei-Statistik*, Vol. II, p. 17; Vol. III, p. 14.

[142] "Schüler des Führers," Richthefte für Adolf-Hitler-Schüler, December 1944, p. 20, Archive of Institut für Zeitgeschichte 1720/55.

IX

The Third Reich and Society

The Third Reich proved that a house divided against itself *can* stand, provided, at least, that the occupants have no alternative place to go and that the landlord pays attention to the wallpaper, if not to the walls.

The German house was no less divided in 1939 or 1945 than it was in 1933 when Hitler took possession of it. The Gemeinschaft invoked by Nazi ideology struck genuinely resonant notes in the hearts of a population desperate for authority and sick unto death of conflict. But real Gemeinschaft was no closer to realization in practice at the end of Nazi rule than it was at the beginning. With all good will, German society was finally united only in a negative community of fear, sacrifice, and ruin. The elimination of class conflict, the Third Reich's major social boast from 1935 on, was at best a half truth. Beneath the cover of Nazi ideology, the historic social groups continued their conflicts like men wrestling under a blanket.[1] Beneath the surface of apparent economic recovery, none of the basic problems of German society had been solved; a more equitable relationship had not been found between capital and labor, between big business and small business, or between industry and agriculture. The problems had at best been postponed, in the case of agriculture even exacerbated.

The division of the Nazi house was built into the Party program. National Socialism was to turn the clocks back, to

[1] According to a contemporary joke, A tells B that "in Britain and America the plutocrats are still in control."

"What are ours then?" B replies. "Cratopluts?"

make the German-speaking world safe for small business, small farmers, and small-towners. The goal was not only political but social revisionism, revision of the tyranny of big industry, big cities, big unions, big banks; and at the same time a revision of Versailles. But the simultaneous revision of Versailles and of the twentieth—not to say the nineteenth—century, *in* the twentieth century, was an attempt to square the circle. Revision of Versailles, in Nazi dimensions, involved at the very least the threat of force. But the threat of force in an industrial age presupposes industry, and there is, as Nazi society conclusively proved, no industry without an industrial society.

The result was an inevitable rapprochement, at first with the industrialists, the generals, the diplomats, and the civil servants, whom the Nazi movement was expected to destroy; not, as should be obvious, because they were admired, but because they were necessary.[2] Then came the inevitable rapprochement with labor, without which there is no industrial society, a rapprochement born of industrial recovery and full employment and sustained with both concessions and ideology. The effective common denominators were the values traditionally called "national"—the efficient administration of the State, the expansion of the economy, the growth of the military establishment, and beyond these, the extension of German markets and frontiers. But the effective lever was the legitimacy and the threat of a mass movement that Hitler had, and that the industrialists, generals, diplomats, and civil servants did not have, and knew they did not have.

Papen's intrigues, Hindenburg's senility, and the hubris of the nationalist Right too contributed to Hitler's success. But the basic justification of Hitler's appointment was that authoritarian government under Papen, who had scorned mass support, and under Schleicher, who had failed to find it, had reached a dead end. If the decision to yield power to this particular mass movement was a fatal illusion, the decision to

[2] Hitler himself admitted this. "When I look at the intellectual classes here in Germany . . . ," he told the press. "But we need them. Otherwise, I don't know, we could wipe them out or something. But unfortunately we need them." Speech of 10 November 1938, in Domarus, op. cit., pp. 975 f.

yield power to a mass movement at all was, in its way, a moment of truth. It was also only a step from here to the conclusive demoralization of the industrialists, the intimidation of the generals, and the capitulation of the civil service that followed.[3] What had not happened in 1918 happened in 1933. Nazi élan had its complement in the shattered self-confidence of the old social elites. Like the figures in an animated cartoon, they had gone over a cliff in 1918, still running though nothing was beneath them. This time they recognized the abyss and fell. With them fell the institutions of German middle-class society—the parties, the universities, and the churches.

But while Hitler opened the door on a vacuum, it was one he could only partially fill. Filling it entirely presupposed the necessary administrative, economic, and military skills that his following basically lacked; it meant the collaboration of those who had themselves created the vacuum. To this they agreed, paving the road to hell with rationalizations of self-interest and national interest, positivist legality, hopes for the best, and hopes of avoiding the worst. What Hitler offered them was what they thought they wanted anyway. What he threatened them with was the achievement of these aims without their help. This characteristic dialectic of "national" ends and mass means was the basis of a new synthesis, the carrot-and-stick principle that was the de facto constitutional premise of the Third Reich.

But this too had paradoxical implications. Its success depended on the assumption that the movement was there as a deterrent and not an object of use. The practical consequence in this case was the schizophrenia typical of Nazi society. So far as could be seen, everything had changed and nothing had changed. Revolution was both imminent and indefinitely suspended. Industry enjoyed record profits, the generals appeared to be unchallenged, and Meissner, for example, who had once sat in Ebert's office and Hindenburg's, now sat in

[3] A revealing illustration of their attitude is Speer's account at Nuremberg of overhearing a group of miners in early 1945 declare their still unbroken faith in Hitler. This made such an impression on him that he dropped plans for an attempt on Hitler's life. Cf. Trevor-Roper, op. cit., pp. 89–91.

Hitler's. Yet industry made concessions not even demanded of it by a revolutionary SPD, the Army capitulated to a civilian administration like no other Army in German history, and the Reich was represented by a set of "new men" compared to whom the revolutionaries of 1792 appear in retrospect like representatives of the ancien régime—abroad by a one-time wine salesman, at home by a neurotic ex-corporal who had failed in the pursuit of everything but power.

What held things together was a combination of ideology and social dynamics on a foundation of charisma and terror. As time went on, even ideology became increasingly unnecessary, particularly for a younger generation of true believers.[4] Behind the entire system was an apparently total lack of alternatives. The official social goals were neither revoked nor seriously pursued, but indefinitely suspended. Symptomatically, Drexler's pamphlet of 1919, like Rosenberg's and Feder's commentaries on the Party program, was still being published in the late 1930s, long after the authors had subsided into one or another form of oblivion. What mattered was faith, and faith was rewarded. In the last analysis, anything could be rationalized with a reference not to Versailles but to 1932. Industrial production did go up, unemployment did go down, Austrians, Sudeten Germans, and Memellanders did come heim ins Reich (home to the Reich), foreign diplomats did capitulate, and foreign armies surrendered. Did it matter that the department stores survived and that big business grew bigger? The Communists, the Jews, and ultimately the war itself were the explanation and the apology. Utopia was suspended for the duration. But if Feder and Darré disappeared, their petit-bourgeois fantasies marched on, all evidences of social reality notwithstanding.

The SS and the Labor Front, the Third Reich's most successful institutional innovations, demonstrate the impact of social necessity on ideological orientation. From beginning to end, Himmler preached "racial" elitism, presided—as he saw it—over a new knightly order, dreamed of feudal do-

[4] Cf. Rauschning, *Die Revolution des Nihilismus,* Zurich-New York, 1938, p. 34; Haffner, op. cit., pp. 79 ff.

mains, new gods, a state of nature. At the same time, his policy precluded anything of the sort. Institutional survival in an industrial society requires administrators, not knights; diplomas, not blue eyes. Himmler consequently recruited administrators and diplomas. The success of his organization itself depended on its abstention from the very ideology it represented and in which at least some of its members really believed. In turn, the SS' success derived from its accommodation to a society its members were sworn to destroy. Only this initial accommodation, the organizational basis of administrators and diplomas, permitted the subsequent recruitment of knights and blue eyes at all. The Ordensideologie (the ideology of a knightly order), to the extent it was ever realized, was necessarily realized in the social vacuum of the occupied Eastern territories, not in Germany.

By comparison, Ley's Ordensburgen, which nominally practiced Ordensideologie at home, which recruited not frustrated officers, civil servants, and doctors, but "ganze Kerle," ("all good fellows," by general agreement, another expression for yokels) vegetated in every sense, including the geographical, on the margins of Nazi society. So did the Hitler Youth with its uncomprehending complaints about the consistently bad results of its own consistently executed selection policy for the Adolf Hitler Schools. Both cases demonstrate the limits imposed even by the Third Reich on careers for the untalented.

If the SS was the bridge that carried the old social elites into the heart of the Third Reich,[5] it was the Labor Front that carried the plebs. In the case of the Labor Front, success was not a result of administrative talent or particular organizational solidarity, but more or less automatic. The premise of mass support in a society resolved and compelled to be industrial made concessions from the regime inevitable. The full employment produced by total industrial mobilization then made concessions from employers inevitable too. In both cases, concessions derived from the decision to reverse Versailles, irrespective of, even despite, the interests and intentions of the respective partners. The lesson

[5] Cf. Chs. VII and VIII.

might be that an industrial society cannot exist without a labor movement. If one does not exist, it has to be invented.

What is striking in both the case of the SS and the Labor Front is the reorientation of support without any equivalent change of ideology, a paradox based on the adaptability of its supporters as well as adaptability of the ideology. In the years before 1933, the SS had lived in the shadow of the SA. The NSBO, predecessor of the Labor Front, had existed in the shadow of the Party and an electorate of irate shopkeepers, small businessmen, and small farmers and their Nazified pressure groups and front organizations. The ascent of the SS and the Labor Front after 1933 was matched by the decline of the SA and the Party. This meant a fundamental shift in the sociological basis of Nazi support. But there was no consequent redefinition of Nazi goals. A movement carried to power by the outsiders of Weimar society was now carried beyond it by the earlier insiders—at least passively. Labor and Bildungsbürgertum (educated middle class) alike surrendered to the stronger battalions by joining them.

This process helps to account for the remarkable durability of Nazi society despite the centrifugal forces it created. In the context of both ideological mobilization and industrial recovery, every social group was integrated, almost overnight, into the new system. The immediate dissatisfactions were wiped out. The unemployed returned to work, the economic curve went up, the farm price index held firm. The new dissatisfactions, to the extent they were perceived at all, were rationalized and sublimated in a system whose very fluidity promised eventual solution to those with enough faith and hard enough elbows. Success promised more success, and war obviated the need for producing it. In the meanwhile, as a kind of advance payment on success, there were opportunities for the taking—by those with talent and those without it, those with education and those without it, those with money and whose without it.

The conflicts that might have arisen from extended reflection on the limits of such successes and the reality of such opportunities were resolved by the genuine conceptual difficulties the new situation presented. In the Third Reich, relative approximation of class and status came to an end.

Discontent presupposes its recognition. The disillusion induced by one's awareness of his own importance or unimportance presupposes that one is aware of it—or at least is made aware of it by one's neighbors. This was next to impossible in the wonderland of Hitler Germany where there were no longer reliable indications of what was up and what was down. How important was a minister, a diplomat, a Party functionary, a Labor Front functionary, a Hitler Youth leader, a member of an Ordensburg? The question was unanswerable.

A few examples indicate the problems involved in trying to answer it. Since the publication of *Mein Kampf,* Hitler had regularly and consistently declared his unambiguous contempt for the businessmen, diplomats, civil servants, and university graduates of official German society. There was no reason to doubt his sincerity. Deviations were never total but always qualified. Each audience was distinguished from "the others," an honorable exception to a general rule. Even at his most conciliatory, as in the famous Industry Club speech in Düsseldorf in 1932, Hitler left no doubt of his real position, tactfully but unmistakably reminding his audience of its share in the disaster of 1918, and leaving no doubt that business in the Third Reich was never again to achieve primacy over politics.[6]

In an expansive moment in 1940, according to Rosenberg, Hitler spoke "very negatively of the civil service," to which a liaison officer of the Foreign Ministry "smilingly" asked whether the Foreign Ministry might be an exception. "It is a remarkable thing," Hitler replied, "that in every operetta the

[6] Domarus, op. cit., pp. 72 f. The first charge alone, coming from a man who maintained that his entire life had been changed by the disaster of 1918, was equivalent to condemning the audience to outer darkness. But the proposition of the primacy of politics was doubly revealing. "In Germany too the power state (Machstaat) created the basic premises of later economic prosperity," Hitler declared, to which members of his audience replied, "Sehr richtig!" This episode reveals not only how Hitler felt about the businessmen in front of him. Their assent also gives some idea of why he felt that way, some idea of the real limits of German capitalism. Even if one could imagine Roosevelt making a comparable statement to a comparable American business audience at the same time, can one imagine a similar response from them?

diplomats are portrayed as stupid (doof). This is no coincidence. The father of several sons let the most efficient take over the estate or something equally sensible. The one who was not all there was sent into the diplomatic service."[7]

But what did all this say about businessmen, about the civil servants or the diplomats, all of whom continued to exist as before? Was it a coincidence that even among the new diplomats there was a von Jagow and a von Killinger? What was the German on the street, whether pro-Nazi or anti-Nazi, to conclude about the status of diplomats or about diplomats as a class? What, considering the labyrinthine diplomatic practices of the Third Reich, was in fact the status of diplomats? What, in the main, were its diplomats as a class?

The same problems arose in the anarchic relations of Party and State. For Frick, Guertner, Ribbentrop, promotion to ministerial rank meant a loss, not a gain, in influence. Compared with their old Party offices, promotion to Governor General of Poland for Frank, to Reichsminister for the Eastern Territories for Rosenberg, "did not signify the climax but the end of their National Socialist careers."[8] On the other hand, to cite two contrary examples, this was not true for Goebbels or for Goering, appointed to ministerial rank in 1933, or for Himmler in 1944. What did this say about the status of ministers and Party officials? Hitler's ministers like Papen's tended to be university graduates, doctors, high civil servants.[9] What did this say about Hitler's government compared with Papen's as a matter of class?

The answers depended on the observer. For the conservative observer, the old guard was the guarantor of continuity, of the historical state that demanded his confidence and his patriotism. For the radical observer, Hitler himself was the guarantor of change, of the new State that demanded his confidence and his patriotism. For even if the old guard was

[7] Rosenberg, *Politisches Tagebuch*, op. cit., p. 134.

[8] Hannah Arendt, op. cit., p. 404.

[9] Nor were Nazis with doctorates, even the most aggressively egalitarian of them like Ley and Goebbels, inhibited about appearing in public with their titles.

still on top,[10] Hitler himself, the corporal and "building worker," was at the very summit. In an economy primed in the meantime with armaments appropriations and building contracts, a society burgeoning with new offices and new opportunities, further reflection could be avoided where objective analysis was in any case impossible. In an extreme case—again the SS—members had the opportunity of humiliating doctors, professors, and judges while being led by doctors, professors, and judges.

In the resultant collision of ideological and industrial revolution, traditional class structure broke down, and with it the traditional structure of political action. If no social group did well in the Third Reich, no social group did badly—or so badly that its discontent was not compensated by the contentment of another group. Labor's defeat was business' triumph, agriculture's frustrations labor's relief, small business' misfortunes the consumer's reward, the consumer's aggravation agriculture's compensation. Kraft durch Freude was supplemented by Kraft durch Schadenfreude. At the same time, at any given moment, some businessmen did well enough, some farmers did well enough, some workers did well enough, to distinguish their interests, their stake in the new regime, from that of their sociological fellows. The classless reality of the Third Reich was mirrored by its opponents, the historically unique coalition of aristocrats, civil servants, clergymen of both Christian churches, and trade unionists who joined forces in 1944 in a final desperate attempt to bring it down.

The net result was not so much a dual state of Nazi politics and capitalist economics as a dual society in which the status of both groups and individuals moved independently of their old objective underpinnings. There was no new class, still less a new elite. There was at best a new set of classes, a set of mutually competitive elites. It was a world that defied the laws of social gravity without replacing them. The average citizen, passive or participant, lived in a world of traditional relationships, forces, and status, and a Nazi world where the

[10] According to a typical contemporary joke, "NSBO=Noch sind die Bonzen oben."

addition of a uniform or a lapel pin could immediately invalidate them.[11] The conflicts of "real" world and "Nazi" world were then reproduced in every kind of combination and permutation. The Wehrmacht rejected the SA; the SA despised the SS; SA and SS deeply resented the Party; SA, SS, and Party resented the power of the incumbent civil service. Everyone seems to have joined in common contempt for the "golden pheasants" of Ley's Ordensburgen. The reports of SS sergeants beating up the graduates of Napolas,[12] of the muffled conflict between generations within the ranks of the Party bureaucracy,[13] indicate lines of division not only between but within institutions. Mutual recognition was the product not of consensus but of quasi-diplomatic negotiations between quasi-sovereignties like the Labor Front and the industrialists at Leipzig in 1935, between the Hitler Youth and the Labor Front, the Hitler Youth and the Party or SS, or between any of them, as in the case of the Four Year Plan, and the relevant branches of the civil service.

The synthesis was a world of frustration and exaltation. But above all it was a world of general perplexity in which, even before the war, "Nazi" and "German" merged indistinctly but inseparably, and the Volksgemeinschaft of official ideology acquired a bizarre reality. In a society accustomed to identify political conflict with class conflict, conflict—in the sense that it had hitherto resulted in organization and action

[11] An example of this in practice can be found in an order of Hess's. "Just as high-ranking Party functionaries, in the performance of their military service, have no right to claim a commission on the basis of their Party rank, Party members who happen to hold high positions in the State or to have spent years in the Wehrmacht have no reason, on that account, to lay claim to comparable Party offices, let alone to get them." *Anordnungen des Stellvertreters des Führers* 36/36 of 3 March 1936, op. cit. Cf. Arendt, op. cit., p. 399: "The inhabitant of Hitler's Third Reich lived not only under the simultaneous and often conflicting authorities of competing powers, such as the civil services, the Party, the SA, and the SS; he could never be sure and he was never explicitly told whose authority he was supposed to place above all others. He had to develop a kind of sixth sense to know at a given moment whom to obey and whom to disregard."

[12] Cf. Ch. VIII.

[13] Cf. Ch. VII.

—seemed to have disappeared altogether. Instead, it reproduced itself in forms so diverse that their only common denominator seems in retrospect to have been the near universality with which they were misunderstood. In a world where the purge of 30 June 1934, for example, meant not the end but the transitional phase of a revolution and where an informed and intelligent foreigner could maintain plausibly in 1937, shortly before the second—if bloodless—purge, that the conservative forces were now regaining control of German society,[14] the contemporary, observer and participant alike, was without a map. Reluctant to return to the original entrance, he not surprisingly plunged ever deeper into a forest he found ever harder to describe. It is revealing that the most profound analysis of the Third Reich in the context of the social history of the preceding century, Thomas Mann's *Doktor Faustus,* was a novel, written by a man who never set foot in the Third Reich at all.

The social consequences of this ultimate disorientation were correspondingly paradoxical. A consistent extension of German history, the Third Reich consistently perpetuated the historic discrepancy between objective social reality and its interpretation. Objective social reality, the measurable statistical consequences of National Socialism, was the very opposite of what Hitler had presumably promised and what the majority of his followers had expected him to fulfill. In 1939 the cities were larger, not smaller; the concentration of capital greater than before; the rural population reduced, not increased; women not at the fireside but in the office and the factory; the inequality of income and property distribution more, not less conspicuous; industry's share of the gross national product up and agriculture's down, while industrial labor had it relatively good and small business increasingly bad. The East Elbian estates continued to be run by the gentry, the civil service by doctors, and the Army by generals whose names began with "von." Not surprisingly, the history of the Third Reich is a story of frustration, cynicism, and resignation, the history of an apparently betrayed

[14] Stephen H. Roberts, *The House That Hitler Built,* London, 1937, pp. 359 ff.

revolution whose one-time supporters, Otto Strasser, Rauschning, Feder, and Rosenberg, one after the other, denounced it as vehemently as its opponents.

Interpreted social reality, on the other hand, reflected a society united like no other in recent German history, a society of opportunities for young and old, classes and masses, a society that was New Deal and good old days at the same time. Like no world since 1914, it was a world of career civil servants and authoritarian paternalism, a world of national purpose and achievement where the Army was once again "the school of the nation." It was no less a world where officers and men ate the same meals and conversed "as men to men."[15]

"Formerly when I went to the theatre with my wife," a prison camp guard told Hans Habe, "there was always trouble. We got a seat in the twentieth row. But Huber, our chief accountant, and his wife were in the tenth row. And afterward all hell broke loose. Why can the Hubers afford the tenth row and not ourselves? Nowadays, six nights a week, all the seats in the theatre cost the same. First come, first served. Sometimes the Hubers sit in the tenth row, and we sit in the twentieth. But my wife knows that's because the Hubers live nearer the theatre."[16]

"For the first time in my life," a Marburg Gymnasium teacher told Milton Mayer after the war, "I was really the peer of men who, in the Kaiser time and in the Weimar time, had always belonged to classes lower or higher than my own, men whom one had always looked down on or up to, but never *at*. . . . National Socialism broke down that separation, that class distinction. Democracy—such democracy as we had had—didn't do it, and is not doing it now."[17]

The interpreted social reality, in turn, had its own objective reality where a Prince of Schaumburg-Lippe served as Goebbels' adjutant and a Prince of Hesse answered Goering's telephone; where Prussian marshals saluted an Austrian cor-

[15] Cf. Shirer, op. cit., pp. 213, 345.

[16] Hans Habe, *A Thousand Shall Fall*, London, 1942, p. 217.

[17] Milton Mayer, *They Thought They Were Free*, Chicago, 1955, p. 105.

poral;[18] where a bourgeois Berlin school girl, fleeing the stuffiness of her German Nationalist home in search of "working youth," sought it in a career in the Hitler Youth and the Labor Service;[19] and an audience of Göttingen law students told a bemused von Salomon, "We don't want a state, we want a Volksgemeinschaft."[20]

It is axiomatic that very few of the participants in this world were seriously alienated from the "real" world, let alone clinically abnormal.[21] Sadists, paranoids, ne'er-do-wells, represented the smallest of minorities, and a minority that tended to be eliminated, not concentrated, from 1933 on.[22] Of the Nuremberg defendants, only two, Hess and Streicher, could be regarded as clinically abnormal, and both were men who had failed in Nazi society rather than succeeded.[23] In both cases, real insanity had proved to be a professional obstacle, not an advantage. The rest, not mad but, in Riesman's phrase, "other-directed" men, were the real executors of the Third Reich, in Hannah Arendt's expression "banal" in their evil, the "normal" representatives of a pathological society.

The basic problem was not political or economic, but social, the problem of an arrested bourgeois-industrial society, convinced by its guilt feelings and its impotence of its own superfluousness, and prepared to destroy itself with the means of the very bourgeois-industrial society it aimed to destroy. The "conservative" motives of so many of the ostensible revolutionaries make the Third Reich a novelty among revolutions since 1789, but a revolution nonetheless, united by a

18 ". . . welche Abdikation des Marschallstabes vor dem Tornister." Karl Kraus, *Die dritte Walpurgisnacht*, Munich, 1955, p. 83.

19 Maschmann, op. cit., p. 25. The Hitler Youth, in 1933 when she joined it, was a particularly unlikely place to find what she was looking for. What makes the story important is that a girl from such a background was looking for this at all.

20 Salomon, op. cit., p. 249.

21 Cf. Bayle, op. cit., pp. 180 f.

22 Many concentration camp survivors report that it was only the earliest generation of SA guards that tortured prisoners for pleasure. The SS guards who followed them tended rather to be "businesslike." Cf. Arendt, op. cit., p. 454.

23 Cf. G. M. Gilbert, *Nuremberg Diary*, New York, 1947.

community of enemies and supported by representatives of every social group. Destruction alone was a common goal after all others—"Beamtenstaat" and Volksgemeinschaft, "back to the land" and back to the boundaries of 1918, the salvation of private property and the achievement of "national socialism"—had eliminated one another in a process of mutual cancellation. In the end, with the achievement of each partial goal, the destruction of unions and aristocracy, of Jews, of the Rights of Man and of bourgeois society, destruction was all that was left.

"The insensate hate which presided over and directed this enterprise," writes Rousset, "derived from the specter of all the frustrations, of all the mean, deceived aspirations, of all the envy and despair engendered by the extraordinary decomposition of the German middle classes between the wars. To pretend to discover in these the atavisms of a race is to echo the mentality of the SS. With each economic catastrophe, with each financial blow, the structure of German society collapsed. Nothing remained but an extraordinary nudity composed of impotent rage and criminal malice, thirsting for vengeance."[24]

In a simultaneous revolution of their situation and their awareness of it, the pillars of society—the Junkers, the industrialists, the Bildungsbürgertum—joined forces with their own enemies to pull down the roof that had hitherto sheltered them. Goebbels invoked the splendid egalitarianism of the bombs falling around him, the total social revolution of total war.[25] His invocation was not only the appropriate elegy of the Third Reich but the elegy of a whole German society.

[24] David Rousset, *L'Univers Concentrationnaire,* Paris, 1946, pp. 114 f.

[25] Cf. Trevor-Roper, op. cit., p. 57. "The bomb terror spares the dwellings of neither rich nor poor; before the labour offices of total war the last class barriers have had to go down."

APPENDIXES

Appendix I

Development of Employee Income 1932 and 1940

Income Group	Employees in 1000s	%	Income In RM 1,000,000	%
		1932		
Under RM 1500	2378	31	2089	12
1500–1800	967	12	1594	9
1800–2400	1754	22	3630	21
2400–3600	1601	21	4610	27
3600–4800	605	8	2498	14
4800–6000	280	4	1479	9
6000–7200	107	1	696	4
Over 7200	87	1	700	4
Total	7779		17296	
		1940		
Under RM 1500	6064	35	5454	15
1500–1800	1510	9	2488	7
1800–2400	3063	18	6416	17
2400–3600	4498	26	13098	35
3600–4800	1339	8	5449	14
4800–6000	487	3	2581	7
6000–7200	173	1	1124	3
Over 7200	79	0	616	2
Total	17213		37226	

RATE OF EMPLOYEE INCOME GROWTH 1932–40

Income Group	*Growth in No. of Employees in %*	*Growth of Income in %*
Under RM 1500	167	161
1500–1800	56	56
1800–2400	74	76
2400–3600	180	182
3600–4800	122	120
4800–6000	76	78
6000–7200	62	62
Over 7200	−9	−12
All Groups	120	115

Appendix II

Income and Income Tax Distribution 1934 and 1938

1934						
Income Group	*Taxpayers in 1000s*	%	*Income in RM 1,000,000*	%	*Tax in RM 1,000,000*	%
Under RM 1500	595	28	662	7	20	2
1500–3000	748	35	1582	17	78	7
3000–5000	351	16	1347	15	97	9
5000–8000	201	9	1261	14	115	10
8000–12,000	121	6	1162	13	125	11
12,000–16,000	47	2	650	7	82	8
16,000–25,000	39	1.4	760	8	119	11
25,000–50,000	22	1.0	731	8	161	15
50,000–100,000	6.3	0.3	423	5	124	11
Over 100,000	2.2	0.1	447	5	167	15
Total	2132.5		9025		1088	

1938						
Under RM 1500	608	17	694	3	23	0.7
1500–3000	1156	32	2522	11	131	4
3000–5000	777	22	3005	13	216	6
5000–8000	456	12	2846	13	260	7
8000–12,000	275	8	2652	12	289	8
12,000–16,000	114	3	1564	7	200	6
16,000–25,000	105	3	2060	9	323	9
25,000–50,000	70	2	2383	11	532	18
50,000–100,000	25	0.7	1713	8	512	14
Over 100,000	12	0.3	2944	13	1128	31
Total	3598		22,383		3614	

RATE OF INCOME GROWTH IN TERMS OF INCOME TAXPAYERS
1934–38

Income Group	*Growth of No. of Taxpayers in %*	*Growth of Income in %*	*Growth of Tax Burden in %*
Under RM 1500	2.5	5	15
1500–3000	55	59	68
3000–5000	122	122	122
5000–8000	127	126	126
8000–12,000	128	128	131
12,000–16,000	143	141	147
16,000–25,000	169	171	171
25,000–50,000	218	227	230
50,000–100,000	297	310	310
Over 100,000	445	557	575
All Groups	68	148	231

BIBLIOGRAPHY

PRIMARY SOURCES

Archival Material

Berlin Document Center. Personnel Files of Gauleiter; Obergruppenführer and Gruppenführer; Oberbefehsleiter der NSDAP; SA Brigadenführer, Obergruppenführer and Gruppenführer; Treuhänder der Arbeit, Gauwalter of Labor Front; and Ordensburg members. Files on Adolf-Hitler-Schulen, Nationalpolitische-Erziehungsanstalten and Reichsschule Feldafing.

Bundesarchiv. Files of NSDAP (Gau Franken), Reichskanzlei, Reichsministerium des Innern, Reichsministerium für Propaganda, Reichsministerium für Wissenschaft, Erziehung und Volksbildung.

Institut für Zeitgeschichte: Police reports on Party and SA; Film 103/1 from Deutsches Zentralarchiv Potsdam, material on Party and civil service.

National Archives Microcopies: T 74, Roll R–15; T 81, Rolls 1, 11, 14, 54, 92, and 166; T 175, Rolls 17, 23, 31, 38, 40, 49, 127.

Document Collections and Reference Works

Anordnungen des Stellvertreters des Führers, Munich, 1937.

Büttner, Johannes, *Der Weg zum nationalsozialistischen Reich,* Berlin, 1943.

Domarus, Max, *Hitler: Reden und Proklamationen, 1932–38,* Würzburg, 1962.

Das Führerlexikon, Munich, 1934.
Hofer, Walter, *Der Nationalsozialismus,* Frankfurt, 1957.
Homeyer, Alfred, *Die Neuordnung des höheren Schulwesens im Dritten Reich,* Berlin, 1943.
International Military Tribunal, *Proceedings,* Vols. I–XXIII, Nuremberg, 1947–49.
Jochmann, Werner, *Im Kampf um die Macht* (Hitlers Rede vor dem Hamburger Nationalklub von 1919), Stuttgart, 1960.
Lorenz, Charlotte, *Zehnjahres-Statistik des Hochschulbesuchs und der Abschlussprüfungen,* Berlin, 1943.
Meier-Benneckenstein, Paul (ed.), *Dokumente der deutschen Politik,* Vol. 5, Berlin, 1938.
Picker, Henry, *Hitlers Tischgespräche,* Bonn, 1951.
Podzun, H. H. (ed.), *Das deutsche Heer,* Bad Nauheim, 1953.
Reichsorganisationsleiter, *Partei-Statistik,* Vols. I–III.
Reichstags-Handbücher, 1930–36.
Rühle, Gerd (ed.), *Das dritte Reich, 1934,* Berlin, 1935.
Statistische Jahrbücher für das deutsche Reich, 1937–42.
Statistisches Jahrbuch für Deutschland, Munich, 1949.
Statistisches Jahrbuch der Schutzstaffel der NSDAP, 1937–38.
Teschemacher, Hermann, *Handbuch des Aufbaus der gewerblichen Wirtschaft,* Leipzig, 1936.
Vorschriftenhandbuch der Hitler-Jugend, Vol. III.
Zeitschrift des bayerischen statistischen Landesamtes.

Basic Nazi Works

Drexler, Anton, *Mein politisches Erwachen,* Munich, 1937.
Feder, Gottfried, *Das Programm der NSDAP,* Munich, 1931.
Goebbels, Paul Josef, *Angriff,* Munich, 1935.
——*Tagebuch, 1925–6,* Stuttgart, 1961.
——*Die zweite Revolution,* Zwickau, 1926.
Goering, Hermann, *Reden und Aufsätze,* Munich, 1940.
Hitler, Adolf, *Mein Kampf* (1925, 1928), Munich, 1939.
——*Zweites Buch,* Stuttgart, 1961.
Röhm, Ernst, *Die Geschichte eines Hochverräters,* Munich, 1934.
Rosenberg, Alfred, *Wesen, Grundsätze und Ziele der NSDAP,* Munich, 1937.
Strasser, Gregor, *Kampf um Deutschland,* Munich, 1932.

LITERATURE PUBLISHED IN THE THIRD REICH

Newspapers and Periodicals

Der Angriff
Das Berliner Tageblatt
Die Fränkische Tageszeitung
Die Frankfurter Zeitung
Das Hakenkreuzbanner (Mannheim)
Der Illustrierte Beobachter
Schüler des Führers, Richthefte für Adolf-Hitler-Schüler
Der Schulungsbrief
Das Schwarze Korps
Soziale Praxis
Der Völkische Beobachter (Munich edition)
Der Westdeutsche Beobachter

Articles

"Agrarpreissteigerung—Wo und Warum," *Die Wirtschaftskurve,* December 1936.

Altstädter, Wilfried, "Sippe und berufliche Herkunft der Studierenden an der Universität München im Winterhalbjahr 1935/36," *Zeitschrift des bayerischen statististischen Landesamtes,* 1937.

"Arbeitseinkommen—Unternehmereinkommen," *Die deutsche Volkswirtschaft,* February 1935.

Arnhold, Karl, "Lehrling—einst und jetzt," *Soziale Praxis,* 23 July 1937.

"Auslese der wirklich Tüchtigen," *Die deutsche Volkswirtschaft,* February 1935.

Bauer, Wilhelm, und Peter Dehem, "Landwirtschaft und Volkseinkommen," *Vierteljahreshefte zur Konjunkturforschung,* 1938–39.

Behrens, Gustav, "Stillstand in der Erzeugungsschlacht," *Odal,* 1939.

Best, Werner, "Neubegründung des Polizeirechts," *Jahrbuch der Akademie für deutsches Recht,* 1937.

Blomeyer, Karl, "Neuerungen im Erbhofrecht," *Jahrbücher für Nationalökonomie und Statistik,* Vol. 146, October 1937.

Bramesfeld, E., "Frauenarbeit in der Industrie," *Werkstattstechnik und Werksleiter,* 1937.

Brandenburg, Hans, "Nationalsozialismus und Bürgertum," *Blut und Boden,* No. 3, 1933.

von der Decken, Hans, "Die Mechanisierung in der Landwirtschaft," *Vierteljahreshefte zur Konjunkturforschung,* 1938–39.

"Deutscher Sozialismus," *Monatshefte für nationalsozialistische Sozialpolitik,* April 1938.

Eckert, Harald, "Sozialismus der Ehrengerichte und das Arbeitsrecht," *Die Tat,* April 1934.

——"Erbhofrecht und Kapitalismus," *Die Tat,* June 1934.

Eschmann, Ernst-Wilhelm, "Die Stunde der Soziologie," *Die Tat,* March 1934.

Frauendorfer, Max, "Ständischer Aufbau," *Grundlagen, Aufbau und Wirtschaftsordnung des nationalsozialistischen Staates,* Vol. III, No. 47, Berlin-Vienna, 1936.

Freyer, Hans, "Gegenwartsaufgaben der deutschen Soziologie," *Zeitschrift für die gesamte Staatswissenschaft,* 1935.

Hagen, Harro, "Die Erziehung in der Hitlerjugend," *Süddeutsche Monatshefte,* March 1935.

Graf Helldorff, W. F., "Adel und Nationalsozialismus," *Das neue Deutschland,* October 1935.

Höhn, Reinhard, "Die Wandlung in der Soziologie," *Süddeutsche Monatshefte,* August 1934.

Höpker, Wolfgang, "Studenten und Arbeiter," *Die Tat,* February 1934.

Huber, E. R., "Die Rechtsstellung des Volksgenossen," *Zeitschrift für die gesamte Staatswissenschaft,* 1936.

Hunke, "Gedanken zum Reichsberufswettkampf," *Die deutsche Volkswirtschaft,* February 1935.

Ibing, Erwin, "Auslese durch Wettkampf," *Der Hoheitsträger,* January 1939.

Kilian, Friedrich, "Der unsterbliche Bürger," *Die Tat,* December 1933.

Kleiner, W., "Der alte Mittelstand," *Die deutsche Volkswirtschaft,* August 1935.

Klug, Oskar, "Möglichkeit und Grenzen des deutschen Handwerks," *Die deutsche Volkswirtschaft,* February 1935.

Kühbacher, Otto Chr., "Vierzig Buchdrucker nehmen den Spaten in die Hand," *Süddeutsche Monatshefte,* March 1935.

Kühne, Hans, "Der Arbeitseinsatz im Vierjahresplan," *Jahrbücher für Nationalökonomie und Statistik,* 1937.

Kuhr, Theodor, "Begriff und Problem der Marktordnung in der liberalistischen und in der nationalsozialistischen Wirtschaftstheorie," *Kartell-Rundschau,* November 1936.

Kummer, Kurt, "Der Weg der deutschen Bauernsiedlung," *Odal,* November 1939.

Ley, Robert, Notice in *Das Archiv,* August 1934.

Mansfeld, Werner, "Sicherung des Gefolgschaftsbestandes," *Der Vierjahresplan,* March 1937.

——"Drei Lohnthesen," *Der deutsche Volkswirt,* 25 August 1939.

Maunz, Theodor, "Die Entwicklung des deutschen Verwaltungsrechts seit dem Jahre 1933," *Zeitschrift für die gesamte Staatswissenschaft,* 1935.

——"Zur Neugestaltung des Enteignungsrechtes," *Deutsche Juristen-Zeitung,* 1935.

Miksch, Leonhard, "Wo herrscht noch freier Wettbewerb," *Die Wirtschaftskurve,* December 1936.

Mirgeler, Albert, "Der Nationalsozialismus als Ausdruck der politischen Landschaft des Reiches," *Deutsches Volkstum,* October 1933.

Pfenning, Andreas, "Das Eliten-Problem in seiner Bedeutung für den Kulturbereich der Wirtschaft," *Zeitschrift für die gesamte Staatswissenschaft,* July 1936.

——"Gemeinschaft und Staatswissenschaft," *Zeitschrift für die gesamte Staatswissenschaft,* 1936.

"Reaktionäre Volkswirtschaftslehre," *Die deutsche Volkswirtschaft,* August 1935.

Reischle, Hermann, "Der Weg der nationalsozialistischen Wirtschaft," *Odal,* October 1939.

Ruban, Hans, "Die Lage," *Die deutsche Volkswirtschaft,* November 1935.

——"Mehr Sozialismus," *Die deutsche Volkswirtschaft,* December 1935.

Russell, Claire, "Die Praxis des Zwangskartellgesetzes," *Zeitschrift für die gesamte Staatswissenschaft,* May 1939.

Scheidt, H. W., "Aussenpolitischer Nachwuchs aus den Reihen der Partei," *Der Hoheitsträger,* June 1939.

Scheuner, Ulrich, "Der Gleichheitsgedanke in der völkischen Verfassungsordnung," *Zeitschrift für die gesamte Staatswissenschaft,* February 1939.

Schmitt, Carl, "Was bedeutet der Streit um den Rechtsstaat," *Zeitschrift für die gesamte Staatswissenschaft,* Vol. 195.

Schultz, Rudolf, "Erziehung oder Auslese," *Der Hoheitsträger,* September 1939.

Seraphim, Hans-Jürgen, "Neuschaffung deutschen Bauerntums," *Zeitschrift für die gesamte Staatswissenschaft,* November 1934.

"Die Sicherstellung des Führernachwuchses der Partei," *Der Zeitspiegel,* 6 March 1936.

Six, F. A., "Nachwuchs und Auslese auf den deutschen Hochschulen," *Der deutsche Student,* March 1935.

Stein, H., "Erziehung zur Selbstverantwortung im Betrieb," *Werkstattstechnik und Werksleiter*, July 1937.

——"Arbeiter bestimmen selbst Zeitvorgabe und Stückpreis," *Zeitschrift für Organisation*, Vol. 11, No. 1, 25 January 1937 and No. 4, 25 April 1937.

Stein, Johannes, "Universität und Auslese," *Süddeutsche Monatshefte*, October 1934.

Stritzke, Otto, "Die Ordnung des graphischen Gewerbes als Beispiel," *Kartell Rundschau*, December 1936.

——"Das Elektro-Abkommen," *Kartell Rundschau*, June 1936.

Syrup, Friedrich, "Arbeitseinsatz gegen Landflucht," *Odal*, July 1939.

Tiessler, Walter, "Klassenkampf," *Der Hoheitsträger*, June 1939.

Völtzer, Friedrich, "Vom Werden des deutschen Sozialismus," *Zeitschrift für die gesamte Staatswissenschaft*, January 1936.

"Die Wirtschaftslage in Deutschland," *Vierteljahreshefte zur Wirtschaftsforschung*, Vol. 13, 1938–39.

Ziegler, Hans Willi, "Erziehung zur Volksgemeinschaft," *Süddeutsche Monatshefte*, March 1935.

Books

Die Adolf-Hitler-Schule, 1941.

Arnhold, Karl, *Das Ringen um die Arbeitsidee*, Berlin, 1938.

Axmann, Artur, *Der Reichsberufswettkampf*, Berlin, 1938.

Benn, Gottfried, *Der neue Staat und die Intellektuellen*, Stuttgart-Berlin, 1933.

Bente, Hermann, *Deutsche Bauernpolitik*, Berlin-Stuttgart, 1940.

Bohn, Hans, *Schwäbische Kleinbauern und Arbeiter der Gemeinde Frommern*, Stuttgart, 1940.

Bojunga, *Zur Steigerung der Leistungen in den Berufs- und Fachschulen*, Berlin, 1937.

Bremhorst, A., und W. Bachmann, *Ordnung des Berufseinsatzes*, Berlin-Leipzig, 1937.

Deutsche Musterbetriebe (Arbeitswissenschaftliches Institut der deutschen Arbeitsfront), Berlin-Stuttgart, 1940.

Drescher, Leo, *Entschuldung der ostdeutschen Landwirtschaft*, Berlin, 1938.

Fried, Ferdinand (Ferdinand Friedrich Zimmermann), *Die soziale Revolution*, Leipzig, 1942.

Günther, Hans, F. K., *Führeradel durch Sippenpflege*, Berlin, 1941.

Das Handwerk in Staat und Wirtschaft, Berlin, 1939.

Heberle, Rudolf, and Fritz Meyer, *Die Grossstädte im Strome der Binnenwanderung*, Leipzig, 1937.

von Hellermann, Friedrich Carl, *Landmaschinen gegen Landflucht*, Berlin, 1939.
Holtz, Achim, *Nationalsozialistische Arbeitspolitik*, Würzburg, 1938.
——*Nationalsozialist—Warum?*, Munich, 1936.
Horsten, Franz, *Die nationalsozialistische Leistungsauslese*, Würzburg, 1938.
Huber, Hans, *Die Begabtenprüfung als Mittel der Begabtenauslese und Begabtenförderung*, Reichsministerium für Wissenschaft, Erziehung und Volksbildung, 1940.
Jaensch, Erich, *Zur Neugestaltung des deutschen Studententums und der Hochschule*, Leipzig, 1937.
Karrasch, Alfred, *Parteigenosse Schmiedecke*, Berlin, 1934.
Marr, Heinz, *Die Massenwelt im Kampf um ihre Form*, Hamburg, 1934.
Mehringer, Helmut, *Die NSDAP als politische Ausleseorganisation*, Munich, 1938.
Mitze, Wilhelm, *Die strukturtypologische Gliederung einer westdeutschen Grossstadt*, Leipzig, 1941.
Müller, Josef, *Deutsches Bauerntum zwischen Gestern und Morgen*, Würzburg, 1940.
——*Ein deutsches Bauerndorf im Umbruch der Zeit*, Würzburg, 1939.
Müller, Willy, *Führertum und soziale Ehre*, Berlin, 1935.
——*Das soziale Leben im neuen Deutschland*, Berlin, 1938.
Müller-Brandenburg, *Die Leistungen des deutschen Arbeitsdienstes*, Stuttgart-Berlin, 1940.
Preiss, Ludwig, *Die Wirkung von Preisen und Preisveränderungen auf die Produktion in der Landwirtschaft*, Berichte über Landwirtschaft, Vol. XXIII, No. 4, Berlin, 1938.
Röpke, Alfred, *Was musst du wissen vom Dritten Reich?*, Berlin, 1935.
Rumpf, Max, and Hans Behringer, *Bauerndorf am Grossstadtrand*, Stuttgart-Berlin, 1940.
Prinz zu Schaumburg-Lippe, Friedrich Christian (ed.), *Wo War der Adel?* Berlin, 1934.
Schwarz van Berk, Hans, *Die sozialistische Auslese*, Breslau, 1934.
Starcke, Gerhard, *Die deutsche Arbeitsfront*, Berlin, 1940.
Wagner, Josef, *Hochschule für Politik: Ein Leitfaden*, Munich, 1934.
Winnig, August, *Der Arbeiter im Dritten Reich*, Berlin-Charlottenburg, 1934.
Was Wir jeden Tag erleben, undated, probably Munich, 1937.
Der Weggzur Ordensburg, undated, probably 1936 or 1937.

Dissertations

Albrecht, Otto, "Die Möglichkeiten des sozialen Aufstieges in den Vereinigten Staaten und in Deutschland," Frankfurt, 1937.

Alvermann, Fritz, "Die Verbrauchergenossenschaften im Dritten Reich," Cologne, 1938.

Bauer, Karl, "Querverbindungen von Partei und Staatsbehörden," Tübingen, 1936.

Fischer, Hellmuth, "Das Eliteprinzip des Faschismus," Erlangen, 1935.

Gauer, Hermann, "Vom Bauerntum, Bürgertum und Arbeitertum in der Armee," Heidelberg, 1935.

Haas, Walter, "Bedeutung, Aufgaben und Durchführung der Neubildung deutschen Bauerntums östlich der Elbe im nationalsozialistischen Staat," Heidelberg, 1936.

Hyllus, Werner, "Die Neuordnung der Berufszulassung und Berufsausübung seit der nationalsozialistischen Revolution," Göttingen, 1935.

Käss, Friedrich, "Nationalsozialismus und Gewerkschaftsgedanke," Munich, 1934.

Kost, Walter, "Die bündischen Elemente in der deutschen politischen Gegenwartsideologie," Greifswald, 1934.

Krapfenbauer, Hans, "Die sozialpolitische Bedeutung der nationalsozialistischen Gemeinschaft 'Kraft durch Freude.'" Nuremberg, 1938.

Meister, Angela, "Die deutsche Industriearbeiterin," Munich, 1938.

Müller-Stork, Karl, "Die Überwindung der Klassengegensätze und der Staatseinfluss in der faschistischen und der nationalsozialistischen Arbeitsordnung," Marburg, 1943.

Peikow, Richard, "Die soziale und wirtschaftliche Stellung der deutschen Frau in der Gegenwart," Berlin, 1937.

Piper, Kunibert, "Das Wesen des Angestellten," Greifswald, 1939.

Roesler, Hans, "Die weltanschauliche Entwicklung der gewerblichen Kreditgenossenschaften und der Konsumvereine Deutschlands," Berlin (Wirtschaftschochschule), 1936.

Schreiber, Max, "Die nationalsozialistische Ständeentwicklung im Vergleich mit der faschistischen Wirtschaftsverfassung," Leipzig Handels-Hochschule, 1935.

Schrewe, Ernst, "Der Streit um die berufsständische Ordnung," Hamburg, 1934.

Steiner, Elisabeth, "Agrarwirtschaft und Agrarpolitik," Munich, 1939.

Sticht, Artur, "Stände und Klassen in der deutschen soziologischen

und ökonomischen Literatur der letzten 80 Jahre," Heidelberg, 1934.
Tisch, Heinrich, "Das Problem des sozialen Auf- und Abstieges im deutschen Volk," Heidelberg, 1937.
Vocke, Annemarie, "Grundrechte und Nationalsozialismus," Heidelberg, 1938.

SECONDARY WORKS

Pre-1933 Literature

PERIODICALS AND ARTICLES

Bauer-Mengelberg, Käthe, "Stand und Klasse," *Kölner Vierteljahreshefte für Soziologie*, Vol. III, 1924.
Dirks, Walter, "Katholizismus und Nationalsozialismus," *Die Arbeit*, March 1932, reprinted in *Frankfurter Hefte*, August 1963.
Endres, Franz Carl, "Soziologische Struktur des deutschen Offizierkorps vor dem Weltkriege," Archiv für Sozialwissenschaft und Sozialpolitik, October 1927.
Lederer, Emil, and Jakob Marschak, "Der neue Mittelstand," *Grundriss der Sozialökonomik*, Vol. IX, Tübingen, 1926.
Michels, Robert, "Psychologie der antikapitalistischen Massenbewegungen," *Grundriss der Sozialökonomik*, Vol. IX, Tübingen, 1926.
Mombert, P., "Die Tatsachen der Klassenbildung," *Schmollers Jahrbuch*, Vol. 44, 1920.
Nothaas, J., "Sozialer Auf- und Abstieg im deutschen Volke," *Kölner Vierteljahreshefte für Soziologie*, Vol. IX, No. ½, 1930.
Pesl, L. D., "Mittelstandsfragen," *Grundriss der Sozialökonomik*, Vol. IX, Tübingen, 1926.
Schumpeter, Joseph A., "Das soziale Antlitz des deutschen Reiches" (1929), *Aufsätze zur Soziologie*, Tübingen, 1953.
"Die soziale Schichtung der Studierenden an den bayerischen Hochschulen," *Zeitschrift des bayerischen statistischen Landesamts*, 1929.

BOOKS AND DISSERTATIONS

Bernays, Marie, *Auslese und Anpassung der Arbeiterschaft der geschlossenen Grossindustrie*, Leipzig, 1910.
Bernhardi, Friedrich von, *Denkwürdigkeiten aus meinem Leben*, Berlin, 1927.
Demeter, Karl, *Das deutsche Offizierkorps*, Berlin, 1930.

Fried, Ferdinand (Ferdinand Friedrich Zimmermann), *Das Ende des Kapitalismus,* Jena, 1931.

Geiger, Theodor, *Die soziale Schichtung des deutschen Volkes,* Stuttgart, 1932.

Heuss, Theodor, *Hitlers Weg, Eine historisch-politische Studie über den Nationalsozialismus,* Stuttgart, 1932.

Most, Otto, *Zur Wirtschafts- und Sozialstatistik der höheren Beamten in Preussen,* Munich-Leipzig, 1916.

von Schlange-Schöningen, Hans, *Bauer und Boden,* Hamburg, 1933.

Schreiner, Walter, "Agrarpolitische Untersuchungen im Landkreis Kassel," Giessen dissertation, 1929.

Schumpeter, Joseph A., *"Imperialism" and "Social Classes,"* ed. Paul Sweezy, tr. Heinz Norden, Oxford, 1951. (The essay on imperialism was written during World War I, the one on social classes in the '20s.)

Speier, Hans, "The Salaried Employees in German Society," mimeographed, Columbia University Department of Social Sciences and WPA, New York, 1939.

Emigré Literature, 1933–45

PERIODICALS

Brandt, Karl, "Junkers to the Fore Again," *Foreign Affairs,* October 1935.

Gerth, Hans, "The Nazi Party, Its Composition and Leadership," *American Journal of Sociology,* January 1940.

Heinrichsen, Karl, "Hitler ohne Hintermänner," *Zeitschrift für Sozialismus,* November–December 1935.

Hertz, Paul, "Das Ende der deutschen Konsumgenossenschaftsbewegung," *Zeitschrift für Sozialismus,* May–June 1935.

Obermann, Karl, "Studienbedingungen und Möglichkeiten im Dritten Reich," *Zeitschrift für freie deutsche Forschung,* Paris, July 1938.

Sering, Paul (Richard Lowenthal), "Der Faschismus," *Zeitschrift für Sozialismus,* September–October, November–December 1935.

Wachenheim, Hedwig, "Hitler's Transfers of Population in Eastern Europe," *Foreign Affairs,* July 1942.

BOOKS

Borkenau, Franz, *Pareto,* London, 1936.

——*The Totalitarian Enemy,* London, 1940.

Fraenkel, Ernst, *The Dual State,* New York, 1941.

Grzesinski, Albert C., *Inside Germany*, New York, 1939.
Haffner, Sebastian, *Germany: Jekyll and Hyde*, London, 1940.
Hamburger, L., *How Nazi Germany Has Controlled Business*, Washington, 1943.
Heberle, Rudolf, *From Democracy to Nazism*, Baton Rouge, 1945.
Heiden, Konrad, *Geburt des dritten Reiches*, Zurich, 1934.
Kahle, Paul E., *Bonn University in Pre-Nazi and Nazi Times*, London, 1945.
Lederer, Emil, *State of the Masses, The Threat of the Classless Society*, New York, 1940.
Neumann, Franz, *Behemoth*, New York, 1942.
Rauschning, Hermann, *Gespräche mit Hitler*, Zurich-New York, 1940. (Page references are to German original.)
——*Die Revolution des Nihilismus*, Zurich-New York, 1938. (Page references are to German original.)
Röpke, Wilhelm, *International Economic Disintegration*, London, 1942.
Stolper, Gustav, *The German Economy, 1870–1940*, New York, 1940. (Page references are to German translation, *Deutsche Wirtschaft*, Stuttgart, 1950.)

Foreign Literature, 1933–45

NEWSPAPERS

Algemeen Handelsblad, Amsterdam
Le Temps, Paris

PERIODICALS AND ARTICLES

"Anti-Socialistic Socialists," *The Economist*, 14 December 1935.
"Dr. Schacht and the Nazis," *The Economist*, 7 December 1935.
Lasswell, Harold D., "The Psychology of Hitlerism" (1933), in *The Analysis of Political Behaviour*, London, 1949.

BOOKS

Brady, Robert A., *The Spirit and Structure of German Fascism*, London, 1937.
Gerschenkron, Alexander, *Bread and Democracy in Germany*, Berkeley, 1943.
Guillebaud, C. W., *The Economic Recovery of Germany*, London, 1939.
——*The Social Policy of Nazi Germany*, Cambridge, 1942.
Gurland, A. R. L., Otto Kirchheimer, and Franz Neumann, *The Fate of Small Business in Nazi Germany*, Senate Committee Print No. 14, Washington, 1943.

Kirkpatrick, Clifford, *Nazi Germany: Its Women and Family Life,* Indianapolis-New York, 1938.
Kraus, Karl, *Die dritte Walpurgisnacht,* Munich, 1955. (Written in Vienna in 1933 and left unpublished until 1952.)
Michels, Robert, *Umschichtungen in den herrschenden Klassen nach dem Krieg,* Stuttgart, 1934. (Michels lived permanently in Italy.)
Roberts, Stephen H., *The House That Hitler Built,* London, 1937.
Shirer, William L., *Berlin Diary,* London, 1941.
Smith, Howard K., *Last Train From Berlin,* London, 1942.
Welles, Sumner, *The Time for Decision,* Cleveland & New York, 1944. (Page ref. to 1945 edition.)
West, Rebecca, *Black Lamb and Grey Falcon,* New York, 1953. (First edition, London, 1942.)

Memoirs and Diaries

Frank, Hans, *Im Angesicht des Galgens,* Munich, 1953.
Habe, Hans, *A Thousand Shall Fall,* London, 1942.
von Hassell, Ulrich, *Vom anderen Deutschland,* Zurich, 1946. (Page references to Frankfurt, 1964, paperback.)
Höss, Rudolf, *Kommandant in Auschwitz,* ed. Martin Broszat, Munich, 1963.
Kersten, Felix, *Totenkopf und Treue,* Hamburg, 1952.
Klemperer, Viktor, *LTI, Notizbuch eines Philologen,* Berlin, 1946.
Krebs, Albert, *Tendenzen und Gestalten der NSDAP,* Stuttgart, 1959.
Leber, Julius, *Ein Mann geht seinen Weg,* ed. Gustav Dahrendorf, Berlin, 1952.
von Manstein, Erich, *Aus einem Soldatenleben,* Bonn, 1958.
Maschmann, Melita, *Fazit,* Stuttgart, 1963.
Rosenberg, Alfred, *Das politische Tagebuch,* Göttingen, 1956. (Page references to the paperback edition, ed. Hans-Günther Seraphim, Munich, 1964.)
von Salomon, Ernst, *Der Fragebogen,* Hamburg, 1951.
Prinz zu Schaumburg-Lippe, Friedrich Christian, *Zwischen Krone und Kerker,* Wiesbaden, 1952.
Strasser, Otto, *Hitler und ich,* Konstanz, 1948.
——"Meine Aussprache mit Hitler," in *Aufbau des deutschen Sozialismus,* Prague, 1936.
Syrup, Friedrich, *Hundert Jahre staatliche Sozialpolitik,* ed. Julius Scheuble, Stuttgart, 1957.
Thyssen, Fritz, *I Paid Hitler,* New York, 1941.
Wahl, Karl, *. . . es ist das deutsche Herz,* Augsburg, 1954.

Postwar Literature, 1945–65

PERIODICALS AND ARTICLES

Bendix, Reinhard, "Social Stratification and Political Power," *American Political Science Review*, June 1952.

Broszat, Martin, "Dokumentation," *Vierteljahrshefte für Zeitgeschichte*, 1960.

Buchheim, Hans, "Die SS in der Verfassung des dritten Reiches," *Vierteljahrshefte für Zeitgeschichte*, 1955.

Eschenburg, Theodor, "Dokumentation," *Vierteljahreshefte für Zeitgeschichte*, 1955.

Hale, Oron James, "Gottfried Feder Calls Hitler to Order," *Journal of Modern History*, December 1958.

König, René, "Die Soziologie der zwanziger Jahre," *Die Zeit ohne Eigenschaften*, ed. Leonhard Reinisch, Stuttgart, 1961.

Lipset, S. M., "Faschismus," *Kölner Zeitschrift für Soziologie und Sozialpsychologie*, 1959.

Maus, Heinz, "Bericht über die Soziologen in Deutschland, 1933 bis 1945," *Kölner Zeitschrift für Soziologie und Sozialpsychologie*, 1959.

Paetel, Karl O., "Geschichte und Soziologie der SS," *Vierteljahreshefte für Zeitgeschichte*, 1954.

Rämisch, Raimund, "Der berufsständische Gedanke als Episode in der nationalsozialistischen Politik," *Zeitschrift für Politik*, 1957.

Schweitzer, Arthur, "Depression and War: Nazi Phase," *Political Science Quarterly*, September 1947.

——"Organisierter Kapitalismus und Parteidiktatur," *Schmollers Jahrbuch*, 1959.

——"Der ursprüngliche Vierjahresplan," *Jahrbücher für Nationalökonomie und Statistik*, Vol. 168, Stuttgart, 1956.

Simpson, Amos E., "The Struggle for Control of the German Economy," *Journal of Modern History*, March 1959.

BOOKS AND DISSERTATIONS

Arendt, Hannah, *The Origins of Totalitarianism*, New York, 1958.

Bayle, François, *Psychologie et Ethique du National-Socialisme*, Paris, 1953.

Bolte, Karl Martin, *Sozialer Aufstieg und Abstieg*, Stuttgart, 1959.

von Borch, Herbert, *Obrigkeit und Widerstand: zur politischen Soziologie des Beamtentums*, Tübingen, 1954.

Graf von Borcke-Stargordt, Henning, *Der ostdeutsche Landbau zwischen Fortschritt, Krise und Politik*, Würzburg, 1957.

Bracher, Karl Dietrich, Gerhard Schulz, and Wolfgang Sauer, *Die nationalsozialistische Machtergreifung*, Cologne and Opladen, 1960.

Brenner, Hildegard, *Die Kunstpolitik des Nationalsozialismus*, Rohwolts deutsche Enzyklopädie, Reinbeck, bei Hamburg, 1963.

Broszat, Martin, *Der Nationalsozialismus*, Stuttgart, 1961.

Bry, Gerhard, *Wages in Germany*, Princeton, 1960.

Bullock, Alan, *Hitler: A Study in Tyranny*, New York, 1962. (Page references to Penguin, 1962, paperback.)

Croner, Fritz, *Soziologie der Angestellten*, Cologne-Berlin, 1962.

Dahrendorf, Ralf, *Gesellschaft und Freiheit*, Munich, 1961.

Dallin, Alexander, *German Rule in Russia*, London, 1957.

Demeter, Karl, *Das deutsche Offizierkorps*, Frankfurt, 1962.

Djilas, Milovan, *The New Class*, New York, 1957.

Dubail, René, *Une Expérience d'Économie Dirigée: L'Allemagne National-Socialiste*, Paris, 1962.

Eilers, Rolf, *Die nationalsozialistische Schulpolitik*, Cologne, 1963.

Erbe, René, *Die nationalsozialistische Wirtschaftspolitik im Lichte der modernen Theorie*, Zurich, 1958.

von Ferber, Christian, *Die Entwicklung des Lehrkörpers der deutschen Universitäten und Hochschulen, 1864–1954*, Göttingen, 1956.

Graf Finck von Finckenstein, H. W., *Die Entwicklung der Landwirtschaft in Preussen und Deutschland, 1800–1930*, Würzburg, 1960.

Foertsch, Hermann, *Schuld und Verhängnis*, Stuttgart, 1951.

Franz-Willing, Georg, *Die Hitler-Bewegung: Der Ursprung 1919–22*, Hamburg-Berlin, 1962.

Führungsschicht und Eliteproblem, Jahrbuch III der Ranke Gesellschaft, Frankfurt-Berlin-Bonn, 1957.

Gamm, Hans-Jochen, *Der braune Kult*, Hamburg, 1962.

Georg, Enno, *Die Wirtschaftlichen Unternehmungen der SS*, Stuttgart, 1963.

Gilbert, G. M., *Nuremberg Diary*, New York, 1947.

Görlitz, Walter, *Die Junker*, Glücksburg, 1956.

Gruchmann, Lothar, *Nationalsozialistische Grossraumordnung*, Stuttgart, 1962.

Hale, Oron J., *The Captive Press in the Third Reich*, Princeton, 1964.

Hallgarten, G. W. F., *Why Dictators?* New York, 1954.

Hofstadter, Richard, *The Age of Reform*, New York, 1955.

Jacobsen, Hans-Adolf, *1939–1945*, Darmstadt, 1961.

Jetzinger, Franz, *Hitler's Youth*, London, 1958.

Klein, Burton H., *Germany's Economic Preparations for War*, Cambridge, Massachusetts, 1959.

Klönne, Arno, *Die Hitlerjugend*, Hanover-Frankfurt, 1956.
Kogon, Eugen, *Der SS-Staat*, Munich, 1946.
Kohn, Hans, *The Mind of Germany*, London, 1961.
Laqueur, Walter Z., *Young Germany*, London, 1962.
Lerner, Daniel, *The Nazi Elite*, Stanford University Press, 1951.
Lipset, S. M., and Reinhard Bendix, *Social Mobility in Industrial Society*, Berkeley and Los Angeles, 1960.
Litt, Theodor, *Das Verhältnis der Generationen*, Wiesbaden, 1947.
Mannheim, Karl, *Mensch und Gesellschaft im Zeitalter des Umbaues*, Darmstadt, 1958.
Manvell, Roger, and Heinrich Fraenkel, *Doctor Goebbels*, London, 1960.
Mayer, Milton, *They Thought They Were Free*, Chicago, 1955.
Meinecke, Friedrich, *Die deutsche Katastrophe*, Wiesbaden, 1949.
Mühlen, Norbert, *The Incredible Krupps*, New York, 1959.
Neusüss-Hunkel, Ermenhild, *Die SS*, Hanover-Frankfurt, 1956.
Nolte, Ernst, *Der Faschismus in seiner Epoche*, Munich, 1963.
Orb, Heinrich, *Nationalsozialismus, 13 Jahre Machtrausch*, Olten, 1945.
Parsons, Talcott, *Essays in Sociological Theory*, Glencoe, 1949.
Plessner, Helmuth, *Die verspätete Nation*, Stuttgart, 1959.
Pross, Harry, *Vor und nach Hitler: Zur deutschen Sozialpathologie*, Olten-Freiburg im Breisgau, 1962.
Reichhardt, Hans Joachim, "Die deutsche Arbeitsfront," Freie Universität Berlin dissertation, 1956.
Reichmann, Eva, *Hostages of Civilization*, London, 1950.
Reitlinger, Gerald, *The SS*, London, 1956.
Ritter, Gerhard, *Carl Goerdeler und die deutsche Widerstandsbewegung*, Stuttgart, 1954.
Roloff, Ernst-August, *Bürgertum und Nationalsozialismus*, Hanover, 1961.
Rousset, David, *L'Univers Concentrationnaire*, Paris, 1946.
Schäfer, Wolfgang, *Die NSDAP: Entwicklung und Struktur der Staatspartei des dritten Reiches*, Hanover-Frankfurt, 1957.
Schumann, Hans-Gerd, *Nationalsozialismus und Gewerkschaftsbewegung*, Hanover-Frankfurt, 1958.
Schweitzer, Arthur, *Big Business in the Third Reich*, Bloomington, 1964.
Seabury, Paul, *The Wilhelmstrasse*, Berkeley, 1954.
Specht, Karl-Gustav, "Die NSDAP als organisiertes soziales Gebilde," Cologne dissertation, 1949.
Sternberger, Dolf, Gerhard Storz, and W. E. Süskind, *Aus dem Wörterbuch des Unmenschen*, Hamburg, 1957. (Page references to Munich, 1962, paperback.)

Stucken, Rudolf, *Deutsche Geld- und Kreditpolitik*, Tübingen, 1953.
Trevor-Roper, H. R., *The Last Days of Hitler*, London, 1958.
Uhlig, Heinrich, *Die Warenhäuser im Dritten Reich*, Cologne-Opladen, 1956.
Untersuchungen zur Geschichte des Offizierkorps, Anciennität und Beförderung nach Leistung, Militärgeschichtliches Forschungsamt, Stuttgart, 1962.
Zapf, Wolfgang, *Wandlungen der deutschen Elite*, Munich, 1965.

INDEX

MODERN GERMAN HISTORY TITLES IN

NORTON PAPERBOUND EDITIONS

The Kaiser and His Times
by Michael Balfour

The Origins of Modern Germany by Geoffrey Barraclough

Arms, Autarky, and Aggression: A Study in German Foreign Policy, 1933-1939 by William Carr

Society and Democracy in Germany by Ralf Dahrendorf

Bismarck and the German Empire by Erich Eyck

Germany's Aims in the First World War by Fritz Fischer

War of Illusions by Fritz Fischer

Hitler's War Aims: Ideology, the Nazi State, and the Course of Expansion by Norman Rich

Hitler's Social Revolution by David Schoenbaum

Germany's First Bid for Colonies, 1884-1885: A Move in Bismarck's European Policy by A. J. P. Taylor